TAO TE CHING

THE CLASSIC BOOK OF INTEGRITY AND THE WAY

LAO TZU

AN ENTIRELY NEW TRANSLATION BASED ON THE
RECENTLY DISCOVERED MA-WANG-TUI MANUSCRIPTS.

Translated, annotated, and with an Afterword
by Victor H. Mair
WOODCUTS BY DAN HEITKAMP

BANTAM BOOKS
NEW YORK · TORONTO · LONDON · SYDNEY · AUCKLAND

TAO TE CHING

A Bantam Book / September 1990

Published simultaneously in hardcover and trade paperback.

Bantam New Age and the accompanying figure design as well as "the search for meaning, growth and change" are trademarks of Bantam Books, a division of Bantam Doubleday Dell Publishing Group, Inc.

Library of Congress Cataloging-in-Publication Data
Lao-tzu.
  [Tao te ching. English]
  Tao te ching : the classic book of integrity and the way / by Lao
Tzu ; translated, annotated, and with an afterword by Victor H.
Mair; woodcuts by Dan Heitkamp.
      p. cm.
  "An entirely new translation based on the recently discovered Ma-
wang-tui manuscripts."
  Includes bibliographical references.
  ISBN 0-553-07005-3. — ISBN 0-553-34935-X (pbk.)
  I. Mair, Victor H., 1943–   II. Title.
BL1900.L26E5   1990
299'.51482—dc20
                                                      90-242
                                                      CIP

Published simultaneously in the United States and Canada

PRINTED IN THE UNITED STATES OF AMERICA

DH   0 9 8 7 6 5 4

FOR DAVE,

who dances with the Tao.

The supreme perfection of actionlessness
He attains through renunciation.

Nāiṣkarmyasiddhiṁ paramāṁ
Saṁnyāsenādhigacchati.

Bhagavad Gītā, XVIII.49.3–4

While you . . .
    Focus your breath until it is supremely soft,
    Can you be like a baby?

Tai . . .
    Chuan ch'i chih jou,
    Neng ying-erh hu?

Tao Te Ching, 54.1, 4–5

What is the use of running when we are not on the right way?

Was hilft laufen, wenn man nicht auf den rechten Weg ist?

German proverb

CONTENTS

PREFACE

Next to the Bible and the *Bhagavad Gītā*, the *Tao Te Ching* is the most translated book in the world. Well over a hundred different renditions of the Taoist classic have been made into English alone, not to mention the dozens in German, French, Italian, Dutch, Latin, and other European languages. There are several reasons for the superabundance of translations. The first is that the *Tao Te Ching* is considered to be the fundamental text of both philosophical and religious Taoism. Indeed, the Tao, or Way, which is at the heart of the *Tao Te Ching*, is also the centerpiece of all Chinese religion and thought. Naturally, different schools and sects bring somewhat different slants to the Tao, but all subscribe to the notion that there is a single, overarching Way that encompasses everything in the universe. As such, the *Tao Te Ching* shares crucial points of similarity with other major religious scriptures the world over.

The second reason for the popularity of the *Tao Te Ching* is its brevity. There are few bona fide classics that are so short, yet so packed with food for thought. One can read and reread the *Tao Te Ching* scores of times without exhausting the insights it offers.

The third aspect that accounts for the wide repute of the *Tao Te Ching* is its deceptive simplicity: In the words of the author himself, it is supposedly "very easy to understand," when actually it is quite difficult to comprehend fully. Paradox is the essence of the *Tao Te Ching*, so much so that even scholars with a solid grounding in classical Chinese cannot be sure they have grasped what the Old Master is really saying in his pithy maxims. For this reason, I vowed two decades ago that I would never attempt to translate the *Tao Te Ching*. However, an unexpected event forced me to recant: The recent discovery of two ancient manuscripts in China made it possible to produce a totally new translation of the *Tao Te Ching* far more accurate and reliable than any published previously. These manuscripts are at least a half a millennium older than commonly translated versions.

This translation of the *Tao Te Ching* is based wholly on these new-found manuscripts. Their availability has made it possible to strip away the distortions and obfuscations of a tradition that has striven for two millennia to "improve" the text with commentaries and interpretations more amenable to various religious, philosophical, and political persuasions. And they have provided me with the means to make the translation in this book significantly different from all other previously existing translations.

In late 1973, when Chinese archaeologists working at Ma-wang-tui, in central China about a hundred miles south of the Yangtze River, unearthed two silk manuscripts of the *Tao Te Ching*, scholars of ancient China around the world were overjoyed. Forty-nine other important items, including the earliest extant version of the *Book of Changes*, were also found. It will be many years before sinologists fully absorb the wealth of new materials made available by the Ma-wang-tui manuscript finds, but we are already beginning to reap important benefits.

By relying on the Ma-wang-tui manuscripts for the present translation of the *Tao Te Ching*, I have solved a number of problems that have puzzled interpreters of the text for centuries. For example, line 8 of chapter 77 reads "To die but not be forgotten. . . ." In previously available editions of the *Tao Te Ching*, this read "To die but not perish . . . ," which does not really make sense even in a religious Taoist context. There are dozens of such instances where the Ma-wang-tui manuscripts are much more intelligible than the old standard editions, which are the basis of almost all other translations. I have pointed out several of these cases in the Notes.

The Ma-wang-tui manuscripts have also enabled me to make break-throughs in determining the origin and composition of the text. In the Afterword and in my translation, I view the core of the *Tao Te Ching*, as having derived from oral tradition rather than from a single author. This characteristic is obscured by the explanatory comments in all other versions of the text and even more frequently by the use of misleading Chinese characters that has resulted from phonological change over the course of many centuries. Since the Ma-wang-tui manuscripts are much nearer to the date of the composition of the original *Tao Te Ching*, it is natural that they preserve more faithfully many of the features of the oral wisdom on which it was based.

Working on the relatively unstudied Ma-wang-tui manuscripts is more difficult than resorting to the ready solutions of the standard editions, which have been repeatedly commented upon and translated. It is also much more inspiring to come to grips with the Ma-wang-tui materials than to rehash the standard version yet again. One is conscious of being in the presence of manuscripts written close to the time when the *Tao Te Ching* crystallized as the foundation of both religious and philosophical Taoism. Without the discovery of the Ma-wang-tui manuscripts, I would never have been prompted to translate the *Tao Te Ching*; with them, reinterpreting the *Tao Te Ching* has become a stimulating challenge.

Once I assumed the task of creating an entirely fresh translation of the *Tao Te Ching*, I became preoccupied with endless details, such as how to convey the meaning of the second word in the title. I spent two full months trying to arrive at a satisfactory translation of *te*. Walking through the woods, riding on the train, buying groceries, chopping wood—the elusive notion of *te* was always on my mind. The final choice of "integrity" is based on a thorough etymological study of the word, together with a careful consideration of each of its forty-four occurrences in the text. In certain instances perhaps another word such as "self," "character," "personality," "virtue," "charisma," or "power" might have been more befitting. But "integrity" is the only word that seems plausible throughout. By "integrity," I mean the totality of an individual including his or her moral stance, whether good or bad.

We shall return to explore this concept in much greater depth in Part II of the Afterword, but I should like to add here that the Ma-wang-tui manuscripts were instrumental in helping me decide upon "integrity" as the right translation for *te* in the *Tao Te Ching*. In the first place, the archaic forms of the Chinese character for *te* used in the manuscripts caused me to realize that this term signified the holistic inner quality or character of a person. The basic components of the

Chinese graph at the time of the writing of the *Tao Te Ching* were an eye looking straight ahead, and the heart, and a sign for movement or behavior. Visually, these components are much clearer on the Ma-wang-tui manuscripts than they are in later stylized forms of the character for *te*, which become far more abstract and arbitrary. Secondly, several of the previously unknown texts among the Ma-wang-tui manuscripts, especially those dealing with metaphysical questions, also contain elaborate discussions of *te*. These, too, served to sharpen my appreciation of *te* as it was used in the intellectual milieu in which the *Tao Te Ching* took shape.

Whether seeking the right English word for *te* or coping with unusual Chinese graphs that were not to be found in any dictionary, my paramount guide has been historical linguistics. Only by the most rigorous application of this discipline can we hope to come close to a full understanding of ancient texts. At the same time I also sought inspiration from the muse so as not to betray the poetic beauty of the *Tao Te Ching*. My aim has been to create an authentic English version of the *Tao Te Ching* that is both eminently readable and sinologically precise. Because the original is in many places maddeningly obscure and frustratingly ambiguous, this was no mean task. Nonetheless, I am satisfied that the final result has been worth all the effort and that the present rendition comes closer than any other to affording someone who knows no classical Chinese the thought-provoking, mind-bending experience of reading the original.

An unusual feature of the present translation is its format. The layout of the words on the page is very carefully calculated to reflect the linguistic structure of the classical Chinese text. By paying attention to the arrangement of the words of the translation, the reader will be able to discern various grammatical, syntactical, and stylistic features of the original. Placement of particles, parallelism, antithesis, and so forth are all more or less evident in the physical appearance of the translation. Most, but not all, of the *Tao Te Ching* may be divided into rhymed sections. The rhyme schemes, in turn, fall into many different categories. Only occasionally do I employ rhyme in the translation, instead approximating its effects for the modern American reader by such devices as consonance, assonance, and other familiar poetic techniques.

The primary duty of the translator is to convey, as nearly as possible, a semblance of the original text in his or her own language. To do so, one must pay attention to form, content, style, diction, and sound. It is not enough merely to transfer the meaning of the original text; one also needs to replicate its effects. If a text is somewhat rough in places, one should resist the temptation to ameliorate it; if it is lyrical, one's own verse should sing. Because of the history of its composition, the style of the *Tao Te Ching* varies greatly. I have striven to recreate in my own rendition the various voices we hear speaking out of the past—the Taoist mystic, the political strategist, the utopian architect, the anti-Confucian philosopher, the clairvoyant poet, the meditative Yogin. If the reader is able to hear with any degree of fidelity more than one of the strains in this thought-provoking *concertstück*, my efforts will have been amply rewarded.

In the Afterword I again endeavor to break virgin territory. The first part shows how the *Tao Te Ching* represents the accumulated wisdom of centuries, not the enterprise of one author. As such, the real title of this book should be something like *Sayings of the Old Masters*. For the sake of convenience and familiarity, nonetheless, I continue to refer to it as the *Tao Te Ching*. The Afterword provides an etymological examination of the three words that make up the customary title of the book, together with explanations of the name of the presumed author and several other key terms.

Another radical departure from the past is my recognition of the *Tao Te Ching*'s intimate relationship to that other well-known oriental classic the *Bhagavad Gītā*. Having read both of them in their original languages repeatedly and attentively over the past two decades, I have come to believe that they are connected in an essential way. In the Afterword and Notes I have also discussed many similarities between Indian Yoga and Chinese Taoism, schools of religion and philosophy with which both books are closely associated.

At present there are only three conceivable explanations for how this relationship could have developed: (1) China borrowed the Yogic system and its attendant practices from India; (2) India borrowed Taoism and its attendant practices from China; (3) both India and China were the recipients of inspiration from a third source. Much research remains to be done, of course, before a conclusive answer can be given. We must also await the results of more thorough archaeological excavations, particularly in Sinkiang (the Chinese part of Central Asia), through which the famous silk roads passed, and along the southeast coast of China, where ships from India and Arabia regularly arrived. Nonetheless, presently available data indicate an Indian priority that can be traced back to at least the beginning of the first millennium B.C.

It is ultimately of little consequence whether Taoism is indebted to Yoga or Yoga to Taoism. What really matters is that they are both unique manifestations of a common human heritage. That is the light in which I have endeavored to view them in this little volume.

ACKNOWLEDGMENT

I would like to thank my editor, Linda Loewenthal, for managing to be both gentle and firm in helping me to make this book more accessible to the people for whom it was written.

NOTE ON THE NUMBERING OF CHAPTERS

The numbers running consecutively from 1 to 81 follow the sequence of the Ma-wang-tui manuscripts. The numbers in parentheses indicate the corresponding chapters of the previous standard text.

NOTE ON THE USE OF PRONOUNS

The third person pronoun is often omitted in classical Chinese, but even when it is explicitly stated, rarely is the sense of gender implied. The translator not only has to supply a subject to satisfy the requirements of English grammar, but is forced to decide in each instance whether "he," "she," or "it" is more appropriate. To avoid overemphasis on the masculine, I have used impersonal or feminine pronouns for the third person whenever possible. When referring to the "sage king," however, I have had to use the masculine form because it is a simple fact of history that in ancient Chinese society this term always referred to men.

TE

INTEGRITY

1
(38)

The person of superior integrity
         does not insist upon his integrity;
For this reason, he has integrity.
The person of inferior integrity
         never loses sight of his integrity;
For this reason, he lacks integrity.

The person of superior integrity takes no action,
   nor has he a purpose for acting.
The person of superior humaneness takes action,
   but has no purpose for acting.
The person of superior righteousness takes action,
   and has a purpose for acting.
The person of superior etiquette takes action,
   but others do not respond to him;
Whereupon he rolls up his sleeves
   and coerces them.

Therefore,
   When the Way is lost,
      afterward comes integrity.
   When integrity is lost,
      afterward comes humaneness.
   When humaneness is lost,
      afterward comes righteousness.
   When righteousness is lost,
      afterward comes etiquette.

Now,

> Etiquette is the attenuation of trustworthiness,
>> and the source of disorder.
> Foreknowledge is but the blossomy ornament of the Way,
>> and the source of ignorance.

For this reason,

> The great man resides in substance,
>> not in attenuation.
> He resides in fruitful reality,
>> not in blossomy ornament.

Therefore,

> He rejects the one and adopts the other.

2
(39)

In olden times, these attained unity:
 Heaven attained unity,
  and thereby became pure.
 Earth attained unity,
  and thereby became tranquil.
 The spirits attained unity,
  and thereby became divine.
 The valley attained unity,
  and thereby became full.
 Feudal lords and kings attained unity,
  and thereby all was put right.

Yet, pushed to the extreme,
It implies that,
 If heaven were ever pure,
  it would be likely to rend.
It implies that,
 If earth were ever tranquil,
  it would be likely to quake.
It implies that,
 If the spirits were ever divine,
  they would be likely to dissipate.
It implies that,
 If the valley were ever full,
  it would be likely to run dry.
It implies that,
 If feudal lords and kings were ever noble
   and thereby exalted,
  they would be likely to fall.

Therefore,
>   It is necessary to be noble,
>   and yet take humility as a basis.
>   It is necessary to be exalted,
>   and yet take modesty as a foundation.

Now, for this reason,
>   Feudal lords and kings style themselves
>   "orphaned," "destitute," and "hapless."
>   Is this not because they take humility as their basis?

Therefore,
>   Striving for an excess of praise,
>   one ends up without praise.
Consequently,
>   Desire not to be jingling as jade
>   nor stolid as stone.

3
(41)

When the superior man hears the Way,
    he is scarcely able to put it into practice.
When the middling man hears the Way,
    he appears now to preserve it, now to lose it.
When the inferior man hears the Way,
    he laughs at it loudly.
If he did not laugh,
    it would not be fit to be the Way.

For this reason,
There is a series of epigrams that says:
    "The bright Way seems dim.
    The forward Way seems backward.
    The level Way seems bumpy.
    Superior integrity seems like a valley.
    The greatest whiteness seems grimy.
    Ample integrity seems insufficient.
    Robust integrity seems apathetic.
    Plain truth seems sullied.

    The great square has no corners.
    The great vessel is never completed.
    The great note sounds muted.
    The great image has no form.

    The Way is concealed and has no name."

Indeed,
    The Way alone is good at beginning
        and good at completing.

4
(40)

Reversal is the movement of the Way;
Weakness is the usage of the Way.

All creatures under heaven are born from being;
Being is born from nonbeing.

5
(42)

The Way gave birth to unity,
Unity gave birth to duality,
Duality gave birth to trinity,
Trinity gave birth to the myriad creatures.

The myriad creatures bear yin on their backs
        and embrace yang in their bosoms.
They neutralize these vapors
        and thereby achieve harmony.

That which all under heaven hate most
Is to be orphaned, destitute, and hapless.
Yet kings and dukes call themselves thus.

Things may be diminished by being increased,
        increased by being diminished.

Therefore,
    That which people teach,
    After deliberation, I also teach people.

Therefore,
    "The tyrant does not die a natural death."
    I take this as my mentor.

6
(43)

The softest thing under heaven
    gallops triumphantly over
The hardest thing under heaven.

Nonbeing penetrates nonspace.
Hence,
    I know the advantages of nonaction.

The doctrine without words,
The advantage of nonaction—
    few under heaven can realize these!

7
(44)

Name or person,
    which is nearer?
Person or property,
    which is dearer?
Gain or loss,
    which is drearier?

Many loves entail great costs,
Many riches entail heavy losses.

Know contentment and you shall not be disgraced,
Know satisfaction and you shall not be imperiled;
    then you will long endure.

8
(45)

Great perfection appears defective,
    but its usefulness is not diminished.
Great fullness appears empty,
    but its usefulness is not impaired.

Great straightness seems crooked,
Great cleverness seems clumsy,
Great triumph seems awkward.

Bustling about vanquishes cold,
Standing still vanquishes heat.

Pure and still,
    one can put things right everywhere under heaven.

9
(46)

When the Way prevails under heaven,
   swift horses are relegated to fertilizing fields.
When the Way does not prevail under heaven,
   war-horses breed in the suburbs.

No guilt is greater than giving in to desire,
No disaster is greater than discontent,
No crime is more grievous than the desire for gain.

Therefore,
   Contentment that derives from knowing
         when to be content
      is eternal contentment.

10
(47)

Without going out-of-doors,
   one may know all under heaven;
Without peering through windows,
   one may know the Way of heaven.

The farther one goes,
The less one knows.

For this reason,
   The sage knows without journeying,
        understands without looking,
        accomplishes without acting.

11
(48)

The pursuit of learning results in daily increase,
Hearing the Way leads to daily decrease.
Decrease and again decrease,
   until you reach nonaction.
Through nonaction,
   no action is left undone.

Should one desire to gain all under heaven,
One should remain ever free of involvements.
For,
   Just as surely as one becomes involved,
   One is unfit for gaining all under heaven.

12
(49)

The sage never has a mind of his own;
He considers the minds of the common people to be his mind.

Treat well those who are good,
Also treat well those who are not good;
    thus is goodness attained.

Be sincere to those who are sincere,
Also be sincere to those who are insincere;
    thus is sincerity attained.

The sage
    is self-effacing in his dealings with all under heaven,
    and bemuddles his mind for the sake of all under heaven.

The common people all rivet their eyes and ears upon him,
And the sage makes them all chuckle like children.

13
(50)

A person comes forth to life and enters into death.
Three out of ten are partners of life,
Three out of ten are partners of death,
And the people whose every movement leads them to the
        land of death because they cling to life
Are also three out of ten.

Now,
    What is the reason for this?
    It is because they cling to life.

Indeed,
I have heard that
    One who is good at preserving life
      does not avoid tigers and rhinoceroses
        when he walks in the hills;
        nor does he put on armor and take up weapons
        when he enters a battle.
    The rhinoceros has no place to jab its horn,
    The tiger has no place to fasten its claws,
    Weapons have no place to admit their blades.

Now,
    What is the reason for this?
    Because on him there are no mortal spots.

14
(51)

The Way gives birth to them and integrity nurtures them.
Matter forms them and function completes them.

For this reason,
   The myriad creatures respect the Way and esteem integrity.
   Respect for the Way and esteem for integrity
      are by no means conferred upon them
         but always occur naturally.

   The Way gives birth to them,
      nurtures them,
      rears them,
      follows them,
      shelters them,
      toughens them,
      sustains them,
      protects them.
   It gives birth but does not possess,
      acts but does not presume,
      rears but does not control.

   This is what is called "mysterious integrity."

15
(52)

Everything under heaven has a beginning
   which may be thought of as the mother
      of all under heaven.
Having realized the mother,
   you thereby know her children.
Knowing her children,
   go back to abide with the mother.
To the end of your life,
   you will not be imperiled.

Stopple the orifices of your heart,
Close your doors;
   your whole life you will not suffer.
Open the gate of your heart,
Meddle with affairs;
   your whole life you will be beyond salvation.

Seeing what is small is called insight,
Abiding in softness is called strength.

Use your light to return to insight,
Be not an inheritor of personal calamity.

This is called "following the constant."

16
(53)

If I were possessed of the slightest knowledge,
    traveling on the great Way,
My only fear would be to go astray.
The great Way is quite level,
    but the people are much enamored of mountain trails.

The court is thoroughly deserted,
The fields are choked with weeds,
The granaries are altogether empty.

Still there are some who
    wear clothes with fancy designs and brilliant colors,
    sharp swords hanging at their sides,
    are sated with food,
    overflowing with possessions and wealth.

This is called "the brazenness of a bandit."
The brazenness of a bandit is surely not the Way!

What is firmly established cannot be uprooted;
What is tightly embraced cannot slip away.

Thus sacrificial offerings made by sons and grandsons
        will never end.

Cultivated in the person, integrity is true.
Cultivated in the family, integrity is ample.
Cultivated in the village, integrity lasts long.
Cultivated in the state, integrity is abundant.
Cultivated everywhere under heaven, integrity is vast.

Observe other persons through your own person.
Observe other families through your own family.
Observe other villages through your own village.
Observe other states through your own state.
Observe all under heaven through all under heaven.

How do I know the nature of all under heaven?
Through this.

18
(55)

He who embodies the fullness of integrity
    is like a ruddy infant.

Wasps, spiders, scorpions, and snakes
    will not sting or bite him;
Rapacious birds and fierce beasts
    will not seize him.

His bones are weak and his sinews soft,
    yet his grip is tight.
He knows not the joining of male and female,
    yet his penis is aroused.
His essence has reached a peak.

He screams the whole day without becoming hoarse;
His harmony has reached perfection.

Harmony implies constancy;
Constancy requires insight.

Striving to increase one's life is ominous;
To control the vital breath with one's mind entails force.

Something that grows old while still in its prime
    is said to be not in accord with the Way;
Not being in accord with the Way
    leads to an early demise.

19
(56)

One who knows does not speak;
One who speaks does not know.

He

Stopples the openings of his heart,
Closes his doors,
Diffuses the light,
Mingles with the dust,
Files away his sharp points,
Unravels his tangles.

This is called "mysterious identity."

Therefore,
Neither can one attain intimacy with him,
Nor can one remain distant from him;
Neither can one profit from him,
Nor can one be harmed by him;
Neither can one achieve honor through him,
Nor can one be debased by him.

Therefore,
He is esteemed by all under heaven.

20
(57)

Rule the state with uprightness,
Deploy your troops with craft,
Gain all under heaven with noninterference.

How do I know this is actually so?

Now,
    The more taboos under heaven,
        the poorer the people;
    The more clever devices people have,
        the more confused the state and ruling house;
    The more knowledge people have,
        the more strange things spring up;
    The more legal affairs are given prominence,
        the more numerous bandits and thieves.

For this reason,
The sage has a saying:
    "I take no action,
        yet the people transform themselves;
    I am fond of stillness,
        yet the people correct themselves;
    I do not interfere in affairs,
        yet the people enrich themselves;
    I desire not to desire,
        yet the people of themselves become
                simple as unhewn logs."

21
(58)

When government is anarchic,
    the people are honest;
When government is meddlesome,
    the state is lacking.

Disaster is that whereon good fortune depends,
Good fortune is that wherein disaster lurks.
    Who knows their limits?

When there is no uprightness,
    correct reverts to crafty,
    good reverts to gruesome.

The delusion of mankind,
How long have been its days!

For this reason, be
    Square but not cutting,
    Angular but not prickly,
    Straight but not arrogant,
    Bright but not dazzling.

22
(59)

To rule men and serve heaven,
    there is nothing like thrift.
Now,
    Only through thrift
      can one be prepared;
    Being prepared
      means having a heavy store of integrity;
    With a heavy store of integrity,
      he can overcome everything.
    Able to overcome everything,
      no one knows his limits;
    If no one knows his limits,
      he can have the kingdom;
    Having the mother of the kingdom,
      he can long endure.
    This is called "sinking roots firm and deep,
      the Way of long life and lasting vision."

23
(60)

Ruling a big kingdom is like cooking a small fish.
If one oversees all under heaven in accord with the Way,
    demons have no spirit.
It is not that the demons have no spirit,
    but that their spirits do not harm people.
It is not merely that their spirits do not harm people,
    but that the sage also does not harm them.

Now,
    When neither harms the other,
        integrity accrues to both.

24
(61)

A large state is like a low-lying estuary,
    the female of all under heaven.
In the congress of all under heaven,
    the female always conquers the male through her stillness.
Because she is still,
    it is fitting for her to lie low.
By lying beneath a small state,
    a large state can take over a small state.
By lying beneath a large state,
    a small state can be taken over by a large state.

Therefore,
    One may either take over or be taken over by lying low.

Therefore,
    The large state wishes only to annex and nurture others;
    The small state wants only to join with and serve others.

Now,
    Since both get what they want,
    It is fitting for the large state to lie low.

25
(62)

The Way is the cistern of the myriad creatures;
It is the treasure of the good man,
And that which is treasured by the bad man.

Beautiful words can be traded,
Noble deeds can be used as gifts for others.
Why should we reject even what is bad about men?

Therefore,
    When the son of heaven is enthroned
            or the three ministers are installed,
    Although they may have large jade disks
    And be preceded by teams of four horses,
    It would be better for them to sit down
            and make progress in this.

    What was the reason for the ancients
            to value this so highly?
Did they not say:
    "Seek and thou shalt receive;
    Sin and thou shalt be forgiven"?

Therefore,
    It is valued by all under heaven.

Act through nonaction,
Handle affairs through noninterference,
Taste what has no taste,
Regard the small as great, the few as many,
Repay resentment with integrity.

Undertake difficult tasks
　　by approaching what is easy in them;
Do great deeds
　　by focusing on their minute aspects.

All difficulties under heaven arise from what is easy,
All great things under heaven arise from what is minute.

For this reason,
　　The sage never strives to do what is great.
Therefore,
　　He can achieve greatness.

One who lightly assents
　　will seldom be believed;
One who thinks everything is easy
　　will encounter much difficulty.

For this reason,
　　Even the sage considers things difficult.
Therefore,
　　In the end he is without difficulty.

27
(64)

What is secure is easily grasped,
What has no omens is easily forestalled,
What is brittle is easily split,
What is minuscule is easily dispersed.

Act before there is a problem;
Bring order before there is disorder.

A tree that fills the arms' embrace
   is born from a downy shoot;
A terrace nine layers high
   starts from a basketful of earth;
An ascent of a hundred strides
   begins beneath one's foot.

Who acts fails;
Who grasps loses.

For this reason,
   The sage does not act.
Therefore,
   He does not fail.

He does not grasp.
Therefore,
   He does not lose.

In pursuing their affairs,
>   people often fail when they are close to success.
Therefore,
>   If one is as cautious at the end as at the beginning,
>   there will be no failures.

For this reason,
>   The sage desires to be without desire
>   and does not prize goods that are hard to obtain;
>   He learns not to learn
>   and reverts to what the masses pass by.

>   Thus, he can help the myriad creatures be natural,
>   but dares not act.

28
(65)

The ancients who practiced the Way
    did not enlighten the people with it;
They used it, rather, to stupefy them.

The people are hard to rule
    because they have too much knowledge.
Therefore,
    Ruling a state through knowledge is to rob the state;
    Ruling a state through ignorance
        brings integrity to the state.

One who is always mindful of these two types
        grasps a paradigm;
Mindfulness of this paradigm is called "mysterious integrity."

Deep and distant is this mysterious integrity!
It runs counter to things
    until it reaches the great confluence.

29
(66)

The river and sea can be kings of
                    the hundred valley streams
            because they are good at lying below them.
For this reason,
        They can be kings of the hundred valley streams.
For this reason, too,
        If the sage wants to be above the people,
            in his words, he must put himself below them;
        If he wishes to be before the people,
            in his person, he must stand behind them.
Therefore,
        He is situated in front of the people,
            but they are not offended;
        He is situated above the people,
            but they do not consider him a burden.
        All under heaven happily push him forward without
                    wearying.
        Is this not because he is without contention?
Therefore,
        No one under heaven can contend with him.

30
(80)

Let there be a small state with few people,
    where military devices find no use;
Let the people look solemnly upon death,
    and banish the thought of moving elsewhere.

They may have carts and boats,
    but there is no reason to ride them;
They may have armor and weapons,
    but they have no reason to display them.

Let the people go back to tying knots
    to keep records.
Let their food be savory,
    their clothes beautiful,
    their customs pleasurable,
    their dwellings secure.

Though they may gaze across at a neighboring state,
    and hear the sounds of its dogs and chickens,
The people will never travel back and forth,
    till they die of old age.

31
(81)

Sincere words are not beautiful,
Beautiful words are not sincere.
He who knows is not learned,
He who is learned does not know.
He who is good does not have much,
He who has much is not good.

The sage does not hoard.
The more he does for others,
    the more he has himself;
The more he gives to others,
    the more his own bounty increases.

Therefore,
    The Way of heaven benefits but does not harm,
    The Way of man acts but does not contend.

32
(67)

All under heaven say that I am great,
   great but unconventional.
Now,
   Precisely because I am unconventional,
      I can be great;
   If I were conventional,
      I would long since have become a trifle.

I have always possessed three treasures
   that I guard and cherish.
The first is compassion,
The second is frugality,
The third is not daring to be ahead of all under heaven.

Now,
   Because I am compassionate,
      I can be brave;
   Because I am frugal,
      I can be magnanimous;
   Because I dare not be ahead of all under heaven,
      I can be a leader in the completion of affairs.

If, today, I were to
   Be courageous while forsaking compassion,
   Be magnanimous while forsaking frugality,
   Get ahead while forsaking the hindmost,
      that would be death!

For compassion
    In war brings victory,
    In defense brings invulnerability.

    Whomsoever heaven would establish,
    It surrounds with a bulwark of compassion.

33
(68)

A good warrior is not bellicose,
A good fighter does not anger,
A good conqueror does not contest his enemy,
One who is good at using others puts himself below them.
This is called "integrity without competition,"
This is called "using others,"
This is called "parity with heaven,"
    —the pinnacle of the ancients.

34
(69)

The strategists have a saying:
    "I dare not be host,
        but would rather be guest;
    I advance not an inch,
        but instead retreat a foot."

This is called
    Marching without ranks,
    Bearing nonexistent arms,
    Flourishing nonexistent weapons,
    Driving back nonexistent enemies.

    There is no greater misfortune
        than not having a worthy foe;
    Once I believe there are no worthy foes,
        I have well-nigh forfeited my treasures.

Therefore,
    When opposing forces are evenly matched,
    The one who is saddened will be victorious.

35
(70)

My words are
   very easy to understand,
   very easy to practice.
But no one is able to understand them,
And no one is able to practice them.

Words have authority.
Affairs have an ancestry.

It is simply because of their ignorance,
   that they do not understand me;
Those who understand me are few,
   thus I am ennobled.

For this reason,
   The sage wears coarse clothing over his shoulders,
   but carries jade within his bosom.

36
(71)

To realize that you do not understand is a virtue;
Not to realize that you do not understand is a defect.

The reason why
    The sage has no defects,
    Is because he treats defects as defects.

Thus,
    He has no defects.

37
(72)

When the people do not fear the majestic,
Great majesty will soon visit them.

Do not limit their dwellings,
Do not suppress their livelihood.
Simply because you do not suppress them,
    they will not grow weary of you.

For this reason,
    The sage is self-aware,
        but does not flaunt himself;
    He is self-devoted,
        but does not glorify himself.

Therefore,
    He rejects the one and adopts the other.

38
(73)

He who is brave in daring will be killed,
He who is brave in not daring will survive.
One of these two courses is beneficial,
The other is harmful.

Who knows the reason for heaven's dislikes?
The Way of heaven
    does not war
      yet is good at conquering,
    does not speak
      yet is good at answering,
    is not summoned
      yet comes of itself,
    is relaxed
      yet good at making plans.

Heaven's net is vast;
Though its meshes are wide,
    nothing escapes.

39
(74)

If the people never fear death,
    what is the purpose of threatening to kill them?
If the people ever fear death,
    and I were to capture and kill those who are devious,
        who would dare to be so?
If the people must be ever fearful of death,
    then there will always be an executioner.

Now,
    To kill in place of the executioner
Is like
    Hewing wood in place of the master carpenter;
    Few indeed will escape cutting their own hands!

Human hunger
　　is the result of overtaxation.
For this reason,
　　There is hunger.

The common people are not governable
　　because of their superiors' actions.
For this reason,
　　They are not governable.

The people make light of death
　　because of too much emphasis on the quest for life.
For this reason,
　　They make light of death.

Now,
　　Only she who acts not for the sake of life
　　Is wiser than those who value life highly.

41
(76)

Human beings are
  soft and supple when alive,
  stiff and straight when dead.

The myriad creatures, the grasses and trees are
  soft and fragile when alive,
  dry and withered when dead.

Therefore, it is said:
  The rigid person is a disciple of death;
  The soft, supple, and delicate are lovers of life.

  An army that is inflexible will not conquer;
  A tree that is inflexible will snap.

  The unyielding and mighty shall be brought low;
  The soft, supple, and delicate will be set above.

42
(77)

The Way of heaven is like the bending of a bow—
    the upper part is pressed down,
    the lower part is raised up,
    the part that has too much is reduced,
    the part that has too little is increased.
Therefore,
    The Way of heaven
        reduces surplus to make up for scarcity;
    The Way of man
        reduces scarcity and pays tribute to surplus.

Who is there that can have a surplus
    and take from it to pay tribute to heaven?
Surely only one who has the Way!

For this reason,
    The sage
        acts but does not possess,
        completes his work but does not dwell on it.
    In this fashion,
        he has no desire to display his worth.

43
(78)

Nothing under heaven is softer or weaker than water,
 and yet nothing is better
  for attacking what is hard and strong,
   because of its immutability.

The defeat of the hard by the soft,
The defeat of the strong by the weak—
 this is known to all under heaven,
  yet no one is able to practice it.

Therefore, in the words of the sage, it is said:
 "He who bears abuse directed against the state
  is called 'lord of the altars for the gods of soil and grain';
 He who bears the misfortunes of the state
  is called the 'king of all under heaven.' "

True words seem contradictory.

44
(79)

Compromise with great resentment
   will surely yield lingering resentment;
How can this be seen as good?

For this reason,
     The sage holds the debtor's side of a contract
       and does not make claims upon others.

Therefore,
     The man of integrity attends to his debts;
     The man without integrity attends to his exactions.

     The Way of heaven is impartial,
       yet is always with the good person.

TAO

THE WAY

45
(1)

The ways that can be walked are not the eternal Way;
The names that can be named are not the eternal name.
The nameless is the origin of the myriad creatures;
The named is the mother of the myriad creatures.

Therefore,
    Always be without desire
      in order to observe its wondrous subtleties;
    Always have desire
      so that you may observe its manifestations.

Both of these derive from the same source;
They have different names but the same designation.

Mystery of mysteries,
The gate of all wonders!

When all under heaven know beauty as beauty,
    already there is ugliness;
When everyone knows goodness,
    this accounts for badness.

Being and nonbeing give birth to each other,
Difficult and easy complete each other,
Long and short form each other,
High and low fulfill each other,
Tone and voice harmonize with each other,
Front and back follow each other—
    it is ever thus.

For these reasons,
    The sage
        dwells in affairs of nonaction,
        carries out a doctrine without words.
    He lets the myriad creatures rise up
        but does not instigate them;
    He acts
        but does not presume;
    He completes his work
        but does not dwell on it.

Now,
    Simply because he does not dwell on them,
        his accomplishments never leave him.

47
(3)

Not exalting men of worth
   prevents the people from competing;
Not putting high value on rare goods
   prevents the people from being bandits;
Not displaying objects of desire
   prevents the people from being disorderly.

For these reasons,
   The sage, in ruling,
      hollows their hearts,
      stuffs their stomachs,
      weakens their wills,
      builds up their bones,
   Always causing the people
      to be without knowledge and desire.
   He ensures that
      the knowledgeable dare not be hostile,
               and that is all.
Thus,
   His rule is universal.

The Way is empty,
      yet never refills with use;
Bottomless it is,
      like the forefather of the myriad creatures.
It files away sharp points,
      unravels tangles,
      diffuses light,
      mingles with the dust.
Submerged it lies,
      seeming barely to subsist.
I know not whose child it is,
      only that it resembles the predecessor of God.

49
(5)

Heaven and earth are inhumane;
    they view the myriad creatures as straw dogs.
The sage is inhumane;
    he views the common people as straw dogs.

The space between heaven and earth,
    how like a bellows it is!
Empty but never exhausted,
The more it pumps, the more comes out.

Hearing too much leads to utter exhaustion;
Better to remain in the center.

50
(6)

_____

The valley spirit never dies—
    it is called "the mysterious female";
The gate of the mysterious female
    is called "the root of heaven and earth."
Gossamer it is,
    seemingly insubstantial,
     yet never consumed through use.

51
(7)

Heaven is long and earth is lasting.
Heaven and earth can be long and lasting
because they do not live for themselves.
Therefore,
They can be long-lived.

For this reason,
The sage
withdraws himself
but comes to the fore,
alienates himself
but is always present.

Is this not because he is free of private interests?
Therefore,
He can accomplish his private interests.

52
(8)

The highest good is like water;
Water is good at benefiting the myriad creatures
        but also struggles
   to occupy the place loathed by the masses.
Therefore,
    It is near to the Way.

The quality of an abode is in its location,
The quality of the heart is in its depths,
The quality of giving lies in trust,
The quality of correct governance lies in orderly rule,
The quality of an enterprise depends on ability,
The quality of movement depends on timing.

Now,
    It is precisely because one does not compete
       that there is no blame.

53
(9)

Instead of keeping a bow taut while holding it straight,
    better to relax.
You may temper a sword until it is razor sharp,
    but you cannot preserve the edge for long.
When gold and jade fill your rooms,
    no one will be able to guard them for you.
If wealth and honor make you haughty,
    you bequeath misfortune upon yourself.
To withdraw when your work is finished,
    that is the Way of heaven.

54
(10)

While you
>Cultivate the soul and embrace unity,
>>can you keep them from separating?
>Focus your vital breath until it is supremely soft,
>>can you be like a baby?
>Cleanse the mirror of mysteries,
>>can you make it free of blemish?
>Love the people and enliven the state,
>>can you do so without cunning?
>Open and close the gate of heaven,
>>can you play the part of the female?
>Reach out with clarity in all directions,
>>can you refrain from action?

It gives birth to them and nurtures them,
It gives birth to them but does not possess them,
It rears them but does not control them.
>This is called "mysterious integrity."

55
(11)

Thirty spokes converge on a single hub,
  but it is in the space where there is nothing
    that the usefulness of the cart lies.
Clay is molded to make a pot,
  but it is in the space where there is nothing
    that the usefulness of the clay pot lies.
Cut out doors and windows to make a room,
  but it is in the spaces where there is nothing
    that the usefulness of the room lies.
Therefore,
  Benefit may be derived from something,
    but it is in nothing that we find usefulness.

56
(12)

The five colors
   make a man's eyes blind;
Horseracing and hunting
   make a man's mind go mad;
Goods that are hard to obtain
   make a man's progress falter;
The five flavors
   make a man's palate dull;
The five tones
   make a man's ears deaf.

For these reasons,
   In ruling, the sage
      attends to the stomach, not to the eye.
Therefore,
   He rejects the one and adopts the other.

57
(13)

"Being favored is so disgraceful that it startles,
Being honored is an affliction as great as one's body."

What is the meaning of
"Being favored is so disgraceful that it startles"?

Favor is debasing;
To find it is startling,
To lose it is startling.

This is the meaning of
"Being favored is so disgraceful that it startles."

What is the meaning of
"Being honored is an affliction as great as one's body"?

The reason I suffer great afflictions is because I have a body;
If I had no body, what affliction could I suffer?

Therefore,
When a man puts more emphasis on caring for his body
than on caring for all under heaven,
then all under heaven can be entrusted to him.
When a man is sparing of his body in caring
for all under heaven,
then all under heaven can be delivered to him.

58
(14)

We look for it but do not see it;
  we name it "subtle."
We listen for it but do not hear it;
  we name it "rare."
We grope for it but do not grasp it;
  we name it "serene."

These three cannot be fully fathomed,
Therefore,
  They are bound together to make unity.

Of unity,
  its top is not distant,
  its bottom is not blurred.
Infinitely extended
  and unnameable,
It returns to nonentity.
This is called
  "the form of the formless,
  the image of nonentity."
This is called "the amorphous."

Following behind it,
  you cannot see its back;
Approaching it from the front,
  you cannot see its head.

Hold to the Way of today
    to manage the actualities of today,
    thereby understanding the primeval beginning.
This is called "the thread of the Way."

59
(15)

Those of old who were adept in the Way
  were subtly profound and mysteriously perceptive,
So deep
  they could not be recognized.

Now,
  Because they could not be recognized,
One can describe their appearance only with effort:
  hesitant,
    as though crossing a stream in winter;
  cautious,
    as though fearful of their neighbors all around;
  solemn,
    as though guests in someone else's house;
  shrinking,
    as ice when it melts;
  plain,
    as an unhewn log;
  muddled,
    as turbid waters;
  expansive,
    as a broad valley.

If turbid waters are stilled,
  they will gradually become clear;
If something inert is set in motion,
  it will gradually come to life.

Those who preserved this Way did not wish to be full.
Now,
    Simply because they did not wish to be full,
      they could be threadbare and incomplete.

60
(16)

Attain utmost emptiness,
Maintain utter stillness.

The myriad creatures arise side by side,
    thus I observe their renewal.
Heaven's creatures abound,
    but each returns to its roots,
        which is called "stillness."
This is termed "renewal of fate."
Renewal of fate is perpetual—
To know the perpetual is to be enlightened;
Not to know the perpetual is to be reckless—
    recklessness breeds evil.
To know the perpetual is to be tolerant—
    tolerance leads to ducal impartiality,
    ducal impartiality to kingliness,
    kingliness to heaven,
    heaven to the Way,
    the Way to permanence.

To the end of his days,
    he will not be imperiled.

61
(17)

Preeminent is one whose subjects barely know he exists;
The next is one to whom they feel close and praise;
The next is one whom they fear;
The lowest is one whom they despise.

When the ruler's trust is wanting,
    there will be no trust in him.
Cautious,
    he values his words.
When his work is completed and his affairs finished,
    the common people say,
        "We are like this by ourselves."

62
(18)

Therefore,
> When the great Way was forsaken,
>> there was humaneness and righteousness;
> When cunning and wit appeared,
>> there was great falsity;
> When the six family relationships lacked harmony,
>> there were filial piety and parental kindness;
> When the state and royal house were in disarray,
>> there were upright ministers.

63
(19)

"Abolish sagehood and abandon cunning,
    the people will benefit a hundredfold;
Abolish humaneness and abandon righteousness,
    the people will once again be filial and kind;
Abolish cleverness and abandon profit,
    bandits and thieves will be no more."

These three statements
    are inadequate as a civilizing doctrine;
Therefore,
    Let something be added to them:

Evince the plainness of undyed silk,
Embrace the simplicity of the unhewn log;
Lessen selfishness,
Diminish desires;
Abolish learning
    and you will be without worries.

64
(20)

Between "yes sir" and "certainly not!"
    how much difference is there?
Between beauty and ugliness,
    how great is the distinction?

He whom others fear,
    likewise cannot but fear others.

How confusing,
    there is no end to it all!

Joyful are the masses,
    as though feasting after the great sacrifice of oxen,
    or mounting a terrace in spring.

Motionless am I,
    without any sign,
    as a baby that has yet to gurgle.
How dejected!
    as though having nowhere to return.

The masses all have more than enough;
I alone am bereft.

I have the heart of a fool.
How muddled!

The ordinary man is luminously clear,
I alone seem confused.
The ordinary man is searchingly exact,
I alone am vague and uncertain.

How nebulous!
    as the ocean;
How blurred!
    as though without boundary.

The masses all have a purpose,
I alone am stubborn and uncouth.

I desire to be uniquely different from others
    by honoring the mother who nourishes.

65

(21)

The appearance of grand integrity
    is that it follows the Way alone.
The Way objectified
    is blurred and nebulous.

How nebulous and blurred!
Yet within it there are images.
How blurred and nebulous!
Yet within it there are objects.
How cavernous and dark!
Yet within it there is an essence.
Its essence is quite real;
Within it there are tokens.

From the present back to the past,
Its name has been imperishable.
Through it we conform to the father of the masses.

How do I know what the father of the masses is like?
Through this.

66
(24)

Who is puffed up cannot stand,
Who is self-absorbed has no distinction,
Who is self-revealing does not shine,
Who is self-assertive has no merit,
Who is self-praising does not last long.

As for the Way, we may say these are
    "excess provisions and extra baggage."
Creation abhors such extravagances.

Therefore,
    One who aspires to the Way,
        does not abide in them.

67
(22)

___

If it
      is bent,
            it will be preserved intact;
      is crooked,
            it will be straightened;
      is sunken,
            it will be filled;
      is worn-out,
            it will be renewed;
      has little,
            it will gain;
      has much,
            it will be confused.

For these reasons,
      The sage holds on to unity
            and serves as the shepherd of all under heaven.
      He is not self-absorbed,
            therefore he shines forth;
      He is not self-revealing,
            therefore he is distinguished;
      He is not self-assertive,
            therefore he has merit;
      He does not praise himself,
            therefore he is long-lasting.

Now,
    Simply because he does not compete,
      No one can compete with him.

    The old saying about the bent being preserved intact
      is indeed close to the mark!

    Truly, he shall be returned intact.

68
(23)

To be sparing of speech is natural.

A whirlwind does not last the whole morning,
A downpour does not last the whole day.
Who causes them?
If even heaven and earth cannot cause them to persist,
    how much less can human beings?

Therefore,
    In pursuing his affairs,
        a man of the Way identifies with the Way,
        a man of integrity identifies with integrity,
        a man who fails identifies with failure.

To him who identifies with integrity,
    the Way awards integrity;
To him who identifies with failure,
    the Way awards failure.

69
(25)

There was something featureless yet complete,
    born before heaven and earth;
Silent—amorphous—
    it stood alone and unchanging.

We may regard it as the mother of heaven and earth.
Not knowing its name,
    I style it the "Way."
If forced to give it a name,
    I would call it "great."
Being great implies flowing ever onward,
Flowing ever onward implies far-reaching,
Far-reaching implies reversal.

The Way is great,
Heaven is great,
Earth is great,
The king, too, is great.

Within the realm there are four greats,
    and the king is one among them.

Man
    patterns himself on earth,
Earth
    patterns itself on heaven,
Heaven
    patterns itself on the Way,
The Way
    patterns itself on nature.

Heavy is the root of light;
Calm is the ruler of haste.

For these reasons,
    The superior man may travel the whole day
      without leaving his heavy baggage cart.
    Though inside the courtyard walls of a noisy inn,
      he placidly rises above it all.

How then should a king with ten thousand chariots
    conduct himself lightly before all under heaven?

If he treats himself lightly,
    he will lose the taproot;
If he is hasty,
    he will lose the rulership.

71
(27)

He who is skilled at traveling
  leaves neither tracks nor traces;
He who is skilled at speaking
  is flawless in his delivery;
He who is skilled in computation
  uses neither tallies nor counters;
He who is skilled at closing things tightly
  has neither lock nor key,
    but what he closes cannot be opened;
He who is good at binding
  has neither cord nor string,
    but what he binds cannot be untied.

For these reasons,
  The sage
    is always skilled at saving others
    and does not abandon them,
    nor does he abandon resources.
  This is called "inner intelligence."

Therefore,
  Good men are teachers for the good man,
  Bad men are foils for the good man.
  He who values not his teacher
    and loves not his foil,
  Though he be knowledgeable,
    is greatly deluded.

This is called "the wondrous essential."

72
(28)

Know masculinity,
Maintain femininity,
  and be a ravine for all under heaven.
By being a ravine for all under heaven,
Eternal integrity will never desert you.
If eternal integrity never deserts you,
You will return to the state of infancy.

Know you are innocent,
Remain steadfast when insulted,
  and be a valley for all under heaven.
By being a valley for all under heaven,
Eternal integrity will suffice.
If eternal integrity suffices,
You will return to the simplicity of the unhewn log.

Know whiteness,
Maintain blackness,
  and be a model for all under heaven.
By being a model for all under heaven,
Eternal integrity will not err.
If eternal integrity does not err,
You will return to infinity.

When the unhewn log is sawn apart,
  it is made into tools;
When the sage is put to use,
  he becomes the chief of officials.

For
  Great carving does no cutting.

73
(29)

Of those who wish to take hold of all-under-heaven
and act upon it,
I have seen that they do not succeed.
Now,
All-under-heaven is a sacred vessel,
Not something that can be acted upon;
Who acts upon it will be defeated,
Who grasps it will lose it.

Of creatures,
some march forward, others follow behind;
some are shiveringly silent, others are all puffed up;
some are strong, others are meek;
some pile up, others collapse.

For these reasons,
The sage
rejects extremes,
rejects excess,
rejects extravagance.

74
(30)

One who assists the ruler of men with the Way
     does not use force of arms against all under heaven;
Such a course is likely to boomerang.

Where armies have been stationed,
     briars and brambles will grow.

A good general fulfills his purpose
         and that is all.
He does not use force
     to seize for himself.

He fulfills his purpose,
     but is not proud;
He fulfills his purpose,
     but is not boastful;
He fulfills his purpose,
     but does not brag;
He fulfills his purpose
     only because he has no other choice.

This is called "fulfilling one's purpose without using force."

If something grows old while still in its prime,
This is called "not being in accord with the Way."
Not being in accord with the Way
     leads to an early demise.

75
(31)

Now,
> Weapons are instruments of evil omen;
> Creation abhors them.

Therefore,
> One who aspires to the Way
>> does not abide in them.

> The superior man
>> at home honors the left,
>> on the battlefield honors the right.

Therefore,
> Weapons are not instruments of the superior man;
> Weapons are instruments of evil omen,
>> to be used only when there is no other choice.

> He places placidity above all
>> and refuses to prettify weapons;
> If one prettifies weapons,
>> this is to delight in the killing of others.

Now,
> One who delights in the killing of others
> Cannot exercise his will over all under heaven.

For this reason,
> On occasions for celebration,
>> the left is given priority;
> On occasions for mourning,
>> the right is given priority.

Therefore,
    A deputy general stands on the left,
    The general-in-chief stands on the right.
In other words,
    They stand in accordance with mourning ritual.

    The killing of masses of human beings,
      we bewail with sorrow and grief;
    Victory in battle,
      we commemorate with mourning ritual.

76
(32)

The Way is eternally nameless.

Though the unhewn log is small,
No one in the world dares subjugate it.
If feudal lords and kings could maintain it,
The myriad creatures would submit of themselves.

Heaven and earth unite
    to suffuse sweet dew.
Without commanding the people,
    equality will naturally ensue.

As soon as one begins to divide things up,
    there are names;
Once there are names,
    one should also know when to stop;
Knowing when to stop,
    one thereby avoids peril.

In metaphorical terms,
    The relationship of all under heaven to the Way
        is like that of valley streams
            to the river and sea.

77
(33)

Understanding others is knowledge,
Understanding oneself is enlightenment;
Conquering others is power,
Conquering oneself is strength;
Contentment is wealth,
Forceful conduct is willfulness;
Not losing one's rightful place is to endure,
To die but not be forgotten is longevity.

78
(34)

Rippling is the Way, flowing left and right!
Its tasks completed, its affairs finished,
Still it does not claim them for its own.
The myriad creatures return to it,
But it does not act as their ruler.

Eternally without desire,
It may be named among the small;
The myriad creatures return to it,
But it does not act as their ruler;
It may be named among the great.

For these reasons,
    The sage can achieve greatness,
    Because he does not act great.
Therefore,
    He can achieve greatness.

Hold fast to the great image
    and all under heaven will come;
They will
    come but not be harmed,
    rest in safety and peace;
Music and fine food
    will make the passerby halt.

Therefore,
    When the Way is expressed verbally,
We say such things as
    "how bland and tasteless it is!"
"We look for it,
    but there is not enough to be seen."
"We listen for it,
    but there is not enough to be heard."
Yet, when put to use,
    it is inexhaustible!

80
(36)

When you wish to contract something,
    you must momentarily expand it;
When you wish to weaken something,
    you must momentarily strengthen it;
When you wish to reject something,
    you must momentarily join with it;
When you wish to seize something,
    you must momentarily give it up.
This is called "subtle insight."

The soft and weak conquer the strong.

Fish cannot be removed from the watery depths;
The profitable instruments of state
              cannot be shown to the people.

81
(37)

The Way is eternally nameless.
If feudal lords and kings preserve it,
The myriad creatures will be transformed by themselves.
After transformation, if they wish to rise up,
I shall restrain them with the nameless unhewn log.
By restraining them with the nameless unhewn log,
They will not feel disgraced;
Not feeling disgraced,
They will be still,
Whereupon heaven and earth will be made right by themselves.

NOTES AND COMMENTARY

1.7—**humaneness** Like "righteousness" and "etiquette" in lines 9 and 11 below, this is an important element of Confucian ideology. It is obvious that the author of this chapter takes a rather dim view of all three. *Jen* (humaneness) is cognate with the homonymous *jen* (human [being]), and both are probably ultimately related to Proto-Indo-European *dhghem*, the root for "human," which means basically "earth." Compare Persian *zamīn* (earth, land), Russian *zemlya* (land), and Old Chinese *zim* (= modern standard Mandarin *jen*). Hence, we may think of humans and *jen* as "earthlings," or those who spring from humus. The character for *jen* (humaneness) shows a man with the sign for "two," thus "[the way] a man [should relate to or treat] others." The usual translations for *jen* are "benevolence," "charity," "altruism," "kindness," and so forth. Although several of them are closely associated with certain historical, secular, and theological movements, I believe the use of some such terms as "humanism," "humanitarianism," "humaneness," or "humanity" as a rendering for *jen* is almost obligatory to show the intimate relationship of this Confucian ethical concept to *jen* (human [being]). The Confucian ideal of humanism and the Western tradition of Humanism share an emphasis on the achievements and concerns of mankind, but we may distinguish them by following the usual practice of capitalizing the latter. The other word for man or people in the *Tao Te Ching*, modern standard Mandarin *min*, is obviously cognate with English "man." Compare Indo-European *man* or *mon* and Old Chinese *myuhn*, Sanskrit *manu* (the thinking one, the creature with a mind), etc.

107

2.11—**right** The usual sinological translation of this term is "rectitude." Here and elsewhere it might well be interpreted as "correct governance," with which it is closely cognate in Sinitic languages.

4.1—**Reversal** Compare *Muṇḍaka Upaniṣad*, II.i.1, where all kinds of creatures are said to issue forth from the immutable (*brahman*) and return to it. Also see *Tao Te Ching*, 27.31, 60.3–4, 69.12, etc.

4.4—Compare this line with *Chāndogya Upaniṣad*, VI.ii.1.

5.5–6—I have left the technical terms yin and yang untranslated because they have already become a part of English vocabulary. While their significance in Chinese dualistic cosmology is known as the passive, female principle and the active, male principle, respectively, it may also be useful to understand these terms in their more primitive senses of shadeward and sunward, hence lunar and solar.

5.7—**vapors** Modern standard Mandarin *ch'i* (vital breath), for a discussion of which see the Afterword, pp. 137–138.

12.1—**mind** The Chinese word *hsin* means both "heart" and "mind."

13.19—This line bears a striking resemblance to the *Bhagavad Gītā*, II.23: "Weapons do not cut it."

14.18—**control** That is to say, it does not exercise dominion over them.

14.19—Almost identical to the last line of chapter 54.

15.9—**orifices of your heart** In ancient Chinese medicine, it was thought that the life breath (*ch'i*) flowed through the openings of the heart. It would seem that the author of the *Tao Te Ching* is grappling here with the problem of how to preserve one's vital energy. Because of the oddly arresting quality of the vocabulary here and in the parallel passage below (19.4–5), I have intentionally employed slightly obscure English phraseology.

15.10—Referring, presumably, to the senses. The same narrowing of consciousness is frequently described in very early Indian texts in almost exactly the same terms. See Feuerstein, p. 104. Compare *Kaṭha Upaniṣad*, II.ii.1; *Chāndogya Upaniṣad*, III.xiii.1–7, where the different types of vital breath that pass through these gates are outlined with precision; the *Bhagavad Gītā*, V.13, and especially VIII.12, which is quoted in the Afterword, pp. 144–145.

16.15—There is an obvious pun here between "bandit" (*tao*) and "the Way" (*Tao*). For similar reasons the thief is mentioned in the *Bhagavad Gītā*, III.12.

17.15—"This" signifies the Way. One knows the nature of all under heaven through observing things in accordance with the Way. Compare 65.17 and the note to 20.4.

18.11—**essence** The character may also quite literally be interpreted as "semen."

18.14–17—**implies, requires, is, entails** The Chinese text has the same word (modern standard Mandarin *yüeh*, "to say, call") for all of these English verbs.

19.4—**openings of his heart** Compare 15.9 above. The character as it appears here shows a heart inside of a gate. This is conventionally interpreted as meaning "depression" or "melancholy" (that is, the heart-mind closed up). From context, comparison with other manuscripts and early editions, and above all from the parallel passage cited at the beginning of this note, it is evident that this is not precisely what the author had in mind here. He intended, rather, to indicate the apertures of the heart.

19.4–6—See commentary to 15.9.

19.7—**the dust** The mundane world.

20.4—Neither of the two manuscripts from Ma-wang-tui answers this question, but the Fu I text has the concise rejoinder "Through this," implying the Way. Compare 17.15 and 65.17.

22.2, 4—**thrift** The author may have chosen the wrong word, but he wrote *se*, which means "stingy, mean, miserly, grasping." It sounds odd to have the Old Master advocating such behavior to one who would "rule men and serve heaven." He is not, however, advocating extreme parsimony or frugality here. Instead, he is advising the potential ruler to husband his own integrity. This becomes clear in lines 7ff.

23.3—**demons** Modern standard Mandarin *kuei*, often rendered as "ghost." A more exact translation might be "specters" or "lemures," as in ancient Roman religion.

25.8—**son of heaven** The emperor.

25.12—**to sit down** Presumably to meditate.

25.12—**this** The Way.

25.15—Compare Matt. 7:7 ("seek, and ye shall find") and 7:8 ("he that seeketh findeth"). These sayings of Jesus surely must be based on pre-Christian sentiments since we find them voiced in the *Tao Te Ching*, which originated at the other end of the continent.

25.16—Compare Apocrypha, Eccles. 2:1 ("the Lord . . . forgiveth sins").

26.3—Closely reminiscent of the *Bhagavad Gītā*, II.59.3.

26.5—Compare Saint Paul's injunction to "overcome evil with good" in Rom. 12:21.

30.9–10—Compare the quipu of various primitive societies.

32.4—Everywhere the word *hsiao* ([un]conventional) appears in this passage, it is meant to be a pun with the homophonous *hsiao* (small).

32.8—**three treasures** This expression is identical to the ancient Indian *triratna* or *ratnatraya*. Indeed, when Chinese Buddhists later translated these terms into their own language, they used the same two words (modern standard Mandarin *san-pao*) as here. In India, the notion of Three Jewels was common to various religious persuasions, each of which interpreted it in different ways. To the Buddhists it referred, of course, to the Buddha, the Dharma (his law or doctrine), and the Sangha (the Buddhist community). For the Jains, it signified *samyag-darśana* (correct perception or insight), *samyag-jñāna* (correct knowledge), and *samyag-cāritra* (correct conduct). The expression *ratnatraya* occurs in the titles of numerous Buddhist and Jain texts and even in those of some Vedānta and Śaivite (Hindu) treatises. It is not at all strange that the Taoists would take over this widespread ancient Indian expression and use it for their own purposes.

32.10—**compassion** Compare Sanskrit *karuṇa*, which the Chinese Buddhists subsequently translated with the same character as that used here by Lao Tzu.

34.2—**be host** Take the initiative.

34.14—**treasures** Compare line 32.8 and its note.

35.1–5—Compare the candid comments of Ssu-ma T'an, father of the great historian Ssu-ma Ch'ien (145–90? B.C.): "The Taoists propound 'non-action' which is also called 'non-inaction.' In reality, it is easy to practice but their words are hard to understand." See *Records of the Grand Historian* (K'ai-ming ed.), 130.279a.

35.8—**ignorance** Compare Sanskrit *ajñāna*, a key term in the *Bhagavad Gītā*.

38.15—**Heaven's net** This seems to be a veiled reference to *indrajāla* ("Indra's net"), mentioned several times already in the *Atharvaveda*. Compare also the net of Brahman in *Śvetāśvatara Upaniṣad*, V.3.

40.10—Many ancient Chinese rulers were almost fanatical in their pursuit of longevity. They resorted to all sorts of bizarre regimens and extravagant practices, including the ingestion of cinnabar (mercuric sulfide) which, of course, had the opposite effect on their life spans of what they desired, and the dispatching of innocent youths into the ocean to find the Isles of Immortality. It is ironic that Lao Tzu, the supposed author of this indictment against longevity (cf. also 33.8), would be made the emblem of life extension by many of his devotees. In truth, however, there are contradictory statements concerning the prolongation of life in *Tao Te Ching* (cf. 7.11, 13.12, 18.21, 41.9, 66.5, 74.22).

42.1—The bow is a favorite metaphor in early Indian texts. Compare *Muṇḍaka Upaniṣad*, II.ii.3–4.

42.15–17—Compare 46.18–21.

44.5—**contract** The imagery employed here is that of the system of tallies in ancient China whereby debtors were given the left-hand side of a piece of wood or bamboo that was split in half and creditors were given the right-hand side. When the latter wanted to collect from the former, they went with their side of the tally as proof of the loan and demanded payment.

45.1—Compare the title of the small book by Swami Ramdas: *The Pathless Path*.

45.2—Reminiscent of the famous Vedānta formula *neti neti* (not this, not that) indicating that Brahman is not designatable. See *Bṛhad-āraṇyaka Upaniṣad*, II.iii.6. Compare also the *Kena Upaniṣad*, I.5, where it is said that Brahman cannot be expressed in speech.

45.3–4—There would appear to be a contradiction between these two lines because "origin" and "mother" seem to mean the same thing. The editor(s) of the received text accordingly changed "myriad creatures" in the third line to "heaven and earth" in order to make it look like there was a difference in content between the predicates of the two lines. Yet both of the Ma-wang-tui manuscripts clearly have "myriad creatures" in both of the lines. This powerfully confirms the very careful scholarship of Ma Hsü-lun and Chiang Hsi-ch'ang, who earlier in this century proved by referring to citations in Ssu-ma Ch'ien's "biography" of the Old Master, Wang Pi's commentary, the *Wen Tzu*, and to other sources that both lines should definitely read "myriad creatures." The real distinction between the two lines lies in the fact that the "nameless" refers to the Tao (the "origin") while the "named" signifies the fecund phenomenal universe ("mother") as it evolves after the primal beginning. Thus we see that although "origin" and "mother" are grammatically and syntactically parallel, they are not semantically identical.

46.13—**sage** The homophonous orthographical error here (the graph for "sound" is written instead of that for "sage"—both are pronounced *sheng* in modern standard Mandarin) may be telling. The percipient sage is one who is aware of the voices of the people. This reminds us of the Bodhisattva of Compassion, Avalokiteśvara (Kuan[-shih-]yin), whose name literally means "Perceiving the Sounds [of the World]."

48.1—Compare 8.3.

49.2, 4—**straw dogs** Used for sacrificial purposes, these were discarded indifferently at the conclusion of the ritual.

49.6—**bellows** The bellows (Sanskrit *bhastrikā*) is a basic form of *prāṇāyāma* (see Appendix, p. 160) going back at least to the *Yoga Upaniṣad* in which the vital breath is forcibly drawn in and out with a kind of pumping action.

49.9—The expression "hear much" in Chinese means "to be learned."

50—The best analysis of this short but very important chapter is by Conrady (1932).

50.6—**insubstantial** The manuscripts read simply "seem to exist."

51.3—**they do not live for themselves** Literally, "not self live," which could also mean "are not born of themselves" (self-generated).

53.1—See note to 42.1.

53.3—**temper** Literally, "to test [by running the finger over the edge of the blade]."

54.1—**While** The character that I have translated as "while" has caused so much consternation among translators and commentators that one famous modern scholar interpreted it as meaning "carrying [one's perplexed bodily soul] on one's head," and the renowned T'ang emperor, Hsüan-tsung, shifted it to the end of the previous chapter as a sort of exclamation point (!)! The majority of less daring scholars have simply pretended that it does not exist. Without here going into all of the painstaking philological proof that would be necessary to demonstrate it fully, the function of this particle standing at the head of the chapter is to serve as what may technically be called an initial aspectual auxiliary, or a particle for beginning a dependent clause.

54.2—**soul** The male and female / yang and yin / light and dark / spiritual and physical souls.

54.4—**Focus your vital breath** This phrase serves well as a translation of *prāṇāyāma* (see Appendix, p. 160).

54.6—**mirror** The heart. Ample justification for this interpretation may be found in the commentary of Ch'en Ku-ying (1984), p. 99 n. 6. See also the brilliant and learned article by Paul Demiéville on the spiritual mirror. Compare *Katha Upaniṣad*, II.iii.5.

54.7—**make it free of blemish** See the Afterword, p. 144.

54.9—**cunning** Literally "knowledge"; compare 28.5, 7. It is curious that "cunning" and "know[ing]" are cognate, both deriving from the Indo-European root *gno*. The equivalent Sinitic word (modern standard Mandarin *chih*) usually means "to know," but occasionally in the *Tao Te Ching* (see also 62.4) is better translated as "cunning."

54.10—**gate of heaven** There is a tremendous variety of opinion among the commentators over the signification of this expression. Some hold that it refers to the sense organs (ear, mouth, eyes, nose [cf. the note to 15.10 above]), others that it stands for the institutions of government, the processes of nature, the place where the soul goes in and comes out, the place in the Polar Star where the Lord of Heaven sits, a particular trigram of the *Book of Changes*, and so on. Still others see in this passage a sexual metaphor or a description of Taoist Yoga. In truth, several levels of interpretation are possible. The ambiguity may well have been intentional.

54.11—**Remain passive.** Literally, "can be female (bird)?"

113

54.15–17—Compare chapter 14.16–19, which ascribe the same attributes to the Way.

55.1—This celebrated metaphor of thirty spokes converging on a single hub was almost certainly inspired by the Indian fondness for using wheel images to demonstrate philosophical concepts. See, for example, *Śvetāśvatara Upaniṣad*, I.4; *Praśna Upaniṣad*, VI.6; *Muṇḍaka Upaniṣad*, II.ii.6; and especially *Praśna Upaniṣad*, II.6, which puts *prāṇa* at the center of the hub.

55.4—**pot** Compare *Chāndogya Upaniṣad*, VI.i.4.

56.1—**five** This chapter has three pentads (items listed in groups of five), but later Chinese authors elaborated many more. They are all ultimately based on the notion of Five Phases / Elements / Agents (water, fire, wood, metal, earth) that became popular in China about the same time as the *Tao Te Ching* was taking shape. It is noteworthy that the notion of Five Elements also occupies a prominent place in Indian metaphysics. Indeed, there were two sets (or, perhaps more accurately, two aspects) of the Five Elements in India, a greater and a lesser. The lesser are the five rudimentary, or subtle, elements (*pañca-tanmātrāṇi*): *śabda* (sound), *sparśa* (touch), *rūpa* (color), *rasa* (flavor), and *gandha* (smell). Three of these are represented in this chapter of *Tao Te Ching*. The greater are the five gross elements (*pañca-mahābhūtāni*): *pṛthivī* (earth), *ap* or *āpas* (water), *tejas* (fire), *vāyu* (wind), and *ākāśa* (ether). In rare Indian enumerations, the same Five [Gross] Elements occur as in the standard Chinese list (metal, wood, water, fire, earth). A similar conception existed in ancient Greek and Iranian philosophy and probably reflects an underlying pan-Eurasian system of thought.

56.1—**five colors** Sanskrit *pañca-varṇa* or *pañca-kāma-guṇā*. These are the five primary colors: *nīla* (blue), *pīta* (yellow), *lohita* (red), *avadāta* (white), and *kṛṣṇa* (black). They are the same as the five colors in China. Note that the Brahman wears over his shoulder a cord made up of threads of these five colors.

56.7—**five flavors** Salty, bitter, sour, acrid, sweet. Compare Sanskrit *pañca-rasa*.

56.9—**five tones** Traditional Chinese scales have five notes (*do, re, mi, sol, la*). Compare Sanskrit *pañca-tūrya*.

56.13—This formulation obliquely recalls our saying about a man's eyes (appetite) being bigger than his stomach (real needs). In other words, the sage understands human psychology with regard to desires.

57.1–2—These two enigmatic sayings have never before been interpreted in such a fashion that they both make some sense and fit with the following sentences. More literally, "favor is a disgrace comparable to being startled; honor is a great disaster comparable to the body." I suspect that these are very old sayings that were far from transparent even to the contemporaries of the *Tao Te Ching* author or compiler. That explains why he makes such an obvious effort (not altogether successful) in this chapter to explain them.

On the human body being an affliction, compare the following passage from the Buddhist text attributed to Nāgasena and entitled *Milindapañha [Questions of Menander]*, 73.24:

> The body, your majesty [Menander, an Indo-Greek king], has been likened to a wound by The Blessed One [the Buddha]; and, therefore, they who have retired from the world take care of their bodies as though they were wounds, without thereby becoming attached to them. And The Blessed One, your majesty, has spoken as follows:
>
> > "This monstrous wound hath outlets nine,
> > A damp, wet skin doth clothe it o'er;
> > At every point this unclean thing
> > Exudeth nasty, stinking smells."
>
> (Warren, p. 423)

57.6, 7—More literally, "To find it is, as it were, startling, / To lose it is, as it were, startling." This entire chapter is fraught with awkward scholarly explanations. The original core of the chapter probably consists solely of the first two lines. All of the rest is commentary, much of it quite pedestrian.

57.19—**then** More literally, "[in] such [a case] . . . ."

58.2, 4, 6—**"subtle," "rare," "serene"** The Chinese syllables for the three imperceptible qualities of the One enunciated at the beginning of this chapter all rhyme. Their order in later editions (including the Fu I text) of the *Tao Te Ching* is "serene," "rare," "subtle." The sounds of these syllables were approximately *yuh-hsyuh-wuh* in late Old Chinese. The *yuh-hsyuh-wuh* sequence led to the interesting (and provocative) speculation on the part of several distinguished nineteenth-century sinologists that Yahweh (Jehovah, the Tetragrammaton [YHWH] which seems to mean "the one who exists") or Īśvara (the self-existent divine power of Hinduism) may have been the ultimate inspiration for the triune Chinese epithet. In fact, *yuh-hsyuh-wuh* sounds more like Joshua (from a Hebrew expression meaning "the Lord is salvation") than it does like Yahweh. Be that as it may, the discovery of the

Ma-wang-tui texts, which have the sequence *wuh-hsyuh-yuh*, casts doubt on this particular attempt to link Chinese conceptions of Unity with notions of ineffable godhead elsewhere in Asia. Nonetheless, the question of how to account for the arrangement *yuh-hsyuh-wuh* in the received tradition remains. Furthermore, this is a typical Chinese method of analyzing polysyllabic foreign words: breaking what was originally a phonetic transcription into its component syllables and then assigning Chinese characters with superficially appropriate meanings to each of them. The same device has long been common in India as well for explicating technical terms. See *Chāndogya Upaniṣad*, I.iii.6–7; VIII.iii.5; *Advaya-tārakopaniṣad*, 16–17 (Ayyaṅgār, p. 8); and the well-known but wholly false etymologizing of the two syllables of *hatha* (literally "violence" or "force") as "solar" and "lunar." Finally, the *Tao Te Ching* itself says unmistakably just below in line 9 of this chapter that the three qualities are bound together as one unit. For all of these and other reasons which must be omitted because they are even more complex, the three syllables for "subtle," "rare," and "serene" should be thought of as constituting a single word whose identity has not yet been firmly established.

59.21—**valley** The word "broad" has been added to the translation both for cadence and to reflect the implied meaning of the Chinese line.

60.1—I view the final particles of this and the next line as emphatics, not as copulatives. Literally, "arrive empty limit indeed" and "maintain stillness thorough indeed."

60.14—**ducal impartiality** The author is playing on the two meanings of *kung* ("duke" and "public, just, fair, equitable").

61.11—Literally, "We [are] self-so." The word for "self-so" in Chinese languages is *tzu-jan* (modern standard Mandarin pronunciation given). It is often translated as "nature." See the Afterword, p. 140, for additional information.

62.1—**Therefore** See the Afterword, pp. 123–124 and 152.

62.6.—**six family relationships** Those between father and son, elder and younger brother, husband and wife. These sentiments are exactly the opposite of Confucianism, which stressed that humaneness and righteousness, especially as applied to familial and other hierarchical relationships, were responsible for the preservation of the Way in society.

63.15–16—The last two lines of this chapter are attached to the beginning of the following chapter in the received text. Nonetheless, the rhyme scheme, the structure, the argument, and the wording all indicate that they belong here. If, however, we understand lines 1–4 of chapter 64 as an attack on pedantry (as Master Chuang seems to have done), it is conceivable that they should be placed ahead of them in that chapter. In any event, few of the chapter divisions in the received text of the *Tao Te Ching* have any validity (see pp. 151–152).

65.17—Compare the Upaniṣadic formula *etad vai tat* (this verily is that). Compare 25.12.

66.9–11—Compare 75.4–6.

68.13—There is a pun with "obtains" for "[awards] integrity," both of which have the same sound.

69.24–25—Literally, "The Way [takes as its] law [being] self-so." Compare note to 61.11.

70.4—Compare *Katha Upaniṣad*, I.ii.21: "Sitting, he travels afar; lying, he goes everywhere." Compare *Tao Te Ching*, 10.8.

72.21—**infinity** Literally "limitless[ness]."

72.23—"Implements [of government]," in other words, "tools" or "subordinates."

72.27—The Chinese word for "carving" is a double pun in that the character used also means "to institute" and sounds like another word that means "to rule."

73.10—**puffed up** Compare the first line of chapter 66. "Shiveringly silent" is derived from a word whose most basic signification is "breath catches."

73.11—**meek** More literally, "may be filed down."

74.22—Compare the end of chapter 18.

75.4–6—Compare 66.9–11.

76.13—In dividing up the undifferentiated cosmos.

76.17–19—These lines offer but the barest glimpse of the magnificent parable recorded by Master Chuang at the beginning of his seventeenth chapter en-

117

titled "Autumn Waters" (*Master Chuang*). Compare 29.1–2. The image of many streams (individual entities) flowing into the ocean (*Brahman*) was a favorite of ancient Indian authors. See, for example, *Chāndogya Upaniṣad*, VI.x.1; *Bṛhad-āraṇyaka*, II.iv.11; IV.v.12; *Praśna Upaniṣad*, VI.5; *Muṇḍaka Upaniṣad*, III.ii.8; the *Bhagavad Gītā*, XI.28.1–2; and especially the *Bhagavad Gītā*, II.70 (Miller p. 38):

As the mountainous depths
of the ocean
are unmoved when waters
rush into it,
so the man unmoved
when desires enter him
attains a peace that eludes
the man of many desires.

77.8—**To die but not be forgotten** The received text reads this as "To die but not perish" where "perish" is homophonous and cognate with "forget" (still evident in modern standard Mandarin where both are pronounced *wang*). Here is a good example of the imposition of a religious interpretation on the *Tao Te Ching* that was not present in the original. Few commentators have questioned the absurdity and illogicality that result from the unwarranted emendation "He who dies but does not perish has longevity."

79.12–15—Compare 58.1, 3.

AFTERWORD

Part I:
Did Lao Tzu Exist? The *Tao Te Ching* and Its Oral Background

There is universal acceptance among both scholars and devotees of the *Tao Te Ching* that its author was Lao Tzu (pronounced *lau dze* in modern standard Mandarin). This is a rather peculiar name for the presumed author of one of the most influential books ever written, for it means no more than "Old Master." Some have interpreted Lao Tzu as meaning "Old Boy" and have concocted weird tales of his having been born with a full head of white hair. However, there are so many precedents for Chinese thinkers being called master (*tzu*)—K'ung Tzu (Master K'ung, Confucius), Meng Tzu (Master Meng, Mencius), Mo Tzu (Master Mo, Mecius or Macius)—that there is little point in making other conjectures.

There is not a single shred of reliable biographical information concerning the identity of the Old Master. Despite frantic efforts to identify him with such shadowy figures as Lao P'eng, an archivist of the Chou dynasty, and others about whom next to nothing substantial other than their names is known, we simply do not know who Lao Tzu was, where or when he was born, what his occupation was, or anything else about him. All we have is a collection of sayings attributed to him that seems to have coalesced beginning sometime during the fourth century B.C. and was probably written down during the second half of the third century B.C.

119

There must have been a prototype for the Old Master. After all, someone did create a group of more or less coherent sayings that espouse a minimalist political strategy heavily laden with mystical overtones. Ultimately these sayings came to be written down in terse, codelike classical Chinese and were identified first as the book of the Old Master and much later as the *Tao Te Ching*.

But it is quite possible that more than one individual was responsible for formulating the sayings now attributed to the Old Master. Our philosopher may actually have been a composite personality. Many quotes attributed to an old master in books that predate the written versions of the *Tao Te Ching* do not appear in the latter text itself. Combined with other evidence that I will explore, this implies that the *Tao Te Ching* is a selection of proverbial wisdom from a larger body of sayings attributed to one or more old masters. However, because adherents of Taoist religion and philosophy think of the Old Master as an individual and since it would be awkward to make constant reference to "one or more old masters," I shall use the singular throughout this Afterword. This is by no means to recognize the historicity of a given old master as the sole author of the *Tao Te Ching* or even as the sole originator of these sayings.

If the *Tao Te Ching* was not the product of an identifiable author, then how do we explain its existence? The answer to this question is fairly straightforward: The *Tao Te Ching* is the result of a period of oral composition that lasted approximately three centuries (from circa 650–350 B.C.) During this period, it was common for philosophers to travel from state to state within the disintegrating Chinese empire, looking for a king who would put their ideas into practice. Initially their doctrines were formulated orally and transmitted in the same fashion from generation to generation among their followers. Finally, one of the adherents would take it upon himself to record the teachings of his master or school in short, pithy, classical Chinese statements. Still later, others might make additions or corrections. Thus the *Tao Te Ching* came about as a result of an editorial and commentarial process that is still going on today. But it was essentially completed by the end of the third century B.C. with some significant revisions and "improvements" some 500 years later.

Numerous vestiges of oral composition remain in the *Tao Te Ching* and fall into several different categories. One of the most striking

120

features of the *Tao Te Ching* is that, in spite of its brevity, it includes a great deal of repetition. The reoccurrence of similar or identical passages might conceivably be the result of a conscious attempt to emphasize certain important doctrines, but textual analysis reveals that such repetitiousness is in fact endemic to oral recitations.

Sometimes the repetition is very close:

> Diffuses the light,
> Mingles with the dust,
> Files away his sharp points,
> Unravels his tangles.
> (19.6–9)

> files away sharp points,
> unravels tangles,
> diffuses light,
> mingles with the dust.
> (48.5–8)

At other times it is exact: "The Way is eternally nameless" (chapter 76, line 1 and chapter 81, line 1). Occasionally there is a replication of what is essentially the same metaphor, even when it is quite complicated:

> Thirty spokes converge on a single hub,
>> but it is in the space where there is nothing
>> that the usefulness of the cart lies.
> Clay is molded to make a pot,
>> but it is in the space where there is nothing
>> that the usefulness of the clay pot lies.
> Cut out doors and windows to make a room,
>> but it is in the spaces where there is nothing
>> that the usefulness of the room lies.
> (55.1–9)

Such modifications and variations are hallmarks of oral delivery, which relies upon them to assist the memory (additional instances of repetition are cited in the notes).

A detailed examination of the Ma-wang-tui silk manuscripts of the

Tao Te Ching—which date from around the beginning of the second century B.C.—shows that they are full of obvious writing errors. This is further indication that they had only recently evolved from an oral tradition. The scribes who copied them were often simply not certain of how to write a given utterance, and many of the errors reveal plainly that they were still very much influenced by the sounds of the words they were trying to record instead of just the meanings. By the third century A.D., with the establishment of the received text, all of the miswritings are "corrected." Unfortunately the "corrections" themselves are often wrong, causing much difficulty and confusion among later interpreters.

The *Tao Te Ching* is full of other examples that prove it to be a collection of proverbial wisdom which previously must have circulated orally. On the one hand we encounter completely isolated adages: "The soft and weak conquer the strong" (chapter 80, line 10). On the other hand we come across obvious quotations:

> There is a series of epigrams that say:
>   "The bright Way seems dim.
>   The forward Way seems backward.
>   The level Way seems bumpy. . . ."
>
>   (3.10ff.)

In several instances, traces of editorial activity are obvious. Chapter 67, for example, consists of two very different types of material: proverbial adages and editorial comments. The chapter begins: "If it is bent, it will be preserved intact. . . ." Lines 28–29 of the same chapter identify this statement as an "old saying" and declare that it is quite true. It is not always easy to identify editorial comments in other chapters because they are seldom so clearly marked. Nonetheless, evidence of editorial tampering abounds. Most often, it is displayed in the jarring juxtaposition of dull explanation and poetic wisdom.

In addition, frequent statements of definition—such as "This is called . . ."—betray the heavy hand of an editor or compiler who is afraid his reader will not comprehend the message of the poetry he has gathered. It is difficult to imagine the Old Master himself making such clumsy remarks. Moreover, the inclusion of explanatory comment (for example, "What is the reason for this? It is because . . .") in the text is frequently obtrusive and can hardly be ascribed to a mystic or poet.

Further evidence of the oral origins of the *Tao Te Ching* is the use of mnemonic devices and formulaic language. They are relics of a stage when the sayings of the Old Master were handed down by word of mouth, rather than with brush and ink. Often the same grammatical pattern recurs over and over again in successive lines. Chain arguments are favored so that a whole series of propositions are linked together thus: if A then B, if B then C, if C . . . There is, in addition, extensive employment of parallel grammatical and syntactical structures. All of these devices helped people remember and retell the adages that were subsequently incorporated in the *Tao Te Ching*.

The Old Master is perhaps best represented in chapters such as 77, which consist entirely of a series of apothegms and maxims uncontaminated by any editorial insertions:

Understanding others is knowledge,
Understanding oneself is enlightenment;
Conquering others is power,
Conquering oneself is strength;
Contentment is wealth;
Forceful conduct is willfulness;
Not losing one's rightful place is to endure,
To die but not be forgotten is longevity.

A few chapters are carefully crafted and appear to be integral poetic sketches. Chapter 30, for example, is of deservedly high literary value. This chapter presents a simple, well-constructed picture of an imaginary primordial utopia with no discernible traces of oral composition. Chapters such as this were probably created expressly for the *Tao Te Ching* by the individual(s) responsible for the first written version(s) of the Old Master's sayings. Some chapters, however, barely cohere.

In order to understand better the matter of editorial intervention, let us look in greater depth at the mock conclusions that permeate the *Tao Te Ching*. Chapter 5, for example, contains two "conclusions" that follow one another in immediate succession. Both begin with "therefore," which implies a logical progression from what precedes. However, the first supposed conclusion does not seem to follow from the previous statements, and the second is even more fallacious. Chapter 62 even begins with the conclusional marker "therefore," although it is unrelated to the preceding chapter. All later editors simply removed the marker, but such omissions seriously distort the true composition of the text.

Another extreme example of a mock conclusion may be found in chapter 36 where the statement "Thus, he has no defects" serves no other purpose than to give the appearance of deductive argumentation. Indeed, more often than not, markers such as "therefore," "thus," and "for this reason" in the *Tao Te Ching* do not really serve to connect an argument with its conclusion.

How then do we explain their common occurrence at what seem to be crucial junctures? The answer lies in the very nature of the text itself. The first compilers of the scattered bits of proverbial wisdom attributed to the Old Master used these and other devices to give the appearance of a coherent text. They undoubtedly hoped to produce an integral text that could serve as the basis for the emerging school of Taoist thought. In fact, a critical reading of the *Tao Te Ching*—even in the Ma-wang-tui versions—reveals that it is burgeoning with non sequiturs, repetitions, and other obvious signs of homiletic derivation.

Dedicated readers of the *Tao Te Ching*—particularly after the founding of Taoist religious sects from the late second century A.D. on—have always assumed that the classic was constructed from start to finish by a single guiding intelligence. As a result they have tried to interpret it as they would any other closely reasoned philosophical discourse. The results—while displaying valiant determination to make sense of the book as a whole and of its constituent parts—are often sheer gibberish. The very frustration of the exegetes at not being able to make everything in the *Tao Te Ching* fit together snugly has only served to fuel further obscurity. For instance, no one is absolutely certain whether the following line should come at the end of chapter 63 or the beginning of chapter 64: "Abolish learning and you will be without worries." Nevertheless, partisans of both placements construct elaborate arguments defending their own preference. Indeed, a substantial measure of the fascination this small scripture has harbored for adherents of Taoism for more than two millennia stems from their inability to comprehend its overall structure.

It has been commonly thought that the Old Master lived from about 580–500 B.C. The main foundation for these dates is a pious legend of an encounter between him and Confucius, the founder of Confucianism, which was the orthodox system of Chinese thought until the first part of this century (naturally the Old Master comes out on top). Yet neither the Old Master nor his book is ever mentioned in the *Analects* of Confucius (551–479 B.C.). The same is true of the *Chronicle of Tso* (completed in 463 B.C. or later), which was a commentary on Confucius' *Spring and Autumn Annals*. Likewise we find no mention of the Old Master or his book in the work attributed to Mencius (372–289 B.C.), the second great Confucian sage. There is also no sign of the Old Master in the *Mecius (Master Mo)*, the canons of a noteworthy populist philosopher who lived (480–400? B.C.) between the times of Confucius and Mencius. We would expect that Master Chuang (355?–275? B.C.)—who was roughly contemporary with Mencius—might have mentioned a book by the Old Master should one have existed during his lifetime, since he is generally considered to have been a follower of the Way of the Old Master. Although he fails to do so, he does refer to the Old Master in the last chapter (33) of his book entitled "All Under Heaven," which is a survey of the major thinkers in China up to and including Master Chuang himself.

If the sayings of the Old Master had already been committed to writing by the time of Master Chuang, one would expect that he (or his successors) would have taken especial care to record their wording accurately. Yet in his exposition of the Old Master's thought, there is only one instance where Master Chuang comes close to quoting his presumed predecessor exactly (insofar as the Old Master is represented in the *Tao Te Ching*). All of Master Chuang's other quotations from the Old Master reflect well enough the general principles of his presumed guru but present his sayings in a jumbled fashion—again, if we take the *Tao Te Ching* as a standard. Virtually all other quotations purporting to come from the Old Master in sources that date from before the second half of the third century B.C. are similarly unreliable. Only in extremely rare cases do they tally exactly with his words as recorded in the *Tao Te Ching*, and in most cases they only vaguely approximate various parts of the classic. The situation improves drastically as we approach the second century B.C.

The sayings of the Old Master are first quoted or referred to in Warring States and Western Han period works such as *Master Chuang, Records of the Grand Historian,* and *Intrigues of the Warring States.* It therefore seems highly improbable that a work attributed to the Old Master could have been compiled before 476 B.C., the advent of the Warring States period. In terms of intellectual history, the Old Master represents a quietist reaction against the hierarchical, bureaucratic ideology of Confucius and his followers. The Old Master's digs at humaneness (*jen*), righteousness (*i*), etiquette (*li*), filial piety (*hsiao*), and so forth are plainly directed at the Confucian school. Such attacks most likely could not have come to pass before about the middle of the fourth century B.C., because until then Confucianism itself had not solidified sufficiently to be viewed as a threat to more spiritually minded individuals.

The composition of the *Master Chuang* book and other comparable works at the beginning of the third century may have provided the stimulus to assemble the wise sayings attributed to the Old Master during the course of the previous three centuries. The codification of the *Tao Te Ching* was probably essentially finished by the middle of the third century, and the first written exemplars must have appeared by about that time, setting the stage for the Ma-wang-tui silk manuscripts.

During the latter part of 1973, thirty silk manuscripts were excavated from a Han period tomb at Ma-wang-tui (literally "Horse King Mound") in the city of Changsha, Hunan province. They had been buried in the tomb of the son of Li Ts'ang, Marquis of Tai (a small southern feudal estate) and Prime Minister of Changsha. The son died in 168 B.C., so the manuscripts recovered from his tomb must date from before that time. Among them were two nearly complete texts of the *Tao Te Ching.* Based on the style of the calligraphy and other paleographical considerations, these texts have been dated to approximately the end of the third century and the beginning of the second century B.C. This means that they are roughly five centuries older than any previously available text of the *Tao Te Ching.*

The next stage in the evolution of the *Tao Te Ching* was the appearance around the beginning of the third century A.D. of the standard, or received, text, together with three notable commentaries upon it, the Hsiang-erh, the Wang Pi, and the Ho-shang Kung. Only the first half of the Hsiang-erh commentary survives. We know nothing of its author except that he leaned strongly in the direction of Yoga, a spiritual discipline emphasizing integration of mind and body. The oldest complete commentary is that of the brilliant Wang Pi (226–249) who died at the age of twenty-three. After it comes the Ho-shang Kung (translated as "Gentleman Who Lives by the River"), about whose author we are also totally in the dark. Where the Wang Pi commentary is more philosophical and metaphysical, the Ho-shang Kung commentary is more religious and emphasizes longevity.

Both commentaries bring their own agendas to the *Tao Te Ching* and, as a result, are not wholly reliable guides to the original text. Aside from minor details, the versions of the *Tao Te Ching* that they present are nearly identical and may be collectively referred to as the received text, although the Wang Pi version is favored by most scholars. Before the discovery of the Ma-wang-tui manuscripts, there were altogether half a dozen major versions of the text that date from before the ninth century A.D. Yet even when all six are consulted, a host of baffling questions remains.

It is only with the emergence of the Ma-wang-tui manuscripts that a substantial number of these problems can be solved. The chief reason for this is that they preserve many credible readings that later editors and commentators changed for their own political, polemical, or philosophical purposes, or simply because they could not comprehend them. The Ma-wang-tui manuscripts are not necessarily the primary text of the *Old Master*, but they do bring us much closer to it than any of the previously available versions.

Since the second century A.D., more than fifteen hundred commentaries have been devoted to the *Tao Te Ching*. Most of these commentaries do not significantly alter the received text itself, but there have been repeated attempts, even in this century, to remold the *Tao Te Ching* for one reason or another. Because ancient Chinese texts are difficult to read, the commentaries and subcommentaries attached to them can have a huge impact on a reader's understanding. A commentator might rearrange the chapters or parts to make the work as a whole seem more logical. Problematic characters might be replaced with more easily intelligible ones. When looking at the early commentaries, we must guard against their misleading or erroneous interpretations. These commentaries often give a false sense of security to the uncritical reader. We would do well to heed the words of the British sinologist Arthur Waley:

> All the commentaries, from Wang Pi's onwards down to the eigh-teenth century, are "scriptural"; that is to say that each commentator reinterprets the text according to his own particular tenets, without any intention or desire to discover what it meant originally. From my point of view they are therefore useless.
>
> From *The Way and Its Power* by Arthur Waley, p. 129.

By no means does this imply that the various commentaries have no value as records for the study of intellectual and religious history. Indeed, since 1949 it has even become possible to read the Old Master as espousing a materialist philosophy acceptable to Marxism! And there are numerous instances where the political and governmental concerns of the Ma-wang-tui manuscripts have been changed to meet more mystical and religious ends. In the early stages of the evolution of the *Tao Te Ching*, this sort of willful interpretation was commonplace.

The original *Tao Te Ching* is actually a very political book—oth-erwise, why so much attention to gaining all under heaven? Clearly, the aim of the author(s) was to show how to achieve hegemony over the empire. The sage who appears so often in the *Tao Te Ching* is the ideal ruler with the heart of a Yogin, an unlikely blend of India and China. The best way to control is through minimal interference and by keeping the people simple, without knowledge and without desires—two pervasive themes of the *Tao Te Ching*. As members of a modern, democratic society we may find reprehensible chapters such as 47, which advocate filling the bellies and emptying the minds of the people. But if we understand them as exemplifying a kind of third-century B.C. realpolitik, they begin to make sense as antidotes to the turbulent conditions that prevailed in society.

Although there is much in the *Tao Te Ching* of a mystical, met-aphysical quality, the text as a whole is designed to serve as a handbook for the ruler. Perhaps this is the most intriguing aspect of the *Tao Te Ching* for a late-twentieth-century reader—the audacity of combining cosmic speculation and mundane governance in a single, slender tome. Some of the mundanity has been leached out of the received text by the religious preoccupations of those who were responsible for it, but in the Ma-wang-tui manuscripts it is still quite obvious.

Next to the Ma-wang-tui manuscripts the most important edition by far for anyone who strives to comprehend the *Tao Te Ching* as it existed during the late third century B.C. is that of Fu I (A.D. 555–640), which is usually referred to as the "ancient text" (*ku-pen*). It is based largely on a text of the *Tao Te Ching* said to have been found in the year 574 in the tomb of one of Hsiang Yü's concubines. Hsiang Yü was a renowned military and political personage at the end of the Chou dynasty who lived from 232–202 B.C. and was from the state of Ch'u. This is additional evidence that the *Tao Te Ching* probably first came to be written down during the latter part of the third century B.C. and in what were then considered to be the southern reaches of Chinese civilization. This puts the apparent source of the *Tao Te Ching* in a region that had access to Indian Yoga both by land and by sea, a factor that will receive due attention in the next two parts of the Afterword. It is also highly significant that Fu I's ancient text derives from the very same area as do the Ma-wang-tui manuscripts. It is possible that the Ma-wang-tui and Fu I texts were among the very first attempts to write down the *Tao Te Ching*.

While there are significant differences between the Ma-wang-tui and the received texts of the *Tao Te Ching*, they resemble each other to such a degree that we may conclude they are part of the same broad textual tradition. That is to say, they most likely constitute different versions of a single, parent work. Therefore, even the received text —when used judiciously—is of some value in our reading of the Ma-wang-tui manuscripts. Furthermore, certain studies of the *Tao Te Ching* carried out after the advent of "evidential learning" during the eighteenth century under the partial tutelage of the Jesuits and other Western scholars are occasionally useful in our efforts to understand the original *Tao Te Ching*. However, the solutions to most of the problems confronting the researcher can usually be found in the Ma-wang-tui manuscripts and the Fu I text together with other, contemporaneous materials.

Because of the discovery of the Ma-wang-tui manuscripts and the advancement of critical modern scholarship, specialists are currently in a better position to elucidate the original *Tao Te Ching* than at any time during the past two millennia and more. By closely analyzing the text and studying comparative religion, we now realize that oral composition played a significant role in the rise of the *Tao Te Ching*.

Part II:
The Meaning of the Title
and Other Key Words

Now that we have become acquainted with the historical background of the *Tao Te Ching*, the most pressing task is to familiarize ourselves with the title and a few key terms. By exploring in depth the three words that make up the title and three other basic words that are intimately connected to the book, we will gain a more profound understanding of its overall import. Several additional concepts vital to the thought of the Old Master will also be introduced.

It may come as a bit of a shock to those who are fond of the *Tao Te Ching* to learn that, strictly speaking, the title is something of a misnomer. In the first place, the book was originally known simply as the *Old Master*, just as numerous other works of the Warring States period went by the names of the thinkers with whom they were most closely associated. The appellation "classic" only became attached to it during the succeeding Han period (206 B.C.–A.D.220) by followers of Taoist religious sects. We can be fairly certain that orthodox Confucians would never have awarded it that honor.

Tao Te Ching or the *Way [and] Integrity Classic* is actually a plausible enough name for the book, except that the Ma-wang-tui manuscripts begin with the thirty-eighth chapter of the received text, which focuses on integrity, whereas the first chapter speaks of the Way; a more proper designation would actually be *Te Tao Ching* or *Integrity [and] Way Classic*. For the convenience of readers who are accustomed to the conventional title and to make it easier for those who might wish to consult previous scholarship on the classic, I have retained the wording *Tao Te Ching*.

The exact date on which the classic became known as the *Tao Te Ching* is unclear. Some scholars claim that this title was already used during the Western Han period (206 B.C.–A.D. 8), but all the sources they cite are actually from a much later time, even though they purport to draw on Han texts. According to his biography in the *History of* the Chin Dynasty (Chin-shu, written during the first half of the seventh century), the famous calligrapher Wang Hsi-chih (321–379) once copied out the Tao Te Ching in exchange for some fine geese that had been raised by a Taoist who lived in the mountains. This is probably the first explicit mention of the classic by this title. The next reliable occurrence of the title Tao Te Ching is in the "Bibliographical Treatise" (Ching-chi Chih) by Chang-sun Wu-chi (d. 659) et al., which is included in the History of the Sui Dynasty. This would seem to indicate that the classic was well known by its now customary title by no later than the Sui period (589–618).

The Tao Te Ching is also known popularly as the Classic of Five Thousand Characters, but the number five thousand is entirely whimsical. Extant versions actually range from 5,227 to 5,722 characters in length. The repeated attempts to prune the classic down to exactly five thousand characters are but another example of the impulse to shape the thinker and his book into a neat, preconceived package.

One of the most exciting recent developments in Chinese historical linguistics has a direct bearing on our investigation of the title. This is the discovery that there are unmistakable linkages between Old Chinese and Indo-European languages. Tsung-tung Chang, a Chinese scholar who has lived in Germany for three decades, recently published over two hundred proposed equivalences and is preparing a common lexicon for Old Chinese and Indo-European that will include more than fifteen hundred basic words. Since the work of Chang and others is still in its infancy, we do not yet know the exact nature of the relationship (that is, whether it is due to extensive borrowing, to some more fundamental kind of kinship, or a combination of the two). Nonetheless, investigators are heartened by the corroboration their work is receiving from archeology. It is now universally accepted, for example, that the chariots of the Shang dynasty burials in China from around 1200 B.C. are virtually identical with those of the Caucasus area between the Black and Caspian seas two centuries earlier.

Various distinctive metal implements (knives, axes, arrowheads, toggles, etc.) have been excavated from a continuum of easily traveled steppe land that runs all the way from northern China, through south Siberia, to northern Europe. Wherever goods are exchanged, so too are ideas and words. Thus, I feel fully justified in pointing out the Indo-European cognates to all of the key terms that will be discussed in the remainder of this part of the Afterword. I also believe that this analysis will serve to illuminate powerfully the meanings of these terms for readers as well as to demonstrate the nonexotic, nonperipheral quality of Chinese civilization. No longer may China be excluded from discussions of world history, for it has always been very much a part of the ebb and flow of human events and ideas. It is only our limited historiography that has underestimated China's place in the evolution of mankind.

THE WAY/*Tao* (pronounced *dow*)

The central concept of the *Tao Te Ching*, of Taoist philosophy and religion, and indeed of all Chinese thought is Tao. The translation of Tao as "Way" is an easy matter. But our understanding of the term is heightened by a closer look at its early history, which shows that the Tao is deeply imbedded in elemental human experience. The archaic pronunciation of Tao sounded approximately like *drog* or *dorg*. This links it to the Proto-Indo-European root *drogh* (to run along) and Indo-European *dhorg* (way, movement). Related words in a few modern Indo-European languages are Russian *doroga* (way, road), Polish *droga* (way, road), Czech *draha* (way, track), Serbo-Croatian *draga* ([path through a] valley), and Norwegian dialect *drog* (trail of animals; valley). The latter two examples help to account for the frequent and memorable valley imagery of the *Tao Te Ching;* ways and valleys, it would appear, are bound together in our consciousness.

The nearest Sanskrit (Old Indian) cognates to Tao (*drog*) are *dhrajas* (course, motion) and *dhraj* (course). The most closely related English words are "track" and "trek," while "trail" and "tract" are derived from other cognate Indo-European roots. Following the Way, then, is like going on a cosmic trek. Even more unexpected than the panoply of Indo-European cognates for Tao (*drog*) is the Hebrew root *d-r-g* for the same word and Arabic *t-r-q*, which yields words meaning "track, path, way, way of doing things" and is important in Islamic philosophical discourse.

As a religious and philosophical concept, Tao is the all-pervading, self-existent, eternal cosmic unity, the source from which all created things emanate and to which they all return. This description could serve equally well for Brahman, the central principle of Indian philosophy and religion. Just as the Tao exists in the myriad creatures, so is Brahman present in all living beings. Brahman, like the Tao, is unborn or birthless (Sanskrit *aja;* modern standard Mandarin *wu-sheng*) and without beginning (*anādi; wu-shih*), both important ideas in *Master Chuang* and in later Taoism. *Wu-sheng*, in particular, becomes a standard epithet for the Mother Queen of the West, the main female deity in Taoism.

A frequent image in Indian religions is that of a way leading to unification with Brahman, that is, *Brahma-patha* (*patha* being cognate with "path"). The Buddhists translated this into Chinese as *Fan-tao*, literally "Brahman-Way," a striking expression that brings together these two manifestations of cosmic unity. Yoga, which I will have much to say about in Part III of the Afterword, is often thought of as a discipline that serves as a path to Brahman. In the *Bhagavad Gītā*, Krishna (who is an avatar of the godhead) repeatedly encourages the hero Arjuna to follow his way (*vartman*, also rendered as Tao in Buddhist Chinese). An even more common word for the Way in Indian religions is *mārga*. In Buddhism, for example, it was thought of as the means for escape from the misery of worldly existence. Among the many translations of *mārga* into Chinese were the following: Tao, *sheng-tao* (sagely way), *cheng-tao* (correct way), *sheng-tao* (way of victory), *chin-tao* (way of progress), and so forth. These and other usages make clear the correspondence of Tao to Indian religious concepts, including Brahman.

INTEGRITY/*te* (pronounced *duh*)

The second word in the title of the *Tao Te Ching*, namely *te*, is far more difficult to handle than the first, as is evident from the astonishing sweep of thoughtful renderings of its meaning: power, action, life, inner potency, indarrectitude (inner uprightness), charisma, mana (impersonal supernatural force inherent in gods and sacred objects), sinderesis (conscience as the directive force of one's actions), and virtue, to name only a few of the brave attempts to convey the meaning of *te* in English. Of these, the last is by far the most frequently encountered. Unfortunately, it is also probably the least appropriate of all to serve as an accurate translation of *te* in the *Tao Te Ching*.

Much of the confusion surrounding the term *te* stems from its appropriation by Confucian moralists. Under their auspices it gradually came to mean "virtue" in the positive sense of innate goodness or the source of ethical behavior toward others. It did not connote the Latinate notion of "manliness, strength, capacity" (*virtūs*), which would be a more accurate translation of *te*. Regrettably, the English word "virtue" has taken the same moralistic path of evolution as that followed by modern standard Mandarin *te*.

To illustrate how far we have departed from the Old Master, *tao-te* has come to mean "morality," which is surely not what he had in mind by *tao* and *te*. To return to our exploration of the latter term alone, in the very first chapter of the Ma-wang-tui manuscripts, we encounter the expression *hsia-te*, which means "inferior *te*." Another common expression is *hsiung-te*, which signifies "malevolent *te*." If we were to render *te* as "virtue" in such instances, we would be faced with unwanted and unacceptable oxymorons. Clearly we must seek a more value-neutral term in modern English. I will begin this search by looking intently at the etymology of the Chinese word.

Te was pronounced approximately *dugh* during the early Chou period (about 1100 to 600 b.c.). The meanings it conveys in texts from that era are "character," "[good or bad] intentions," "quality," "disposition," "personality," "personhood," "personal strength," and "worth." There is a very close correlation between these meanings and words deriving from Proto-Indo-European *dhugh* (to be fit, of use, proper; acceptable; achieve). And there is a whole series of words derived from the related Teutonic verbal root *dugan*. These are Old High German *tugan*, Middle High German *tugen*, and modern German *taugen*, all of which mean "to be good, fit, of use." There is another cognate group of words relating to modern English "doughty" (meaning worthy, valiant, stouthearted) that also contribute to our understanding of *te*. They are Middle English *douhti*, *dohti*, or *dühti* (valiant), which goes back to late Old English *dohtig* and earlier Old English *dyhtig* (also "valiant").

As it is used in the *Tao Te Ching*, *te* signifies the personal qualities or strengths of the individual, one's personhood. *Te* is determined by the sum total of one's actions, good and bad. Therefore it is possible to speak of "cultivating one's *te*." Like karma, *te* is the moral weight of a person, which may be either positive or negative. In short, *te* is what you are. *Te* represents self-nature or self-realization, only in relation to the cosmos. It is in fact the actualization of the cosmic principle in the self. *Te* is the embodiment of the Way and is the character of all entities in the universe. Each creature, each object has a *te* which is its own manifestation of the Tao.

The relationship between individual *te* and cosmic Tao is almost exactly parallel with that between the Indian concept of *ātman* (soul) and Brahman (the all-pervading divine reality of the universe; literally "growth, expansion, swelling [of the spirit or soul]"). *Jīvātman* (the living soul) is the self, whereas *paramātman* (the utmost soul) is none other than Brahman: thus the quintessential Hindu formula *tat tvam asi* (that thou art). In other words, you are one with the universe. Tao and Brahman both represent cosmic unity, while *te* and *ātman* stand for the individual personality or character. Just as the *Bhagavad Gītā* portrays the absorption of the separate soul (*ātman*) into the cosmic Unity (Brahman), so the *Tao Te Ching* describes the assimilation of the individual personality (*te*) into the eternal Way (Tao).

The closest English approximation of *te* as used in the *Tao Te Ching* is "integrity." In simplest terms, integrity means no more than the wholeness or completeness of a given entity. Like *te*, it represents the selfhood of every being in the universe. Integrity may also have a moral dimension in the sense of adherence to a set of values. But it lacks the uniformly positive quality of the usual translation, "virtue," which subverts the moral ambiguity so important to our understanding of *te*.

CLASSIC/*ching* (pronounced *jeang*)

Ching is the standard term in Chinese for "classic" or "scripture." However, its basic meaning is "warp of a fabric," and from this is derived the idea of "passing through," "experiencing," "transacting." *Ching* came to mean "classic" because it also signified the threads used to hold manuscripts together. Indeed, translators of Buddhist texts into Chinese used *ching* as an equivalent for Sanskrit *sūtra*, which is usually the final word in the titles of Buddhist scriptures. *Sūtra* literally means "thread" (compare English "suture") and probably derives from the root *siv* (defined by the cognate English word "to sew"), which also applies to the stitching that holds the leaves of a manuscript together. In addition, *sūtra* refers to compositions consisting of short sentences or aphoristic rules.

The Old Chinese sound of *ching* is roughly *gwing*. Without the final nasalization, this is very close to Proto-Indo-European *gwhi* (thread). Another form of the latter is *gwhi-slo*, which appears in Latin as *filum* (thread). English words ultimately derived from the Latin are "filament," "fillet," and "file" (in the sense of "line"). The latter may be traced back through Middle English *filen* and Middle French *filer*, which means "to string documents on a thread or wire" and is reminiscent of Chinese *ching* (book held together by thread). Other Indo-European cognates are Lithuanian *gysla* and Old Prussian *gislo*, both of which mean "vein," as well as Lithuanian *gija* (thread) and Welsh *gewyn* (sinew, nerve). Note that the latter, like Chinese *ching* (*gwing*), has a nasal ending. The character used for Chinese *ching* (*gwing*) almost certainly depicts the warp of a fabric on a loom.

Therefore, in strictly etymological terms, *Tao Te Ching* means "track-doughtiness-file." It would originally have been pronounced roughly as *drog-dugh-gwing*, had the title in its current form already existed during the Chou period. It is clear that all three words of the title *Tao Te Ching* are conceptually linked to Indian notions such as Brahman or *mārga*, karma or *ātman*, and *sūtra*. But etymologically they appear to be more closely related to European terms. It is thus conceivable that both China and India may have received the ideas these words represent from some such Europoids as the Tocharians or their predecessors who lived in central Asia before the formation of the *Tao Te Ching*. And China may have received these concepts more directly than did India. However, these are speculations that await the findings of archaeology for confirmation.

To complete our etymological journey, let us look briefly at several key terms from the body of the *Tao Te Ching* text.

SAGE/*sheng-jen* (pronounced *shuhng-zren*)

This term, which occurs over thirty times in the text, represents the ideal Taoist ruler. There are a whole series of interesting parallels between Chinese *sheng* (Old Chinese *syang*, "sage") and English "sage." The first and most obvious is the similarity of their sounds. Still more striking is the fact that both of them are related to perceptiveness. The character used to write *sheng* (*syang*) shows this clearly by having an ear as its semantic classifier. The Proto-Indo-European root for "sage" is *sap-* (to taste, perceive). Several related English words are derived from this root (through Latin *sapere*—"to taste, have [good] taste, be sensible, wise"): sapid, sapient, sapor, savant, savor, savvy. "Sage" itself goes back to the same Latin word through Old French *sage*. *Jen* simply means "human" (see p. 107 for further discussion). Thus, *sheng-jen* means "sagacious person."

VITAL BREATH/*ch'i* (pronounced *chee*)

While it only appears three times in the text, this term is key due to its role in the development of Taoist meditation techniques. These methods for calming the mind and prolonging life are described in the next part of the Afterword and in the Appendix.

The analogies between Chinese *ch'i* ("vital breath") and its Western and Indian equivalents are even more uncanny than in the case of *sheng-jen*. *Ch'i* refers to the metaphysical concept of material energy coursing through the body and the universe. The same concept exists in the Indian tradition as *prāṇa*, in the Greek tradition as *pneuma*, in the Latin tradition as *spiritus*, and in the Hebrew tradition as *ruaḥ*.

Moreover, there is evidence of a relationship between the Chinese word and certain Western terms. The archaic sound of *ch'i* is roughly *k'ied*, although the oldest Sinitic form of the word may have been something like *kvept*. There is little question about the early Chinese meaning of *ch'i* (*kvept*), because the pictograph used to represent it shows a few wisps of vapor rising. This calls to mind the Proto-Indo-European root *kwēp* (to smoke, to be emotionally agitated, etc.) and its derivatives. Most prominent among these derivatives is English "vapor" itself, which has lost the initial consonant and added an ending. Other Indo-European cognates are Lithuanian *kvė̃pti* (to blow the breath), Lettish *kvēpt* (steam, smoke), Greek *kapnós* (smoke, vapor), and so forth. Most amazing is the cognate Sanskrit verb *kupyati* (he swells with rage, is angry), which literally means "he is smoking, steaming [mad]." This is precisely the same, very common idiomatic usage as in modern standard Mandarin *t'a sheng ch'i[-le]* (he is angry)—literally "he is generating vapors," the origin of which has long puzzled even native speakers.

BEING, NONBEING/*yu, wu* (pronounced *yo, woo*)

This pair of terms literally means "there is" and "there is not." Together, these words constitute the ontological ground upon which the phenomenal world is played out. The Tao, ineffable and without attribute, is identified with nonbeing, yet it is the source of all creation, which is characterized as being. The Old Chinese pronunciation of *yu* was approximately *yex*. This seems to link it with English "is," which goes back to the Indo-European root *es* (to be). *Wu* is the same word with a negative prefix.

NONACTION/*wu-wei* (pronounced *woo-weigh*)

If Tao and *te* are the most significant static or nounal concepts in the *Tao Te Ching*, *wu-wei* is certainly the most important dynamic or verbal notion set forth in the classic. Of all the Old Master's ideas, it is also the most difficult to grasp. *Wu-wei* does not imply absence of action. Rather, it indicates spontaneity and noninterference; that is, letting things follow their own natural course. For the ruler, this implies reliance on capable officials and the avoidance of an authoritarian posture. For the individual, it means accomplishing what is necessary without ulterior motive. Some commentators have explained *wu-wei* as connoting "nonpurposive" or "nonassertive" action. The Old Chinese pronunciation of *wei*, which means "to act as, be, make, do," was roughly *wjar*. This is quite likely related to "were" in English. *Wu* is simply the negative, which I have already discussed above.

MYRIAD CREATURES/*wan-wu* (pronounced *wawn-woo*)

Literally "ten thousand objects," this expression refers to all things in the universe that have existence or being, in contrast to their origin —the Tao—which is without existence. The figure "ten thousand" signifies the vast variety of creatures and things in the world. It stands in opposition to the unity of the Tao from which they spring. The Old Chinese pronunciation of *wan-wu* was roughly *myanh-var*. This expression is clearly related to English "many varieties." The connection between *myanh* and "many" is obvious without having to cite earlier Indo-European antecedents. Still more striking is the affinity between Chinese *var* and the Indo-European root *var* of "variety," since both originally referred to the multicolored fur of animals (compare English "vair" and "miniver"). The earliest character used to write *wu* actually depicts a speckled bovine.

UNHEWN LOG/*p'u* (pronounced *pooh*)

P'u (also translated as "uncarved block") is the most frequent metaphor in the *Tao Te Ching* for expressing the utter simplicity of the Way. Those who coined the phrase "Tao of Pooh" have captured a deeper truth than they may be aware of. The Old Chinese pronunciation of *p'u* was *phluk*. This is almost certainly related to the English word "block," which probably derives from the Indo-European root *bhelk* (beam).

REVERSAL, RETURN, RENEWAL/*fan, kuei, fu* (pronounced *fawn, gway, foo*)

All of these terms suggest the continual return of the myriad creatures to the cosmic principle from which they arose. This is the "myth of the eternal return" so well analyzed by the great authority on comparative religion Mircea Eliade. The Old Chinese reconstruction of *kuei* is roughly *kwyed* and that of *fan* roughly *pran*. Since there are Sino-Tibetan roots for both (respectively *kwyerd* [turn in a circle] and *pran* [turn around]), we should not expect to find any immediate Indo-

European cognates. The Old Chinese reconstruction of *fu* (literally "go/come back") is roughly *byok*. A close cognate, written with the same character, may be tentatively reconstructed as *byog* and means "again." This reminds us of words such as *paky* (again) in Church Slavonic and *öfugr* (turned backward) in Old Norse that derive from Indo-European *apo*.

NATURE/*tzu-jan* (pronounced *dze-zrawn*)

Tzu-jan literally means "self-so." This expression is also sometimes translated as "spontaneous." It implies that things are what they are by themselves; no agent causes them to be so. The Old Chinese reconstruction is approximately *sdyelv-lyan*, which resembles the old Germanic equivalent *selbh-lik* (self-like).

At the end of Part III and in the Appendix, I shall provide justification from the history of civilization for the wide-ranging approach to core Taoist terminology advocated here. But first we must examine more closely the rudiments of Taoist religion and thought. A good point of departure for this subject is the comparison of Taoism with the Hindu spiritual discipline known as Yoga ("union" or, more literally, "yoking [with godhead]"). We shall find that they agree in such varied aspects as the philosophies they espouse and the religious practices they advocate. Studying either is valuable for gaining an understanding of the other.

Part III:
Parallels Between Taoism and Yoga

From our examination of the oral background and of the title of the *Tao Te Ching*, we have already seen hints of Indian influence on its formation. In this part of the Afterword, I will provide evidence of a close relationship between the *Tao Te Ching* and the *Bhagavad Gītā*, widely considered to be the most important scripture of Hindu religion. Furthermore, as B. K. S. Iyengar and other experts hold, the basic philosophical premises of Yoga were given their first authoritative expression in the *Bhagavad Gītā*, just as Taoists regard the *Tao Te Ching* as the fountainhead of their tradition. Although a few earlier scholars have hinted at the possibility of a connection between Taoism and Yoga and between the *Bhagavad Gītā* and the *Tao Te Ching*, no one has been able to prove that they are actually related. I believe that the materials I present in this section, the Appendix, and the textual notes constitute convincing evidence that the obvious resemblances between the two traditions are not merely happenstance.

Since we are by now familiar with the rise of the *Tao Te Ching*, I will begin this section with a brief glimpse at the history of the *Bhagavad Gītā*. Unlike the *Tao Te Ching*, the *Bhagavad Gītā* has an explicit narrative context; it forms an essential part of *parvan* (book) VI of the great Indian epic *Mahābhārata*. This fact is also evident from its very title, which means "Song of the Lord [that is, Krishna]." The *Mahābhārata* (*Great Epic of the Bhārata Dynasty*) recounts events that took place between about 1400 and 800 B.C. The *Bhagavad Gītā* and the epic of which it is a part were probably written down sometime between about the fourth century B.C. and the second century A.D. Complicating their dating is the fact that both the epic and the *Bhagavad Gītā* must have undergone a long period of oral transmission before they were committed to writing. In any case, the core of the *Bhagavad Gītā* is probably at least one or two centuries older than the *Tao Te Ching*.

The *Bhagavad Gītā* consists of a very long dialogue between the warrior prince Arjuna and Krishna, a manifestation of the god Vishnu, who doubles as Arjuna's counselor and charioteer. This takes place on the battleground called Kurukṣetra (Field of the Kurus) as the war between the Pāndavas and the Kauravas, two ancient Indian clans, is about to commence. When the two armies draw up their ranks and face off, Arjuna becomes depressed at the thought of having to fight against many of his acquaintances and relatives who are in the opposing camp. He questions whether he should throw away his weapons and submit to a sure death or participate in a war that, no matter how just, is certain to result in much slaughter. Krishna reminds him that it is his duty to be a warrior and embarks upon a long discourse on action.

The chief lesson Krishna has to offer Arjuna is that altruistic or disinterested action (*niṣkāma karma*) leads to realization of Brahma. That is to say, one should act without regard or desire for the fruits

141

(*phala*) of one's action. This idea is repeated over and over again in countless different formulations. These passages are of great importance for understanding the enigmatic concept of "nonaction" that is so prominent in the *Tao Te Ching*. "The person of superior integrity takes no action," says the Old Master, "nor has he a purpose for acting." We are told straightaway to "act through nonaction" and that "through nonaction, no action is left undone." In spite of the fact that this idea appears a dozen times and is obviously central to the Old Master's teachings, we can only vaguely surmise from the *Tao Te Ching* the specific implications of *wu-wei* (nonaction).

However, when we read the *Bhagavad Gītā*, we discover an exceedingly elaborate analysis of the nature and purpose of nonaction. The ideal of action without attachment is conveyed in many guises throughout the *Bhagavad Gītā*, for example, *akṛta* (nonaction), *akarma* (inaction), *naiṣkarmya* (freedom from action or actionlessness), *karmaṇām anārambhān* (noncommencement of action), and so forth. Krishna refers to himself as the "eternal nondoer" and states that the Yogin should think, "I do not do anything." He declares that he "sits indifferently unattached by these actions." Elsewhere, he condemns sitting and remembering. All of this reminds us of the "sitting and forgetting" advocated by the Taoists that later developed into a type of meditative practice.

If one acts in Brahman, he has abandoned attachment and will not be defiled by evil "any more than a lotus leaf by water," an eloquent image that subsequently became very popular in China. It is not actions themselves that are to be eschewed; it is only undue concern for their results ("fruits," in the language of the *Bhagavad Gītā*), which binds one to desires. Repeatedly, Krishna enjoins Arjuna to relinquish actions prompted by desire. There is a linkage between actions and desires in the *Tao Te Ching* as well, although it is not spelled out so explicitly.

Krishna makes clear his views on action and nonaction in the following passage:

> I desire no fruit of actions,
> and actions do not defile me;
> one who knows this about me
> is not bound by actions.

Knowing this, even ancient seekers
of freedom performed action—
do as these seers
did in ancient times.

What is action? What is inaction?
Even the poets were confused—
what I shall teach you of action
will free you from misfortune.

One should understand action,
understand wrong action,
and understand inaction too;
the way of action is obscure.

A man who sees inaction in action
and action in inaction
has understanding among men,
disciplined in all action he performs.

The wise say a man is learned
when his plans lack constructs of desire,
when his actions are burned
by the fire of knowledge.

Abandoning attachment to fruits
of action, always content, independent,
he does nothing at all
even when he engages in action.

He incurs no guilt if he has no hope,
restrains his thought and himself,
abandons possessions,
and performs actions with his body only.

Content with whatever comes by chance,
beyond dualities, free from envy,
impartial to failure and success,
he is not bound even when he acts.

      (IV.14–22, trans. Barbara Stoler Miller)

In the end, Krishna counsels Arjuna to rise above the dichotomy of
action and nonaction.

143

Aside from this striking fundamental resemblance between the *Tao Te Ching* and the *Bhagavad Gītā* with regard to nonaction, there are numerous other affinities between the two works. One is a shared concern for the relationship between the multitude, or aggregate, of created beings and the eternal cosmic principle that is their origin. Both focus on being and nonbeing. Both are preoccupied with the significance of wisdom, or knowledge, and nescience, or ignorance. Both texts strongly emphasize becoming free from desires and not prizing rare and costly goods. Both are concerned with birth, (long) life, and death. Like the *Bhagavad Gītā*, the *Tao Te Ching* openly discusses the purposes of war and the obligations of a soldier. Just a few of the key terms encountered in both texts are those for "return," "subtlety" (or "fineness"), "disorder," "affairs," "desire," "tranquility" (or "calm"), "taste," "supreme," "percipient sage," and "peace."

Entire stanzas of the *Bhagavad Gītā* read like miniature foreshadowings of the *Tao Te Ching*. In a burst of nominatives that would have warmed the heart of the Old Master when contemplating the Way, Krishna unfolds his all-encompassing nature:

Understanding, knowledge, nondelusion,
patience, truth, control, tranquility,
joy, suffering, being, nonbeing,
fear, and fearlessness . . .

Nonviolence, equanimity, contentment,
penance, charity, glory, disgrace,
these diverse attitudes
of creatures arise from me.

(X.4-5, Miller)

There are whole passages in the *Tao Te Ching* where the imagery and wording are very close to those of the *Bhagavad Gītā*. In book 3, stanza 38, of the *Bhagavad Gītā*, the obscuring of a mirror by dust as a metaphor for the clouding of the mind is almost identical to chapter 54, lines 6–7, of the *Tao Te Ching*. Even more startling is the likeness between book 8, stanza 12 of the *Bhagavad Gītā* and chapter 19, lines 4–5, of the *Tao Te Ching*: The former begins with "closing all the doors [of the body], shutting up the mind in the heart" and then goes on to direct the practitioner to channel his vital breath (*prāṇa*) up into his head to establish himself in Yogic concentration. The latter states that the practitioner "stopples the openings of his heart, closes his doors." Since these two lines are repeated verbatim in chapter 15, lines 9–10 of the *Tao Te Ching*, it appears as if they were taken over directly from Indian Yoga into Chinese Taoism. The manifestly Yogic content of the *Tao Te Ching* is also to be seen in the beginning of chapter 54, especially lines 4–5, which advise the practitioner to focus the breath until it is supremely soft.

By no means am I implying that the "author" of the *Tao Te Ching* sat down with a copy of the *Bhagavad Gītā* in hand and proceeded to translate it into Chinese. The fact that both texts evolved from oral traditions precludes such a simplistic scenario. Moreover, the sayings of the Old Master have a style and socioreligious character all their own. The *Tao Te Ching* was as much, if not far more, the product of internal sociopolitical conditions as it was the reaction to radically new religious and philosophical stimuli from without. As a result, it comes to very different conclusions from those of the *Bhagavad Gītā*. The Chinese classic emphasizes political skills and social harmony in preference to the theistic orientation of the Indian scripture. The *Bhagavad Gītā* is essentially a manual of spiritual discipline that has applications in the real world; the *Tao Te Ching* is basically a handbook for the ruler with mystical overtones. The *Bhagavad Gītā* advocates control of the mind and ultimate liberation; adherents of the *Tao Te Ching* espouse the indefinite protraction of the physical body.

Yet it remains that there are many remarkable correspondences between the *Bhagavad Gītā* and the *Tao Te Ching*. The most probable explanation is that the *Bhagavad Gītā* was transmitted to China in the same fashion that it was initially transmitted within India—by word of mouth. Particularly memorable images and powerful expressions would have been transferred virtually verbatim. In most instances, however, what the founders of Taoism absorbed from Yoga were radically new ideas concerning man and his place in the universe and a complementary physiological regimen (meditational discipline, dietary practices, flexing exercises, and so forth). Considering the immense linguistic, social, and philosophical differences between China and India, it is astounding that the kindredness of the *Bhagavad Gītā* and the *Tao Te Ching* shines through so conspicuously.

I must now address the sensitive issue of the precedence of Yoga

145

versus that of Taoism. Given the complexities of the dating of the *Tao Te Ching* and the *Bhagavad Gītā*, if we rely strictly on these two sources alone, it is conceivable (though unlikely) that the Chinese classic might have influenced the Indian scripture. Certain distinctive aspects of Yoga that also show up in Taoism can be traced back to India beyond the first millennium B.C. and are systematically described over and over at great length (see the Appendix). However, in China they only begin to appear at the earliest around the middle of the first millennium B.C. And they are presented in a confused and cursory fashion until after the advent of Buddhism around the first century A.D. when they are reinforced by a new and more coherently conveyed wave of Indian influence. In short, if Indian Yoga did not exert a shaping force upon Chinese Taoism, the only other logical explanation is that both were molded by a third source. Since no such source is known, we can only assume an Indian priority and wait for additional data from future archaeological discoveries. However, it is improbable that new data would significantly alter our present understanding, because the case in favor of Indian priority is already massive (see the Appendix for a sampling of the evidence).

There are so many correspondences between Yoga and Taoism—even in the smallest and oddest details—throughout the history of their development that we might almost think of them as two variants of a single religious and philosophical system. Both conceive of conduits, tracts, channels, or arteries through which the vital breath, or energy, flows. They view the main channel as originating in the "root," or "tail," region of the body, then passing through the spinal column and flanked by two subsidiary channels. At death, the energized soul of both the Yogin and the Taoist emerges from the bregma (junction of the sagittal and coronal sutures at the top of the skull) to merge with the world-soul (Brahman, Tao). This is called the Way to Brahman by Yogis and the Marrow Way by Taoists.

Both Yoga and Taoism maintain that there are certain points in the body where energy is held, or bound, and that there are supports that guide the vital breath. Both envisage wheels or fields where this energy generates heat. Practitioners of both disciplines are said to possess an outer radiance that reflects a refined inner essence. In their esoteric forms, both are obsessed with semen retention (said to repair the brain)—not a preoccupation of religious practitioners that one might expect to find springing up spontaneously in two such different cultures.

Yoga and Taoism also share a close association with internal and external alchemy. Both resort to the use of various charms, sacred syllables, and talismans as aids in meditation and for conveying secret knowledge. And both maintain that advanced accomplishment in their respective disciplines affords the practitioner special powers such as the ability to walk on water without sinking or on fire without getting burned. Claims of levitation have also been announced by those who style themselves Taoists and Yogins. These are only a few of the more obvious analogies between Taoism and Yoga.

By now, it is hoped that even the most hardened skeptic and the most ardent Chinese isolationist will admit that Yoga and Taoism bear such striking affinities to each other that they must be related in some fashion. But how do we account for this historically? It is commonly held that China was virtually cut off from the rest of humanity until about the middle of the second century B.C. This is simply wrong; fortunately archaeological discoveries and anthropological fieldwork are beginning to prove beyond the shadow of a doubt that, with rare exceptions, all of mankind—including China—has been continuously interacting across the face of the globe since the origin of the species.

It is also often claimed that China and India did not have any significant cultural intercourse until the first century A.D. This, too, is false, for there is now available artifactual evidence of Buddhism in China from no later than the middle of the first century B.C. China is mentioned by name, particularly as the source of silk, in a number of still earlier Indian texts. Trade between India and China, through a variety of overland and ocean routes, flourished well before the sayings of the Old Master came to be written down. As suggested earlier, whenever trade occurs between two countries, mutual cultural borrowing is inevitable.

The flow of Indian intellectual and spiritual influence into China that resulted in the rise of Taoism was undoubtedly mediated by a complex mix of peoples from western and central Asia. The same process was repeated later during the penetration of Buddhism into the heartland of China when Persian-speaking peoples, among others, played a crucial role in its transmission. Also, just as with Buddhism, Indian ideas instrumental in the rise of Taoism must have been brought

147

to the south and central Chinese coast by trading ships that sometimes carried religious personages, paraphernalia, and scriptures.

In any event, Taoism (as well as other aspects of Chinese civilization) certainly did not materialize in a vacuum. As more thorough archaeological and anthropological studies are carried out on the periphery of China and as more unrestricted philological studies are undertaken on early Chinese texts, it becomes increasingly apparent that Chinese civilization is an integral part of the development of world civilization. Those who attempt to seal it off hermetically from the rest of mankind, for whatever purpose, not only distort Chinese history but fail to comprehend the true nature of human history outside of China.

The *Bhagavad Gītā* and the *Tao Te Ching* are not the only instances of Sino-Indian interaction in the development of Taoism. Master Chuang, Master Lieh, and other early Taoist thinkers also reveal distinct Indian philosophical and thematic proclivities at the same time as they are quintessentially Chinese. Taoist religion, too, shares much with Indian Buddhism. Its canon, ecclesiastical establishment, hierarchy of deities, ritual, and rules for communal living were all inspired by Indian models, and yet they have been assimilated in a way that makes them seem very much at home in China. Taoism, in turn, laid the foundations for the rise of perhaps the most genuinely Chinese of all Buddhist sects, Ch'an, which we know in its Japanese guise as Zen (both of which names are truncated transcriptions of Sanskrit *dhyāna* [meditation]). The circles and cycles of cultural interflow never cease.

Part IV:
Sinological Usages
and Principles of Translation

The topics that need to be discussed in this section are somewhat technical. However, for the sinologist and for those who are curious about what sinologists do, the following observations are vital.

Since there are so many different systems available for spelling out Chinese languages, I must first say a few words about the crucial distinction between spoken language and written script so that I can explain my own choice. Ideally, the Chinese script is a device for recording on a surface the sentiments and sounds of the languages.

The script is definitely not equivalent to any of the spoken languages and, in many instances, there is an enormous gap between the two. We must be wary of using visual analysis of the ideographic and pictographic components of a character alone to arrive at the presumed meaning of the word from the spoken language it is meant to convey. The phonology of Chinese takes precedence over the script as it does with any language when one is trying to extract meaning. We also need to make a distinction between the various forms of extremely terse classical Chinese, which may never have been spoken, and the vernacular Sinitic languages, most of which have never been written down. The *Tao Te Ching*, naturally, is written in classical Chinese.

The transcription system used in this book is a slightly modified form of Wade-Giles romanization. Its chief competitor is Pinyin, which is the official romanization of the People's Republic of China and is used mainly by students whose work focuses on China during the second half of this century. I have picked Wade-Giles because it remains the sinological standard for the spelling of Mandarin and because nearly all libraries continue to use it for the cataloguing of Chinese authors, titles, and subjects. Furthermore, of the various competing systems, Wade-Giles is actually closer than most to scientific notations such as the International Phonetic Alphabet. Above all, the title of the classic is already widely known in the English-speaking world by its Wade-Giles transcription. Conversion to another romanization would render the title unrecognizable to many who are already familiar with it as the *Tao Te Ching*.

There are only two transcribed terms (yin and yang) in the entire text, and these have already been accepted into English. Thus there is no need to set forth here the whole Wade-Giles system, but it does behoove us at least to learn the correct pronunciation of the title and the name of the presumed author, Lao Tzu (see pp. 119, 133–134). *Tao* sounds exactly like Dow (as in Dow-Jones), *Te* is pronounced like Duh (as in "Duh, I dunno" but with a rising intonation), and *Ching* is almost the same as Jean with a -g sound stuck on at the end. Hence, *Tao Te Ching* might be phonetically transcribed for American speakers as *Dow Duh Jeang*. The Lao part of Lao Tzu sounds like "louse" minus the final sibilant. Tzu sounds not like "zoo," as many Americans tend to pronounce it, but rather like "adze" with the initial vowel missing.

As a matter of fact, neither the title *Tao Te Ching* nor the name Lao Tzu originally sounded the way we pronounce it now. The archaic reconstruction of the former is roughly *drog-dugh-gwing* and that of the latter is roughly *ruwh-tsyuh*. It is purely a sinological convention to cite ancient terms according to their modern standard Mandarin pronunciations. However, this is often quite misleading, since modern standard Mandarin is so far removed from the sounds of ancient Chinese languages that any resemblance between them is usually unrecognizable by all but those who are highly trained specialists. The problem is less severe for other modern Sinitic languages such as Cantonese, Taiwanese, and Shanghainese, which have preserved the ancient sounds to a much greater extent.

The dissonances between the realms of oral and written discourse in China pose enormous difficulties for the philologist, especially when he is dealing with a text like the *Tao Te Ching*, which had its origins in proverbial wisdom that first circulated orally and only came to be written down much later. During the transition from oral expression to written formulation in characters, a profound transformation occurred. What were once purely strings of sound possessed of rhythm, tone, accent, and pause that elicited in the mind of the auditor certain associated meanings became visual patterns spaced equidistantly on a flat surface that provided truncated semantic and phonetic clues to the thought of the author. Loquaciousness gave way to laconicism, affording great latitude to the imaginative interpreter.

The central role of imagination and intuition in the reading of classical Chinese accounts for the great diversity of opinion among the exegetes. It is for this reason that I have tried to reach beyond the commentators to the text of the *Tao Te Ching* and even, whenever possible, to get beyond the written text to the spoken language that inspired it. This may seem an impossible task to the novice, but there are rigorous linguistic methods that permit us to extrapolate from the terse written statements of the classics significant features of the oral formulations from which they were drawn. It is rather like the paleontologist's recreation of a Devonian amphibian on the basis of a few fossilized bones, or the forensic reconstruction of an entire skull on the basis of a molar, a bicuspid, a mandible, half a maxilla, one ethmoid, and a quarter of the occipital bone.

Unlike nearly all other sinological translators of the *Tao Te Ching*,

I place very little credence in the traditional commentators. More often than not, they simply lead one astray if one's objective is to understand the *Tao Te Ching* itself rather than the commentator's philosophical and religious programs. Because of a series of startling archaeological discoveries (oracle bones, bronze inscriptions, jade plaques, pottery marks, etc.) during the course of this century, we know far more today about the development of the Chinese script and Sinitic languages than did scholars at any time in the past. This is not to deny that there are items of value in the work of the early commentators, only to caution that they are often egregiously wrong because they were limited both by their sources and their methods. Most important of all, we are in possession of the Ma-wang-tui manuscripts, which are hundreds of years older and far more reliable than any previously known texts of the *Tao Te Ching*. Consequently, even though forty or fifty later editions sometimes agree on a certain reading, they may all be wrong simply because they did not have access to the early manuscripts.

The first principle of translation subscribed to herein is always to use the oldest available manuscript except when it is defective (that is, when it has lacunae, is torn, is illegible, etc.) or can be proven to be in error, in which case I rely on the next oldest text. When none of the early texts makes sense, I search for homophonous and near-homophonous cognates. Only when that fails to yield a reasonable reading do I suspect an orthographical error and begin to look for a character whose shape might have been mistaken for the one in question. My first assumption (borne out by many years of work on other ancient Chinese manuscripts) is that the author or scribe knew very well the sound of the word he wanted to record but was not always certain of the proper character that should be used to write it. I emend the text only as a last resort, which, fortunately, happens rarely in the present work.

This leads to the thorny matter of the chapters in the *Tao Te Ching* and whether or not they are legitimately applied to the Ma-wang-tui manuscripts, which are not marked consistently. I have numbered the chapters consecutively, according to the sequence they were found in the Ma-wang-tui manuscripts, while retaining in parentheses the conventional chapter divisions for easy reference for those already familiar with the *Tao Te Ching*. Readers will quickly notice that the order of the chapters in the Ma-wang-tui manuscripts is not the same as that of the received text. For example, the Ma-wang-tui manuscripts begin with chapter 38 of the received text, chapter 40 is preceded by 41, chapters 80 and 81 (the final chapters of the received text) come before 67, and so forth.

While not fully punctuated, the older of the two Ma-wang-tui manuscripts occasionally has scribal marks that indicate where pauses should be made and stanzas separated. This is often helpful for understanding the text, and it contrasts with the vast majority of classical Chinese texts written before this century that consist solely of very long strings of characters spaced equidistantly. It should be noted that the breaks marked on the older of the two Ma-wang-tui manuscripts do not always coincide with the chapter divisions of the received text.

The division into eighty-one chapters has no validity whatsoever in terms of the original collection of the Old Master's sayings. Most of the chapters consist of two or more parts and are joined together for no particular reason other than the editors' desire to have a neat package. Conversely, in several cases, portions of the *Tao Te Ching* that are separated by chapter breaks in the received text might better be joined together. One chapter (62), for example, begins with a conclusion ("Therefore . . .").

It is futile to attempt to provide any rational basis for the division into eighty-one chapters since the number is purely arbitrary and has no organic bearing on the systematic ordering of the text. This particular number (*ekāśīti* in Sanskrit) was probably picked up from the Buddhists who favored it because it is the square of nine, which was itself fraught with all manner of symbolic significance for Indian mystics. One of the most hallowed Buddhist scriptures, the *Prajñāpāramitā-sūtra*, also had eighty-one divisions. Even in the few sporadic instances where chapter divisions are marked in the Ma-wang-tui manuscripts, they do not always coincide with those in the received text. Nonetheless, for purposes of comparison and analysis I have divided my translation into the customary eighty-one chapters.

As for annotations, there are two different approaches that might have been followed. On the one hand, there is the heavily annotated translation that so bristles with technical flourishes as to scare away all nonsinologists. On the other hand, there is the translation that is totally devoid of commentary and that often leaves the lay reader guessing and wondering at every turn. I have tried to strike a happy balance between these two extremes by providing notes that would satisfy the curiosity or puzzlement of the beginner and the legitimate needs of the sinologist, but they appear at the back of the book so as not to clutter up the pages of the translation. For the same reason, the Notes are keyed to the text by line and word rather than by superscript numbers. In general, my aim has been to make the translation completely integral and self-explanatory. Thus, there should be no need to consult the Notes or the Afterword upon a first reading of the *Tao Te Ching* itself. The Notes and the Afterword are intended for those who reread the text and require additional commentary in the course of their deeper analysis and reflection.

My chief goal in undertaking this translation has been to create a thoroughly new English version of the *Tao Te Ching*. During its preparation, I intentionally avoided consulting other translations so that I would not be influenced by them. Aside from not wanting to be repetitive and stale, I did not wish to be trapped by facile solutions bequeathed by the received text, its editors, commentators, and translators. As a tribute to the unexpected re-emergence of the Ma-wang-tui manuscripts, I have endeavored to provide a fresh examination on their own terms, one not burdened by two millennia of religious and philosophical exegesis. If others wish to amalgamate the Ma-wang-tui manuscripts with the received text, that is their prerogative, but it is not what I have set out to do here. For those who are interested in learning about later interpretations of the *Tao Te Ching*, several previous translations that include extensive commentaries and explanations are listed in the bibliography.

APPENDIX

This Appendix is designed for those who want additional information on the relationship between Yoga and Taoism.

In his landmark comparative study *Sufism and Taoism*, Toshihiko Izutsu discerns what he calls "the two pivots of a world-view," namely "the Absolute and the Perfect Man." Izutsu sees these twin pivots (Tao and *te*, as it were) developing independently in different places and ages. Nonetheless, it would be difficult to prove that Sufism and Taoism were absolutely unrelated. This is especially the case when we consider that both Persia and China had commercial, cultural, and political ties with each other and with India during the period when Sufism developed. Similarly, given the unmistakable resemblances between Taoism and Yoga, it would be virtually impossible to prove that they have no historical connections whatsoever. Even Joseph Needham (pp. 257–88), the great advocate of the autonomy of Chinese technology, is persuaded by the evidence to admit that there must have been some sort of influence operating between these two systems of thought. The difficulty is in trying to sort out which came first.

Because the question of priority is too complicated to include in the main body of the Afterword, I have gathered in this Appendix some of the more pertinent material. The first item of evidence from the Chinese side is an isolated inscription on ten pieces of jade making up a small knob that is datable to approximately the year 380 B.C.:

In moving the vital breath (*hsing ch'i*) [through the body, hold it deep and] thereby accumulate it. Having accumulated it, let it extend (*shen*). When it extends, it goes downward. After it goes downward, it settles. Once it is settled, it becomes firm. Having become firm, it sprouts [compare Yogic *bīja* ("seed" or "germ")]. After it sprouts, it grows. Once grown, then it withdraws. Having withdrawn, it becomes celestial [that is, yang]. The celestial potency presses upward, the terrestrial potency presses downward. [He who] follows along [with this natural propensity of the vital breath] lives; [he who] goes against it dies.

(Kuo Mo-jo, p. 9)

Without addressing the choppy, convoluted style in which it is written, I need only point out that every essential element of this inscription can be traced to Indian texts that date from 900 to 200 B.C. Among these are the thirteen classical *Upaniṣads* (c. 700–300 B.C.), which are supplementary teachings attached to the *Vedas*, India's most ancient body of knowledge. For example, the *Maitrī Upaniṣad* offers an elaborate exposition of the five types of breath (*prāṇa, apāna, samāna, udāna, vyāna*), their movement upward and downward and throughout each limb, as well as their relationship to life and death. The whole second *khaṇḍa* (section) of the *Muṇḍaka Upaniṣad* has so many close parallels to the *Tao Te Ching* that it deserves the most thorough study by serious students of the Taoist classic. Here I shall cite only a part of the sixth stanza, which bears obvious resemblance to one of the most celebrated images of the Old Master:

Where the channels (*nāḍi*) come together
Like spokes in the hub of a wheel,
Therein he (imperishable Brahman as manifested
    in the individual soul [*ātman*]) moves about
Becoming manifold.

The corresponding passage from the *Tao Te Ching* (chapter 55, lines 1–3) has a slightly different application, but the common inspiration is evident:

Thirty spokes converge on a single hub,
    but it is in the space where there is nothing
    that the usefulness of the cart lies.

156

In one of the earliest *Upaniṣads*, the *Chāndogya*, we find an exposition of the microcosmology of the human body that certainly prefigures Taoist notions of a much later period:

A hundred and one are the arteries (*nāḍi*) of the heart,
One of them leads up to the crown of the head;
Going upward through that, one becomes immortal (*amṛta*),
The others serve for going in various directions. . . .

(translation adapted from Radhakrishnan, p. 501)

This is not just an isolated occurrence, for the same conception is restated in the *Kaṭha Upaniṣad*, the *Taittīrīya Upaniṣad*, and the *Praśna Upaniṣad*.

Yogic concentration of all the senses upon the self is clearly evident in the *Chāndogya Upaniṣad*. In the *Maitrī Upaniṣad*, Yoga is mentioned specifically by name and defined in a manner that would fit Taoism almost as well:

The oneness of the breath, the mind, and likewise of the senses,
The abandonment of all conditions of existence, this is designated Yoga.

(translation adapted from Radhakrishnan, p. 835)

By the time of the *Yoga Sūtras* and *Yoga Upaniṣads* (the earliest layers of which date to no later than the second century B.C.), the complete pre–Tantric Yogic system had received explicit and elaborate codification in written form. Patañjali, who wrote the first three books of the *Yoga Sūtras* around the second century B.C., recognizes (I.1) that he was not the creator of Yogic techniques but only wanted to present them in a rigorously systematic fashion. Those who take the trouble to read attentively the early Indian texts just cited, particularly the classical *Upaniṣads*, will realize that they foreshadow the entire philosophical, religious, and physiological foundations of Taoism, but not its social and political components, which are distinctively Chinese.

Still farther back in time, the *Atharva Veda* (900 B.C. or before) has a very long chapter dealing exclusively with the vital breath and its circulation (to mention only one aspect that is pertinent to Taoism). Although the entire chapter deserves quotation and careful examination by all conscientious students of Taoism, I have space to present only nine stanzas here:

When breath with thunder roars at the plants, they are fertilized, they receive the germ, consequently they are born abundantly.

Rained upon, the plants spoke with breath (saying): You have extended our life, you have made us all fragrant.

Homage, breath, be to you breathing up, homage to you breathing down; homage to you turning away, homage to you turning hither; here is homage to all of you.

Your dear form, breath, and your even dearer form, also the healing power that is yours, of that put in us, that we may live.

Breath is the shining One (the Queen), breath the Directress, all revere breath; breath is the sun and the moon, breath they say is the Lord of Creatures.

Man, while still in the womb, functions with nether and upper breath [compare the "womb breathing" of the Taoists]; when you, breath, quicken him, then he is born again.

When breath has rained with rain upon the great earth, plants are generated, and all herbs that exist.

Who is lord over this (all) of every source, over all that moves, whose bow is swift among (against?) the unwearied ones,—O breath, homage be to thee.

O breath, turn not away from me; you shall be no other than myself. I bind you to myself, breath, like the child of the waters, that I may live.

(XI.iv.3, 6, 8–9, 12, 14, 17, 23, 26; trans. Edgerton)

If there were still any doubts about the vast antiquity of Yogic physiological discipline in comparison with similar Taoist practices, one need only recall that *āsana* (postures) have been found represented on seals and statuettes from Mohenjo Daro and Harappā, sites of the Indus Valley civilization that date back to about 2500 B.C. Although we cannot be certain that the individuals so depicted are actually engaged in meditation (*dhyāna*), it is noteworthy that some elements of Yoga, as Eliade has asserted, must have preceded the arrival of the

Aryans in the south Asian subcontinent. Yoga is reflected as well in many ancient archaeological monuments of India, Indochina, and Indonesia (see Pott). Specific meditational postures are already mentioned by name in the Indian epic *Mahābhārata* of which the *Bhagavad Gītā* forms a part. These include the *maṇḍūkayoga* (frog yoga) and *vīrāsana* (posture of a hero).

The next piece of evidence from the Chinese side is quite well known and has been cited by most competent authorities as providing crucial data for the origins of Taoist physical exercises. It comes from one of the later chapters of the *Master Chuang* and may be dated roughly to 250 B.C., just about the time when the *Tao Te Ching* came to be written down:

> Blowing and breathing, exhaling and inhaling, expelling the old and taking in the new, bear strides and bird stretches—[these activities are designed] to achieve longevity and that is all. They are favored by those who [through] channeling [of the vital breath] and flexions [of the muscles and the joints wish to emulate] the longevity of Methuselah.
>
> (*Concordance to Chuang Tzu*, ch. 15, p. 40)

The odd expression "bear strides" is illustrated on another recently unearthed document from Ma-wang-tui. A silk manuscript from the same Han tomb that yielded the manuscripts of the *Tao Te Ching* consists of painted designs of gymnastic exercises that date to 168 B.C. or before. Originally, the manuscript showed over forty exercises, but only twenty-eight survive intact in its present fragmentary condition.

One striking feature of the twenty-eight exercises depicted on the fragmentary silk manuscript is that many of them are named after birds and animals (wolf, kite, sparrow hawk, ape, crane, and so on). This immediately reminds us of Yogic *āsana* (postures) that are patterned after the movements or poses of similar (and sometimes even identical) creatures: eagle, swan, peacock, crane, heron, cock, pigeon, partridge, tortoise, fish, monkey, lion, camel, frog, horse, cow, dog, crocodile, snake, locust, scorpion, and so on. One might say it is natural for man to imitate animals when devising physical exercises, but there are other grounds for believing that Taoist gymnastics and Yogic postures have a common origin.

159

Let us discuss the native designations for this type of exercise in India and in China. The Chinese word is the bisyllabic *tao-yin*, which means leading, guiding, channeling, or duction (an obsolete English term that we may revive for this purpose) and basically signifies the directed movement through the body of *ch'i* (vital breath) as well as the controlled extension or drawing out of the limbs, muscles, and joints of the body. This sounds suspiciously close to Yogic breath control (*prāṇāyāma*, from *prāṇa* [vital breath] and *āyāma* [lengthening, extension]). *Prāṇāyāma* is the rhythmically restrained drawing in and out of the breath.

To return to our discussion of the passage from *Master Chuang*, after "bear strides" comes "bird stretches." While not among the surviving postures and labels on the silk manuscript from Ma-wang-tui, it clearly echoes several Indian *āsana*. The next phrases show that Master Chuang disparages the pursuit of physical longevity, perhaps a sly dig at the Old Master and his ilk. At least one strand of the *Tao Te Ching* itself, however, is definitely opposed to conscientious life extension and breath control (see chapter 18, lines 16–17; chapter 40, lines 9–15 and the note to line 10; and chapter 77, line 8).

I have cited above many early Indian texts that outline Yoga philosophy, yet they can only have constituted but a small fraction of what was transmitted orally in fuller form. Hence it is not possible in every case to provide specific textual references for the sources of Indian influence on the development of Taoism. For example, it would be difficult to pinpoint a single Indian source for the microcosmic physiological conception of the human body so characteristic of Taoism, yet we know that it was already securely in place in India long before being elaborated in China. So pervasive was the Indian impact upon the growth of Taoist metaphysics that the latter—especially in its formative stages—is not wholly intelligible without consulting its Yogic background. Our appreciation of Chinese thought in general is enhanced by the recognition that, in fact, it is intimately connected to world philosophy.

The rise of Taoism is not just a matter of Sino-Indian cultural relations. A tremendous intellectual ferment convulsed all of Eurasia around the middle of the first millennium B.C. Within a brief span of approximately a century, the following major systems of thought were articulated or adumbrated: pre-Socratic Greek philosophy (Thales and

Anaximander of Miletus), Confucianism, Mohism, Upaniṣadic Hinduism, Jainism, Taoism, Buddhism, Zoroastrianism, and Biblical Judaism. It is highly unlikely that these great movements were utterly independent phenomena (see Benjamin Schwartz's comments on the Axial Age in his *The World of Thought in Ancient China*, pp. 2–3). Indeed, they were probably closely tied to the explosive growth in the use of iron during the preceding two centuries, which caused tremendous social and political rearrangements (see Calder, p. 169).

The political manifestation of the widespread use of iron in China was the breakup of the feudal Chou empire into seven main and many lesser states about 475 B.C. After more than 250 years of prolonged fighting, the state of Ch'in emerged as the leading power to reunite China in 221 B.C. It is significant both that the original Ch'in base was far to the northwest and that her soldiers were well equipped with iron and advanced metallic alloy weapons. The procurement of these new technologies enabled the Ch'in armies to defeat the other warring states farther east that had splintered off from the Chou dynasty. The consolidation of the Chinese state under the First Emperor (Shih-huang) of the Ch'in probably thus represents the last eastward wave of the conquests of Darius the Great of Persia (558?–486 B.C.) and Alexander the Great of Macedonia (356–323 B.C.). This interpretation has been forcefully corroborated by the recent discovery in Sinkiang ("New Borders"—the Chinese-controlled part of central Asia) of a large copper statue of a west Asiatic warrior that is preserved in the regional museum at Urumchi. He dates to approximately the fourth century B.C. and is depicted in a kneeling posture almost identical to that of many infantrymen in the terra cotta army of the First Emperor of the Ch'in. The existence of a large Roman military encampment even farther east in Kansu province during the first century B.C. has also recently been documented. It was through these soldiers that the transfer of iron technology and the ideas that came in its wake were achieved.

Note: Scholars who wish to obtain complete documentation for all points raised in the Afterword and who desire fuller annotations for the text may write to the author for a separate, sinologically oriented publication concerning the *Tao Te Ching*.

SELECTED
BIBLIOGRAPHY

Ames, Roger T. *The Art of Rulership: A Study in Ancient Chinese Political Thought.* Honolulu: University of Hawaii Press, 1983.

Ayyaṅgār, T. R. Śrīnivāsa, trans. *The Yoga-Upaniṣad-s.* Edited by Paṇḍit S. Subrahmaṇya Śāstrī. Madras: The Adyar Library, 1938.

Boltz, William G. "The *Lao tzu* Text that Wang Pi and Ho-shang Kung Never Saw." *Bulletin of the School of Oriental and African Studies* 48, no. 3 (1985):493–501.

————. "The Religious and Philosophical Significance of the 'Hsiang erh' *Lao tzu* in the Light of the Ma-wang-tui Silk Manuscripts." *Bulletin of the School of Oriental and African Studies* 45, no. 1 (1982):95–117.

————. "Textual Criticism and the Ma-wang-tui *Lao tzu.*" *Harvard Journal of Asiatic Studies* 44, no. 1 (June 1984):185–224.

Calder, Nigel. *Timescale: An Atlas of the Fourth Dimension.* New York: Viking, 1983.

Chan, Wing-tsit, trans. and annot. *The Way of Lao Tzu (Tao-te ching).* Indianapolis: Bobbs-Merrill, 1963.

Chang, Tsung-tung. "Indo-European Vocabulary in Old Chinese: A New Thesis on the Emergence of Chinese Language and Civilization in the Late Neolithic Age." *Sino-Platonic Papers* 7 (January 1988), 56 pages.

Chatterji, Suniti Kumar. "India and China: Ancient Contacts—What India Received from China." *Journal of the Asiatic Society* [Calcutta] 1, no. 1 (1959):89–122.

Chen, Ellen M. *The* Tao Te Ching: *A New Translation with Commentary*. New York: Paragon, 1989.

Ch'en Ku-ying. *Lao Tzu Chu I chi P'ing-chieh* [Lao Tzu: Commentary, translation, and critique]. Peking: Chung-hua Shu-chü, 1984.

————. *Lao Tzu: Text, Notes, and Comments*. Translated by Rhett Y. W. Young and Roger T. Ames. San Francisco: Chinese Materials Center, 1977.

Ch'en Yin-k'o. "*San-kuo Chih* Ts'ao Ch'ung Hua-t'o Chuan yü Fo-chiao Ku-shih [Buddhist Tales and the Biographies of Ts'ao Ch'ung and Hua-t'o in the *History of the Three Kingdoms*]." In *Ch'en Yin-k'o Hsien-sheng Lun-wen Chi* [Collected works of Ch'en Yin-k'o], pp. 417–20. Vol. 2. Taipei: San-jen-hsing Ch'u-pan-she, 1974.

Chiang Hsi-ch'ang. *Lao Tzu Chiao-ku* [Lao Tzu: Collation and commentary]. Shanghai: Commercial Press, 1937.

Conrady, A. "Indischer Einfluss in China im 4-Jahrhundert v. Chr." *Zeitschrift der Deutscher Morgenländischen Gesellschaft* 60 (1906):335–51.

————. "Zu *Lao-Tze*, cap. 6." *Asia Major* 7 (1932):150–56.

DeFrancis, John. *The Chinese Language: Fact and Fantasy*. Honolulu: University of Hawaii Press, 1984.

————. *Visible Speech: The Diverse Oneness of Writing Systems*. Honolulu: University of Hawaii Press, 1989.

Demiéville, Paul. "Le miroir spirituel." *Sinologica* 1, no. 2 (1947):112–37.

Duyvendak, J. J. L., trans. and annot. *Tao Te Ching: The Book of the Way and Its Virtue*. The Wisdom of the East Series. London: John Murray, 1954.

Edgerton, Franklin, trans., intro., and notes. *The Beginnings of Indian Philosophy: Selections from the Rig Veda, Atharva Veda, Upaniṣads, and Mahābhārata*. Cambridge, Mass.: Harvard University Press, 1965.

Eliade, Mircea. *The Myth of the Eternal Return*, trans. from the French by Willard R. Trask. Bollingen Series, 46. New York: Pantheon, 1954.

————. *Yoga: Immortality and Freedom*, trans. from the French by Willard R. Trask. Bollingen Series, 56. 2d ed. Princeton: Princeton University Press, 1970.

Encyclopaedia Britannica, fifteenth ed., s.v. "Taoism," "Taoism, history of," and "Taoist literature."

Erkes, Eduard. *Ho-shang-kung's Commentary on Lao-tse*. Ascona, Switz.: Artibus Asiae, 1958.

Feuerstein, G. A. *The Essence of Yoga: A Contribution to the Psychohistory of Indian Civilisation*. London: Rider, 1974.

Filliozat, J. "Taoïsme et Yoga." *Dan Viet Nam* 3 (1949):113–20; and *Journal Asiatique* 257, nos. 1, 2 (1969):41–87.

Giles, Herbert A. *A History of Chinese Literature*. London: William Heinemann, 1901.

————. *The Remains of Lao Tzŭ*. Hong Kong: China Mail, 1886.

Harvard-Yenching Institute. *A Concordance to Chuang Tzu*. Sinological Index Series, Supplement no. 20. Cambridge, Mass.: Harvard University Press, 1956.

Henricks, Robert G. "Character Variants in the Ma-wang-tui Texts of the *Lao-tzu*." *Tsing Hua Journal of Chinese Studies*, n.s. 13, nos. 1, 2 (December 1981):221–84.

————. "Examining the Ma-wang-tui Silk Texts of the *Lao-tzu*: With Special Note of Their Differences from the Wang Pi Text." *T'oung Pao* 65, nos. 4, 5 (1979):166–99.

————. *Lao-Tzu: Te-Tao Ching: A New Translation Based on the Recently Discovered Ma-wang-tui Texts*. New York: Ballantine, 1989.

————. "A Note on the Question of Chapter Divisions in the Ma-wang-tui Manuscripts of the *Lao-tzu*." *Early China* 4 (1978–79):49–51.

————. "On the Chapter Divisions in the *Lao-tzu*." *Bulletin of the School of Oriental and African Studies* 45, no. 3 (1982):501–24.

————. "The Philosophy of Lao-tzu Based on the Ma-wang-tui Texts: Some

Preliminary Observations." *Society for the Study of Chinese Religions Bulletin* 9 (Fall 1981):59–78.

Iyengar, B. K. S. *Light on Yoga: Yoga Dipika*. London: George Allen and Unwin, 1965. Reprint. New York: Shocken, 1975.

Izutsu, Toshihiko. *Sufism and Taoism: A Comparative Study of Key Philosophical Concepts*. Berkeley: University of California Press, 1984.

Kaltenmark, Max. *Lao Tzu and Taoism*. Translated from the French by Roger Greaves. Stanford: Stanford University Press, 1969.

Kuo Mo-jo. "Ku-tai Wen-tzu chih Pien-cheng te Fa-chan [The Development of the Dialectics of Ancient Script]." *K'ao-ku* [Archaeology] 3 (1972):2–13.

Kuvalayananda, Svami. *Prāṇāyāma*. Bombay: Popular Prakashan, 1966.

Lau, D. C., trans. and annot. *Tao Te Ching*. Hong Kong: Chinese University Press, 1982.

Lin, Paul J. *A Translation of Lao Tzu's Tao Te Ching and Wang Pi's Commentary*. Ann Arbor: University of Michigan Center for Chinese Studies, 1977.

Ma Hsü-lun. *Lao Tzu Chiao-ku* [Lao Tzu: Collation and commentary]. Peking: Ku-chi Ch'u-pan-she, 1956.

Mair, Victor H. *T'ang Transformation Texts: A Study of the Buddhist Contribution to the Rise of Vernacular Fiction and Drama in China*. Harvard-Yenching Institute Monograph Series, no. 28. Cambridge, Mass.: Harvard University Council on East Asian Studies, 1989.

————, trans., annot., and intro. *Tun-huang Popular Narratives*. Cambridge: Cambridge University Press, 1983.

Ma-wang-tui Han Mu Po-shu (I) [Silk Manuscripts from the Han Tombs at Ma-wang-tui], I. Peking: Wen-wu Ch'u-pan-she, 1974. Includes complete photofacsimiles of the manuscripts.

Miller, Barbara Stoler, trans. *The Bhagavad-Gita: Krishna's Counsel in Time of War*. New York: Columbia University Press and Bantam, 1986.

Needham, Joseph, with the collaboration of Lu Gwei-Djen. *Science and Civ-*

ilisation in China. Vol. 5, *Chemistry and Chemical Technology;* Part V, "Spagyrical Discovery and Invention: Physiological Alchemy." Cambridge: Cambridge University Press, 1983.

Pott, P.H. *Yoga and Yantra: Their Interrelation and Their Significance for Indian Archaeology.* Translated from the Dutch by Rodney Needham. Koninklijk Instituut voor Taal-, Land- en Volkenkunde, Translation Series, no. 8. The Hague: Martinus Nijhoff, 1966.

Radhakrishnan, S., ed., trans., and annot. *The Principal Upaniṣads.* London: George Allen and Unwin, 1953.

Ramdas, Swami. *The Pathless Path.* Bombay: Bharatiya Vidya Bhavan, 1964.

Rump, Ariane, in collaboration with Wing-tsit Chan. *Commentary on the Lao Tzu by Wang Pi.* Society for Asian and Comparative Philosophy Monograph no. 6. Honolulu: University of Hawaii Press, 1979.

Sargeant, Winthrop, trans. *The Bhagavad Gītā.* Rev. ed. by Christopher Chapple. Albany: State University of New York Press, 1984.

Schwartz, Benjamin I. *The World of Thought in Ancient China.* Cambridge, Mass.: Belknap (Harvard University Press), 1985.

Seidel, Anna K. "Taoism." Macropaedia of *The New Encyclopaedia Britannica.* Chicago: Encyclopaedia Britannica, 1983. Vol. 17, pp. 1034b–1044b.

Shaughnessy, Edward L. "Historical Perspectives on the Introduction of the Chariot into China." *Harvard Journal of Asiatic Studies* 48, no. 1 (June 1988):189–237.

———. "Western Cultural Innovations in China, 1200 B.C." *Sino-Platonic Papers* 11 (July 1989).

Shima Kunio. *Rōshi Kōsei* [Variorum Edition of the Laozi]. Tokyo: Kyūko Shoin, 1973.

Strickmann, Michel. "History of Taoism" and "Taoist Literature." Macropaedia of *The New Encyclopaedia Britannica.* Chicago: Encyclopaedia Britannica, 1983. Vol. 17, pp. 1044b–1050b and 1051a–1055a.

Vasilyev, L. S. "Dao i Brakhman: Fenomen Iznachal'noi Verkhovnoi Vseobshchnosti." In *Dao i Daosizm v Kitae.* Akademiya Nauk SSSR, Ordena Tru-

dovogo Krasnogo Znameni Institut Vostokovedeniya. Moscow: "Nauka,"
Glavnaya Redaktsiya Vostochnoi Literatur'i, 1982.

Waley, Arthur. *The Way and Its Power: A Study of the Tao Te Ching and Its
Place in Chinese Thought.* New York: Grove, 1958.

Warren, Henry Clarke, trans. *Buddhism in Translations.* Cambridge, Mass.:
Harvard University, 1909.

Watson, Burton, trans. *The Complete Works of Chuang Tzu.* New York: Columbia University Press, 1968.

Praise for *Why Evolution Is True*

"[Coyne] makes an unassailable case."
— *The New York Times*

"In nine crisp chapters . . . the respected evolutionary biologist lays out an airtight case that Earth is unspeakably old and that new species evolve from previous ones." — *The Boston Globe*

"Coyne's book ... ... w of and deserves its success as a bestseller."
—R. C. Lewontin, *The New York Review of Books*

"I recommend that Mr. Coyne's insightful and withering assessment of evolutionary studies of human psychology and behavior be taped to the bathroom mirrors of all those (perhaps especially journalists) inclined to be swept into excited announcements of What Evolution Shows About Us."
—Philip Kitcher, *The Wall Street Journal*

"With logic and clarity, Coyne presents the vast trove of scientific evidence that supports Darwin's theory." — *The Cleveland Plain Dealer*

"It's always a pleasure to tell people about a wonderful book, especially when the subject of the book is of universal and critical importance. Evolutionary geneticist Jerry A. Coyne has given us such a book. . . . A book that may change the way you look at things—if you dare." —The Huffington Post

"In this two hundredth anniversary year of Darwin's birth, *Why Evolution Is True* ranks among the best of new titles flooding bookstores."
— *The Christian Science Monitor*

"I once wrote that anybody who didn't believe in evolution must be stupid, insane or ignorant, and I was then careful to add that ignorance is no crime. I should now update my statement. Anybody who doesn't believe in evolution is stupid, insane or hasn't read Jerry Coyne. I defy any reasonable person to read this marvelous book and still take seriously the inanity that is intelligent design 'theory' or its country cousin, young earth creationism."
—Richard Dawkins, author of *The God Delusion*

"Many recent writers, from Stephen Jay Gould and Richard Dawkins through Sean B. Carroll and Neil Shubin, have made wonderful contributions to the public understanding of evolution, but Coyne has done the best job of simply laying out the evidence."
—*Library Journal* (starred review)

"Its ignorant opponents like to say that the process of evolution is 'only a theory.' (That's how they prove their ignorance.) Jerry Coyne shows with elegance and rigor that it is a hypothesis that meets and withstands all tests, and strengthens itself as a theory thereby. Once could almost say that it had the distinct merit of being true."
—Christopher Hitchens, author of *God Is Not Great*

"With great care, attention to the scientific evidence and a wonderfully accessible style, Coyne, an evolutionary geneticist at the University of Chicago, presents an overwhelming case for evolution."
—*Publishers Weekly* (starred review)

"For anyone who wishes a clear, well-written explanation of evolution by one of the formost scientists working on the subject, *Why Evolution Is True* should be your choice."
—Edward O. Wilson, author of *Consilience, On Human Nature* and *Sociobiology*

"Scientists don't use the word 'true' lightly, but in this lively and engrossing book, Jerry Coyne shows why biologists are happy to use it when it comes to evolution. Evolution is 'true' not because the experts say it is, nor because some worldview demands it, but because the evidence overwhelmingly supports it. There are many superb books on evolution, but this one is superb in a new way—it explains the latest evidence for evolution lucidly, thoroughly, and with devastating effectiveness."
—Steven Pinker, author of *The Stuff of Thought*

"Richly detailed evidence to counter the Intelligent Design argument."
—*Kirkus Reviews*

"At a time when good evolution books are rife, Coyne has given general readers one of the best."
—*Booklist*

PENGUIN BOOKS

WHY EVOLUTION IS TRUE

Jerry A. Coyne has been a professor at the University of Chicago in the Department of Ecology and Evolution for the past twenty years, where he specializes in evolutionary genetics and the origin of new species. He is a regular contributor to *The New Republic*, *The Times Literary Supplement*, and NPR.

Why
Evolution
Is True

Jerry A. Coyne

PENGUIN BOOKS

VIKING
Published by the Penguin Group
Penguin Group (USA) Inc., 375 Hudson Street, New York, New York 10014, U.S.A.
Penguin Group (Canada), 90 Eglinton Avenue East, Suite 700, Toronto,
Ontario, Canada M4P 2Y3 (a division of Pearson Penguin Canada Inc.)
Penguin Books Ltd, 80 Strand, London WC2R 0RL, England
Penguin Ireland, 25 St Stephen's Green, Dublin 2, Ireland (a division of Penguin Books Ltd)
Penguin Group (Australia), 250 Camberwell Road, Camberwell,
Victoria 3124, Australia (a division of Pearson Australia Group Pty Ltd)
Penguin Books India Pvt Ltd, 11 Community Centre, Panchsheel Park, New Delhi – 110 017, India
Penguin Group (NZ), 67 Apollo Drive, Rosedale, North Shore 0632,
New Zealand (a division of Pearson New Zealand Ltd)
Penguin Books (South Africa) (Pty) Ltd, 24 Sturdee Avenue, Rosebank, Johannesburg 2196, South Africa

Penguin Books Ltd, Registered Offices:
80 Strand, London WC2R 0RL, England

First published in the United States of America by Viking Penguin,
a member of Penguin Group (USA) Inc. 2009
Published in Penguin Books 2010

5   7   9   10   8   6   4

Illustration credits appear on page 271.

Illustrations by Kalliopi Monoyios. Copyright © Kalliopi Monoyios, 2009.

THE LIBRARY OF CONGRESS HAS CATALOGED
THE HARDCOVER EDITION AS FOLLOWS:
Coyne, Jerry A., 1949–
Why evolution is true / by Jerry A. Coyne.
p.   cm.
Includes bibliographical references.
ISBN 978-0-670-02053-9 (hc.)
ISBN 978-0-14-311664-6 (pbk.)
1. Evolution (Biology)   I. Title.
QH366.2.C74 2009
576.8—dc22   2008033973

Printed in the United States of America
Set in Warnock Pro
Designed by Amy Hill

For Dick Lewontin

il miglior fabbro

Contents

Preface

December 20, 2005. Like many scientists on that day, I awoke feeling anxious. John Jones III, a federal judge in Harrisburg, Pennsylvania, was due to issue his ruling in the case of *Kitzmiller et al. vs. Dover Area School District et al*. It had been a watershed trial, and Jones's judgment would decide how American schoolchildren would learn about evolution.

The educational and scientific crisis had begun modestly enough, when administrators of the Dover, Pennsylvania, school district met to discuss which biology textbooks to order for the local high school. Some religious members of the school board, unhappy with the current text's adherence to Darwinian evolution, suggested alternative books that included the biblical theory of creationism. After heated wrangling, the board passed a resolution requiring biology teachers at Dover High to read the following statement to their ninth-grade classes:

> The Pennsylvania Academic Standards require students to learn about Darwin's Theory of Evolution and eventually to take a standardized test of which evolution is a part. Because Darwin's Theory is a theory, it continues to be tested as new evidence is discovered. The Theory is not a fact. Gaps in the Theory exist for which there is no evidence. . . . Intelligent design is an explanation of the origin of life that differs from Darwin's view. The reference book *Of Pandas and People* is available for students to see if they would like to explore this view in an effort to gain an understanding of what intelligent design actually involves. As is true with any theory, students are encouraged to keep an open mind.

This ignited an educational firestorm. Two of the nine school board members resigned, and all the biology teachers refused to read the statement to their classes, protesting that "intelligent design" was religion rather than science. Since offering religious instruction in public schools violates the United States Constitution, eleven outraged parents took the case to court.

The trial began on September 26, 2005, lasting six weeks. It was a colorful affair, justifiably billed as the "Scopes Trial of our century," after the famous 1925 trial in which high school teacher John Scopes, from Dayton, Tennessee, was convicted for teaching that humans had evolved. The national press descended on the sleepy town of Dover, much as it had eighty years earlier on the sleepier town of Dayton. Even Charles Darwin's great-great-grandson, Matthew Chapman, showed up, researching a book about the trial.

By all accounts it was a rout. The prosecution was canny and well prepared, the defense lackluster. The star scientist testifying for the defense admitted that his definition of "science" was so broad that it could include astrology. And in the end, *Of Pandas and People* was shown to be a put-up job, a creationist book in which the word "creation" had simply been replaced by the words "intelligent design."

But the case was not open and shut. Judge Jones was a George W. Bush appointee, a devoted churchgoer, and a conservative Republican—not exactly pro-Darwinian credentials. Everyone held their breath and waited nervously.

Five days before Christmas, Judge Jones handed down his decision—in favor of evolution. He didn't mince words, ruling that the school board's policy was one of "breathtaking inanity," that the defendants had lied when claiming they had no religious motivations, and, most important, that intelligent design was just recycled creationism:

> It is our view that a reasonable, objective observer would, after reviewing both the voluminous record in this case, and our narrative, reach the inescapable conclusion that ID is an interesting theological argument, but that it is not science. . . . In summary, the [school board's] disclaimer singles out the theory of evolution for special treatment, misrepresents its status in the scientific community, causes students to doubt its validity without scientific justification, presents students with a religious

alternative masquerading as a scientific theory, directs them to consult a creationist text [*Of Pandas and People*] as though it were a science resource, and instructs students to forego scientific inquiry in the public school classroom and instead to seek out religious instruction elsewhere.

Jones also brushed aside the defense's claim that the theory of evolution was fatally flawed:

> To be sure, Darwin's theory of evolution is imperfect. However, the fact that a scientific theory cannot yet render an explanation on every point should not be used as a pretext to thrust an untestable alternative hypothesis grounded in religion into the science classroom to misrepresent well-established scientific propositions.

But scientific truth is decided by scientists, not by judges. What Jones had done was simply prevent an established truth from being muddled by biased and dogmatic opponents. Nevertheless, his ruling was a splendid victory for American schoolchildren, for evolution, and, indeed, for science itself.

All the same, it wasn't a time to gloat. This was certainly not the last battle we'd have to fight to keep evolution from being censored in the schools. During more than twenty-five years of teaching and defending evolutionary biology, I've learned that creationism is like the inflatable roly-poly clown I played with as a child: when you punch it, it briefly goes down, but then pops back up. And while the Dover trial is an American story, creationism isn't a uniquely American problem. Creationists—who aren't necessarily Christians—are establishing footholds in other parts of the world, especially the United Kingdom, Australia, and Turkey. The battle for evolution seems never-ending. And the battle is part of a wider war, a war between rationality and superstition. What is at stake is nothing less than science itself and all the benefits it offers to society.

The mantra of evolution's opponents, whether in America or elsewhere, is always the same: "The theory of evolution is in crisis." The implication is that there are some profound observations about nature that conflict with Darwinism. But evolution is far more than a "theory," let alone a theory in crisis. Evolution is a fact. And far from casting doubt on Darwinism, the evidence gathered by scientists over the past century and a half supports it completely, showing that evolution happened, and that it happened largely as Darwin proposed, through the workings of natural selection.

This book lays out the main lines of evidence for evolution. For those who oppose Darwinism purely as a matter of faith, no amount of evidence will do—theirs is a belief not based on reason. But for the many who find themselves uncertain, or who accept evolution but are not sure how to argue their case, this volume gives a succinct summary of why modern science recognizes evolution as true. I offer it in the hope that people everywhere may share my wonder at the sheer explanatory power of Darwinian evolution, and may face its implications without fear.

Any book on evolutionary biology is necessarily a collaboration, for the field enfolds areas as diverse as paleontology, molecular biology, population genetics, and biogeography; no one person could ever master them all. I am grateful for the help and advice of many colleagues who have patiently instructed me and corrected my errors. These include Richard Abbott, Spencer Barrett, Andrew Berry, Deborah Charlesworth, Peter Crane, Mick Ellison, Rob Fleischer, Peter Grant, Matthew Harris, Jim Hopson, David Jablonski, Farish Jenkins, Emily Kay, Philip Kitcher, Rich Lenski, Mark Norell, Steve Pinker, Trevor Price, Donald Prothero, Steve Pruett-Jones, Bob Richards, Callum Ross, Doug Schemske, Paul Sereno, Neil Shubin, Janice Spofford, Douglas Theobald, Jason Weir, Steve Yanoviak, and Anne Yoder. I apologize to those whose names have been inadvertently omitted, and exculpate all but myself for any remaining errors. I am especially grateful to Matthew Cobb, Naomi Fein, Hopi Hoekstra, Latha Menon, and Brit Smith, who read and critiqued the entire manuscript. The book would have been substantially poorer without the hard work and artistic acumen of the illustrator, Kalliopi Monoyios. Finally, I am grateful to my agent, John Brockman, who agreed that people needed to hear the evidence for evolution, and to my editor at Viking Penguin, Wendy Wolf, for her help and support.

Introduction

Darwin matters because evolution matters. Evolution matters
because science matters. Science matters because it is the
preeminent story of our age, an epic saga about who we are,
where we came from, and where we are going.

—Michael Shermer

Among the wonders that science has uncovered about the universe in which we dwell, no subject has caused more fascination and fury than evolution. That is probably because no majestic galaxy or fleeting neutrino has implications that are as personal. Learning about evolution can transform us in a deep way. It shows us our place in the whole splendid and extraordinary panoply of life. It unites us with every living thing on the earth today and with myriads of creatures long dead. Evolution gives us the true account of our origins, replacing the myths that satisfied us for thousands of years. Some find this deeply frightening, others ineffably thrilling.

Charles Darwin, of course, belonged to the second group, and expressed the beauty of evolution in the famous final paragraph of the book that started it all—*On the Origin of Species* (1859):

There is grandeur in this view of life, with its several powers, having been originally breathed into a few forms or into one; and that, whilst this planet has gone cycling on according to the fixed law of gravity, from so simple a beginning endless forms most beautiful and most wonderful have been, and are being, evolved.

But there is even more cause for wonder. For the *process* of evolution—natural selection, the mechanism that drove the first naked, replicating molecule into the diversity of millions of fossil and living forms—is a mechanism of staggering simplicity and beauty. And only those who understand it can experience the awe that comes with realizing how such a straightforward process could yield features as diverse as the flower of the orchid, the wing of the bat, and the tail of the peacock. Again in *The Origin*, Darwin—imbued with Victorian paternalism—described this feeling:

When we no longer look at an organic being as a savage looks at a ship, as something wholly beyond his comprehension; when we regard every production of nature as one which has had a long history; when we contemplate every complex structure and instinct as the summing up of many contrivances, each useful to the possessor, in the same way as any great mechanical invention is the summing up of the labour, the experience, the reason, and even the blunders of numerous workmen; when we thus view each organic being, how far more interesting—I speak from experience—does the study of natural history become!

Darwin's theory that all of life was the product of evolution, and that the evolutionary process was driven largely by natural selection, has been called the greatest idea that anyone ever had. But it is more than just a good theory, or even a beautiful one. It also happens to be true. Although the idea of evolution itself was not original to Darwin, the copious evidence he mustered in its favor convinced most scientists and many educated readers that life had indeed changed over time. This took only about ten years after *The Origin* was published in 1859. But for many years thereafter, scientists remained skeptical about Darwin's key innovation: the theory of natural selection.

Indeed, if ever there was a time when Darwinism was "just a theory," or was "in crisis," it was the latter half of the nineteenth century, when evidence for the mechanism of evolution was not clear, and the means by which it worked—genetics—was still obscure. This was all sorted out in the first few decades of the twentieth century, and since then the evidence for both evolution and natural selection has continued to mount, crushing the scientific opposition to Darwinism. While biologists have revealed many phenomena that Darwin never imagined—how to discern evolutionary relationships from DNA sequences, for one thing—the theory presented in *The Origin of Species* has, in the main, held up steadfastly. Today scientists have as much confidence in Darwinism as they do in the existence of atoms, or in microorganisms as the cause of infectious disease.

Why then do we need a book that gives the evidence for a theory that long ago became part of mainstream science? After all, nobody writes books explaining the evidence for atoms, or for the germ theory of disease. What is so different about evolution?

Nothing—and everything. True, evolution is as solidly established as any scientific fact (it is, as we will learn, more than "just a theory"), and scientists need no more convincing. But things are different outside scientific circles. To many, evolution gnaws at their sense of self. If evolution offers a lesson, it seems to be that we're not only related to other creatures but, like them, are also the product of blind and impersonal evolutionary forces. If humans are just one of many outcomes of natural selection, maybe we aren't so special after all. You can understand why this doesn't sit well with many people who think that we came into being differently from other species, as the special goal of a divine intention. Does our existence have any purpose or meaning that distinguishes us from other creatures? Evolution is also thought to erode morality. If, after all, we are simply beasts, then why not *behave* like beasts? What can keep us moral if we're nothing more than monkeys with big brains? No other scientific theory produces such angst, or such psychological resistance.

It's clear that this resistance stems largely from religion. You can find religions without creationism, but you never find creationism without religion. Many religions not only deem humans as special, but deny evolution by asserting that we, like other species, were objects of an instantaneous creation by a deity. While many religious people have found a way to accommodate evolution with their spiritual beliefs, no such reconciliation is possible if one adheres to the literal truth of a special creation. That is why opposition to evolution is so strong in the United States and Turkey, where fundamentalist beliefs are pervasive.

Statistics show starkly how resistant we are to accepting the plain scientific fact of evolution. Despite incontrovertible evidence for evolution's truth, year after year polls show that Americans are depressingly suspicious about this single branch of biology. In 2006, for example, adults in thirty-two countries were asked to respond to the assertion "Human beings, as we know them, developed from earlier species of animals," by answering whether they considered it true, false, or were unsure. Now, this statement is flatly true: as we will see, genetic and fossil evidence shows that humans descend from a primate lineage that split off from our common ancestor with the chimpanzees roughly seven million years ago. And yet only 40 percent of Americans—four in ten people—judge the statement true (down 5 percent from 1985). This figure is nearly matched by the proportion of people who say it's false: 39 percent. And the rest, 21 percent, are simply unsure.

This becomes even more remarkable when we compare these statistics to those from other Western countries. Of the thirty-one other nations surveyed, only Turkey, rife with religious fundamentalism, ranked lower in accepting evolution (25 percent accept, 75 percent reject). Europeans, on the other hand, score much better, with over 80 percent of French, Scandinavians, and Icelanders seeing evolution as true. In Japan, 78 percent of people agree that humans evolved. Imagine if America ranked next to last among countries accepting the existence of atoms! People would immediately go to work improving education in the physical sciences.

And evolution gets bumped down even further when it comes to deciding not whether it's true, but whether it should be taught in the public schools. Nearly two-thirds of Americans feel that if evolution is taught in the science classroom, creationism should be as well. Only 12 percent—one in eight people—think that evolution should be taught without mentioning a creationist alternative. Perhaps the "teach all sides" argument appeals to the American sense of fair play, but to an educator it's truly disheartening. Why teach a discredited, religiously based theory, even one widely believed, alongside a theory so obviously true? It's like asking that shamanism be taught in medical school alongside Western medicine, or astrology be presented in psychology class as an alternative theory of human behavior. Perhaps the most frightening statistic is this: despite legal prohibitions, nearly one in eight American high school biology teachers admits to presenting creationism or intelligent design in the classroom as a valid scientific alternative to Darwinism. (This may not be surprising given that one in six teachers believes that "God created human beings pretty much in their present form within the last 10,000 years.")

Sadly, antievolutionism, often thought to be a peculiarly American problem, is now spreading to other countries, including Germany and the United Kingdom. In the UK, a 2006 poll by the BBC asked two thousand people to describe their view of how life formed and developed. While 48 percent accepted the evolutionary view, 39 percent opted for either creationism or intelligent design, and 13 percent didn't know. More than 40 percent of the respondents thought that either creationism or intelligent design should be taught in school science classes. That isn't so different from the statistics from America. And some schools in the UK do present intelligent design as an alternative to evolution, an educational tactic illegal in the United States. With evangelical Christianity gaining a foothold in mainland Europe, and Muslim fundamentalism spreading through the Middle East, creationism follows in their wake. As I write, Turkish biologists are fighting a rearguard action against well-funded and vociferous creationists in their own country. And—the ultimate irony—creationism has even established a foothold on the Galápagos archipelago. There, on the very land that symbolizes evolution, the iconic islands that inspired Darwin, a Seventh-day Adventist school dispenses undiluted creationist biology to children of all faiths.

Aside from its conflict with fundamentalist religion, much confusion and misunderstanding surrounds evolution because of a simple lack of awareness of the weight and variety of evidence in its favor. Doubtless some simply aren't interested. But the problem is more widespread than this: it's a lack of information. Even many of my fellow biologists are unacquainted with the many lines of evidence for evolution, and most of my university students, who supposedly learned evolution in high school, come to my courses knowing almost nothing of this central organizing theory of biology. In spite of the wide coverage of creationism and its recent descendant, intelligent design, the popular press gives almost no background on why scientists accept evolution. No wonder then that many people fall prey to the rhetoric of creationists and their deliberate mischaracterizations of Darwinism.

Although Darwin was the first to compile evidence for the theory, since his time scientific research has uncovered a stream of new examples showing evolution in action. We are observing species splitting into two, and finding more and more fossils capturing change in the past—dinosaurs that have sprouted feathers, fish that have grown limbs, reptiles turning into mammals. In this book I weave together the many threads of modern work in genetics, paleontology, geology, molecular biology, anatomy, and development that demonstrate the "indelible stamp" of the processes first proposed by Darwin. We will examine what evolution is, what it is not, and how one tests the validity of a theory that inflames so many.

We will see that while recognizing the full import of evolution certainly requires a profound shift in thinking, it does not inevitably lead to the dire consequences that creationists always paint when trying to dissuade people from Darwinism. Accepting evolution needn't turn you into a despairing nihilist or rob your life of purpose and meaning. It won't make you immoral, or give you the sentiments of a Stalin or Hitler. Nor need it promote atheism, for enlightened religion has always found a way to accommodate the advances of science. In fact, understanding evolution should surely deepen and enrich our appreciation of the living world and our place in it. The truth—that we, like lions, redwoods, and frogs, all resulted from the slow replacement of one gene by another, each step conferring a tiny reproductive advantage—is surely more satisfying than the myth that we were suddenly called into being from nothing. As so often happens, Darwin put it best:

> When I view all beings not as special creations, but as the lineal descendants of some few beings which lived long before the first bed of the Cambrian system was deposited, they seem to me to become ennobled.

Why Evolution Is True

Chapter 1

What Is Evolution?

A curious aspect of the theory of evolution is that
everybody thinks he understands it.

—Jacques Monod

I f anything is true about nature, it is that plants and animals seem intricately and almost perfectly designed for living their lives. Squids and flatfish change color and pattern to blend in with their surroundings, becoming invisible to predator and prey. Bats have radar to home in on insects at night. Hummingbirds, which can hover in place and change position in an instant, are far more agile than any human helicopter, and have long tongues to sip nectar lying deep within flowers. And the flowers they visit also appear designed—to use hummingbirds as sex aids. For while the hummingbird is busy sipping nectar, the flower attaches pollen to its bill, enabling it to fertilize the next flower that the bird visits. Nature resembles a well-oiled machine, with every species an intricate cog or gear.

What does all this seem to imply? A master mechanic, of course. This conclusion was most famously expressed by the eighteenth-century English philosopher William Paley. If we came across a watch lying on the ground, he said, we would certainly recognize it as the work of a watchmaker. Likewise, the existence of well-adapted organisms and their intricate features surely implied a conscious, celestial designer—God. Let's look at Paley's argument, one of the most famous in the history of philosophy:

> When we come to inspect the watch, we perceive . . . that its several parts are framed and put together for a purpose, *e.g.* that they are so formed and adjusted as to produce motion, and that motion so regulated as to point out the hour of the day; that, if the different parts had been differently shaped from what they are, if a different size from what they are, or placed after any other manner, or in any other order than that in which they are placed, either no motion at all would have been carried on in the machine, or none which would have answered the use that is now served by it. . . . Every indication of contrivance, every manifestation of design, which existed in the watch, exists in the works of nature; with the difference, on the side of nature, of being greater and more, and that in a degree which exceeds all computation.

The argument Paley put forward so eloquently was both commonsensical and ancient. When he and his fellow "natural theologians" described plants and animals, they believed that they were cataloging the grandeur and ingenuity of God manifested in his well-designed creatures.

Darwin himself raised the question of design—before disposing of it— in 1859.

> How have all those exquisite adaptations of one part of the organization to another part, and to the conditions of life, and of one distinct organic being, been perfected? We see these beautiful co-adaptations most plainly in the woodpecker and missletoe; and only a little less plainly in the humblest parasite which clings to the hairs of a quadruped or feathers of a bird; in the structure of the beetle which dives though the water; in the plumed seed which is wafted by the gentlest breeze; in short, we see beautiful adaptations everywhere and in every part of the organic world.

Darwin had his own answer to the conundrum of design. A keen naturalist who originally studied to be a minister at Cambridge University (where, ironically, he occupied Paley's former rooms), Darwin well knew the seductive power of arguments like Paley's. The more one learns about plants and animals, the more one marvels at how well their designs fit their ways of life. What could be more natural than inferring that this fit reflects *conscious* design? Yet Darwin looked beyond the obvious, suggesting—and supporting with copious evidence—two ideas that forever dispelled the idea of deliberate design. Those ideas were evolution and natural selection. He was not the first to think of evolution—several before him, including his own grandfather Erasmus Darwin, floated the idea that life had evolved. But Darwin was the first to use data from nature to convince people that evolution was true, and his idea of natural selection was truly novel. It testifies to his genius that the concept of natural theology, accepted by most educated Westerners before 1859, was vanquished within only a few years by a single five-hundred-page book. *On the Origin of Species* turned the mysteries of life's diversity from mythology into genuine science.

So what is "Darwinism"?[1] This simple and profoundly beautiful theory, the theory of evolution by natural selection, has been so often misunderstood, and even on occasion maliciously misstated, that it is worth pausing for a moment to set out its essential points and claims. We'll be coming back to these repeatedly as we consider the evidence for each.

In essence, the modern theory of evolution is easy to grasp. It can be summarized in a single (albeit slightly long) sentence: Life on earth evolved gradually beginning with one primitive species—perhaps a self-replicating molecule—that lived more than 3.5 billion years ago; it then branched out over time, throwing off many new and diverse species; and the mechanism for most (but not all) of evolutionary change is natural selection.

When you break that statement down, you find that it really consists of six components: evolution, gradualism, speciation, common ancestry, natural selection, and nonselective mechanisms of evolutionary change. Let's examine what each of these parts means.

The first is the idea of *evolution* itself. This simply means that a species undergoes genetic change over time. That is, over many generations a species can evolve into something quite different, and those differences are based on changes in the DNA, which originate as mutations. The species of animals and plants living today weren't around in the past, but are descended from those that lived earlier. Humans, for example, evolved from a creature that was apelike, but not identical to modern apes.

Although all species evolve, they don't do so at the same rate. Some, like horseshoe crabs and gingko trees, have barely changed over millions of years. The theory of evolution does not predict that species will constantly be evolving, or how fast they'll change when they do. That depends on the evolutionary pressures they experience. Groups like whales and humans have evolved rapidly, while others, like the coelacanth "living fossil," look almost identical to ancestors that lived hundreds of millions of years ago.

The second part of evolutionary theory is the idea of *gradualism*. It takes many generations to produce a substantial evolutionary change, such as the evolution of birds from reptiles. The evolution of new features, like the teeth and jaws that distinguish mammals from reptiles, does not occur in just one or a few generations, but usually over hundreds or thousands—even millions— of generations. True, some change can occur very quickly. Populations of microbes have very short generations, some as brief as twenty minutes. This means that these species can undergo a lot of evolution in a short time, accounting for the depressingly rapid rise of drug resistance in disease-causing bacteria and viruses. And there are many examples of evolution known to occur within a human lifetime. But when we're talking about really *big* change, we're usually referring to change that requires many thousands of years. Gradualism does not mean, however, that each species evolves at an even pace. Just as different species vary in how fast they evolve, so a single species evolves faster or slower as evolutionary pressures wax and wane. When natural selection is strong, as when an animal or plant colonizes a new environment, evolutionary change can be fast. Once a species becomes well adapted to a stable habitat, evolution often slows down.

The next two tenets are flip sides of the same coin. It is a remarkable fact that while there are many living species, all of us—you, me, the elephant, and the potted cactus—share some fundamental traits. Among these are the biochemical pathways that we use to produce energy, our standard four-letter DNA code, and how that code is read and translated into proteins. This tells us that every species goes back to a single common ancestor, an ancestor who had those common traits and passed them on to its descendants. But if evolution meant only gradual genetic change within a species, we'd have only one species today—a single highly evolved descendant of the first species. Yet we have many: well over ten million species inhabit our planet today, and we know of a further quarter million as fossils. Life is diverse. How does this diversity arise from one ancestral form? This requires the third idea of evolution: that of *splitting*, or, more accurately, *speciation*.

Look at figure 1, which shows a sample evolutionary tree that illustrates the relationships between birds and reptiles. We've all seen these, but let's examine one a bit more closely to understand what it really means. What exactly happened when node X, say, split into the lineage that leads to modern reptiles like lizards and snakes on the one hand and to modern birds and their dinosaurian relatives on the other? Node X represents a *single ances-*

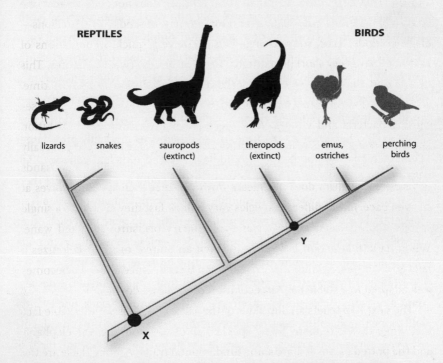

FIGURE 1. An example of common ancestry in reptiles. X and Y are species that were the common ancestors between later-evolved forms.

tral species, an ancient reptile, that split into two descendant species. One of the descendants went on its own merry path, eventually splitting many times and giving rise to all dinosaurs and modern birds. The other descendant did the same, but produced most modern reptiles. The common ancestor X is often called the "missing link" between the descendant groups. It is the genealogical connection between birds and modern reptiles—the intersection you'd finally reach if you traced their lineages all the way back. There's a more recent "missing link" here too: node Y, the species that was the common ancestor of bipedal meat-eating dinosaurs like *Tyrannosaurus rex* (all now extinct) and modern birds. But although common ancestors are no longer with us, and their fossils nearly impossible to document (after all, they represent but a single species out of thousands in the fossil record), we can sometimes discover fossils closely related to them, species having features that show common ancestry. In the next chapter, for example, we'll learn about the "feathered dinosaurs" that support the existence of node Y.

What happened when ancestor X split into two separate species? Nothing much, really. As we'll see later, speciation simply means the evolution of different groups that can't interbreed—that is, groups that can't exchange genes. What we would have seen had we been around when this common ancestor began to split is simply two populations of a single reptilian species, probably living in different places, beginning to evolve slight differences from each other. Over a long time, these differences gradually grew larger. Eventually the two populations would have evolved sufficient genetic difference that members of the different populations could not interbreed. (There are many ways this can happen: members of different animal species may no longer find each other attractive as mates, or if they do mate with each other, the offspring could be sterile. Different plant species can use different pollinators or flower at different times, preventing cross-fertilization.)

Millions of years later, and after more splitting events, one of the descendant dinosaur species, node Y, itself split into two more species, one eventually producing all the bipedal, carnivorous dinosaurs and the other producing all living birds. This critical moment in evolutionary history—the birth of the ancestor of all birds—wouldn't have looked so dramatic at the time. We wouldn't have seen the sudden appearance of flying creatures from reptiles, but merely two slightly different populations of the same dinosaur, probably no more different than members of diverse human populations are today. All the important change occurred thousands of generations after the split, when selection acted on one lineage to promote flight and on the other to promote the traits of bipedal dinosaurs. It is only in retrospect that we can identify species Y as the common ancestor of *T. rex* and birds. These evolutionary events were slow, and seem momentous only when we arrange in sequence all the descendants of these diverging evolutionary streams.

But species don't *have* to split. Whether they do depends, as we'll see, on whether circumstances allow populations to evolve enough differences that they are no longer able to interbreed. The vast majority of species—more than 99 percent of them—go extinct without leaving any descendants. Others, like gingko trees, live millions of years without producing many new species. Speciation doesn't happen very often. But each time one species splits into two, it doubles the number of opportunities for *future* speciation, so the number of species can rise exponentially. Although speciation is slow, it happens sufficiently often, over such long periods of history, that it can easily explain the stunning diversity of living plants and animals on earth.

Speciation was so important to Darwin that he made it the title of his most famous book. And that book did give some evidence for the splitting. The only diagram in the whole of *The Origin* is a hypothetical evolutionary tree resembling figure 1. But it turns out that Darwin didn't really explain how new species arose, for, lacking any knowledge of genetics, he never really understood that explaining species means explaining barriers to gene exchange. Real understanding of how speciation occurs began only in the 1930s. I'll have more to say about this process, which is my own area of research, in chapter 7.

It stands to reason that if the history of life forms a tree, with all species originating from a single trunk, then one can find a common origin for every pair of twigs (existing species) by tracing each twig back through its branches until they intersect at the branch they have in common. This node, as we've seen, is their common ancestor. And if life began with one species and split into millions of descendant species through a branching process, it follows that every pair of species shares a common ancestor sometime in the past.

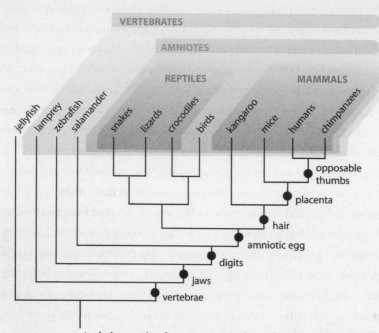

FIGURE 2. A phylogeny (evolutionary tree) of vertebrates, showing how evolution produces a hierarchical grouping of features, and thus of species containing these features. The dots indicate where on the tree each trait arose.

Closely related species, like closely related people, had a common ancestor that lived fairly recently, while the common ancestor of more distantly related species, like that of distant human relatives, lived further back in the past. Thus, the idea of *common ancestry*—the fourth tenet of Darwinism—is the flip side of speciation. It simply means that we can always look back in time, using either DNA sequences or fossils, and find descendants joining at their ancestors.

Let's examine one evolutionary tree, that of vertebrates (figure 2). On this tree I've put some of the features that biologists use to deduce evolutionary relationships. For a start, fish, amphibians, mammals, and reptiles all have a backbone—they are "vertebrates"—so they must have descended from a common ancestor that also had vertebrae. But within vertebrates, reptiles and mammals are united (and distinguished from fish and amphibians) by having an "amniotic egg"—the embryo is surrounded by a fluid-filled membrane called the amnion. So reptiles and mammals must have had a more recent common ancestor that itself possessed such an egg. But this group also contains two subgroups, one with species that all have hair, are warm-blooded, and produce milk (that is, mammals), and another with species that are cold-blooded, scaly, and produce watertight eggs (that is, reptiles). Like all species, these form a nested hierarchy: a hierarchy in which big groups of species whose members share a few traits are subdivided into smaller groups of species sharing more traits, and so on down to species, like black bears and grizzly bears, that share nearly all their traits.

Actually, the nested arrangement of life was recognized long before Darwin. Starting with the Swedish botanist Carl Linnaeus in 1735, biologists began classifying animals and plants, discovering that they consistently fell into what was called a "natural" classification. Strikingly, different biologists came up with nearly identical groupings. This means that these groupings are not subjective artifacts of a human need to classify, but tell us something real and fundamental about nature. But nobody knew what that something was until Darwin came along and showed that the nested arrangement of life is precisely what evolution predicts. Creatures with recent common ancestors share many traits, while those whose common ancestors lay in the distant past are more dissimilar. The "natural" classification is itself strong evidence for evolution.

Why? Because we don't see such a nested arrangement if we're trying to arrange objects that haven't arisen by an evolutionary process of splitting and descent. Take cardboard books of matches, which I used to collect. They don't fall into a natural classification in the same way as living species. You could, for example, sort matchbooks hierarchically beginning with size, and then by country within size, color within country, and so on. Or you could start with the type of product advertised, sorting thereafter by color and then by date. There are many ways to order them, and everyone will do it differently. There is no sorting system that all collectors agree on. This is because rather than evolving, so that each matchbook gives rise to another that is only slightly different, each design was created from scratch by human whim.

Matchbooks resemble the kinds of creatures expected under a creationist explanation of life. In such a case, organisms would not have common ancestry, but would simply result from an instantaneous creation of forms designed de novo to fit their environments. Under this scenario, we wouldn't expect to see species falling into a nested hierarchy of forms that is recognized by all biologists.[2]

Until about thirty years ago, biologists used visible features like anatomy and mode of reproduction to reconstruct the ancestry of living species. This was based on the reasonable assumption that organisms with similar features also have similar genes, and thus are more closely related. But now we have a powerful, new, and independent way to establish ancestry: we can look directly at the genes themselves. By sequencing the DNA of various species and measuring how similar these sequences are, we can reconstruct their evolutionary relationships. This is done by making the entirely reasonable assumption that species having more similar DNA are more closely related—that is, their common ancestors lived more recently. These molecular methods have not produced much change in the pre–DNA era trees of life: both the visible traits of organisms and their DNA sequences usually give the same information about evolutionary relationships.

The idea of common ancestry leads naturally to powerful and testable predictions about evolution. If we see that birds and reptiles group together based on their features and DNA sequences, we can predict that we should find common ancestors of birds and reptiles in the fossil record. Such predictions have been fulfilled, giving some of the strongest evidence for evolution. We'll meet some of these ancestors in the next chapter.

The fifth part of evolutionary theory is what Darwin clearly saw as his greatest intellectual achievement: the idea of *natural selection*. This idea was not in fact unique to Darwin—his contemporary, the naturalist Alfred Russel Wallace, came up with it at about the same time, leading to one of the most famous simultaneous discoveries in the history of science. Darwin, however, gets the lion's share of credit because in *The Origin* he worked out the idea of selection in great detail, gave evidence for it, and explored its many consequences.

But natural selection was also the part of evolutionary theory considered most revolutionary in Darwin's time, and it is still unsettling to many. Selection is both revolutionary and disturbing for the same reason: it explains apparent design in nature by a purely materialistic process that doesn't require creation or guidance by supernatural forces.

The idea of natural selection is not hard to grasp. If individuals within a species differ genetically from one another, and some of those differences affect an individual's ability to survive and reproduce in its environment, then in the next generation the "good" genes that lead to higher survival and reproduction will have relatively more copies than the "not so good" genes. Over time, the population will gradually become more and more suited to its environment as helpful mutations arise and spread through the population, while deleterious ones are weeded out. Ultimately, this process produces organisms that are well adapted to their habitats and way of life.

Here's a simple example. The wooly mammoth inhabited the northern parts of Eurasia and North America, and was adapted to the cold by bearing a thick coat of hair (entire frozen specimens have been found buried in the tundra).[3] It probably descended from mammoth ancestors that had little hair—like modern elephants. Mutations in the ancestral species led to some individual mammoths—like some modern humans—being hairier than others. When the climate became cold, or the species spread into more northerly regions, the hirsute individuals were better able to tolerate their frigid surroundings, and left more offspring than their balder counterparts. This enriched the population in genes for hairiness. In the next generation, the average mammoth would be a bit hairier than before. Let this process continue over some thousands of generations, and your smooth mammoth gets replaced by a shaggy one. And let many different features affect your resistance to cold (for example, body size, amount of fat, and so on), and those features will change concurrently.

The process is remarkably simple. It requires only that individuals of a species vary genetically in their ability to survive and reproduce in their environment. Given this, natural selection—and evolution—are inevitable. As we shall see, this requirement is met in every species that has ever been examined. And since many traits can affect an individual's adaptation to its environment (its "fitness"), natural selection can, over eons, sculpt an animal or plant into something that looks designed.

It's important to realize, though, that there's a real difference in what you'd expect to see if organisms were consciously designed rather than if they evolved by natural selection. Natural selection is not a master engineer, but a tinkerer. It doesn't produce the absolute perfection achievable by a designer starting from scratch, but merely the best it can do with what it has to work with. Mutations for a perfect design may not arise because they are simply too rare. The African rhinoceros, with its two tandemly placed horns, may be better adapted at defending itself and sparring with its brethren than is the Indian rhino, graced with but a single horn (actually, these are not true horns, but compacted hairs). But a mutation producing two horns may simply not have arisen among Indian rhinos. Still, one horn is better than no horns. The Indian rhino is better off than its hornless ancestor, but accidents of genetic history may have led to a less than perfect "design." And, of course, every instance of a plant or animal that is parasitized or diseased represents a failure to adapt. Likewise for all cases of extinction, which represent well over 99 percent of species that ever lived. (This, by the way, poses an enormous problem for theories of intelligent design (ID). It doesn't seem so intelligent to design millions of species that are destined to go extinct, and then replace them with other, similar species, most of which will also vanish. ID supporters have never addressed this difficulty.)

Natural selection must also work with the design of an organism as a whole, which is a compromise among different adaptations. Female sea turtles dig their nests on the beach with their flippers—a painful, slow, and clumsy process that exposes their eggs to predators. Having more shovel-like flippers would help them do a better and faster job, but then they couldn't swim as well. A conscientious designer might have given the turtles an extra pair of limbs, with retractable shovel-like appendages, but turtles, like all reptiles, are stuck with a developmental plan that limits their limbs to four.

Organisms aren't just at the mercy of the luck of the mutational draw, but are also constrained by their development and evolutionary history. Mutations are changes in traits that already exist; they almost never create brand-new features. This means that evolution must build a new species starting with the design of its ancestors. Evolution is like an architect who cannot design a building from scratch, but must build every new structure by adapting a preexisting building, keeping the structure habitable all the while. This leads to some compromises. We men, for example, would be better off if our testes formed directly outside the body, where the cooler temperature is better for sperm.[4] The testes, however, begin development in the abdomen. When the fetus is six or seven months old, they migrate down into the scrotum through two channels called the inguinal canals, removing them from the damaging heat of the rest of the body. Those canals leave weak spots in the body wall that make men prone to inguinal hernias. These hernias are bad: they can obstruct the intestine, and sometimes caused death in the years before surgery. No intelligent designer would have given us this tortuous testicular journey. We're stuck with it because we inherited our developmental program for making testes from fishlike ancestors, whose gonads developed, and remained, completely within the abdomen. We begin development with fishlike internal testes, and our testicular descent evolved later, as a clumsy add-on.

So natural selection does not yield perfection—only improvements over what came before. It produces the *fitter*, not the *fittest*. And although selection gives the appearance of design, that design may often be imperfect. Ironically, it is in those imperfections, as we'll see in chapter 3, that we find important evidence for evolution.

This brings us to the last of evolutionary theory's six points: *processes other than natural selection can cause evolutionary change.* The most important is simple random changes in the proportion of genes caused by the fact that different families have different numbers of offspring. This leads to evolutionary change that, being random, has nothing to do with adaptation. The influence of this process on important evolutionary change, though, is probably minor, because it does not have the molding power of natural selection. Natural selection remains the only process that can produce adaptation. Nevertheless, we'll see in chapter 5 that genetic drift may play some evolutionary role in small populations and probably accounts for some non-adaptive features of DNA.

These, then, are the six parts of evolutionary theory.[5] Some parts are intimately connected. If speciation is true, for instance, then common ancestry must also be true. But some parts are independent of others. Evolution might occur, for example, but it need not occur gradually. Some "mutationists" in the early twentieth century thought that a species could instantly produce a radically different species via a single monster mutation. The renowned zoologist Richard Goldschmidt, for example, once argued that the first creature recognizable as a bird might have hatched from an egg laid by an unambiguous reptile. Such claims can be tested. Mutationism predicts that new groups should arise instantly from old ones, without transitions in the fossil record. But the fossils tell us that this is not the way evolution works. Nevertheless, such tests show that different parts of Darwinism can be tested independently.

Alternatively, evolution might be true, but natural selection might not be its cause. Many biologists, for instance, once thought that evolution occurred by a mystical and teleological force: organisms were said to have an "inner drive" that made species change in certain prescribed directions. This kind of drive was said to have propelled the evolution of the huge canine teeth of saber-toothed tigers, making the teeth get larger and larger, regardless of their usefulness, until the animal could not close its mouth and the species starved itself to extinction. We now know that there's no evidence for teleological forces—saber-toothed tigers did not in fact starve to death, but lived happily with oversized canines for millions of years before they went extinct for other reasons. Yet the fact that evolution might have different causes was one reason why biologists accepted evolution many decades before accepting natural selection.

So much for the claims of evolutionary theory. But here's an important and commonly heard refrain: Evolution *is* only a theory, isn't it? Addressing an evangelical group in Texas in 1980, presidential candidate Ronald Reagan characterized evolution this way: "Well, it is a theory. It is a scientific theory only, and it has in recent years been challenged in the world of science and is not yet believed in the scientific community to be as infallible as it once was believed."

The key word in this quote is "only." *Only* a theory. The implication is that there is something *not quite right* about a theory—that it is a mere speculation, and very likely wrong. Indeed, the everyday connotation of "theory" is "guess," as in, "My theory is that Fred is crazy about Sue." But in science the word "theory" means something completely different, conveying far more assurance and rigor than the notion of a simple guess.

According to the *Oxford English Dictionary*, a *scientific* theory is "a statement of what are held to be the general laws, principles, or causes of something known or observed." Thus we can speak of the "theory of gravity" as the proposition that all objects with mass attract one another according to a strict relationship involving the distance between them. Or we talk of the "theory of relativity," which makes specific claims about the speed of light and the curvature of space-time.

There are two points I want to emphasize here. First, in science, a theory is much more than just a speculation about how things are: it is a well-thought-out group of propositions meant to explain facts about the real world. "Atomic theory" isn't just the statement that "atoms exist"; it's a statement about how atoms interact with one another, form compounds, and behave chemically. Similarly, the theory of evolution is more than just the statement that "evolution happened": it is an extensively documented set of principles—I've described six major ones—that explain *how and why* evolution happens.

This brings us to the second point. For a theory to be considered scientific, it must be *testable* and *make verifiable predictions*. That is, we must be able to make observations about the real world that either support it or disprove it. Atomic theory was initially speculative, but gained more and more credibility as data from chemistry piled up supporting the existence of atoms. Although we couldn't actually *see* atoms until scanning-probe microscopy was invented in 1981 (and under the microscope they do look like the little balls we envision), scientists were already convinced long before that atoms were real. Similarly, a good theory makes predictions about what we should find if we look more closely at nature. And if those predictions are met, it gives us more confidence that the theory is true. Einstein's general theory of relativity, proposed in 1916, predicted that light would be bent as it passed by a large celestial body. (To be technical, the gravity of such a body distorts space-time, which distorts the path of nearby photons.) Sure enough, Arthur Eddington verified this prediction in 1919 by showing, during a solar eclipse, that light coming from distant stars was bent as it went by the sun, shifting the stars' apparent positions. It was only when this prediction was verified that Einstein's theory began to be widely accepted.

Because a theory is accepted as "true" only when its assertions and predictions are tested over and over again, and confirmed repeatedly, there is no one moment when a scientific theory suddenly becomes a scientific fact. A theory becomes a fact (or a "truth") when so much evidence has accumulated in its favor—and there is no decisive evidence against it—that virtually all reasonable people will accept it. This does not mean that a "true" theory will never be falsified. All scientific truth is provisional, subject to modification in light of new evidence. There is no alarm bell that goes off to tell scientists that they've finally hit on the ultimate, unchangeable truths about nature. As we'll see, it is possible that despite thousands of observations that support Darwinism, new data might show it to be wrong. I think this is unlikely, but scientists, unlike zealots, can't afford to become arrogant about what they accept as true.

In the process of becoming truths, or facts, scientific theories are usually tested against *alternative* theories. After all, there are usually several explanations for a given phenomenon. Scientists try to make key observations, or conduct decisive experiments, that will test one rival explanation against another. For many years, the position of the earth's landmasses was thought to have been the same throughout the history of life. But in 1912, the German geophysicist Alfred Wegener came up with the rival theory of "continental drift," proposing that continents had moved about. Initially, his theory was inspired by the observation that the shapes of continents like South America and Africa could be fitted together like pieces of a jigsaw puzzle. Continental drift then became more certain as fossils accumulated and paleontologists found that the distribution of ancient species suggested that the continents were once joined. Later, "plate tectonics" was suggested as a mechanism for continental movement, just as natural selection was suggested as the mechanism for evolution: the plates of the earth's crust and mantle floated about on more liquid material in the earth's interior. And although plate tectonics was also greeted with skepticism by geologists, it was subject to rigorous testing on many fronts, yielding convincing evidence that it is true. Now,

thanks to global positioning satellite technology, we can even *see* the continents moving apart, at a speed of two to four inches per year, about the same
rate that your fingernails grow. (This, by the way, combined with the unassailable evidence that the continents were once connected, is evidence
against the claim of "young-earth" creationists that the earth is only six to
ten thousand years old. If that were the case, we'd be able to stand on the
west coast of Spain and see the skyline of New York City, for Europe and
America would have moved less than a mile apart!)

When Darwin wrote *The Origin*, most Western scientists, and nearly
everyone else, were creationists. While they might not have accepted every
detail of the story laid out in Genesis, most thought that life had been created pretty much in its present form, designed by an omnipotent creator,
and had not changed since. In *The Origin*, Darwin provided an alternative
hypothesis for the development, diversification, and design of life. Much of
that book presents evidence that not only supports evolution but at the same
time refutes creationism. In Darwin's day, the evidence for his theories was
compelling but not completely decisive. We can say, then, that evolution was
a theory (albeit a strongly supported one) when first proposed by Darwin,
and since 1859 has graduated to "facthood" as more and more supporting
evidence has piled up. Evolution is still called a "theory," just like the theory
of gravity, but it's a theory that is also a fact.

So how do we test evolutionary theory against the still popular alternative view that life was created and remained unchanged thereafter? There
are actually two kinds of evidence. The first comes from using the six tenets
of Darwinism to make *testable predictions*. By predictions, I don't mean that
Darwinism can predict how things will evolve in the future. Rather, it predicts what we should find in living or ancient species when we study them.
Here are some evolutionary predictions:

- Since there are fossil remains of ancient life, we should be able to find
  some evidence for evolutionary change in the fossil record. The deepest (and oldest) layers of rock would contain the fossils of more primitive species, and some fossils should become more complex as the
  layers of rock become younger, with organisms resembling present-day

species found in the most recent layers. And we should be able to see some species changing over time, forming lineages showing "descent with modification" (adaptation).

• We should be able to find some cases of speciation in the fossil record, with one line of descent dividing into two or more. And we should be able to find new species forming in the wild.

• We should be able to find examples of species that link together major groups suspected to have common ancestry, like birds with reptiles and fish with amphibians. Moreover, these "missing links" (more aptly called "transitional forms") should occur in layers of rock that date to the time when the groups are supposed to have diverged.

• We should expect that species show genetic variation for many traits (otherwise there would be no possibility of evolution happening).

• Imperfection is the mark of evolution, not of conscious design. We should then be able to find cases of imperfect adaptation, in which evolution has not been able to achieve the same degree of optimality as would a creator.

• We should be able to see natural selection acting in the wild.

In addition to these predictions, Darwinism can also be supported by what I call *retrodictions*: facts and data that aren't necessarily predicted by the theory of evolution but *make sense only in light of the theory of evolution*. Retrodictions are a valid way to do science: some of the evidence supporting plate tectonics, for example, came only after scientists learned to read ancient changes in the direction of the earth's magnetic field from patterns of rocks on the seafloor. Some of the retrodictions that support evolution (as opposed to special creation) include patterns of species distribution on the earth's surface, peculiarities of how organisms develop from embryos, and the existence of vestigial features that are of no apparent use. These are the subjects of chapters 3 and 4.

Evolutionary theory, then, makes predictions that are bold and clear.

Darwin spent some twenty years amassing evidence for his theory before publishing *The Origin*. That was more than a hundred and fifty years ago. So much knowledge has accumulated since then! So many more fossils found; so many more species collected and their distributions mapped around the world; so much more work in uncovering the evolutionary relationships of different species. And whole new branches of science, undreamt of by Darwin, have arisen, including molecular biology and systematics, the study of how organisms are related.

As we'll see, all the evidence—both old and new—leads ineluctably to the conclusion that evolution is true.

Chapter 2

Written in the Rocks

The crust of the earth is a vast museum;
but the natural collections have been made only
at intervals of time immensely remote.

—*Charles Darwin*, On the Origin of Species

The story of life on earth is written in the rocks. True, this is a history book torn and twisted, with remnants of pages scattered about, but it is there, and significant portions are still legible. Paleontologists have worked tirelessly to piece together the tangible historical evidence for evolution: the fossil record.

When we admire breathtaking fossils such as the great dinosaur skeletons that grace our natural history museums, it is easy to forget just how much effort has gone into discovering, extracting, preparing, and describing them. Time-consuming, expensive, and risky expeditions to remote and inhospitable corners of the world are often involved. My University of Chicago colleague Paul Sereno, for instance, studies African dinosaurs, and many of the most interesting fossils lie smack in the middle of the Sahara Desert. He and his colleagues have braved political troubles, bandits, disease, and of course the rigors of the desert itself to discover remarkable new species such as *Afrovenator abakensis* and *Jobaria tiguidensis*, specimens that have helped rewrite the story of dinosaur evolution.

Such discoveries involve true dedication to science, many years of painstaking work, persistence, and courage—as well as a healthy dose of luck. But many paleontologists would risk their lives for finds like these. To biologists, fossils are as valuable as gold dust. Without them, we'd have only a sketchy outline of evolution. All we could do would be to study living species and try to infer evolutionary relationships through similarities in form, development, and DNA sequence. We would know, for example, that mammals are more closely related to reptiles than to amphibians. But we wouldn't know what their common ancestors looked like. We'd have no inkling of giant dinosaurs, some as large as trucks, or of our early australopithecine ancestors, small-brained but walking erect. Much of what we'd like to know about evolution would remain a mystery. Fortunately, advances in physics, geology, and biochemistry, along with the daring and persistence of scientists throughout the world, have provided these precious insights into the past.

Making the Record

FOSSILS HAVE BEEN KNOWN since ancient times: Aristotle discussed them, and fossils of the beaked dinosaur *Protoceratops* may have given rise to the mythological griffin of the ancient Greeks. But the real meaning of fossils wasn't appreciated until much later. Even in the nineteenth century, they were simply explained away as products of supernatural forces, organisms buried in Noah's flood, or remains of still-living species inhabiting remote and uncharted parts of the globe.

But within these petrified remains lies the history of life. How can we decipher that history? First, of course, you need the fossils—lots of them. Then you have to put them in the proper order, from oldest to youngest. And then you must find out exactly when they were formed. Each of these requirements comes with its own set of challenges.

The formation of fossils is straightforward, but requires a very specific set of circumstances. First, the remains of an animal or plant must find their way into water, sink to the bottom, and get quickly covered by sediment so that they don't decay or get scattered by scavengers. Only rarely do dead plants and land-dwelling creatures find themselves on the bottom of a lake or ocean. This is why most of the fossils we have are of marine organisms, which live on or in the ocean floor, or naturally sink to the floor when they die.

Once buried safely in the sediments, the hard parts of fossils become infiltrated or replaced by dissolved minerals. What remains is a cast of a living creature that becomes compressed into rock by the pressure of sediments piling up on top. Because soft parts of plants and animals aren't easily fossilized, this immediately creates a severe bias in what we can know about ancient species. Bones and teeth are abundant, as are shells and the hard outer skeletons of insects and crustaceans. But worms, jellyfish, bacteria, and fragile creatures like birds are much rarer, as are all terrestrial species compared to aquatic ones. Over the first 80 percent of the history of life, all species were soft-bodied, so we have only a foggy window into the earliest and most interesting developments in evolution, and none at all into the origin of life.

Once a fossil is formed, it has to survive the endless shifting, folding, heating, and crushing of the earth's crust, processes that completely obliterate most fossils. Then it must be discovered. Buried deeply beneath the earth's surface, most are inaccessible to us. Only when the sediments are raised and exposed by the erosion of wind or rain can they be attacked with the paleontologist's hammer. And there is only a short window of time before these semiexposed fossils are themselves effaced by wind, water, and weather.

Taking into account all of these requirements, it's clear that the fossil record *must* be incomplete. How incomplete? The total number of species that ever lived on earth has been estimated to range between 17 million (probably a drastic underestimate given that at least 10 million species are alive today) and 4 billion. Since we have discovered around 250,000 different fossil species, we can estimate that we have fossil evidence of only 0.1 percent to 1 percent of all species—hardly a good sample of the history of life! Many amazing creatures must have existed that are forever lost to us. Nevertheless, we have enough fossils to give us a good idea of how evolution proceeded, and to discern how major groups split off from one another.

Ironically, the fossil record was originally put in order not by evolutionists but by geologists who were also creationists, and who accepted the account of life given in the book of Genesis. These early geologists simply ordered the different layers of rocks that they found (often from canal excavations that accompanied the industrialization of England) using principles based on common sense. Because fossils occur in sedimentary rocks that begin as silt in oceans, rivers, or lakes (or more rarely as sand dunes or glacial deposits), the deeper layers, or "strata," must have been laid down before the shallower ones. Younger rocks lie atop older ones. But not all layers are laid down at any one place—sometimes there's no water to form sediments.

To establish a complete ordering of rock layers, then, you must cross-correlate the strata from different localities around the world. If a layer of the same type of rock, containing the same type of fossils, appears in two different places, it's reasonable to assume that the layer is of the same age in both places. So, for example, if you find four layers of rock in one location (let's label them, from shallowest to deepest, as ABDE), and then you find just two of those same layers in another place, interspersed with yet another layer—BCD—you can infer that this record includes at least five layers of rock, in the order, from youngest to oldest, of ABCDE. This *principle of superposition* was first devised in the seventeenth century by the Danish polymath Nicolaus Steno, who later became an archbishop and was beatified by Pope John Paul II in 1987—surely the only case of a future saint making an important scientific contribution. Using Steno's principle, the geological record was painstakingly ordered in the eighteenth and nineteenth centuries: all the way from the very old Cambrian to the Recent. So far, so good. But this tells you only the relative ages of rocks, not their *actual* ages.

Since about 1945 we have been able to measure the actual ages of some rocks—using radioactivity. Certain radioactive elements ("radioisotopes") are incorporated into igneous rocks when they crystallize out of molten rock from beneath the earth's surface. Radioisotopes gradually decay into other elements at a constant rate, usually expressed as the "half-life"—the time required for half of the isotope to disappear. If we know the half-life, how much of the radioisotope was there when the rock formed (something that geologists can accurately determine), and how much remains now, it's relatively simple to estimate the age of the rock. Different isotopes decay at different rates. Old rocks are often dated using uranium-235 (U-235), found in the common mineral zircon. U-235 has a half-life of around 700 million years. Carbon-14, with a half-life of 5,730 years, is used for much younger materials like wood, bone, or human artifacts such as the Dead Sea Scrolls. Several radioisotopes usually occur together, so the dates can be cross-checked, and the ages invariably agree. The rocks that bear fossils, however, are not igneous but sedimentary, and can't be dated directly. But we can obtain the ages of fossils by bracketing the sedimentary layers with the dates of adjacent igneous layers that contain radioisotopes.

Opponents of evolution often attack the reliability of these dates by saying that rates of radioactive decay might have changed over time or with the physical stresses experienced by rocks. This objection is often raised by "young-earth" creationists, who hold the earth to be six to ten thousand years old. But it is specious. Since the different radioisotopes in a rock decay in different ways, they wouldn't give consistent dates if decay rates changed. Moreover, the half-lives of isotopes don't change when scientists subject them to extreme temperatures and pressures in the laboratory. And when radiometric dates can be checked against dates from the historical record, as with the carbon-14 method, they invariably agree. It is radiometric dating of meteorites that tells us that the earth and solar system are 4.6 billion years old. (The oldest earth rocks are a bit younger—4.3 billion years in samples from northern Canada—because older rocks have been destroyed by movements of the earth's crust.)

There are yet other ways to check the accuracy of radiometric dating. One of them uses biology, and involved an ingenious study of fossil corals by John Wells of Cornell University. Radioisotope dating showed that these corals lived during the Devonian period, about 380 million years ago. But Wells could also find out when these corals lived simply by looking closely at them. He made use of the fact that the friction produced by tides gradually slows the earth's rotation over time. Each day—one revolution of the earth— is a tiny bit longer than the last one. Not that you would notice: to be precise, the length of a day increases by about two seconds every 100,000 years. Since the duration of a year—the time it takes the earth to circle the sun—doesn't change over time, this means that the number of days per year must be decreasing over time. From the known rate of slowing, Wells calculated that when his corals were alive—380 million years ago if the radiometric dating was correct—each year would have contained about 396 days, each 22 hours long. If there was some way that the fossils themselves could tell how long each day was when they were alive, we could check whether that length matched up with the 22 hours predicted from radiometric dating.

But corals can do this, for as they grow they record in their bodies how many days they experience each year. Living corals produce both daily and annual growth rings. In fossil specimens, we can see how many daily rings separate each annual one: that is, how many days were included in each year when that coral was alive. Knowing the rate of tidal slowing, we can cross check the "tidal" age against the "radiometric" age. Counting rings in his Devonian corals, Wells found that they experienced about 400 days per year, which means that each day was 21.9 hours long. That's only a tiny deviation from the predicted 22 hours. This clever biological calibration gives us additional confidence in the accuracy of radiometric dating.

The Facts

WHAT WOULD CONSTITUTE EVIDENCE for evolution in the fossil record? There are several types. First, the big evolutionary picture: a scan through the entire sequence of rock strata should show early life to be quite simple, with more complex species appearing only after some time. Moreover, the youngest fossils we find should be those that are most similar to living species.

We should also be able to see cases of evolutionary change within lineages: that is, one species of animal or plant changing into something different over time. Later species should have traits that make them look like the descendants of earlier ones. And since the history of life involves the splitting of species from common ancestors, we should be able to see this splitting—and find evidence of those ancestors—in the fossil record. For example, nineteenth-century anatomists predicted that, from their bodily similarities, mammals evolved from ancient reptiles. So we should be able to find fossils of reptiles that were becoming more mammal-like. Of course because the fossil record is incomplete, we can't expect to document *every* transition between major forms of life. But we should at least find some.

When writing *The Origin*, Darwin bemoaned the sketchy fossil record. At that time we lacked transitional series of fossils or "missing links" between major forms that could document evolutionary change. Some groups, like whales, appeared suddenly in the record, without known ancestors. But Darwin still had some fossil evidence for evolution. This included the observation that ancient animals and plants were very different from living species, resembling modern species more and more as one moved up to more recently formed rocks. He also noted that fossils in adjacent layers were more similar to each other than to those found in layers more widely separated, implying a gradual and continuous process of divergence. What's more, at any given place, the fossils in the most recently deposited rocks tended to resemble the modern species living in that area, rather than the species living in other parts of the world. Fossil marsupials, for instance, were found in profusion only in Australia, and that's where most modern marsupials live. This suggested that modern species descended from the fossil ones. (Those fossil marsupials include some of the most bizarre mammals that ever lived, including a giant ten-foot kangaroo with a flat face, huge claws, and a single toe on each foot.)

What Darwin didn't have were enough fossils to show clear evidence of gradual changes within species, or of common ancestors. But since his time, paleontologists have turned up fossils galore, fulfilling all the predictions mentioned above. We can now show continuous changes within lineages of animals; we have lots of evidence for common ancestors and transitional forms (those missing ancestors of whales, for instance, have turned up); and we have dug deep enough to see the very beginnings of complex life.

Big Patterns

Now that we have put all the strata in order and estimated their dates, we can read the fossil record from bottom to top. Figure 3 shows a simplified timeline of life's history, depicting the major biological and geological events that occurred since the first organisms arose around 3.5 billion years ago.[6] This record gives an unambiguous picture of change, starting with the simple and proceeding to the more complex. Although the figure shows the "first appearances" of groups like reptiles and mammals, this shouldn't be

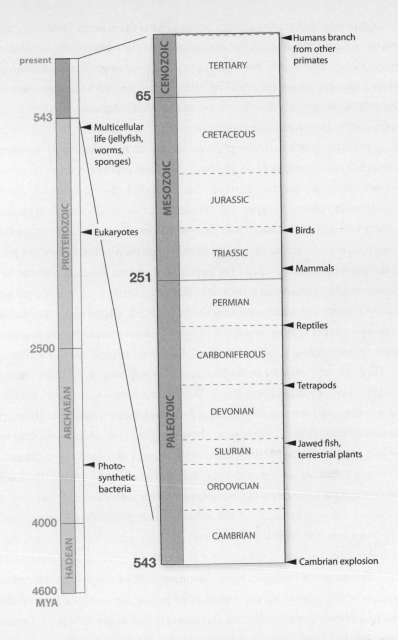

FIGURE 3. The fossil record showing first appearance of various forms of life that arose since the earth formed 4,600 million years ago (MYA). Note that multicellular life originated and diversified only in the last 15 percent of life's history. Groups appear on the scene in an orderly evolutionary fashion, with many arising after known fossil transitions from ancestors.

taken to mean that modern forms appear in the fossil record suddenly, arising out of nowhere. Instead, for most groups we see gradual evolution from earlier forms (birds and mammals, for example, evolved over millions of years from reptilian ancestors). The existence of gradual transitions between major groups, which I discuss below, means that assigning a date to a "first appearance" becomes somewhat arbitrary.

The first organisms, simple photosynthetic bacteria, appear in sediments about 3.5 billion years old, only about a billion years after the planet was formed. These single cells were all that occupied the earth for the next 2 billion years, after which we see the first simple "eukaryotes": organisms having true cells with nuclei and chromosomes. Then, around 600 million years ago, a whole gamut of relatively simple but multicelled organisms arise, including worms, jellyfish, and sponges. These groups diversify over the next several million years, with terrestrial plants and tetrapods (four-legged animals, the earliest of which were lobe-finned fish) appearing about 400 million years ago. Earlier groups, of course, often persisted: photosynthetic bacteria, sponges, and worms appear in the early fossil record, and are still with us.

Fifty million years later we find the first true amphibians, and after another 50 million years reptiles come along. The first mammals show up around 250 million years ago (arising, as predicted, from reptilian ancestors), and the first birds, also descended from reptiles, show up 50 million years later. After the earliest mammals appear, they, along with insects and land plants, become ever more diverse, and as we approach the shallowest rocks, the fossils increasingly come to resemble living species. Humans are newcomers on the scene—our lineage branches off from that of other primates only about 7 million years ago, the merest sliver of evolutionary time. Various imaginative analogies have been used to make this point, and it is worth making again. If the entire course of evolution were compressed into a single year, the earliest bacteria would appear at the end of March, but we wouldn't see the first human ancestors until 6 a.m. on December 31. The golden age of Greece, about 500 BC, would occur just thirty seconds before midnight.

Although the fossil record of plants is sparser—they lack easily fossilized hard parts—they show a similar evolutionary pattern. The oldest are mosses and algae, followed by the appearance of ferns, then conifers, then deciduous trees, and, finally, flowering plants.

So the appearance of species through time, as seen in fossils, is far from random. Simple organisms evolved before complex ones, predicted ancestors before descendants. The most recent fossils are those most similar to living species. And we have transitional fossils connecting many major groups. No theory of special creation, or *any* theory other than evolution, can explain these patterns.

Fossilized Evolution and Speciation

To show gradual evolutionary change within a single lineage, you need a good succession of sediments, preferably laid down quickly (so that each time period represents a thick slice of rock, making change easier to see), and without missing layers (a missing layer in the middle makes a smooth evolutionary transition look like a sudden "jump").

Very small marine organisms, such as plankton, are ideal for this. There are billions of them, many with hard parts, and they conveniently fall directly to the seafloor after death, piling up in a continuous sequence of layers. Sampling the layers in order is easy: you can thrust a long tube into the seafloor, pull up a columnar core sample, and read it (and date it) from bottom to top.

Tracing a single fossil species through the core, you can often see it evolve. Figure 4 shows an example of evolution in a tiny, single-celled marine proto-

FIGURE 4. A record of fossils (preserved in a seafloor core) showing evolutionary change in the marine foraminiferan *Globorotalia conoidea* over an eight-million-year period. The scale gives the number of chambers in the final whorl of the shell, averaged among all individuals counted in each section of the core.

zoan that builds a spiral shell, creating more chambers as it grows. These samples come from sections of a two-hundred-meter-long core taken from the ocean floor near New Zealand, representing about eight million years of evolution. The figure shows change over time in one trait: the number of chambers in the final whorl of the shell. Here we see fairly smooth and gradual change over time: individuals have about 4.8 chambers per whorl at the beginning of the sequence and 3.3 at the end, a decrease of about 30 percent.

Evolution, though gradual, need not always proceed smoothly, or at an even pace. Figure 5 shows a more irregular pattern in another marine microorganism, the radiolarian *Pseudocubus vema*. In this case geologists took regularly spaced samples from an eighteen-meter-long core extracted near Antarctica, representing about two million years of sediments. The trait measured was the width of the animal's cylindrical base (its "thorax"). Although size increases by nearly 50 percent over time, the trend is not smooth. There are periods in which size doesn't change much, interspersed with periods of more rapid change. This pattern is quite common in fossils, and is completely understandable if the changes we see were driven by environmental factors such as fluctuations in climate or salinity. Environments

FIGURE 5. Evolutionary change of thorax size in the radiolarian *Pseudocubus vema* over a period of two million years. Values are population averages from each section of the core.

FIGURE 6. Evolutionary change in the number of "pygidial ribs" (segments on the rear section) of five groups of Ordovician trilobites. The number gives the population average at each section of the three-million-year sample of shale. All five species—and three others not shown—displayed a net increase in rib number over the period, suggesting that natural selection was involved over the long term, but that the species did not change in perfect parallel.

themselves change sporadically and unevenly, so the strength of natural selection will wax and wane.

Let's look at evolution in a more complex species: trilobites. Trilobites were arthropods, in the same group as insects and spiders. Since they were protected by a hard shell, they are extremely common in ancient rocks (you can probably buy one in your nearest museum shop). Peter Sheldon, then at Trinity College Dublin, collected trilobite fossils from a layer of Welsh shale spanning about three million years. Within this rock, he found eight distinct lineages of trilobites, and over time each showed evolutionary change in the number of "pygidial ribs"—the segments on the last section of the body. Figure 6 shows the changes in several of these lineages. Although over the entire period of sampling every species showed a net increase in segment number, the changes among different species were not only uncorrelated, but sometimes went in opposite directions during the same period.

Unfortunately, we have no idea what selective pressures drove the evolutionary changes in these plankton and trilobites. It is always easier to document evolution in the fossil record than to understand what caused it, for although fossils are preserved, their environments are not. What we can say is that there was evolution, it was gradual, and it varied in both pace and direction.

Marine plankton give evidence for the splitting of lineages as well as evolution within a lineage. Figure 7 shows an ancestral plankton species dividing into two descendants, distinguishable by both size and shape. Interestingly, the new species, *Eucyrtidium matuyamai*, first evolved in an area to the north of the area from where these cores were taken, and only later invaded the area where its ancestor occurred. As we'll see in chapter 7, the formation of a new species usually begins when populations are geographically isolated from one another.

There are hundreds of other examples of evolutionary change in fossils— both gradual and punctuated—from species as diverse as mollusks, rodents, and primates. And there are also examples of species that barely change over time. (Remember that evolutionary theory does not state that *all* species must evolve!) But listing these cases wouldn't change my point: the fossil record gives no evidence for the creationist prediction that all species appear suddenly and then remain unchanged. Instead, forms of life appear in the record in evolutionary sequence, and then evolve and split.

"Missing Links"

Changes in marine species may give evidence for evolution, but that's not the only lesson that the fossil record has to teach. What really excites people— biologists and paleontologists among them—are *transitional forms*: those fossils that span the gap between two very different kinds of living organisms. Did birds really come from reptiles, land animals from fish, and whales from land animals? If so, where is the fossil evidence? Even some creationists will admit that minor changes in size and shape might occur over time—a process called *microevolution*—but they reject the idea that

FIGURE 7. Evolution and speciation in two species of the planktonic radiolarian *Eucyrtidium*, taken from a sediment core spanning more than 3.5 million years. The points represent the width of the fourth segment, shown as the average of each species at each section of the core. In areas to the north of where this core was taken, an ancestral population of *E. calvertense* became larger, gradually acquiring the name *E. matuyamai* as it became larger. *E. matuyamai* then reinvaded the range of its relative, as shown on the graph, and both species, now living in the same place, began to diverge in body size. This divergence may have been the result of natural selection acting to reduce competition for food between the two species.

one *very different* kind of animal or plant can come from another (*macro-evolution*). Advocates of intelligent design argue that this kind of difference requires the direct intervention of a creator.[7] Although in *The Origin* Darwin could point to no transitional forms, he would have been delighted by how his theory has been confirmed by the fruits of modern paleontology. These include numerous species whose existence was predicted many years ago, but that have been unearthed in only the last few decades.

But what counts as fossil evidence for a major evolutionary transition? According to evolutionary theory, for every two species, however different, there was once a single species that was the ancestor of both. We could call this one species the "missing link." As we've seen, the chance of finding that single ancestral species in the fossil record is almost zero. The fossil record is simply too spotty to expect that.

But we needn't give up, for we can find some *other* species in the fossil record, close cousins to the actual "missing link," that document common ancestry equally well. Let's take one example. In Darwin's day, biologists conjectured from anatomical evidence, such as similarities in the structure of hearts and skulls, that birds were closely related to reptiles. They speculated that there must have been a common ancestor that, through a speciation event, produced two lineages, one eventually yielding all modern birds and the other all modern reptiles.

What would this common ancestor have looked like? Our intuition is to say that it would have resembled something halfway between a modern reptile and a modern bird, showing a mixture of features from both types of animal. But this need not be the case, as Darwin clearly saw in *The Origin*:

> I have found it difficult, when looking at any two species, to avoid picturing to myself, forms directly intermediate between them. But this is a wholly false view; we should always look for forms intermediate between each species and a common but unknown progenitor; and the progenitor will generally have differed in some respects from all of its modified descendants.

Because reptiles appear in the fossil record before birds, we can guess that the common ancestor of birds and reptiles was an *ancient reptile*, and would have looked like one. Its overall appearance would give few clues that it was indeed a "missing link"—that one lineage of descendants would later give rise to all modern birds, and the other to more dinosaurs. Truly birdlike traits, such as wings and a large breastbone for anchoring the flight muscles, would have evolved only later on the branch leading to birds. And as that lineage itself progressed from reptiles to birds, it sprouted off many species having mixtures of reptilelike and birdlike traits. Some of those species went extinct, while others continued evolving into what are now modern birds. It is to these *groups* of ancient species, the relatives of species near the branch point, that we must look for evidence of common ancestry.

Showing common ancestry of two groups, then, does not require that we produce fossils of the precise single species that was their common ancestor, or even species on the direct line of descent from an ancestor to descendant. Rather, we need only produce fossils having the types of traits that link two groups together, and, importantly, we must also have the dating evidence showing that those fossils occur at the right time in the geological record. A "transitional species" is not equivalent to "an ancestral species"; it is simply a species showing a mixture of traits from organisms that lived both before and after it. Given the patchiness of the fossil record, finding these forms at the proper times in the record is a sound and realistic goal. In the reptile-to-bird transition, for instance, the transitional forms should look like early reptiles, but with some birdlike traits. And we should find these transitional fossils after reptiles had already evolved, but before modern birds appeared. Further, transitional forms don't have to be on the direct line of descent from an ancestor to a living descendant—they could be evolutionary cousins that went extinct. As we'll see, the dinosaurs that gave rise to birds sported feathers, but some feathered dinosaurs continued to persist well after more birdlike creatures had evolved. Those later feathered dinosaurs still provide evidence for evolution, because they tell us something about where birds came from.

The dating and—to some extent—the physical appearance of transitional creatures, then, can be predicted from evolutionary theory. Some of the more recent and dramatic predictions that have been fulfilled involve our own group, the vertebrates.

Onto the Land: From Fish to Amphibians

One of the greatest fulfilled predictions of evolutionary biology is the discovery, in 2004, of a transitional form between fish and amphibians. This is the fossil species *Tiktaalik roseae*, which tells us a lot about how vertebrates came to live on the land. Its discovery is a stunning vindication of the theory of evolution.

Until about 390 million years ago, the only vertebrates were fish. But, 30 million years later, we find creatures that are clearly *tetrapods*: four-footed vertebrates that walked on land. These early tetrapods were like modern amphibians in several ways: they had flat heads and bodies, a distinct neck, and well-developed legs and limb girdles. Yet they also show strong links with earlier fishes, particularly the group known as "lobe-finned fishes," so called because of their large bony fins that enabled them to prop themselves up on the bottom of shallow lakes or streams. The fishlike structures of early tetrapods include scales, limb bones, and head bones (figure 8).

Acanthostega gunnari

Tiktaalik roseae

Eusthenopteron foordi

FIGURE 8. Invasion of the land. An early lobe-finned fish (*Eusthenopteron foordi*) from about 385 million years ago; a land-dwelling tetrapod (*Acanthostega gunnari*) from Greenland, about 365 million years ago; and the transitional form, *Tiktaalik roseae*, from Ellesmere Island, about 375 million years ago. The intermediacy of *Tiktaalik's* body form is mirrored by the intermediacy of its limbs, which have a bone structure in between that of the sturdy fins of the lobe-finned fish and the even sturdier walking limbs of the tetrapod. Shaded bones are those that evolved into the arm bones of modern mammals: the bone with darkest shading will become our humerus, and the medium- and light-shaded bones will become the radius and ulna, respectively.

How did early fish evolve to survive on land? This was the question that interested—or rather obsessed—my University of Chicago colleague Neil Shubin. Neil had spent years studying the evolution of limbs from fins, and was driven to understand the earliest stages of that evolution.

This is where the prediction comes in. If there were lobe-finned fishes but no terrestrial vertebrates 390 million years ago, and clearly terrestrial vertebrates 360 million years ago, where would you expect to find the transitional forms? Somewhere in between. Following this logic, Shubin predicted that if transitional forms existed, their fossils would be found in strata around 375 million years old. Moreover, the rocks would have to be from freshwater rather than marine sediments, because late lobe-finned fish and early amphibians both lived in fresh water.

Searching his college geology textbook for a map of exposed freshwater sediments of the right age, Shubin and his colleagues zeroed in on a paleontologically unexplored region of the Canadian Arctic: Ellesmere Island, which sits in the Arctic Ocean north of Canada. And after five long years of fruitless and expensive searching, they finally hit pay dirt: a group of fossil skeletons stacked one atop another in sedimentary rock from an ancient stream. When Shubin first saw the fossil face poking out of the rock, he knew that he had at last found his transitional form. In honor of the local Inuit people and the donor who helped fund the expeditions, the fossil was named *Tiktaalik roseae* ("Tiktaalik" means "large freshwater fish" in Inuit, and "roseae" is a cryptic reference to the anonymous donor).

Tiktaalik has features that make it a direct link between the earlier lobe-finned fish and the later amphibians (figure 8). With gills, scales, and fins, it was clearly a fish that lived its life in water. But it also has amphibianlike features. For one thing, its head is flattened like that of a salamander, with the eyes and nostrils on top rather than on the sides of the skull. This suggests that it lived in shallow water and could peer, and probably breathe, above the surface. The fins had become more robust, allowing the animal to flex itself upward to help survey its surroundings. And, like the early amphibians, *Tiktaalik* has a neck. Fish don't have necks—their skull joins directly to their shoulders.

Most important, *Tiktaalik* has two novel traits that were to prove useful in helping its descendants invade the land. The first is a set of sturdy ribs that helped the animal pump air into its lungs and move oxygen from its gills (*Tiktaalik* could breathe both ways). And instead of the many tiny bones in the fins of lobe-finned fish, *Tiktaalik* had fewer and sturdier bones in the limbs—bones similar in number and position to those of every land creature that came later, including ourselves. In fact, its limbs are best described as part fin, part leg.

Clearly *Tiktaalik* was well adapted to live and crawl about in shallow waters, peek above the surface, and breathe air. Given its structure, we can envision the next, critical evolutionary step, which probably involved a novel behavior. A few of *Tiktaalik*'s descendants were bold enough to venture out of the water on their sturdy fin-limbs, perhaps to make their way to another stream (as the bizarre mudskipper fish of the tropics does today), to avoid predators, or perhaps to find food among the many giant insects that had already evolved. If there were advantages to venturing onto land, natural selection could mold those explorers from fish into amphibians. That first small step ashore proved a great leap for vertebrate-kind, ultimately leading to the evolution of every land-dwelling creature with a backbone.

Tiktaalik itself was not ready for life ashore. For one thing, it had not yet evolved a limb that would allow it to walk. And it still had internal gills for breathing underwater. So we can make another prediction. Somewhere, in freshwater sediments about 380 million years old, we'll find a very early land-dweller with reduced gills and limbs a bit sturdier than those of *Tiktaalik*.

Tiktaalik shows that our ancestors were flat-headed predatory fish who lurked in the shallow waters of streams. It is a fossil that marvelously connects fish with amphibians. And equally marvelous is that its discovery was not only anticipated, but predicted to occur in rocks of a certain age and in a certain place.

The best way to experience the drama of evolution is to see the fossils for yourself, or better yet, handle them. My students had this chance when Neil brought a cast of *Tiktaalik* to class, passed it around, and showed how it filled the bill of a true transitional form. This was, to them, the most tangible evidence that evolution was true. How often do you get to put your hands on a piece of evolutionary history, much less one that might have been your distant ancestor?

Into Thin Air: The Origin of Birds

Of what use is half a wing? Ever since Darwin, that question has been raised to cast doubt on evolution and natural selection. Biologists tell us that birds evolved from early reptiles, but how could a land-dwelling animal evolve the ability to fly? Natural selection, creationists argue, could not explain this transition, because it would require intermediate stages in which animals have just the rudiments of a wing. This would seem more likely to encumber a creature than to give it a selective advantage.

But if you think a bit, it's not so hard to come up with intermediate stages in the evolution of flight, stages that might have been useful to their possessors. Gliding is the obvious first step. And gliding has evolved independently many times: in placental mammals, marsupials, and even lizards. Flying squirrels do quite well by gliding with flaps of skin that extend along their sides—a good way to get from tree to tree to escape predators or find nuts. And there is the even more remarkable "flying lemur," or colugo, of Southeast Asia, which has an impressive membrane stretching from head to tail. One colugo was seen gliding for a distance of 450 feet—nearly the length of six tennis courts—while losing only forty feet in height! It's not hard to envision the next evolutionary step: the flapping of colugolike limbs to produce true flight, as we see in bats. But we no longer have to only imagine this step: we now have the fossils that clearly show how flying birds evolved.

Since the nineteenth century, the similarity between the skeletons of birds and some dinosaurs led paleontologists to theorize that they had a common ancestor—in particular, the *theropods*: agile, carnivorous dinosaurs that walked on two legs. Around 200 million years ago, the fossil record shows plenty of theropods but nothing that looks even vaguely birdlike. By 70 million years ago, we see fossils of birds that look fairly modern. If evolution is true, then we should expect to see the reptile-bird transition in rocks between 70 and 200 million years old.

And there they are. The first link between birds and reptiles was actually known to Darwin, who, curiously, mentioned it only briefly in later editions of *The Origin*, and then only as an oddity. It is perhaps the most famous of all transitional forms: the crow-sized *Archaeopteryx lithographica*, discovered in a limestone quarry in Germany in 1860. (The name *Archaeopteryx* means "ancient wing," and "lithographica" comes from the Solnhofen limestone, fine-grained enough to make lithographic plates and preserve the impressions of soft feathers.) *Archaeopteryx* has just the combination of traits one would expect to find in a transitional form. And its age, about 145 million years, places it where we would expect.

Archaeopteryx is really more reptile than bird. Its skeleton is almost identical to that of some theropod dinosaurs. In fact, some biologists who didn't look at the *Archaeopteryx* fossils closely enough missed the feathers, and misclassified the beasts as theropods. (Figure 9 shows this similarity between the two types.) The reptilian features include a jaw with teeth, a long bony tail, claws, separate fingers on the wing (in modern birds these bones are fused, as you can see by inspecting a gnawed chicken wing), and a neck attached to its skull from behind (as in dinosaurs) instead of from below (as in modern birds). The birdlike traits number just two: large feathers and an opposable big toe, probably used for perching. It still isn't clear whether this creature, though fully feathered, could fly. But its asymmetrical feathers— one side of each feather is larger than the other—suggest that it could. Asymmetrical feathers, like airplane wings, create the "airfoil" shape necessary for aerodynamic flight. But even if it could fly, *Archaeopteryx* is mainly dinosaurian. It is also what evolutionists call a "mosaic." Rather than having every feature appear halfway between those of birds and reptiles, *Archaeopteryx* has a few bits that are very birdlike, while most bits are very reptilian.

After the discovery of *Archaeopteryx*, no other reptile-bird intermediates were found for many years, leaving a gaping hole between modern birds and their ancestors. Then, in the mid-1990s, a spate of astonishing discoveries from China began to fill in the gap. These fossils, found in lake sediments that preserve the impressions of soft parts, represent a veritable parade of feathered theropod dinosaurs.[8] Some of them have very small filamentous structures covering the whole body—probably early feathers. One is the remarkable *Sinornithosaurus millenii* (*Sinornithosaurus* means "Chinese bird-lizard"), whose whole body was covered with long, thin feathers—feathers so small that they couldn't possibly have helped it fly (figure 10a). And its claws, teeth, and long, bony tail clearly show that this creature was far from

chicken

Archaeopteryx

Compsognathus

FIGURE 9. Skeletons of a modern bird (chicken), a transitional form (*Archaeopteryx*), and a small, bipedal, carnivorous theropod dinosaur (*Compsognathus*), similar to one of *Archaeopteryx*'s ancestors. *Archaeopteryx* has a few features like those of modern birds (feathers and an opposable big toe), but its skeleton is very similar to that of the dinosaur, including teeth, a reptilian pelvis, and a long bony tail. *Archaeopteryx* was about the size of a raven, *Compsognathus* slightly larger.

FIGURE 10A. The feathered dinosaur *Sinornithosaurus millenii*, original fossil from China (about 125 million years old), and artist's reconstruction. The fossil clearly shows the impression of filamentous feathers, especially on the head and forelimbs (arrows).

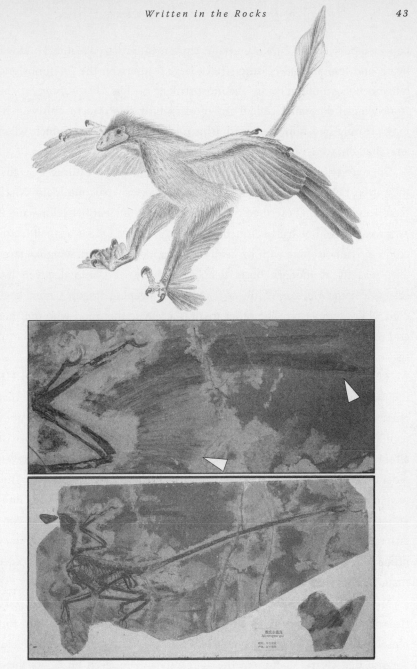

FIGURE 10B. The bizarre "four-winged" dinosaur *Microraptor gui*, which had long feathers on both its fore- and hindlimbs. These feathers (arrows) are clearly visible in the fossil, about 120 million years old. It's not clear whether this animal could fly or only glide, but the rear "wings" almost certainly helped it land, as shown in the drawing.

being a modern bird.⁹ Other dinosaurs show medium-sized feathers on their heads and forelimbs. Still others have large feathers on the forelimbs and tail, much like modern birds. The most striking of all is *Microraptor gui*, the "four-winged dinosaur." Unlike any modern bird, this bizarre, thirty-inch-long creature had fully feathered arms *and* legs (figure 10b), which when stretched out were probably used for gliding.¹⁰

Theropod dinosaurs didn't just have primitive birdlike features, it seems: they even behaved in birdlike ways. The American paleontologist Mark Norell and his team described two fossils showing ancient behavior—and if ever fossils could be called "touching," these are they. One is a small feathered dinosaur sleeping with its head tucked under its folded, winglike forearm—exactly as modern birds sleep (figure 11). The animal, given the scientific name *Mei long* (Chinese for "soundly sleeping dragon"), must have died while slumbering. The other fossil is a female theropod who met her end while sitting on her nest of eggs, showing brooding behavior similar to that of birds.

All the nonflying feathered dinosaur fossils date between 135 and 110 million years ago—later than the 145-million-year-old *Archaeopteryx*. That means that they could not be *Archaeopteryx's* direct ancestors, but they could have been its cousins. Feathered dinosaurs probably continued to exist after one of their kin gave rise to birds. We should, then, be able to find even older feathered dinosaurs that were the ancestors of *Archaeopteryx*. The problem is that feathers are preserved only in special sediments—the fine-grained silt of quiet environments like lake beds or lagoons. And these conditions are very rare. But we can make another testable evolutionary prediction: someday we'll find fossils of feathered dinosaurs that are older than *Archaeopteryx*.¹¹

We're not sure whether *Archaeopteryx* is the one single species that gave rise to all modern birds. It seems unlikely that it was the "missing link." But regardless, it's one of a long string of fossils (some found by the intrepid Paul Sereno) that clearly document the appearance of modern birds. As these fossils get younger, we see the reptilian tail shrinking, the teeth disappearing, the claws fusing together, and the appearance of a large breastbone to anchor the flight muscles.

FIGURE 11. Fossil behavior: the feathered theropod dinosaur *Mei long* (top) fossilized in a birdlike roosting position, sleeping with its head tucked under its forelimb. Middle: a reconstruction of *Mei long* from the fossil. Bottom: a modern bird (juvenile house sparrow) sleeping in the same position.

Put together, the fossils show that the basic skeletal plan of birds, and those essential feathers, evolved *before* birds could fly. There were many feathered dinosaurs, and their feathers are clearly related to those of modern birds. But if feathers didn't arise as adaptations for flying, what on earth were they for? Again, we don't know. They could have been used for ornamentation or display—perhaps to attract mates. It seems more likely, though, that they were used for insulation. Unlike modern reptiles, theropods may have been partially warm-blooded; and even if they weren't, feathers would have helped maintain body temperature. And what feathers evolved *from* is even more mysterious. The best guess is that they derive from the same cells that give rise to reptilian scales, but not everyone agrees.

Despite the unknowns, we can make some guesses about how natural selection fashioned modern birds. Early carnivorous dinosaurs evolved longer forelimbs and hands, which probably helped them grab and handle their prey. That kind of grabbing would favor the evolution of muscles that would quickly extend the front legs and pull them inward: exactly the motion used for the downward stroke in true flight. Then followed the feathery covering, probably for insulation. Given these innovations, there are at least two ways flight could then have evolved. The first is called the "trees down" scenario. There is evidence that some theropods lived at least partly in trees. Feathery forelimbs would help these reptiles glide from tree to tree, or from tree to ground, which would help them escape predators, find food more readily, or cushion their falls.

A different—and more likely—scenario is called the "ground up" theory, which sees flight evolving as an outgrowth of open-armed runs and leaps that feathered dinosaurs might have made to catch their prey. Longer wings could also have evolved as running aids. The chukar partridge, a game bird studied by Kenneth Dial at the University of Montana, represents a living example of this step. These partridges almost never fly, and flap their wings mainly to help them run uphill. The flapping gives them not only extra propulsion, but also more traction against the ground. Newborn chicks can run up 45-degree slopes, and adults can ascend 105-degree slopes—overhangs more than vertical!—solely by running and flapping their wings. The obvious advantage is that uphill scrambling helps these birds escape predators.

The next step in evolving flight would be very short airborne hops, like those made by turkeys and quail fleeing from danger.

In either the "trees down" or "ground up" scenario, natural selection could begin to favor individuals who could fly farther instead of merely gliding, leaping, or flying for short bursts. Then would come the other innovations shared by modern birds, including hollow bones for lightness and that large breastbone.

While we may speculate about the details, the existence of transitional fossils—and the evolution of birds from reptiles—is fact. Fossils like *Archaeopteryx* and its later relatives show a mixture of birdlike and early reptilian traits, and they occur at the right time in the fossil record. Scientists predicted that birds evolved from theropod dinosaurs, and, sure enough, we find theropod dinosaurs with feathers. We see a progression in time from early theropods having thin, filamentous body coverings to later ones with distinct feathers, probably adept gliders. What we see in bird evolution is the refashioning of old features (forelimbs with fingers and thin filaments on the skin) into new ones (fingerless wings and feathers)—just as evolutionary theory predicts.

Back to the Water: The Evolution of Whales

Duane Gish, an American creationist, is renowned for his lively and popular (if wildly misguided) lectures attacking evolution. I once attended one, during which Gish made fun of biologists' theory that whales descended from land animals related to cows. How, he asked, could such a transition occur, since the intermediate form would have been poorly adapted to both land and water, and thus couldn't be built by natural selection? (This resembles the half-a-wing argument against the evolution of birds.) To illustrate his point, Gish showed a slide of a mermaidlike cartoon animal whose front half was a spotted cow and whose rear half was a fish. Apparently puzzled over its own evolutionary fate, this clearly maladapted beast was standing at the water's edge, a large question mark hovering over its head. The cartoon had the intended effect: the audience burst into laughter. How stupid, they thought, could evolutionists be?

Indeed, a "mer-cow" is a ludicrous example of a transitional form between terrestrial and aquatic mammals—an "udder failure," as Gish called it. But let's forget the jokes and rhetoric, and look to nature. Can we find any mammals that live on both land and water, the kind of creature that supposedly could not have evolved?

Easily. A good candidate is the hippopotamus, which, although closely related to terrestrial mammals, is about as aquatic as a land mammal can get. (There are two species, the pygmy hippo and the "regular" hippo, whose scientific name is, appropriately, *Hippopotamus amphibius*.) Hippos spend most of their time submerged in tropical rivers and swamps, surveying their domain with eyes, noses, and ears that sit atop their head, all of which can be tightly closed underwater. Hippos mate in the water, and their babies, who can swim before they can walk, are born and suckle underwater. Because they are mostly aquatic, hippos have special adaptations for coming ashore to graze: they usually feed at night and, because they're prone to sunburn, secrete an oily red fluid that contains a pigment—hipposudoric acid—that acts as a sunscreen and possibly an antibiotic. This has given rise to the myth that hippos sweat blood. Hippos are obviously well adapted to their environment, and it's not hard to see that if they could find enough food in the water, they might eventually evolve into totally aquatic, whalelike creatures.

But we don't just have to imagine how whales evolved by extrapolating from living species. Whales happen to have an excellent fossil record, courtesy of their aquatic habits and robust, easily fossilized bones. And how they evolved has emerged within only the last twenty years. This is one of our best examples of an evolutionary transition, since we have a chronologically ordered series of fossils, perhaps a lineage of ancestors and descendants, showing their movement from land to water.

It's been recognized since the seventeenth century that whales and their relatives, the dolphins and porpoises, are mammals. They are warm-blooded, produce live young whom they feed with milk, and have hair around their blowholes. And evidence from whale DNA, as well as vestigial traits like their rudimentary pelvis and hind legs, show that their ancestors lived on land. Whales almost certainly evolved from a species of the artiodactyls: the group of mammals that have an even number of toes, such as camels and pigs.[12] Biologists now believe that the closest living relative of whales is—you guessed it—the hippopotamus, so maybe the hippo-to-whale scenario is not so far-fetched after all.

But whales have their own unique features that set them apart from their terrestrial relatives. These include the absence of rear legs, front limbs that are shaped like paddles, a flattened flukelike tail, a blowhole (a nostril atop the head), a short neck, simple conical teeth (different from the complex, multicusped teeth of land animals), special features of the ear that allow them to hear underwater, and robust projections on top of the vertebrae to anchor the strong swimming muscles of the tail. Thanks to an amazing series of fossil finds in the Middle East, we can trace the evolution of each of these traits—except for the boneless tail, which doesn't fossilize—from a terrestrial to an aquatic form.

Sixty million years ago there were plenty of fossil mammals, but no fossil whales. Creatures that resemble modern whales show up 30 million years later. We should be able, then, to find the transitional forms within this gap. And once again, that's exactly where they are. Figure 12 shows, in chronological order, some of the fossils involved in this transition, spanning the period between 52 and 40 million years ago.

There is no need to describe this transition in detail, as the drawings clearly speak—if not shout—of how a land-living animal took to the water. The sequence begins with a recently discovered fossil of a close relative of whales, a raccoon-sized animal called *Indohyus*. Living 48 million years ago, *Indohyus* was, as predicted, an artiodactyl. It is clearly closely related to whales because it has special features of the ears and teeth seen only in modern whales and their aquatic ancestors. Although *Indohyus* appears slightly later than the largely aquatic ancestors of whales, it is probably very close to what the whale ancestor looked like. And it was at least partially aquatic. We know this because its bones were denser than those of fully terrestrial mammals, which kept the creature from bobbing about in the water, and because the isotopes extracted from its teeth show that it absorbed a lot of oxygen from water. It probably waded in shallow streams or lakes to graze on vegetation or escape from its enemies, much like a similar animal, the African water chevrotain, does today.[13] This part-time life in water probably put the ancestor of whales on the road to becoming fully aquatic.

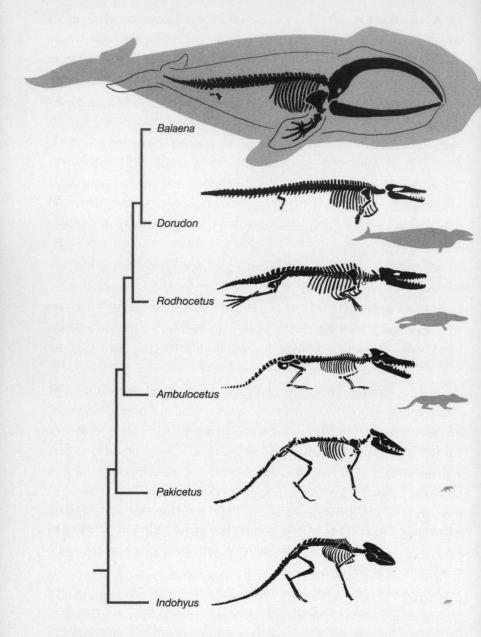

FIGURE 12. Transitional forms in the evolution of modern whales. (*Balaena* is the modern baleen whale, with a vestigial pelvis and hindlimb, while the other forms are transitional fossils.) Relative sizes of the animals are shown in shading to the right. The "tree" shows the evolutionary relationships of these species.

Indohyus was not the ancestor of whales, but was almost certainly its cousin. But if we go back 4 million more years, to 52 million years ago, we see what might well be that ancestor. It is a fossil skull from a wolf-sized creature called *Pakicetus*, which is a bit more whalelike than *Indohyus*, having simpler teeth and whalelike ears. *Pakicetus* still looked nothing like a modern whale, so if you had been around to see it, you wouldn't have guessed that it or its close relatives would give rise to a dramatic evolutionary radiation. Then follows, in rapid order, a series of fossils that become more and more aquatic with time. At 50 million years ago there is the remarkable *Ambulocetus* (literally, "walking whale"), with an elongated skull and reduced but still robust limbs, limbs that still ended in hooves that reveal its ancestry. It probably spent most of its time in shallow water, and would have waddled awkwardly on land, much like a seal. *Rodhocetus* (47 million years ago) is even more aquatic. Its nostrils have moved somewhat backward, and it has a more elongated skull. With stout extensions on the backbone to anchor its tail muscles, *Rodhocetus* must have been a good swimmer, but was handicapped on land by its small pelvis and hindlimbs. The creature certainly spent most if not all of its time at sea. Finally, at 40 million years ago, we find the fossils *Basilosaurus* and *Dorudon*—clearly fully aquatic mammals, with short necks and blowholes atop the skull. They could not have spent any time on land, for their pelvis and hindlimbs were reduced (the fifty-foot *Dorudon* had legs only two feet long) and were unconnected to the rest of the skeleton.

The evolution of whales from land animals was remarkably fast: most of the action took place within only 10 million years. That's not much longer than the time it took us to diverge from our common ancestor with chimpanzees, a transition that involved far less modification of the body. Still, adapting to life at sea did not require the evolution of any brand-new features—only modifications of old ones.

But why did some animals go back to the water at all? After all, millions of years earlier their ancestors had invaded the land. We're not sure why there was a reverse migration, but there are several ideas. One possibility involves the disappearance of the dinosaurs along with their fierce marine cousins, the fish-eating mosasaurs, ichthyosaurs, and plesiosaurs. These creatures would not only have competed with aquatic mammals for food, but probably made a meal of them. With their reptilian competitors extinct, the ancestors of whales may have found an open niche, free from predators and loaded with food. The sea was ripe for invasion. All of its benefits were only a few mutations away.

What the Fossils Say

IF AT THIS POINT you're feeling overwhelmed with fossils, be consoled that I've omitted hundreds of others that also show evolution. There is the transition between reptiles and mammals, so amply documented with intermediate "mammal-like reptiles" that they are the subjects of many books. Then there are the horses, a branching evolutionary bush leading from a small, five-toed ancestor to the proud hoofed species of today. And of course there is the human fossil record, described in chapter 8—surely the best example of an evolutionary prediction fulfilled.

At the risk of overkill, I'll briefly mention a few more important transitional forms. The first is an insect. From anatomical similarities, entomologists had long supposed that ants evolved from nonsocial wasps. In 1967, E. O. Wilson and his colleagues found a "transitional" ant, preserved in amber, bearing almost exactly the combination of antlike and wasplike features that entomologists had predicted (figure 13).

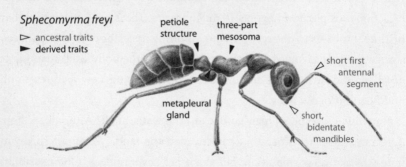

FIGURE 13. Transitional insect: an early ant showing primitive features of wasps— the predicted ancestral group—and derived features of ants. A single specimen of this species, *Sphecomyrma freyi,* was found preserved in amber dating from 92 million years ago.

Similarly, snakes have long been supposed to have evolved from lizard-like reptiles that lost their legs, since reptiles with legs appear in the fossil record well before snakes. In 2006, paleontologists digging in Patagonia found a fossil of the earliest known snake, 90 million years old. Just as predicted, it had a small pelvic girdle and reduced hind legs. And perhaps the most thrilling find of all is a 530-million-year-old fossil from China called *Haikouella lanceolata*, resembling a small eel with a frilly dorsal fin. But it also had a head, a brain, a heart, and a cartilaginous bar along the back—the notochord. This marks it as perhaps the earliest chordate, the group that gave rise to all vertebrates, including ourselves. In this complex, inch-long creature may lie the roots of our own evolution.

The fossil record teaches us three things. First, it speaks loudly and eloquently of evolution. The record in the rocks confirms several predictions of evolutionary theory: gradual change within lineages, splitting of lineages, and the existence of transitional forms between very different kinds of organisms. There is no getting around this evidence, no waving it away. Evolution happened, and in many cases we see how.

Second, when we find transitional forms, they occur in the fossil record precisely where they should. The earliest birds appear after dinosaurs but before modern birds. We see ancestral whales spanning the gap between their own landlubber ancestors and fully modern whales. If evolution were not true, fossils would not occur in an order that makes evolutionary sense. Asked what observation could conceivably *disprove* evolution, the curmudgeonly biologist J. B. S. Haldane reportedly growled, "Fossil rabbits in the Precambrian!" (That's the geological period that ended 543 million years ago.) Needless to say, no Precambrian rabbits, or any other anachronistic fossils, have ever been found.

Finally, evolutionary change, even of a major sort, nearly always involves remodeling the old into the new. The legs of land animals are variations on the stout limbs of ancestral fish. The tiny middle ear bones of mammals are remodeled jawbones of their reptilian ancestors. The wings of birds were fashioned from the legs of dinosaurs. And whales are stretched-out land animals whose forelimbs have become paddles and whose nostrils have moved atop their head.

There is no reason why a celestial designer, fashioning organisms from scratch like an architect designs buildings, should make new species by remodeling the features of existing ones. Each species could be constructed from the ground up. But natural selection can act only by changing what already exists. It can't produce new traits out of thin air. Darwinism predicts, then, that new species will be modified versions of older ones. The fossil record amply confirms this prediction.

Chapter 3

Remnants:
Vestiges, Embryos, and Bad Design

Nothing in biology makes sense except in the light of evolution.

—Theodosius Dobzhansky

In medieval Europe, before there was paper, manuscripts were made by writing on parchment and vellum, thin sheets of dried animal skin. Because these were hard to produce, many medieval writers simply reused earlier texts by scraping off the old words and writing on the newly cleaned pages. These recycled manuscripts are called *palimpsests*, from the Greek *palimpsestos*, meaning "scraped again."

Often, however, minute traces of the earlier writing remained. This has proved critical in our understanding of the ancient world. Many ancient texts are in fact known to us only by peering beneath the stratum of medieval overwriting to recover the original words. Perhaps the most famous of these is the Archimedes Palimpsest, first written in Constantinople in the tenth century and then cleaned and overwritten three centuries later by a monk making a prayer book. In 1906, a Danish classicist identified the original text as the work of Archimedes. Since then, a combination of X-rays, optical character recognition, and other complex methods have been used to decipher the original underlying text. This painstaking work yielded three mathematical treatises of Archimedes written in ancient Greek, two of them previously unknown and enormously important in the history of science. In such arcane ways we recover the past.

Like these ancient texts, organisms are palimpsests of history—evolutionary history. Within the bodies of animals and plants lie clues to their ancestry, clues that are testimony to evolution. And they are many. Hidden here are special features, "vestigial organs," that make sense only as remnants of traits that were once useful in an ancestor. Sometimes we find "atavisms"—throwback traits produced by the occasional reawakening of ancestral genes that have long been silenced. Now that we can read DNA sequences directly, we find that species are also *molecular* palimpsests: in their genomes is inscribed much of their evolutionary history, including the wrecks of genes that once were useful. What's more, in their development from embryos, many species go through contortions of form that are bizarre: organs and other features appear, and then change dramatically or even disappear completely before birth. And species aren't all that well designed, either: many of them show imperfections that are signs not of celestial engineering but of evolution.

Stephen Jay Gould called these biological palimpsests the "senseless signs of history." But they are not really senseless, for they constitute some of the most powerful evidence for evolution.

Vestiges

AS A GRADUATE STUDENT IN BOSTON, I was enlisted to help a senior scientist who had written a paper about whether it was more efficient for warm-blooded animals to run on two legs or four. He planned to submit the paper to *Nature*, one of the most prestigious scientific journals, and asked me to help him take a photograph striking enough to land on the journal cover and call attention to his work. Eager to get out of the laboratory, I spent an entire afternoon chasing a horse and an ostrich around a corral, hoping to get them to run side by side, demonstrating both types of running in a single frame. Needless to say, the animals refused to cooperate, and, all species being exhausted, we finally gave up. Although we never got the picture,[14] the experience did teach me a biology lesson: ostriches can't fly, but they can still use their wings. When they're running, they use their wings for balance, extending them to the sides to keep from toppling over. And when an ostrich becomes agitated—as it tends to do when you chase it around a corral—it runs straight at you, extending its wings in a threat display. That's a sign to get out of the way, for a miffed ostrich can easily disembowel you with one swift kick. They also use their wings in mating displays,[15] and spread them out to shade their chicks from the harsh African sun.

The lesson, though, goes deeper. The wings of the ostrich are a *vestigial trait*: a feature of a species that was an adaptation in its ancestors, but that has either lost its usefulness completely or, as in the ostrich, has been co-opted for new uses. Like all flightless birds, ostriches are descended from flying ancestors. We know this from both fossil evidence and from the pattern of ancestry that flightless birds carry in their DNA. But the wings, though still present, can no longer help the birds take flight to forage or escape predators and bothersome graduate students. Yet the wings are not useless—they've evolved new functions. They help the bird maintain balance, mate, and threaten its enemies.

The African ostrich isn't the only flightless bird. Besides the *ratites*—the large flightless birds that include the South American rhea, the Australian emu, and the New Zealand kiwi—dozens of other bird species have independently lost the ability to fly. These include flightless rails, grebes, ducks, and, of course, penguins. Perhaps the most bizarre is the New Zealand kakapo, a tubby flightless parrot that lives mainly on the ground but can also climb trees and "parachute" gently to the forest floor. Kakapos are critically endangered: fewer than one hundred still exist in the wild. Because they can't fly, they are easy prey for introduced predators like cats and rats.

All flightless birds have wings. In some, like the kiwi, the wings are so small—only a few inches long and buried beneath their feathers—that they don't seem to have any function. They're just remnants. In others, as we saw with the ostrich, the wings have new uses. In penguins, the ancestral wings have evolved into flippers, allowing the bird to swim underwater with amazing speed. Yet they all have exactly the same bones that we see in the wings of species that can fly. That's because the wings of flightless birds weren't the product of deliberate design (why would a creator use exactly the same bones in flying and flightless wings, including the wings of swimming penguins?), but of evolution from flying ancestors.

Opponents of evolution always raise the same argument when vestigial traits are cited as evidence for evolution. "The features are *not* useless," they say. "They are either useful for something, or we haven't yet discovered what they're for." They claim, in other words, that a trait can't be vestigial if it still has a function, or a function yet to be found.

But this rejoinder misses the point. Evolutionary theory doesn't say that vestigial characteristics have no function. A trait can be vestigial and functional at the same time. It is vestigial not because it's functionless, but because *it no longer performs the function for which it evolved.* The wings of an ostrich are useful, but that doesn't mean that they tell us nothing about evolution. Wouldn't it be odd if a creator helped an ostrich balance itself by giving it appendages that just happen to look exactly like reduced wings, and which are constructed in exactly the same way as wings used for flying?

Indeed, we *expect* that ancestral features will evolve new uses: that's just what happens when evolution builds new traits from old ones. Darwin himself noted that "an organ rendered, during changed habits of life, useless or injurious for one purpose, might easily be modified and used for another purpose."

But even when we've established that a trait is vestigial, the questions don't end. In which ancestors was it functional? What was it used for? Why did it lose function? Why is it still there instead of having disappeared completely? And which new functions, if any, has it evolved?

Let's take wings again. Obviously, there are many advantages to having wings, advantages shared by the flying ancestors of flightless birds. So why did some species lose their ability to fly? We're not absolutely sure, but we do have some powerful clues. Most of the birds that evolved flightlessness did so on islands—the extinct dodo on Mauritius, the Hawaiian rail, the kakapo and kiwi in New Zealand, and the many flightless birds named after the islands they inhabit (the Samoan wood rail, the Gough Island moorhen, the Auckland Island teal, and so on). As we'll see in the next chapter, one of the notable features of remote islands is their lack of mammals and reptiles—species that prey on birds. But what about ratites that live on continents, like ostriches? All of these evolved in the Southern Hemisphere, where there were far fewer mammalian predators than in the north.

The long and short of it is this: flight is metabolically expensive, using up a lot of energy that could otherwise be diverted to reproduction. If you're flying mainly to stay away from predators, but predators are often missing on islands, or if food is readily obtained on the ground, as it can be on islands (which often lack many trees), then why do you need fully functioning wings? In such a situation, birds with reduced wings would have a reproductive advantage, and natural selection could favor flightlessness. Also, wings are large appendages that are easily injured. If they're unnecessary, you can avoid injury by reducing them. In both situations, selection would directly favor mutations that led to progressively smaller wings, resulting in an inability to fly.

So why haven't they disappeared completely? In some cases they nearly have: the wings of the kiwi are functionless nubs. But when the wings have assumed new uses, as in the ostrich, they will be maintained by natural selection, though in a form that doesn't allow flight. In other species, wings may be in the process of disappearing, and we're simply seeing them in the middle of this process.

Vestigial eyes are also common. Many animals, including burrowers and cave dwellers, live in complete darkness, but we know from constructing evolutionary trees that they descended from species that lived aboveground and had functioning eyes. Like wings, eyes are a burden when you don't need them. They take energy to build, and can be easily injured. So any mutations that favored their loss would clearly be advantageous when it's just too dark to see. Alternatively, mutations that reduced vision could simply accumulate over time if they neither helped nor hurt the animal.

Just such an evolutionary loss of eyes occurred in the ancestor of the eastern Mediterranean blind mole rat. This is a long, cylindrical rodent with stubby legs, resembling a fur-covered salami with a tiny mouth. This creature spends its entire life underground. Yet it still retains a vestige of an eye—a tiny organ only one millimeter across and completely hidden beneath a protective layer of skin. The remnant eye can't form images. Molecular evidence tells us that, around 25 million years ago, blind mole rats evolved from sighted rodents, and their withered eyes attest to this ancestry. But why do these remnants remain at all? Recent studies show that they contain a photopigment that is sensitive to low levels of light, and helps regulate the animal's daily rhythm of activity. This residual function, driven by small amounts of light that penetrate underground, could explain the persistence of vestigial eyes.

True moles, which are not rodents but insectivores, have independently lost their eyes, retaining only a vestigial, skin-covered organ that you can see by pushing aside the fur on its head. Similarly, in some burrowing snakes the eyes are completely hidden beneath the scales. Many cave animals also have eyes that are reduced or missing. These include fish (like the blind cave fish you can buy at pet stores), spiders, salamanders, shrimp, and beetles. There is even a blind cave crayfish that still has eyestalks, but no eyes atop them!

Whales are treasure troves of vestigial organs. Many living species have a vestigial pelvis and leg bones, testifying, as we saw in the last chapter, to their descent from four-legged terrestrial ancestors. If you look at a complete whale skeleton in a museum, you'll often see the tiny hindlimb and pelvic bones hanging from the rest of the skeleton, suspended by wires. That's because in living whales they're not connected to the rest of the bones, but are simply imbedded in tissue. They once were part of the skeleton, but became disconnected and tiny when they were no longer needed. The list of vestigial organs in animals could fill a large catalog. Darwin himself, an avid beetle collector in his youth, pointed out that some flightless beetles still have vestiges of wings beneath their fused wing covers (the beetle's "shell").

We humans have many vestigial features proving that we evolved. The most famous is the appendix. Known medically as the vermiform ("worm-shaped") appendix, it's a thin, pencil-sized cylinder of tissue that forms the end of the pouch, or caecum, that sits at the junction of our large and small intestines. Like many vestigial features, its size and degree of development are highly variable: in humans, its length ranges from about an inch to over a foot. A few people are even born without one.

In herbivorous animals like koalas, rabbits, and kangaroos, the caecum and its appendix tip are much larger than ours. This is also true of leaf-eating primates like lemurs, lorises, and spider monkeys. The enlarged pouch serves as a fermenting vessel (like the "extra stomachs" of cows), containing bacteria that help the animal break down cellulose into usable sugars. In primates whose diet includes fewer leaves, like orangutans and macaques, the caecum and appendix are reduced. In humans, who don't eat leaves and can't digest cellulose, the appendix is nearly gone. Obviously the less herbivorous the animal, the smaller the caecum and appendix. In other words, our appendix is simply the remnant of an organ that was critically important to our leaf-eating ancestors, but of no real value to us.

Does an appendix do us any good at all? If so, it's not obvious. Removing it doesn't produce any bad side effects or increase mortality (in fact, removal seems to *reduce* the incidence of colitis). Discussing the appendix in his famous textbook *The Vertebrate Body*, the paleontologist Alfred Romer remarked dryly, "Its major importance would appear to be financial support of the surgical profession." But to be fair, it may be of some small use. The appendix contains patches of tissue that may function as part of the immune system. It has also been suggested that it provides a refuge for useful gut bacteria when an infection removes them from the rest of our digestive system.

But these minor benefits are surely outweighed by the severe problems that come with the human appendix. Its narrowness makes it easily clogged, which can lead to its infection and inflammation, otherwise known as appendicitis. If not treated, a ruptured appendix can kill you. You have about one chance in fifteen of getting appendicitis in your lifetime. Fortunately, thanks to the evolutionarily recent practice of surgery, the chance of dying when you get appendicitis is only 1 percent. But before doctors began to remove inflamed appendixes in the late nineteenth century, mortality may have exceeded 20 percent. In other words, before the days of surgical removal, more than one person in a hundred died of appendicitis. That's pretty strong natural selection.

Over the vast period of human evolution—more than 99 percent of it— there were no surgeons, and we lived with a ticking time bomb in our gut.

When you weigh the tiny advantages of an appendix against its huge disadvantages, it's clear that on the whole it is simply a bad thing to have. But apart from whether it's good or bad, the appendix is still vestigial, for it no longer performs the function for which it evolved.

So why do we still have one? We don't yet know the answer. It may in fact have been on its way out, but surgery has almost eliminated natural selection against people with appendixes. Another possibility is that selection simply can't shrink the appendix any more without it becoming even *more* harmful: a smaller appendix may run an even higher risk of being blocked. That might be an evolutionary roadblock to its complete disappearance.

Our bodies teem with other remnants of primate ancestry. We have a vestigial tail: the coccyx, or the triangular end of our spine that's made of several fused vertebrae hanging below our pelvis. It's what remains of the long, useful tail of our ancestors (figure 14). It still has a function (some useful muscles attach to it), but remember that its vestigiality is diagnosed not by its usefulness but because it no longer has the function for which it originally evolved. Tellingly, some humans have a rudimentary tail muscle (the "extensor coccygis"), identical to the one that moves the tails of monkeys and other mammals. It still attaches to our coccyx, but since the bones can't move, the muscle is useless. You may have one and not even know it.

Other vestigial muscles become apparent in winter, or at horror movies. These are the *arrector pili*, the tiny muscles that attach to the base of each body hair. When they contract, the hairs stand up, giving us "goose bumps"— so called because of their resemblance to the skin of a plucked goose. Goose bumps and the muscles that make them serve no useful function, at least in humans. In other mammals, however, they raise the fur for insulation when it's cold, and cause the animal to look larger when it's making or receiving threats. Think of a cat, whose fur bushes out when it's cold or angry. Our vestigial goose bumps are produced by exactly the same stimuli—cold or a rush of adrenaline.

And here's a final example: if you can wiggle your ears, you're demonstrating evolution. We have three muscles under our scalp that attach to our

FIGURE 14. Vestigial and atavistic tails. Top left: in our relatives that have tails, such as the ruffed lemur (*Varecia variegates*), the tail (caudal) vertebrae are unfused (the first four are labeled C1–C4). But in the human "tail," or coccyx (top right), the caudal vertebrae are fused to form a vestigial structure. Bottom: atavistic tail of a three-month-old Israeli infant. X-ray of the tail (right) shows that the three caudal vertebrae are much larger and more well developed than normal, are not fused, and approach the size of the sacral vertebrae (S1–S5). The tail was later surgically removed.

ears. In most individuals they're useless, but some people can use them to wiggle their ears. (I am one of the lucky ones, and every year demonstrate this prowess to my evolution class, much to the students' amusement.) These are the same muscles used by other animals, like cats and horses, to move their ears around, helping them localize sounds. In those species, moving the ears helps them detect predators, locate their young, and so on. But in humans the muscles are good only for entertainment.[16]

To paraphrase the quote from the geneticist Theodosius Dobzhansky that begins this chapter, vestigial traits make sense only in the light of evolution. Sometimes useful, but often not, they're exactly what we'd expect to find if natural selection gradually eliminated useless features or refashioned them into new, more adaptive ones. Tiny, nonfunctional wings, a dangerous appendix, eyes that can't see, and silly ear muscles simply don't make sense if you think that species were specially created.

Atavisms

OCCASIONALLY AN INDIVIDUAL crops up with an anomaly that looks like the reappearance of an ancestral trait. A horse can be born with extra toes, a human baby with a tail. These sporadically expressed remnants of ancestral features are called *atavisms*, from the Latin *atavus*, or "ancestor." They differ from vestigial traits because they occur only occasionally rather than in every individual.

True atavisms must recapitulate an ancestral trait, and in a fairly exact way. They aren't simply monstrosities. A human born with an extra leg, for example, is not an atavism because none of our ancestors had five limbs. The most famous genuine atavisms are probably the legs of whales. We've already learned that some species of whales retain vestigial pelvises and rear leg bones, but about one whale in five hundred is actually born with a rear leg that protrudes outside the body wall. These limbs show all degrees of refinement, with many of them clearly containing the major leg bones of terrestrial mammals—the femur, tibia, and fibula. Some even have feet and toes!

Why do atavisms like this occur at all? Our best hypothesis is that they come from the reexpression of genes that were functional in ancestors but were silenced by natural selection when they were no longer needed. Yet these dormant genes can sometimes be reawakened when something goes awry in development. Whales still contain some genetic information for making legs—not perfect legs, since the information has degraded during the millions of years that it resided unused in the genome—but legs nonetheless. And that information is there because whales descended from four-legged ancestors. Like the ubiquitous whale pelvis, the rare whale leg is evidence for evolution.

Modern horses, which descend from smaller, five-toed ancestors, show similar atavisms. The fossil record documents the gradual loss of toes over time, so that in modern horses only the middle one—the hoof—remains. It turns out that horse embryos begin development with three toes, which grow at equal rates. Later, however, the middle toe begins to grow faster than the other two, which at birth are left as thin "splint bones" along either side of the leg. (Splint bones are true vestigial features. When they become inflamed, a horse gets "the splints.") On rare occasions, though, the extra digits continue developing until they become true extra toes, complete with hoofs. Often these atavistic toes don't touch the ground unless the horse is running. This is exactly what the ancient horse *Merychippus* looked like 15 million years ago. Extra-toed horses were once considered supernatural wonders: both Julius Caesar and Alexander the Great were said to have ridden them. And they are wonders of a sort—wonders of evolution—for they clearly show genetic kinship between ancient and modern horses.

The most striking atavism in our own species is called the "coccygeal projection," better known as the human tail. As we'll learn shortly, early in development human embryos have a sizable fishlike tail, which begins to disappear about seven weeks into development (its bones and tissues are simply reabsorbed by the body). Rarely, however, it doesn't regress completely, and a baby is born with a tail projecting from the base of its spine (figure 14). The tails vary tremendously: some are "soft," without bone, while others contain vertebrae—the same vertebrae normally fused together in our tailbone. Some tails are an inch long, others nearly a foot. And they aren't just simple flaps of skin, but can have hair, muscles, blood vessels, and nerves. Some can even wiggle! Fortunately, these awkward protrusions are easily removed by surgeons.

What could this mean, other than that we still carry a developmental program for making tails? Indeed, recent genetic work has shown that we carry exactly the same genes that make tails in animals like mice, but these genes are normally deactivated in human fetuses. Tails appear to be true atavisms.

Some atavisms can be produced in the laboratory. The most amazing of these is that paragon of rarity, hen's teeth. In 1980, E. J. Kollar and C. Fisher at the University of Connecticut combined the tissues of two species, grafting the tissue lining the mouth of a chicken embryo on top of tissue from the jaw of a developing mouse. Amazingly, the chicken tissue eventually produced toothlike structures, some with distinct roots and crowns. Since the underlying mouse tissue alone could not produce teeth, Kollar and Fisher inferred that molecules from the mouse reawakened a dormant developmental program for making teeth in chickens. This meant that chickens had all the right genes for making teeth, but were missing a spark that the mouse tissue was able to provide. Twenty years later, scientists unraveled the molecular biology and showed that Kollar and Fisher's suggestion was right: birds do indeed have genetic pathways for producing teeth, but don't make them because a single crucial protein is missing. When that protein is supplied, toothlike structures form on the bill. You'll remember that birds evolved from toothed reptiles. They lost those teeth more than 60 million years ago, but clearly still carry some genes for making them—genes that are remnants of their reptilian ancestry.

Dead Genes

ATAVISMS AND VESTIGIAL TRAITS show us that when a trait is no longer used, or becomes reduced, the genes that make it don't instantly disappear from the genome: evolution stops their action by inactivating them, not snipping them out of the DNA. From this we can make a prediction. We expect to find, in the genomes of many species, silenced, or "dead," genes: genes that once were useful but are no longer intact or expressed. In other words, there should be vestigial genes. In contrast, the idea that all species were created from scratch predicts that no such genes would exist, since there would be no common ancestors in which those genes were active.

Thirty years ago we couldn't test this prediction because we had no way to read the DNA code. Now, however, it's quite easy to sequence the complete genome of species, and it's been done for many of them, including humans. This gives us a unique tool to study evolution when we realize that the normal function of a gene is to make a protein—a protein whose sequence of amino acids is determined by the sequence of nucleotide bases that make up the DNA. And once we have the DNA sequence of a given gene, we can usually tell if it is expressed normally—that is, whether it makes a functional protein—or whether it is silenced and makes nothing. We can see, for example, whether mutations have changed the gene so that a usable protein can no longer be made, or whether the "control" regions responsible for turning on a gene have been inactivated. A gene that doesn't function is called a *pseudogene*.

And the evolutionary prediction that we'll find pseudogenes has been fulfilled—amply. Virtually every species harbors dead genes, many of them still active in its relatives. This implies that those genes were also active in a common ancestor, and were killed off in some descendants but not in others.[17] Out of about thirty thousand genes, for example, we humans carry more than two thousand pseudogenes. Our genome—and that of other species—are truly well populated graveyards of dead genes.

The most famous human pseudogene is *GLO*, so called because in other species it produces an enzyme called L-gulono-γ-lactone oxidase. This enzyme is used in making vitamin C (ascorbic acid) from the simple sugar glucose. Vitamin C is essential for proper metabolism, and virtually all mammals have the pathway to make it—all, that is, except for primates, fruit bats, and guinea pigs. In these species, vitamin C is obtained directly from their food, and normal diets usually have enough. If we don't ingest enough vitamin C, we get sick: scurvy was common among fruit-deprived seamen of the nineteenth century. The reason why primates and these few other mammals don't make their own vitamin C is because they don't need to. Yet DNA sequencing tells us that primates still carry most of the genetic information needed to make the vitamin.

It turns out that the pathway for making vitamin C from glucose involves a sequence of four steps, each promoted by the product of a different gene. Primates and guinea pigs still have active genes for the first three steps, but the last step, which requires the GLO enzyme, doesn't take place: *GLO* has been inactivated by a mutation. It has become a pseudogene, called ψ*GLO* (ψ is the Greek letter psi, standing for "pseudo"). ψ*GLO* doesn't work because a single nucleotide in the gene's DNA sequence is missing. And it's exactly the *same* nucleotide missing in other primates. This shows that the mutation that destroyed our ability to make vitamin C was present in the ancestor of all primates, and was passed on to its descendants. The inactivation of *GLO* in guinea pigs happened independently, since it involves different mutations. It's highly likely that since fruit bats, guinea pigs, and primates got plenty of vitamin C in their diet, there was no penalty for inactivating the pathway that made it. This could even have been beneficial since it eliminated a protein that might have been costly to produce.

A dead gene in one species that is active in its relatives is evidence for evolution, but there's more. When you look at ψ*GLO* in living primates, you find out that its sequence is more similar between close relatives than between more distant ones. The sequences of human and chimp ψ*GLO*, for example, resemble each other closely, but differ more from the ψ*GLO* of orangutans, which are more distant relatives. What's more, the sequence of guinea pig ψ*GLO* is very different from that of all primates.

Only evolution and common ancestry can explain these facts. All mammals inherited a functional copy of the *GLO* gene. About 40 million years ago, in the common ancestor of all primates, a gene that was no longer needed was inactivated by a mutation. All primates inherited that same mutation. After *GLO* was silenced, other mutations continued to occur in the gene that was no longer expressed. These mutations accumulated over time—they are harmless if they occur in genes that are already dead—and were passed on to descendant species. Since closer relatives share a common ancestor more recently, genes that change in a time-dependent way follow the pattern of common ancestry, leading to DNA sequences more similar in close than in distant relatives. This occurs whether or not a gene is dead. The sequence of *ψGLO* in guinea pigs is so different because it was inactivated independently, in a lineage that had already diverged from that of primates. And *ψGLO* is not unique in showing such patterns: there are many other such pseudogenes.

But if you believe that primates and guinea pigs were specially created, these facts don't make sense. Why would a creator put a pathway for making vitamin C in all these species, and then inactivate it? Wouldn't it be easier simply to omit the whole pathway from the beginning? Why would the same inactivating mutation be present in all primates, and a different one in guinea pigs? Why would the sequences of the dead gene exactly mirror the pattern of resemblance predicted from the known ancestry of these species? And why do humans have thousands of pseudogenes in the first place?

We also harbor dead genes that came from other species, namely viruses. Some, called "endogenous retroviruses," can make copies of their genome and insert them into the DNA of species they infect. (HIV is a retrovirus.) If the viruses infect the cells that make sperm and eggs, they can be passed on to future generations. The human genome contains thousands of such viruses, nearly all of them rendered harmless by mutations. They are the remnants of ancient infections. But some of these remnants sit in exactly the same location on the chromosomes of humans and chimpanzees. These were surely viruses that infected our common ancestor and were passed on to both descendants. Since there is almost no chance of viruses inserting themselves independently at exactly the same spot in two species, this points strongly to common ancestry.

Another curious tale of dead genes involves our sense of smell, or rather our poor sense of smell, for humans are truly bad sniffers among land mammals. Nevertheless, we can still recognize more than ten thousand different odors. How can we accomplish such a feat? Until recently, this was a complete mystery. The answer lies in our DNA—in our many olfactory receptor (OR) genes.

The OR story was worked out by Linda Buck and Richard Axel, who were awarded the Nobel Prize for this feat in 2004. Let's look at OR genes in a super-sniffer: the mouse.

Mice depend heavily on their sense of smell, not only to find food and avoid predators, but also to detect one another's pheromones. The sensory world of a mouse is vastly different from ours, in which vision is far more important than smell. Mice have about a thousand active OR genes. All of them descend from a single ancestral gene that arose millions of years ago and became duplicated many times, so that each gene differs slightly from the others. And each produces a different protein—an "olfactory receptor"— that recognizes a different airborne molecule. Each OR protein is expressed in a different type of receptor cell in the tissues lining the nose. Different odors contain different combinations of molecules, and each combination stimulates a different group of cells. The cells send signals to the brain, which integrates and decodes the different signals. That's how mice can distinguish the smell of cats from that of cheese. By integrating *combinations* of signals, mice (and other mammals) can recognize far more odors than they have OR genes.

The ability to recognize different smells is useful: it enables you to distinguish kin from nonkin, find a mate, locate food, recognize predators, and see who's been invading your territory. The survival advantages are enormous. How has natural selection tapped them? First, an ancestral gene became duplicated a number of times. Such duplication happens from time to time as an accident during cell division. Gradually, the duplicated copies diverged from each other, with each gene's products binding to a different odor molecule. A different type of cell evolved for each of the thousand OR genes. And at the same time, the brain became rewired to combine the signals from the various kinds of cells to create the sensations of different odors. This is a truly staggering feat of evolution, driven by the sheer survival value of the discerning sniff!

Our own sense of smell comes nowhere close to that of mice. One reason is that we express fewer OR genes—only about four hundred. But we still carry a total of eight hundred OR genes, which make up nearly 3 percent of our entire genome. And fully half of these are pseudogenes, permanently inactivated by mutations. The same is true for most other primates. How did this happen? Probably because we primates, who are active during the day, rely more on vision than on smell, and so don't need to discriminate among so many odors. Unneeded genes eventually get bumped off by mutations. Predictably, primates with color vision, and hence greater discrimination of the environment, have more dead OR genes.

If you look at the sequences of human OR genes, both active and inactive, they are most similar to those of other primates, less similar to those of "primitive" mammals like the platypus, and less similar yet to the OR genes of distant relatives like reptiles. Why should dead genes show such a relationship, if not for evolution? And the fact that we harbor so many inactive genes is even more evidence for evolution: we carry this genetic baggage because it was needed in our distant ancestors who relied for survival on a keen sense of smell.

But the most striking example of the evolution—or de-evolution—of OR genes is the dolphin. Dolphins don't need to detect volatile odors in the air, since they do their business underwater, and they have a completely different set of genes for detecting waterborne chemicals. As one might predict, OR genes of dolphins are inactivated. In fact, *80 percent of them* are inactivated. Hundreds of them still sit silently in the dolphin genome, mute testimony of evolution. And if you look at the DNA sequences of these dead dolphin genes, you'll find that they resemble those of land mammals. This makes sense when we realize that dolphins evolved from land mammals whose OR genes became useless when they took to the water.[18] This makes no sense if dolphins were specially created.

Vestigial genes can go hand in hand with vestigial structures. We mammals evolved from reptilian ancestors that laid eggs. With the exceptions of the "monotremes" (the order of mammals that includes the Australian spiny anteater and duck-billed platypus), mammals have dispensed with egg-laying, and mothers nourish their young directly through the placenta instead of by providing a storehouse of yolk. And mammals carry three genes that, in reptiles and birds, produce the nutritious protein vitellogenin, which fills the yolk sac. But in virtually all mammals these genes are dead, totally inactivated by mutations. Only the egg-laying monotremes still produce vitellogenin, having one active and two dead genes. What's more, mammals like ourselves still produce a yolk sac—but one that is vestigial and yolkless, a large, fluid-filled balloon attached to the fetal gut (figure 15). In the second month of human pregnancy, it detaches from the embryo.

With its ducklike bill, fat tail, poison-tipped spurs on the hind legs of males, and the ability of females to lay eggs, the platypus of Australia is bizarre in many ways. If ever a creature seems *un*intelligently designed—or perhaps devised for a creator's amusement—it would be this one. But the platypus has one more odd feature: it lacks a stomach. Unlike nearly all vertebrates, who have a pouchlike stomach in which digestive enzymes break down food, the platypus "stomach" is just a slight swelling of the esophagus where it joins the

FIGURE 15. Normal and vestigial yolk sacs. Top photos: full yolk sac of the embryonic zebrafish, *Danio rerio*, extracted from the egg case at two days, just before hatching. Bottom photos: empty vestigial yolk sac of a human embryo at about four weeks. The human embryo at bottom right shows the branchial arches, the hindlimb bud, and the "tail" below the hindlimb.

intestine. This stomach completely lacks the glands that produce digestive enzymes in other vertebrates. We're not sure why evolution has eliminated the stomach—perhaps the platypus diet of soft insects doesn't require much processing—but we know that the platypus came from ancestors with stomachs. One reason is that the platypus genome contains two pseudogenes for enzymes related to digestion. No longer needed, they've become inactivated by mutation, but still testify to the evolution of this strange beast.

Palimpsests in Embryos

WELL BEFORE THE TIME OF DARWIN, biologists were busy studying both embryology (how an animal develops) and comparative anatomy (the similarities and differences in the structure of different animals). Their work turned up many peculiarities that, at the time, didn't make sense. For example, all vertebrates begin development in the same way, looking rather like an embryonic fish. As development proceeds, different species begin to diverge—but in weird ways. Some blood vessels, nerves, and organs that were present in the embryos of all species at the start suddenly disappear, while others go through strange contortions and migrations. Eventually, the dance of development culminates in the very different adult forms of fish, reptiles, birds, amphibians, and mammals. Nevertheless, when development begins they look very much alike. Darwin tells the story of how the great German embryologist Karl Ernst von Baer became confused by the similarity of vertebrate embryos. Von Baer wrote to Darwin:

> In my possession are two little embryos in spirit [alcohol], whose names I have omitted to attach, and at present I am quite unable to say to what class they belong. They may be lizards or small birds, or very young mammalia, so complete is the similarity in the mode of formation of the head and trunk in these animals.

And again, it was Darwin who reconciled the disparate facts about embryology that filled the textbooks of his time, and showed that the puzzling features of development suddenly made perfect sense under the unifying idea of evolution:

Embryology rises greatly in interest, when we thus look at the embryo as a picture, more or less obscured, of the common parent-form of each great class of animals.

Let's start with that fishy fetus of all vertebrates—limbless and sporting a fishlike tail. Perhaps the most striking fishlike feature is a series of five to seven pouches, separated by grooves, that lie on each side of the embryo near its future head. These pouches are called the *branchial arches*, but we'll call them "arches" for short (figure 16). Each arch contains tissues that develop into nerves, blood vessels, muscles, and bone or cartilage. As fish and shark

FIGURE 16. Branchial arches of a shark embryo (top left) and a human embryo (bottom left). In sharks and fish (such as the basking shark *Cetorhinus maximus* shown at top right), the arches develop directly into the adult gill structures, while in the human (and other mammals) they develop into diverse structures in the adult head and upper body.

embryos develop, the first arch becomes the jaw and the rest become gill structures: the clefts between the pouches open up to become the gill slits, and the pouches develop nerves to control the movement of the gills, blood vessels to remove oxygen from water, and bars of bone or cartilage to support the gill structure. In fish and sharks, then, the development of gills from the embryonic arches is more or less direct: these embryonic features simply enlarge without much change to form the adult breathing apparatus.

But in other vertebrates that don't have gills as adults, these arches turn into very different structures—structures that make up the head. In mammals, for example, they form the three tiny bones of the middle ear, the Eustachian tube, the carotid artery, the tonsils, the larynx, and the cranial nerves. Sometimes the embryonic gill slits fail to close in human embryos, producing a baby with a cyst on its neck. This condition, an atavistic remnant of our fishy ancestors, can be corrected with surgery.

Our blood vessels go through especially strange contortions. In fish and sharks, the embryonic pattern of vessels develops without much change into the adult system. But as other vertebrates develop, the vessels move around, and some of them disappear. Mammals like ourselves are left with only three main vessels from the original six. The really curious thing is that as our development proceeds, the changes resemble an evolutionary sequence. Our fishlike circulatory system turns into one similar to that of embryonic amphibians. In amphibians, the embryonic vessels turn directly into adult vessels, but ours continue to change—into a circulatory system resembling that of embryonic reptiles. In reptiles, this system then develops directly into the adult one. But ours changes still further, adding a few more twists that turn it into a true mammalian circulatory system, complete with carotid, pulmonary, and dorsal arteries (figure 17).

These patterns raise a lot of questions. First, why do different vertebrates, which wind up looking very different from one another, all begin development looking like a fish embryo? Why do mammals form their heads and faces from the very same embryonic structures that become the gills of fish? Why do vertebrate embryos go through such a contorted sequence of changes in the circulatory system? Why don't human embryos, or lizard embryos, begin development with their adult circulatory system already in place, rather than making a lot of changes in what developed earlier? And why does our sequence

FIGURE 17. The blood vessels of embryonic humans start out resembling those of embryonic fish, with a top and bottom vessel connected by parallel vessels, one on each side ("aortic arches"). In fish, these side vessels carry blood to and from the gills. Embryonic and adult fish have six pairs of arches; this is the basic ground plan that appears at the beginning of development of all vertebrates. In the human embryo, the first, second, and fifth arches form briefly at the beginning of development, but disappear by four weeks of age, when the third, fourth, and sixth arches (distinguished by different shades of gray) form. By seven weeks, the embryonic arches have rearranged themselves, looking much like the embryonic vessels of a reptile. In the final adult configuration, the vessels are rearranged still more, with some having vanished or transformed themselves into different vessels. The aortic arches of fish undergo no such transformation.

of development mimic the order of our ancestors (fish to amphibian to reptile to mammal)? As Darwin argued in *The Origin*, it's not because human embryos experience a series of environments during development to which they must successively adapt—first a fishlike one, then a reptilian one, and so on:

> The points of structure, in which the embryos of widely different animals of the same class resemble each other, often have no direct relation to their conditions of existence. We cannot, for instance, suppose that in the embryos of the vertebrata the peculiar loop-like course of the arteries near the branchial slits are related to similar conditions—in the young mammal which is nourished in the womb of its mother, in the egg of the bird which is hatched in a nest, and in the spawn of a frog under water.

The "recapitulation" of an evolutionary sequence is seen in the developmental sequence of other organs—our kidneys, for example. During development, the human embryo actually forms three different types of kidneys, one after the other, with the first two discarded before our final kidney appears. And those transitory embryonic kidneys are similar to those we find in species that evolved before us in the fossil record—jawless fish and reptiles, respectively. What does this mean?

You could answer this question superficially as follows: each vertebrate undergoes development in a series of stages, and the sequence of those stages happens to follow the evolutionary sequence of its ancestors. So, for example, a lizard begins development resembling an embryonic fish, then somewhat later an embryonic amphibian, and finally an embryonic reptile. Mammals go through the same sequence, but add on the final stage of an embryonic mammal.

This answer is correct but only raises deeper issues. Why *does* development often occur in this way? Why doesn't natural selection eliminate the "fish embryo" stage of human development, since a combination of a tail, fishlike gill arches, and a fishlike circulatory system doesn't seem necessary for a human embryo? Why don't we simply begin development as tiny humans—as some seventeenth-century biologists thought we did—and just get larger and larger until we're born? Why all the transformation and rearrangement?

The probable answer—and it's a good one—involves recognizing that as one species evolves into another, the descendant inherits the developmental program of its ancestor: that is, all the genes that form ancestral structures. And development is a very conservative process. Many structures that form later in development require biochemical "cues" from features that appear earlier. If, for example, you try to tinker with the circulatory system by remodeling it from the very onset of development, you might produce all sorts of adverse side effects in the formation of other structures, like bones, that mustn't be changed. To avoid these deleterious side effects, it's usually easier to simply tack some less drastic changes onto what is already a robust and basic developmental plan. It is best for things that *evolved* later to be programmed to *develop* later in the embryo.

This "adding new stuff onto old" principle also explains why the sequence of developmental changes mirrors the evolutionary sequence of organisms. As one group evolves from another, it often adds its development program on top of the old one.

Noting this principle, Ernst Haeckel, a German evolutionist and Darwin's contemporary, formulated a "biogenetic law" in 1866, famously summarized as "Ontogeny recapitulates phylogeny." This means that the development of an organism simply replays its evolutionary history. But this notion is true in only a limited sense. Embryonic stages don't look like the adult forms of their ancestors, as Haeckel claimed, but like the *embryonic* forms of ancestors. Human fetuses, for example, never resemble adult fish or reptiles, but in certain ways they do resemble embryonic fish and reptiles. Also, the recapitulation is neither strict nor inevitable: not every feature of an ancestor's embryo appears in its descendants, nor do all stages of development unfold in a strict evolutionary order. Further, some species, like plants, have dispensed with nearly all traces of their ancestry during development. Haeckel's law has fallen into disrepute not only because it wasn't strictly true, but also because Haeckel was accused, largely unjustly, of fudging some drawings of early embryos to make them look more similar than they really are.[19] Yet we shouldn't throw out the baby with the bathwater. Embryos still show a form of recapitulation: features that arose earlier in evolution often appear earlier in development. And this makes sense only if species have an evolutionary history.

Now, we're not absolutely sure why some species retain much of their evolutionary history during development. The "adding new stuff onto old" principle is just a hypothesis—an explanation for the facts of embryology. It's hard to prove that it was easier for a developmental program to evolve one way rather than another. But the facts of embryology remain, and make sense only in light of evolution. All vertebrates begin development looking like embryonic fish because we all descended from a fishlike ancestor with a fishlike embryo. We see strange contortions and disappearances of organs, blood vessels, and gill slits because descendants still carry the genes and developmental programs of ancestors. And the sequence of developmental changes also makes sense: at one stage of development mammals have an embryonic circulatory system like that of reptiles; but we don't see the converse situation. Why? Because mammals descended from early reptiles and not vice versa.

When he wrote *The Origin*, Darwin considered embryology his strongest evidence for evolution. Today he'd probably give pride of place to the fossil record. Nevertheless, science continues to accumulate intriguing features about development that support evolution. Embryonic whales and dolphins form hindlimb buds—bulges of tissue that, in four-legged mammals, become the rear legs. But in marine mammals the buds are reabsorbed soon after they're formed. Figure 18 shows this regression in the develop-

FIGURE 18. The disappearing hindlimb structures in the spotted dolphin (*Stenella attenuata*)—evolutionary remnants of its four-legged ancestor. In the twenty-four-day-old embryo (left), the hindlimb bud (indicated by triangle) is well developed, only slightly smaller than the forelimb bud. By forty-eight days (right), the hindlimb buds have almost disappeared, while the forelimb buds continue to develop into what will be the flippers.

ment of the spotted dolphin. Baleen whales, which lack teeth but whose ancestors were toothed whales, develop embryonic teeth that disappear before birth.

One of my favorite cases of embryological evidence for evolution is the furry human fetus. We are famously known as "naked apes" because, unlike other primates, we don't have a thick coat of hair. But in fact for one brief period we do—as embryos. Around sixth months after conception, we become completely covered with a fine, downy coat of hair called *lanugo*. Lanugo is usually shed about a month before birth, when it's replaced by the more sparsely distributed hair with which we're born. (Premature infants, however, are sometimes born with lanugo, which soon falls off.) Now, there's no need for a human embryo to have a transitory coat of hair. After all, it's a cozy 98.6 degrees Fahrenheit in the womb. Lanugo can be explained only as a remnant of our primate ancestry: fetal monkeys also develop a coat of hair at about the same stage of development. Their hair, however, doesn't fall out, but hangs on to become the adult coat. And, like humans, fetal whales also have lanugo, a remnant of when their ancestors lived on land.

The final example from humans takes us into the realm of speculation, but is too appealing to omit. This is the "grasping reflex" of newborn babies. If you have access to an infant, gently stroke the palms of its hands. The baby will show a reflex response by making a fist around your finger. In fact, the grasp is so tight that an infant can, using both hands, hang for several minutes from a broomstick. (Warning: don't try this experiment at home!) The grasping reflex, which disappears several months after birth, may well be an atavistic behavior. Newborn monkeys and apes have the same reflex, but it persists throughout the juvenile stage, allowing the young to hang on to their mother's fur as they're carried about.

It is sad that while embryology provides such a gold mine of evidence for evolution, textbooks of embryology often fail to point this out. I have met obstetricians, for instance, who know everything about the lanugo except why it appears in the first place.

As well as peculiarities of embryonic development, there are also peculiarities of animal structure that can be explained only by evolution. These are cases of "bad design."

Bad Design

IN THE OTHERWISE FORGETTABLE MOVIE *Man of the Year*, comedian Robin
Williams plays a television talk-show host who, through a series of bizarre
accidents, becomes president of the United States. During a preelection
debate, Williams's character is asked about intelligent design. He responds,
"People say intelligent design—we must teach intelligent design. Look at the
human body; is that intelligent? You have a waste processing plant next to a
recreation area!"

It's a good point. Although organisms appear designed to fit their natural
environments, the idea of *perfect* design is an illusion. Every species is imperfect in many ways. Kiwis have useless wings, whales have a vestigial pelvis,
and our appendix is a nefarious organ.

What I mean by "bad design" is the notion that if organisms were built
from scratch by a designer—one who used the biological building blocks of
nerves, muscles, bone, and so on—they would not have such imperfections.
Perfect design would truly be the sign of a skilled and intelligent designer.
Imperfect design is the mark of evolution; in fact, it's precisely what we *expect*
from evolution. We've learned that evolution doesn't start from scratch.
New parts evolve from old ones, and have to work well with the parts that have
already evolved. Because of this, we should expect compromises: some features that work pretty well, but not as well as they might, or some features—
like the kiwi wing—that don't work at all, but are evolutionary leftovers.

A good example of bad design is the flounder, whose popularity as an
eating fish (Dover sole, for instance) comes partly from its flatness, which
makes it easy to bone. There are actually about five hundred species of flatfish—halibut, turbot, flounders, and their kin—all placed in the order Pleu-
ronectiformes. The word means "side-swimmers," a description that's the
key to their poor design. Flatfish are born as normal-looking fish that swim
vertically, with one eye placed on each side of a pancake-shaped body. But a
month thereafter, a strange thing happens: one eye begins to move upward.
It migrates over the skull and joins the other eye to form a pair of eyes on
one side of the body, either right or left, depending on the species. The skull

also changes its shape to promote this movement, and there are changes in the fins and color. In concert, the flatfish tips onto its newly eyeless side, so that both eyes are now on top. It becomes a flat camouflaged bottom-dweller that preys on other fish. When it has to swim, it does so on its side. Flatfish are the world's most asymmetrical vertebrates; check out a specimen the next time you go to the fish market.

If you wanted to design a flatfish, you wouldn't do it this way. You'd produce a fish like the skate, which is flat from birth and lies on its belly—not one that has to achieve flatness by lying on its side, moving its eyes and deforming its skull. Flatfish are poorly designed. But the poor design comes from their evolutionary heritage. We know from their family tree that flounders, like all flatfish, evolved from "normal" symmetrical fish. Evidently, they found it advantageous to tip onto their sides and lie on the seafloor, hiding themselves from both predators and prey. This, of course, created a problem: the bottom eye would be both useless and easily injured. To fix this, natural selection took the tortuous but available route of moving its eye about, as well as otherwise deforming its body.

One of nature's worst designs is shown by the recurrent laryngeal nerve of mammals. Running from the brain to the larynx, this nerve helps us speak and swallow. The curious thing is that it is much longer than it needs to be. Rather than taking a direct route from the brain to the larynx, a distance of about a foot in humans, the nerve runs down into our chest, loops around the aorta and a ligament derived from an artery, and then travels back up ("recurs") to connect to the larynx (figure 19). It winds up being three feet long. In giraffes the nerve takes a similar path, but one that runs all the way down that long neck and back up again: a distance fifteen feet longer than the direct route! When I first heard about this strange nerve, I had trouble believing it. Wanting to see for myself, I mustered up my courage to make a trip to the human anatomy lab and inspect my first corpse. An obliging professor showed me the nerve, tracing its course with a pencil down the torso and back up to the throat.

This circuitous path of the recurrent laryngeal nerve is not only poor design, but might even be maladaptive. That extra length makes it more prone to injury. It can, for example, be damaged by a blow to the chest, mak-

FIGURE 19. The circuitous path of the left recurrent laryngeal nerve in humans is evidence for their evolution from a fishlike ancestor. In fish, the sixth branchial arch, which later becomes a gill, is served by the sixth aortic arch. The fourth branch of the vagus nerve runs behind this arch. These structures remain part of the gill apparatus in adult fish, innervating and bringing blood from the gills. In mammals, however, part of the branchial arch evolved into the larynx. The larynx and its nerve remained connected during this process, but the sixth aortic arch on the left side of the body moved down into the chest to become a nonfunctional remnant, the *ligamentum arteriosum*. Because the nerve remained behind this arch but still connected to a structure in the neck, it was forced to evolve a pathway that travels down into the chest, loops around the aorta and the remnants of the sixth aortic arch, and then travels back up to the larynx. The indirect path of this nerve does not reflect intelligent design but can be understood only as the product of our evolution from ancestors having very different bodies.

ing it hard to talk or swallow. But the pathway makes sense when we understand how the recurrent laryngeal nerve evolved. Like the mammalian aorta itself, it descends from those branchial arches of our fishlike ancestors. In the early fishlike embryos of all vertebrates, the nerve runs from top to bottom alongside the blood vessel of the sixth branchial arch; it is a branch of the larger vagus nerve that travels along the back from the brain. And in adult fish, the nerve remains in that position, connecting the brain to the gills and helping them pump water.

During our evolution, the blood vessel from the fifth arch disappeared, and the vessels from the fourth and sixth arches moved downward into the future torso so that they could become the aorta and a ligament connecting the aorta to the pulmonary artery. But the laryngeal nerve, still behind the sixth arch, had to remain connected to the embryonic structures that become the larynx, structures that remained near the brain. As the future aorta evolved backward toward the heart, the laryngeal nerve was forced to evolve backward along with it. It would have been more efficient for the nerve to detour around the aorta, breaking and then re-forming itself on a more direct course, but natural selection couldn't manage that, for severing and rejoining a nerve is a step that reduces fitness. To keep up with the backward evolution of the aorta, the laryngeal nerve had to become long and recurrent. And that evolutionary path is recapitulated during development, since as embryos we begin with the ancestral fishlike pattern of nerves and blood vessels. In the end, we're left with bad design.

Courtesy of evolution, human reproduction is also full of jerry-rigged features. We've already learned that the descent of male testes, a result of their evolution from fish gonads, creates weak spots in the abdominal cavity that can cause hernias. Males are further disadvantaged because of the poor design of the urethra, which happens to run right through the middle of the prostate gland that produces some of our seminal fluid. To paraphrase Robin Williams, it's a sewage pipe running directly through a recreation area. A large fraction of males develop enlarged prostates later in life, which squeeze the urethra and make urination difficult and painful. (Presumably this wasn't a problem during most of human evolution, when few men lived past thirty.) A smart designer wouldn't put a collapsible tube through an organ prone to infection and swelling. It happened this way because the mammalian prostate gland evolved from tissue in the walls of the urethra.

Women don't fare much better. They give birth through the pelvis, a painful and inefficient process that, before modern medicine, killed appreciable numbers of mothers and babies. The problem is that as we evolved a big brain, the infant's head became very large relative to the opening of the pelvis, which had to remain narrow to allow efficient bipedal (two-legged) walking. This compromise leads to the difficulties and enormous pain of human birth. If you designed a human female, wouldn't you have rerouted the female reproductive tract so it exited through the lower abdomen instead of the pelvis? Imagine how much easier it would be to give birth! But humans evolved from creatures that laid eggs or gave live birth—less painfully than we—through the pelvis. We're constrained by our evolutionary history.

And would an intelligent designer have created the small gap between the human ovary and Fallopian tube, so that an egg must cross this gap before it can travel through the tube and implant in the uterus? Occasionally a fertilized egg doesn't make the leap successfully and implants in the abdomen. This produces an "abdominal pregnancy," almost invariably fatal to the baby and, without surgery, to the mother. The gap is a remnant of our fish and reptilian ancestors, who shed eggs directly from the ovary to the outside of their bodies. The Fallopian tube is an imperfect connection because it evolved later as an add-on in mammals.[20]

Some creationists respond that poor design is not an argument for evolution—that a supernatural intelligent designer could nevertheless have created imperfect features. In his book *Darwin's Black Box*, the ID proponent Michael Behe claims that "features that strike us as odd in a design might have been placed there by the Designer for a reason—for artistic reasons, for variety, to show off, for some as-yet-undetectable practical purpose, or for some unguessable reason—or they might not." But this misses the point. Yes, a designer may have motives that are unfathomable. But the particular bad designs that we see make sense *only if they evolved from features of earlier ancestors*. If a designer did have discernible motives when creating species, one of them must surely have been to fool biologists by making organisms look as though they evolved.

Chapter 4

The Geography of Life

When on board H.M.S. "Beagle" as naturalist,
I was much struck with certain facts in the distribution of
the inhabitants of South America, and in the geological
relations of the present to the past inhabitants of that continent.
These facts seemed to me to throw some light on the origin of
species—that mystery of mysteries, as it has been called
by one of our greatest philosophers.

—*Charles Darwin,* On the Origin of Species

Some of the loneliest places on earth are the isolated volcanic islands of the southern oceans. On one of them—St. Helena, halfway between Africa and South America—Napoleon whiled away his last five years in British captivity, exiled from Europe. But the islands most famous for their isolation are those of the Juan Fernández archipelago: four small specks of land totaling about forty square miles and lying four hundred miles west of Chile. For it was on one of these that Alexander Selkirk, the real-life Robinson Crusoe, lived out his solitary tenure as a castaway.

Born Alexander Selcraig in 1676, Selkirk was a hot-tempered Scot who took to sea in 1703 as sailing master of the *Cinque Ports*, a British privateer deputized to plunder Spanish and Portuguese ships. Worried about the recklessness of his twenty-one-year-old captain and the shoddy condition of the ship, Selkirk demanded to be put ashore, hoping for timely rescue, when the *Cinque Ports* stopped for food and water at Más a Tierra Island in the Juan Fernández group. The captain obliged, and Selkirk was voluntarily marooned, taking ashore only clothes, bedding, some tools, a flintlock, tobacco, a kettle, and a Bible. Thus began four and a half years of solitude.

Más a Tierra was uninhabited, and besides Selkirk the only mammals were goats, rats, and cats, all of them introduced by earlier sailors. But after an initial period of loneliness and depression, Selkirk adapted to his circumstances, hunting goats and shellfish, eating fruits and vegetables planted by his predecessors, making fire by rubbing sticks together, fashioning goatskin clothes, and warding off rats by taming kittens to share his quarters.

Selkirk was finally rescued in 1709 by a British ship, piloted, oddly enough, by the skipper of the original *Cinque Ports*. The crew was startled by the wild man in goatskins, who had been alone so long that his English could barely be understood. After helping replenish the ship with fruit and goat meat, Selkirk went aboard and made his way back to England. There he teamed up with a writer to produce a popular account of his adventures, *The Englishman*, said to have inspired Daniel Defoe's *Robinson Crusoe*.[21] Yet Selkirk could not adapt to a sedentary life ashore. He returned to sea in 1720, and died from fever a year later off the African coast.

The contingencies of time and character produced the story of Selkirk. But contingency is also the lesson of a greater story: the story of the nonhuman inhabitants of the Juan Fernández group and other islands like it. For although Selkirk did not know it, Más a Tierra (now called Alejandro Selkirk Island) was inhabited by descendants of earlier castaways—the Robinson Crusoes of plants, birds, and insects who found their way to the island by accident thousands of years before Selkirk. Unknowingly, he was living in a laboratory of evolutionary change.

Today the three islands of Juan Fernández are a living museum of rare and exotic plants and animals, with many species that are *endemic*—found nowhere else in the world. Among them are five species of birds (including a giant five-inch rust-brown hummingbird, the spectacular and endangered Juan Fernández firecrown), 126 species of plants (including many bizarre members of the sunflower family), a fur seal, and a handful of insects. No comparable area anywhere in the world has so many endemic species. But the island is just as notable for what it is *missing*: it harbors *not a single native species of amphibian, reptile, or mammal*—groups that are common on continents throughout the world. This pattern of bizarre and efflorescent forms of endemic life, with many major groups strikingly absent, is repeated over and over again on oceanic islands. And, as we'll see, the pattern gives striking evidence for evolution.

It was Darwin who first took a hard look at these patterns. Through his own youthful travels on the HMS *Beagle* and his voluminous correspondence with scientists and naturalists, he realized that evolution was necessary to explain not just the origins and forms of plants and animals but also their distributions across the globe. These distributions raised a lot of questions. Why did oceanic islands have such odd and unbalanced floras and faunas compared to continental assemblages? Why were nearly all of Australia's native mammals marsupials, while placental mammals dominated the rest of the world? And if species were created, why did the creator stock distant areas having similar terrain and climate, like the deserts of Africa and of the Americas, with species that were superficially similar in form but showed other, more fundamental differences?

Pondering these questions, others before Darwin laid the groundwork for his own intellectual synthesis—one he considered so important that it occupies two whole chapters in *The Origin*. These chapters are often considered the founding document of the field of *biogeography*—the study of the distribution of species on earth. And their evolutionary explanation of the geography of life, largely correct when first proposed, has only been refined and supported by a legion of later studies. The biogeographic evidence for evolution is now so powerful that I have never seen a creationist book, article, or lecture that has tried to refute it. Creationists simply pretend that the evidence doesn't exist.

Ironically, the roots of biogeography lie deep in religion. The earliest "natural theologians" tried to show how the distribution of organisms could be reconciled with the account of Noah's Ark in the Bible. All living animals were understood as the descendants of the pairs that Noah took aboard, pairs that traveled to their present locations from the Ark's postflood resting place (traditionally near Mount Ararat in eastern Turkey). But this explanation had obvious problems. How did kangaroos and giant earthworms make their way across the oceans to their present home in Australia? Wouldn't the pair of lions have quickly made a meal of the antelopes? And as naturalists continued to discover new species of plants and animals, even the staunchest believer realized that no boat could possibly hold them all, much less their food and water for a six-week voyage.

So another theory arose: that of *multiple* creations distributed across the earth's surface. In the mid-1800s, the renowned Swiss zoologist Louis Agassiz, then at Harvard, asserted that "not only were species immutable and static, but so were their distributions, with each remaining at or near their site of creation." But several developments also made this idea untenable, especially the increasing number of fossils disproving the claim that species were "immutable and static." Geologists such as Charles Lyell, Darwin's friend and mentor, began to find evidence that the earth was not only very old, but in flux. On the *Beagle* voyage, Darwin himself discovered fossil seashells high in the Andes, proving that what is now mountain was once underwater. Lands could rise or sink, and the continents we see today might have been larger or smaller in the past. And there were those unanswered questions about the distribution of species. Why was the flora of southern Africa so similar to that of southern South America? Some biologists proposed that all the continents were once connected by giant land bridges (Darwin grumbled to Lyell that these bridges were conjured up "as easily as a cook does pancakes"), but there was no evidence that they had ever existed.

To deal with these difficulties, Darwin proposed his own theory. The distributions of species, he claimed, were explained not by creation, but by evolution. If plants and animals had ways of dispersing over large distances and could evolve into new species after they dispersed, then this—combined with some ancient shifts in the earth, like periods of glacial expansion—could explain many peculiarities of biogeography that had puzzled his predecessors.

Darwin turned out to be right—but not completely. True, many facts about biogeography made sense if one assumed dispersal, evolution, and a changing earth. But not every fact. The large flightless birds, like ostriches, rheas, and emus, occur in Africa, South America, and Australia, respectively. If they all had a common flightless ancestor, how could they have possibly dispersed so widely? And why do eastern China and eastern North America—widely separated areas—share plants, like tulip trees and skunk cabbage, that don't occur in the intervening lands?

We now have many of the answers that once eluded Darwin, thanks to two developments that he could not have imagined: continental drift and molecular taxonomy. Darwin appreciated that the earth had changed over time, but he had no idea of how much change had actually taken place. Since the 1960s, scientists have known that the past geography of the world was very different from that of the present, as huge supercontinents have shifted about, joined, and separated into pieces.[22]

And, starting about forty years ago, we have accumulated information from DNA and protein sequences that tell us not only the evolutionary relationship between species, but also the approximate times when they diverged from common ancestors. Evolutionary theory predicts, and data support, the notion that as species diverge from their common ancestors, their DNA sequences change in roughly a straight-line fashion with time. We can use this "molecular clock," calibrated with fossil ancestors of living species, to estimate the divergence times of species that have poor fossil records.

Using the molecular clock, we can match the evolutionary relationships between species with the known movements of the continents, as well as the movements of glaciers and the formation of genuine land bridges such as the Isthmus of Panama. This tells us whether the origins of species are concurrent with the origin of new continents and habitats. These innovations have transformed biogeography into a grand detective story: using a variety of tools and seemingly unconnected facts, biologists can deduce why species live where they do. We know now, for instance, that the similarities between African and South American plants are not surprising, for their ancestors once inhabited a supercontinent—Gondwana—that split into several pieces (now Africa, South America, India, Madagascar, and Antarctica) beginning about 170 million years ago.

Every bit of biogeographic detective work turns out to support the fact of evolution. If species didn't evolve, their geographic distributions, both living and fossil, wouldn't make sense. We'll look first at species that live on continents and then at those on islands, for these disparate areas provide different sorts of evidence.

Continents

LET'S BEGIN WITH ONE OBSERVATION that strikes anyone who travels widely. If you go to two distant areas that have similar climate and terrain, you find different types of life. Take deserts. Many desert plants are succulents: they show an adaptive combination of traits that include large fleshy stems to store water, spines to deter predators, and small or missing leaves to reduce water loss. But different deserts have different types of succulents. In North and South America, the succulents are members of the cactus family. But in the deserts of Asia, Australia, and Africa, there are no native cacti, and the succulents belong to a completely different family, the euphorbs. You can tell the difference between the two types of succulents by their flowers and their sap, which is clear and watery in cacti but milky and bitter in euphorbs. Yet despite these fundamental differences, cacti and euphorbs can look very much alike. I have both types growing on my windowsill, and visitors can't tell them apart without reading their tags.

Why would a creator put plants that are fundamentally different, but look so similar, in diverse areas of the world that seem ecologically identical? Wouldn't it make more sense to put the same species of plants in areas with the same type of soil and climate?

You might reply that, although the deserts *appear* similar, the habitats differ in subtle but important ways, and cacti and euphorbs were created to be best suited to their respective habitats. But this explanation doesn't work, for when cacti are introduced into Old World deserts, where they don't occur naturally, they do very well. The North American prickly pear cactus, for example, was introduced into Australia in the early 1800s, as settlers planned to extract a red dye from the cochineal beetle that feeds on the plant (this is the dye that gives the deep crimson color to Persian rugs). By the twentieth century, the prickly pear had spread so rapidly that it became a serious pest, destroying thousands of acres of farmland and prompting drastic—and ineffective—eradication programs. The plant was finally controlled in 1926 by introducing the cactoblastis moth, whose caterpillars devour the cacti: one of the first and most successful examples of biological control. Certainly prickly pear cacti can flourish in Australian deserts, though the native succulents are euphorbs.

The most famous example of different species filling similar roles involves the marsupial mammals, now found mainly in Australia (the Virginia opossum is a familiar exception), and placental mammals, which predominate elsewhere in the world. The two groups show important anatomical differences, most notably in their reproductive systems (almost all marsupials have pouches and give birth to very undeveloped young, while placentals have placentas that enable young to be born at a more advanced stage). Nevertheless, in other ways some marsupials and placentals are astonishingly similar. There are burrowing marsupial moles that look and act just like placental moles, marsupial mice that resemble placental mice, the marsupial sugar glider, which glides from tree to tree just like a flying squirrel, and marsupial anteaters, which do exactly what South American anteaters do (figure 20).

Again one must ask: If animals were specially created, why would the creator produce on different continents fundamentally different animals that nevertheless look and act so much alike? It is not that marsupials are inherently superior to placentals in Australia, because introduced placental mammals have done very well there. Introduced rabbits, for example, are such serious pests in Australia that they are displacing native marsupials such as the bilby (a small mammal with remarkably long ears). To help fund the eradication of rabbits, conservationists are campaigning to switch from the Easter Bunny to the Easter Bilby: each autumn chocolate bilbies fill the shelves of Australian supermarkets.

No creationist, whether of the Noah's Ark variety or otherwise, has offered a credible explanation for why different types of animals have similar forms in different places. All they can do is invoke the inscrutable whims of the creator. But evolution *does* explain the pattern by invoking a well-known process called *convergent evolution*. It's really quite simple. Species

FIGURE 20. Convergent evolution of mammals. Marsupial anteaters, small gliders, and moles evolved in Australia, independent of their placental-mammal equivalents in the Americas, yet their forms are remarkably similar.

that live in similar habitats will experience similar selection pressures from their environment, so they may evolve similar adaptations, or *converge*, coming to look and behave very much alike even though they are unrelated. But these species still retain key differences that give clues to their distant ancestry. (A famous example of convergence is the camouflaging white coloration shared by diverse Arctic animals such as the polar bear and the snowy owl.) The ancestor of marsupials colonized Australia, while placentals dominated the rest of the world. Both placentals and marsupials split into a variety of species, and those species adapted to diverse habitats. If you survive and reproduce better because you burrow underground, natural selection will shrink your eyes and give you large digging claws, be you placental or marsupial. But you'll still retain some characteristic traits of your ancestors.

Cacti and euphorbs also show convergent traits. The ancestor of euphorbs colonized the Old World, and that of cacti the Americas. Those species that happened to wind up in the desert evolved similar adaptations: if you're a plant in a dry climate, you're better off being tough and leafless, with a fat stem to store water. So natural selection molded euphorbs and cacti into similar forms.

Convergent evolution demonstrates three parts of evolutionary theory working together: common ancestry, speciation, and natural selection. Common ancestry accounts for why Australian marsupials share some features (females have two vaginas and a double uterus, for example), while placental mammals share different features (e.g., a long-lasting placenta). Speciation is the process by which each common ancestor gives rise to many different descendants. And natural selection makes each species well adapted to its environment. Put these together, add in the fact that distant areas of the world can have similar habitats, and you get convergent evolution—and a simple explanation of a major biogeographic pattern.

As for how the marsupials got to Australia, that's part of another evolutionary tale, and one that leads to a testable prediction. The earliest marsupial fossils, around 80 million years old, are found not in Australia but in North America. As marsupials evolved, they spread southward, reaching what is now the tip of South America about 40 million years ago. Marsupials made it to Australia roughly 10 million years later, where they began diversi-fying into the two-hundred-odd species that live there today.

But how could they cross the South Atlantic? The answer is that it didn't yet exist. At the time of the marsupial invasion, South America and Austra-lia were joined as part of the southern supercontinent of Gondwana. This landmass had already begun to break apart, unzipping to form the Atlantic Ocean, but the tip of South America was still connected to what is now Ant-arctica, which in turn was connected to what is now Australia (see figure 21). Since marsupials had to go overland from South America to Australia, they must have passed through Antarctica. So we can predict this: there should be fossil marsupials on Antarctica dating somewhere between 30 and 40 million years ago.

This hypothesis was strong enough to drive scientists to Antarctica, looking for marsupial fossils. And, sure enough, they found them: more than a dozen species of marsupials (recognized by their distinctive teeth and jaws) unearthed on Seymour Island, off the Antarctic Peninsula. This area is right on the ancient ice-free pathway between South America and Antarctica. And the fossils are just the right age: 35 to 40 million years old. After a find in 1982, the polar paleontologist William Zinsmeister was exultant: "For years and years people thought marsupials had to be there. This ties together all the suppositions made about Antarctica. The things we found are what you'd expect we would have."

What about the many cases of similar (but not identical) species that live in similar habitats but on different continents? The red deer lives in north-ern Europe, but the elk, which resembles it closely, lives in North America. Tongueless aquatic frogs of the family Pipidae occur in two widely separated places: eastern South America and subtropical Africa. And we already learned about the similar flora of eastern Asia and eastern North America. These observations *would* be puzzling to evolutionists if the continents were always in their present locations. There would have been no way for an ancestral magnolia to disperse from China to Alabama, for freshwater frogs to cross the ocean between Africa and South America, or for an ancestral deer to get from Europe to North America. But we now know precisely how this dispersal did happen: by the existence of ancient land connections between the continents. (These are different from the huge land bridges imagined by early biogeographers.) Asia and North America were once well connected via the Bering land bridge, over which plants and mammals (including humans) colonized North America. And South America and Africa were once part of Gondwana.

As organisms disperse and successfully colonize a new area, they often evolve. And this leads to another prediction that we made in chapter 1. If evolution happened, species living in one area should be the descendants of earlier species that lived in the same place. So if we dig into shallow layers of rocks in a given area, we should find fossils that resemble the organisms treading that ground today.

And this is also the case. Where can we dig up fossil kangaroos that most closely resemble living kangaroos? In Australia. Then there are the armadillos of the New World. Armadillos are unique among mammals in having a carapace of bony armor—*armadillo* in Spanish means "little armored one." They live only in North, Central, and South America. Where do we find fossils resembling them? In the Americas, the home of the *glyptodonts*, armored plant-eating mammals that look just like overgrown armadillos. Some of these ancient armadillos were the size of Volkswagen Beetles, weighed a ton, were covered with two-inch-thick armor, and sported spiky balls on tails wielded like a mace. Creationism is hard-pressed to explain these patterns: to do so, it would have to propose that there were an endless number of successive extinctions and creations all over the world, and that each set of newly created species were made to resemble older ones that lived in the same place. We've come a long way from Noah's Ark.

The co-occurrence of fossil ancestors and descendants leads to one of the most famous predictions in the history of evolutionary biology—Darwin's hypothesis, in *The Descent of Man* (1871), that humans evolved in Africa:

> We are naturally led to enquire, where was the birthplace of man at that stage of descent when our progenitors diverged from the Catarrhine stock [Old World monkeys and apes]? The fact that they belonged to this stock clearly shews that they inhabited the Old World; but not Australia nor any oceanic island, as we may infer from the laws of geograph-

ical distribution. In each great region of the world the living mammals are closely related to the extinct species of the same region. It is therefore probable that Africa was formerly inhabited by extinct apes closely allied to the gorilla and chimpanzee; and as these two species are now man's nearest allies, it is somewhat more probable that our early progenitors lived on the African continent than elsewhere.

At the time Darwin made this prediction, no one had seen any fossils of early humans. As we'll see in chapter 8, they were first found in 1924 in—you guessed it—Africa. The profusion of ape-human transitional fossils unearthed since then, with the earliest ones always African, leaves no doubt that Darwin's prediction was right.

Biogeography not only makes predictions, but solves puzzles. Here's one involving glaciers and fossil trees. Geologists have known for a long time that all the southern continents and subcontinents experienced a massive period of glaciation during the Permian period, about 290 million years ago. We know this because as glaciers move, the rocks and pebbles they carry with them make scratches in the underlying rock. The direction of these scratches tells us which way the glaciers were moving.

Looking at the scratches in Permian rocks of southern lands, you see strange patterns. The glaciers seem to have arisen in areas like Central Africa that are now very warm and, even more confusingly, appear to have moved from the seas onto the continents. (See the direction of the arrows in figure 21.) Now, this is quite impossible: glaciers can form only in persistently cold climates on dry land, when repeated snows become compacted into ice that begins to move under its own weight. So how do we explain these seemingly willy-nilly patterns of glacial striation, and the apparent origin of glaciers in the sea?

And there is one more part of this puzzle, involving the distribution not of scratches but of fossil trees—species in the genus *Glossopteris*. These were conifers that had tongue-shaped leaves instead of needles (*glossa* is Greek for "tongue"). *Glossopteris* was one of the dominant plants of the Permian flora. For several reasons botanists believe that they were deciduous (shedding their leaves each fall and regrowing them in spring): they show growth

FIGURE 21. Continental drift explains the evolutionary biogeography of the ancient tree *Glossopteris*. Top: the present-day distribution of *Glossopteris* fossils (shaded) is broken up into pieces distributed among the continents, making it hard to understand. The patterns of glacial scratches in the rocks are likewise mysterious (arrows). Bottom: the distribution of *Glossopteris* during the Permian period, when the continents were joined in a supercontinent. This pattern makes sense because the trees surrounded the Permian south pole in an area of temperate climate. And the glacial scratches we see today also make sense, as they all pointed away from the Permian south pole.

rings, indicating seasonal cycles, and specialized features indicating that leaves were programmed to separate from the tree. These, and other traits, suggest that *Glossopteris* lived in temperate areas with cold winters.

When you plot the distribution of *Glossopteris* fossils in the Southern Hemisphere—the only region in which they are found (figure 21)—they form a strange pattern, scattered in swatches across the southern continents. The pattern can't be explained by overseas dispersal, because *Glossopteris* had large, heavy seeds that almost certainly couldn't float. Could this be evidence for creation of the plant on different continents? Not so fast.

Both of these puzzles are solved when we realize where the present-day southern continents really were during the late Permian (figure 21): joined like a jigsaw puzzle into Gondwana. And when you put together the pieces, the position of glacial scratches and the distribution of trees suddenly make sense. The scratches now all point away from the center of Antarctica, which happens to be the part of Gondwana that passed over the South Pole during the Permian. The snows would have produced extensive glaciers spreading away from this location, making scratches in exactly the observed directions. And when the distribution of *Glossopteris* trees is superimposed on a map of Gondwana, the pattern is no longer chaotic: the patches connect up, running like a ring around the edges of the glaciers. These are precisely the cool locations where temperate deciduous trees would be found.

It isn't the trees that migrated from continent to distant continent, then: it is the continents themselves that moved, carrying the trees with them. These conundrums make sense in light of evolution, while creationism is at a loss to explain either the pattern of glacial scratches or the peculiarly disjunct distribution of *Glossopteris*.

There's a poignant footnote to this story. When Robert Scott's party was found in 1912, frozen to death after their unsuccessful attempt to be the first at the South Pole (the Norwegian Roald Amundsen got there a bit earlier), thirty-five pounds of *Glossopteris* fossils lay next to their bodies. Despite having discarded much of their equipment in a desperate attempt to stay alive, the party physically dragged these heavy rocks on hand sledges, doubtlessly realizing their scientific value. They were the first specimens of *Glossopteris* found in Antarctica.

The evidence for evolution from patterns of life on continents is strong, but that from life on islands is, as we shall see, even stronger.

Islands

REALIZING THAT THE DISTRIBUTION of species on islands provides conclusive proof of evolution was one of the greatest pieces of sleuthing in the history of biology. This too was the work of Darwin, whose ideas still loom mightily over the field of biogeography. In chapter 12 of *The Origin*, Darwin reports fact after fact, painstakingly gathered over years of observation and correspondence, building his case like a brilliant lawyer. When I teach the evidence for evolution to my students, this is my favorite lecture. It's an hourlong mystery story, an accumulation of seemingly disparate data that in the end resolves into an airtight case for evolution.

But before we get to the evidence, we need to distinguish two types of islands. The first are *continental islands*: those islands once connected to a continent but later separated either by rising sea levels that flooded former land bridges or by moving continental plates. These islands include, among many others, the British Isles, Japan, Sri Lanka, Tasmania, and Madagascar. Some are old (Madagascar parted from Africa about 160 million years ago), others much younger (Great Britain separated from Europe around 300,000 years ago, probably during a catastrophic flood spilling from a large, dammed-up lake to the north). *Oceanic islands*, on the other hand, are those that were never connected to a continent; they arose from the seafloor, initially bereft of life, as growing volcanoes or coral reefs. These include the Hawaiian Islands, the Galápagos archipelago, St. Helena, and the Juan Fernández group described at the beginning of this chapter.

The "island" argument for evolution starts with the following observation: oceanic islands are missing many types of native species that we see on both continents and continental islands. Take Hawaii, a tropical archipelago whose islands occupy about 6,400 square miles, only slightly smaller than the state of Massachusetts. While the islands are well stocked with native birds, plants, and insects, they completely lack native freshwater fish, amphibians, reptiles, and land mammals. Napoleon's island of St. Helena and the archipelago of Juan Fernández lack these same groups, but still have plenty of endemic plants, birds, and insects. The Galápagos Islands do have a few native reptiles (land and marine iguanas, as well as the famous giant tortoises), but they too are missing native mammals, amphibians, and freshwater fish. Over and over again, on the oceanic islands that dot the Pacific, the South Atlantic, and the Indian Ocean, one sees a pattern of missing groups—more to the point, the *same* missing groups.

At first blush, these absences seem bizarre. If you look at even a very small patch of a tropical continent or a continental island, say in Peru, New Guinea, or Japan, you'll find plenty of native fish, amphibians, reptiles, and mammals.

As Darwin noted, this disparity is hard to explain under a creationist scenario: "He who admits the doctrine of creation of each separate species, will have to admit, that a sufficient number of the best adapted plants and animals have not been created on oceanic islands." But how do we know that mammals, amphibians, freshwater fish, and reptiles really are *suited* to oceanic islands? Maybe the creator didn't put them there because they wouldn't do well. One obvious reply is that *continental* islands do have these animals, so why would a creator put different types of animals on continental versus oceanic islands? How the island was formed shouldn't make a difference. But Darwin ends the sentence given above with an even better response: ". . . for man has unintentionally stocked them from various sources far more fully and perfectly than nature."

In other words, mammals, amphibians, freshwater fish, and reptiles often do very well when humans introduce them to oceanic islands. In fact, they often take over, wiping out native species. Introduced pigs and goats have overrun Hawaii, making meals of native plants. Introduced rats and mongooses have destroyed or endangered many of Hawaii's spectacular birds. The cane toad, a huge poisonous amphibian native to tropical America, was introduced to Hawaii in 1932 to control beetles on sugarcane. The toads are now a pest, breeding prolifically and killing cats and dogs who mistake them for a meal. The Galápagos Islands have no native amphibians, but an Ecuadorian tree frog, introduced in 1998, has established itself on three islands. On São Tomé, the volcanic island off the west coast of Africa where I collect fruit flies for my own research, black cobras have been introduced—perhaps accidentally—from the African mainland. They have done so well that we simply won't work in certain areas of the island, as the cobras are so numerous that we can encounter several dozen of these deadly and aggressive snakes in a single day. Land mammals do well on islands too—introduced goats helped Alexander Selkirk stay alive on Más a Tierra, and they also thrive on St. Helena. Throughout the world the story is the same: humans introduce species to oceanic islands where they did not exist, and these species displace or destroy native forms. So much for the argument that oceanic islands are somehow unsuitable for mammals, amphibians, reptiles, and fish.

The next step of the argument is this: although oceanic islands lack many basic kinds of animals, the types that *are* found there are often present in profusion, comprising many similar species. Take the Galápagos. Among its thirteen islands there are twenty-eight species of birds found nowhere else. And of these twenty-eight, fourteen belong to a single group of closely related birds: the famous Galápagos finches. No continent or continental island has a bird fauna so heavily dominated by finches. Yet despite their shared finchlike traits, the Galápagos group is ecologically quite diverse, with different species specializing on foods as different as insects, seeds, and the eggs of other species. The "woodpecker finch" is one of those rare species that uses tools—in this case a cactus spine or twig to pry insects from trees. Woodpecker finches fill the ecological role of woodpeckers, which don't live in the Galápagos. And there's even a "vampire finch" that pecks wounds on the rear ends of seabirds and then laps up the blood.

Hawaii has an even more spectacular radiation of birds, the honeycreepers. When the Polynesians arrived in Hawaii about fifteen hundred years ago, they found about 140 species of native birds (we know this from studies of bird "subfossils": bones preserved in ancient waste dumps and lava tubes). Around sixty of these species—nearly half the bird fauna—were honeycreepers, all descended from a single ancestral finch that arrived on the islands about four million years ago. Sadly, only twenty species of honeycreeper remain, all of them endangered. The rest were destroyed by hunting, habitat loss, and human-introduced predators like rats and mongooses. But even the few remaining honeycreepers show a fantastic diversity of ecological roles, as shown in figure 22. The bill of a bird can tell us a lot about its diet. Some species have curved bills for sipping nectar from flowers, others stout, parrotlike bills for cracking hard seeds or crushing twigs, still others thin pointy bills for picking insects from foliage, and some even have hooked bills for prying insects from trees, filling the role of a woodpecker. As on the Galápagos, we see one group that is overrepresented, with species filling niches occupied by very different species on continents or continental islands.

FIGURE 22. An adaptive radiation: some related species of Hawaiian honeycreepers that evolved after their finchlike ancestor colonized the islands. Each finch has a bill that enables it to use different food. The 'i'iwi's slender bill helps it sip nectar from long tubular flowers, the 'akepa has a slightly crossed bill that allows it to pry open buds to search for insects and spiders, the Maui parrotbill has a massive bill for prying up bark and splitting twigs to find beetle larvae, and the palila's short but strong bill helps it open seed pods and extract the seeds.

Oceanic islands also harbor radiations of plants and insects. St. Helena, though lacking many groups of insects, is home to dozens of species of small, flightless beetles, especially wood weevils. On Hawaii, the group that I study—fruit flies of the genus *Drosophila*—is positively luxuriant. Although the Hawaiian Islands make up only 0.004 percent of earth's land, they contain nearly half of the world's two thousand species of *Drosophila*. And then there are the remarkable radiations of plants in the sunflower family on the Juan Fernández archipelago and St. Helena, some of which have become small woody trees. Only on oceanic islands can small flowering plants, freed from competition with larger shrubs and trees, evolve into trees themselves.

So far we've learned two sets of facts about oceanic islands: they are missing many groups of species that live on continents and continental islands, and yet the groups that *are* found on oceanic islands are replete with many similar species. Together these observations show that, compared to other areas of the world, life on oceanic islands is *unbalanced*. Any theory of biogeography worth its salt has to explain this contrast.

But there's something more here too. Take a look at the following list of the groups that are often native to oceanic islands and those that are usually missing (Juan Fernández is just one group of islands that conforms to the list):

NATIVE	MISSING
Plants	Land mammals
Birds	Reptiles
Insects and other arthropods (e.g., spiders)	Amphibians
	Freshwater fish

What's the difference between the two columns? A moment's thought gives the answer. Species in the first column can colonize an oceanic island through long-distance dispersal; species in the second column lack this ability. Birds are capable of flying great distances over the sea, carrying with them not only their own eggs but also seeds of plants they've eaten (which can germinate from their droppings), parasites in their feathers, and small organisms sticking to mud on their feet. Plants can get to islands as seeds, floating across expanses of sea. Seeds with barbs or sticky coverings can hitchhike to islands on the feathers of birds. The light spores of ferns, fungi, and mosses can be carried huge distances by the wind. Insects too can fly to islands or be taken by winds.

In contrast, animals in the second column have great difficulty crossing expanses of sea. Land mammals and reptiles are heavy and can't swim very far. And most amphibians and freshwater fish simply can't survive in salt water.

So the kinds of species that we find on oceanic islands are precisely those that can arrive across the sea from distant lands. But what is the evidence that they do so? Every ornithologist knows of occasional "visitor" birds found thousands of miles from their normal habitat, the victim of winds or faulty navigation. Some birds have even established breeding colonies on oceanic islands in historical times. The purple gallinule, long an occasional visitor to the remote island of Tristan da Cunha in the South Atlantic, finally started breeding there in the 1950s.

Darwin himself did some simple yet elegant experiments showing that seeds from some plant species could still germinate after prolonged immersion in seawater. Seeds from the West Indies have been found on the distant shores of Scotland, obviously carried by the Gulf Stream, and "drift seeds" from continents or other islands are also found on the shores of South Pacific islands. Caged birds can retain plant seeds in their digestive tracts for a week or more, showing the likelihood of long-distance transport. And there have been many successful attempts to sample insects in the air using traps attached to airplanes or ships far from land. Among the species collected have been locusts, moths, butterflies, flies, aphids, and beetles. Charles Lindbergh, on a 1933 trip across the Atlantic, exposed glass microscope slides to the air, capturing numerous microorganisms and insect parts. Many spiders disperse as juveniles by "ballooning" with parachutes of silk; these wanderers have been found several hundred miles from land.

Animals and plants can also hitch rides to islands on "rafts"—logs or masses of vegetation that float away from continents, usually from the mouths of rivers. In 1995 one of these large rafts, probably blown by a hurricane, deposited a cargo of fifteen green iguanas on the Caribbean island of Anguilla, where they had not previously existed, from a source two hundred miles away. Logs of Douglas fir from North America have been found on Hawaii, and logs from South America have made it to Tasmania. Rafting like this explains the presence of the occasional endemic reptile on oceanic islands, such as the Galápagos iguanas and tortoises.

Further, when you look at the type of insects and plants native to oceanic islands, they are from groups that are the best colonizers. Most of the insects are small, precisely those that would be easily picked up by wind. Compared to weedy plants, trees are relatively rare on oceanic islands, almost certainly because many trees have heavy seeds that neither float nor are eaten by birds. (The coconut palm, with its large, buoyant seeds, is a notable exception, occurring on almost all Pacific and Indian Ocean islands.) The relative rarity of trees, in fact, explains why many plants that are short weeds on continents have evolved into woody treelike forms on islands.

Terrestrial mammals are not good colonizers, and that's why oceanic islands lack them. But they don't lack *all* mammals. This brings up two exceptions that prove the rule. The first was noted by Darwin:

Although terrestrial mammals do not occur on oceanic islands, aërial mammals do occur on almost every island. New Zealand possesses two bats found nowhere else in the world: Norfolk Island, the Viti Archipelago, the Bonin Islands, the Caroline and Marianne [Mariana] Archipelagoes, and Mauritius, all possess their peculiar bats. Why, it may be asked, has the supposed creative force produced bats and no other mammals on remote islands? On my view this question can easily be answered; for no terrestrial mammal can be transported across a wide space of sea, but bats can fly across.

And there are also *aquatic* mammals on islands. Hawaii has one, the endemic monk seal, and the Juan Fernández group has a native fur seal. If native mammals on oceanic islands were not created, but descended from colonists, you'd predict that those ancestral colonists must have been able to fly or swim.

Now, it's clear that long-distance dispersal of a given species to a distant island can't be a frequent event. The chance that an insect or bird could not only traverse vast expanses of sea to land on an island, but also establish a breeding population once it got there (this requires either an already fertilized female or at least two individuals of opposite sex), must be very low. And if dispersal were common, life on oceanic islands would be quite similar to that of continents and continental islands. Nevertheless, most oceanic islands have been around for millions of years, long enough to permit some colonization. As the zoologist George Gaylord Simpson remarked, "Any event that is not absolutely impossible . . . becomes probable if enough time passes." To take a hypothetical example, suppose that a given species has only one chance in a million of colonizing an island each year. It's easy to show that after a million years have passed, there is a large probability that the island would have been colonized at least once: 63 percent, to be exact.

One final observation closes the chain of logic that secures the case for evolution on islands. And that is this: with few exceptions, the animals and plants on oceanic islands are most similar to species found on the nearest mainland. This is true, for example, of the Galápagos Islands, whose species resemble those from the west coast of South America. The similarity can't be explained by the argument that the islands and South America have similar habitats for divinely created species, because the Galápagos are dry, treeless, and volcanic—quite different from the lush tropics that dominate the Americas. Darwin was especially eloquent on this point:

> The naturalist, looking at the inhabitants of these volcanic islands in the Pacific, distant several hundred miles from the continent, feels that he is standing on American land. Why should this be so? Why should the species which are supposed to have been created in the Galápagos Archipelago, and nowhere else, bear so plainly the stamp of affinity to those created in America? There is nothing in the conditions of life, in the geological nature of the islands, in their height or climate, or in the proportions in which the several classes are associated together, which closely resemble the conditions of the South American coast: in fact, there is a considerable dissimilarity in all these respects.... Facts such as these admit of no sort of explanation on the ordinary view of independent creation; whereas on the view here maintained, it is obvious that the Galápagos Islands would be likely to receive colonists from America, whether by occasional means of transport or (though I do not believe in this doctrine) by formerly continuous land . . . such colonists would be liable to modification,—the principle of inheritance still betraying their original birthplace.

What is true of the Galápagos is also true of other oceanic islands. The closest relatives of the endemic plants and animals on Juan Fernández come from the temperate forests of southern South America, the closest continent. Most of the species on Hawaii are similar (but not identical) to those from the nearby Indo-Pacific region—Indonesia, New Guinea, Fiji, Samoa, and Tahiti—or from the Americas. Now, given the vagaries of winds and the direction of ocean currents, we don't expect *every* island colonist to come from the closest source. Four percent of Hawaiian plant species, for example, have their closest relatives in Siberia or Alaska. Still, the similarity of island species to those on the nearest mainland demands explanation.

To sum up, oceanic islands have features that distinguish them from either continents or continental islands. Oceanic islands have unbalanced biotas—

they are missing major groups of organisms, and the same ones are missing on different islands. But the types of organisms that *are* there often comprise many similar species—a *radiation*—and they are the types of species, like birds and insects, that can disperse most easily over large stretches of ocean. And the species most similar to those inhabiting oceanic islands are usually found on the nearest mainland, even though their habitats are different.

How do these observations fit together? They make sense under a simple evolutionary explanation: the inhabitants of oceanic islands descended from earlier species that colonized the islands, usually from nearby continents, in rare events of long-distance dispersal. Once there, accidental colonists were able to form many species because oceanic islands offer lots of empty habitats that lack competitors and predators. This explains why speciation and natural selection go wild on islands, producing "adaptive radiations" like that of the Hawaiian honeycreepers. Everything fits together if you add accidental dispersal, which is known to occur, to the Darwinian processes of selection, evolution, common ancestry, and speciation. In short, oceanic islands demonstrate every tenet of evolutionary theory.

It's important to remember that these patterns do not generally hold for *continental* islands (we'll come to an exception in a second), which share species with the continents to which they once were joined. The plants and animals of Great Britain, for example, form a much more balanced ecosystem, having species largely identical to those of mainland Europe. Unlike oceanic islands, continental islands were cut adrift with most of their species already in place.

Now try to think of a theory that explains the patterns we've discussed by invoking the special creation of species on oceanic islands and continents. Why would a creator happen to leave amphibians, mammals, fish, and reptiles off oceanic islands, but not continental ones? Why did a creator produce radiations of similar species on oceanic islands, but not continental ones? And why were species on oceanic islands created to resemble those from the nearest mainland? There are no good answers—unless, of course, you presume that the goal of a creator was to make species *look* as though they evolved on islands. Nobody is keen to embrace that answer, which explains why creationists simply shy away from island biogeography.

We can now make one final prediction. *Very old* continental islands, which separated from the mainland eons ago, should show evolutionary patterns that fall between those of young continental islands and oceanic islands. Old continental islands such as Madagascar and New Zealand, cut off from their continents 160 million and 85 million years ago, respectively, will have been isolated before many groups like primates and modern plants had evolved. Once these islands parted from the mainland, some of their ecological niches remained unfilled. This opens the door for some later-evolving species to successfully colonize and establish themselves. We can predict, then, that these old continental islands should have a *somewhat* unbalanced flora and fauna, showing some of the biogeographic peculiarities of true oceanic islands.

And indeed, this is just what we find. Madagascar is famous for its unusual fauna and flora, including many native plants and, of course, its unique lemurs—the most primitive of the primates—whose ancestors, after arriving in Madagascar some 60 million years ago, radiated into more than seventy-five endemic species. New Zealand too has many natives, the most well-known being flightless birds: the giant moa, a thirteen-foot-tall monster hunted to extinction by about 1500, the kiwi, and that fat, ground-dwelling parrot, the kakapo. New Zealand also shows some of the "imbalance" of oceanic islands: it has only a few endemic reptiles, only one species of amphibian, and two native mammals, both bats (though a small fossil mammal was recently found). It too had a radiation—there were eleven species of moas, all now gone. And, like oceanic islands, the species on Madagascar and New Zealand are related to those found on the nearest mainland: Africa and Australia, respectively.

Envoi

THE MAIN LESSON OF BIOGEOGRAPHY is that only evolution can explain the diversity of life on continents and islands. But there is another lesson as well: the distribution of life on earth reflects a blend of chance and lawfulness. Chance, because the dispersal of animals and plants depends on unpredictable vagaries such as winds, currents, and the opportunity to colonize. If the first finches had not arrived in the Galápagos or Hawaii, we might see very different birds there today. If an ancestral lemurlike creature hadn't made it to Madagascar, that island (and likely the earth) would have no lemurs. Time and chance alone determine who gets marooned; one might call this the "Robinson Crusoe effect." But there is also lawfulness. Evolutionary theory predicts that many animals and plants arriving in new and unoccupied habitats will evolve to thrive there, and will form new species, filling up ecological niches. And they will usually find their relatives on the nearest island or mainland. This is what we see, over and over again. One cannot understand evolution without grasping its unique interaction between chance and lawfulness—an interaction that, as we'll see in the next chapter, is critically important in understanding the idea of natural selection.

But the lessons of biogeography go further, into the realm of biological conservation. Island plants and animals adapt to their environments isolated from species that live elsewhere, their potential competitors, predators, and parasites. Because species on islands don't experience the diversity of life found on continents, they aren't good at coexisting with others. Island ecosystems, then, are fragile things, easily ravaged by foreign invaders who can destroy habitats and species. The worst of these are humans, who not only chop down forests and hunt, but also bring with them an entourage of destructive prickly pears, sheep, goats, rats, and toads. Many of the unique species on oceanic islands are already gone, victims of human activity, and we can confidently (and sadly) predict that many more will vanish soon. In our lifetime we may see the last of the Hawaiian honeycreepers, the extinction of New Zealand's kakapos and kiwis, the decimation of the lemurs, and the loss of many rare plants that, while perhaps less charismatic, are no less interesting. Each species represents millions of years of evolution and, once gone, can never be brought back. And each is a book containing unique stories about the past. Losing any of them means losing part of life's history.

Chapter 5

The Engine of Evolution

What but the wolf's tooth whittled so fine
The fleet limbs of the antelope?
What but fear winged the birds, and hunger
Jewelled with such eyes the great goshawk's head?

—Robinson Jeffers, "The Bloody Sire"

ne of the marvels of evolution is the Asian giant hornet, a predatory wasp especially common in Japan. It's hard to imagine a more frightening insect. The world's largest hornet, it's as long as your thumb, with a two-inch body bedecked with menacing orange and black stripes. It's armed with fearsome jaws to clasp and kill its insect prey, and a quarter-inch stinger that proves lethal to several dozen Asians a year. And with a three-inch wingspan, it can fly twenty-five miles per hour (far faster than you can run), and can cover sixty miles in a single day.

This hornet is not only ferocious, but voracious. Its young larval grubs are fat, insatiable eating machines, who insistently rap their heads against the hive to signal their hunger for meat. To satisfy their relentless demands for food, adult hornets raid the nests of social bees and wasps.

One of the hornet's prime victims is the introduced European honeybee. The raid on a honeybee nest involves a merciless mass slaughter that has few parallels in nature. It starts when a lone hornet scout finds a nest. With its abdomen, the scout marks the nest for doom, placing a drop of pheromone near the entrance of the bee colony. Alerted by this mark, the scout's nestmates descend on the spot, a group of twenty or thirty hornets arrayed against a colony of up to thirty thousand honeybees.

But it's no contest. Wading into the hive with jaws slashing, the hornets decapitate the bees one by one. With each hornet making bee heads roll at a rate of forty per minute, the battle is over in a few hours: every bee is dead, and body parts litter the hive. Then the hornets stock their larder. Over the next week, they systematically ravage the nest, eating honey and carrying the helpless bee grubs back to their own nests, where they are promptly deposited into the gaping mouths of the hornets' own ravenous offspring.

This is "Nature red in tooth and claw," as the poet Tennyson described.[23] The hornets are fearsome hunting machines, and the introduced bees are defenseless. But there are bees that *can* fight off the giant hornet: honeybees that are native to Japan. And their defense is stunning—another marvel of adaptive behavior. When the hornet scout first arrives at their hive, the honeybees near the entrance rush into the hive, calling nestmates to arms while luring the hornet inside. In the meantime, hundreds of worker bees assemble inside the entrance. Once the hornet is inside, it is mobbed and covered by a tight ball of bees. Vibrating their abdomens, the bees quickly raise the temperature inside the ball to about 117 degrees Fahrenheit. Bees can survive this temperature, but the hornet cannot. In twenty minutes the hornet scout is *cooked to death*, and—usually—the nest is saved. I can't think of another case (save the Spanish Inquisition) in which animals kill their enemies by roasting them.[24]

There are several evolutionary lessons in this twisted tale. The most obvious is that the hornet is marvelously adapted to kill—it looks as though it was *designed* for mass slaughter. Moreover, many traits work together to make the wasp a killing machine. They include body form (large size, stinger, deadly jaws, big wings), chemicals (marking pheromones and deadly venom in the sting), and behavior (rapid flight, coordinated attacks on bee nests, and the larval "I am hungry" behavior that prompts the hornet attacks). And then there is the defense of the native honeybees—the coordinated swarming and subsequent roasting of their enemy—certainly an evolved response to repeated attacks by hornets. (Remember, this behavior is genetically encoded in a brain smaller than a pencil point.)

On the other hand, the recently introduced European honeybees are virtually defenseless against the hornet. This is exactly what we would expect, for those bees evolved in an area lacking giant predatory hornets, and therefore natural selection did not build a defense. We can predict, though, that if the hornets are sufficiently strong predators, the European bees will either die out (unless they are reintroduced), or will find their own evolutionary response to the hornets—and not necessarily the same one as the native bees.

Some adaptations entail even more sinister tactics. One of them involves a roundworm that parasitizes a species of Central American ant. When infected, an ant undergoes a radical change in both behavior and appearance. First, its normally black abdomen turns a bright red. The ant then becomes sluggish and raises its abdomen straight up in the air, like a taunting red flag. The thin junction between the abdomen and the thorax becomes flimsy and weakened. And an infected ant no longer produces alarm pheromones when attacked, so it can't alert its nestmates.

All of these changes are caused by the genes of the parasitic worm as an ingenious ploy to reproduce themselves. The worm alters the appearance and behavior of the ant, which advertises itself to birds as a scrumptious berry, and in so doing brings on its own death. The berrylike red abdomen of the ant is raised up for all birds to see, and easily plucked because of the ant's sluggishness and the weakened junction between the abdomen and the rest of the body. And birds gobble up these abdomens, which are full of worm eggs. The birds then pass the eggs in their droppings, which ants scavenge and take back to their nests to feed the larvae. The worm eggs hatch within the ant larva and grow. When the ant larva becomes a pupa, the worms migrate to the ant's abdomen and mate, producing more eggs. And so the cycle begins again.

It is staggering adaptations like this—the many ways that parasites control their carriers, just to pass on the parasites' genes—that gets an evolutionist's juices flowing.[25] Natural selection, acting on a simple worm, has caused it to commandeer its host and change the host's appearance, behavior, and structure, turning it into a tempting mock fruit.[26]

The list of adaptations like this is endless. There are adaptations in which animals look like plants, camouflaging themselves among the vegetation to hide from enemies. Some katydids, for example, look almost exactly like leaves, complete with leaflike patterns and even "rotten spots" resembling the holes in leaves. The mimicry is so precise that you'd have trouble spotting the insects in a small cage full of vegetation, much less in the wild.

And we have the converse: plants that look like animals. Some species of orchids have flowers that superficially resemble bees and wasps, complete with fake eyespots and petals shaped like wings. The resemblance is good enough to fool many shortsighted male insects, who alight on the flower and try to mate with it. While this is happening, the pollen sacs of the orchid attach to the insect's head. When the frustrated insect departs without consummating his passion, he unwittingly carries the pollen to the next orchid, fertilizing it during the next fruitless "pseudocopulation." Natural selection has molded the orchid into a bogus insect because genes that attract pollinators in this way are more likely to be passed on to the next generation. Some orchids further seduce their pollinators by producing chemicals that smell like the sex pheromones of bees.

Finding food, like finding a mate, can involve complex adaptations. The pileated woodpecker, a crested bird that is the largest woodpecker in North America, makes its living by hammering holes into trees and plucking insects like ants and beetles from the wood. Besides its superb ability to detect prey beneath the bark (probably by hearing or feeling their movements—we're not sure), the woodpecker has a whole group of traits that help it hunt and hammer. Perhaps the most remarkable is its ridiculously long tongue.[27] The base of the tongue attaches to the jawbone, and then the tongue runs up through one nostril, completely over and around the back of the head, and finally reenters the beak from below. Most of the time the tongue is retracted, but it can be extended deep into a tree to probe for ants and beetles. It is pointed and covered with sticky saliva to help extract those tasty insects from holes. Pileated woodpeckers also use their bills to excavate large nest cavities and to drum on trees, attracting mates and defending their territories.

The woodpecker is a biological jackhammer. This poses a problem: how can a delicate creature drill through hard wood without hurting itself? (Think of the force it takes to drive a nail into a plank.) The punishment that a pileated woodpecker's skull takes is astounding—the bird can strike up to fifteen blows *per second* when it's "drumming" for communication, each blow generating a force equivalent to banging your head into a wall at sixteen miles per hour. This is a speed that can crumple your car. There is a real danger of the woodpecker injuring its brain, or even having its eyes pop out of its skull under the extreme force.

To prevent brain damage, the woodpecker's skull is specially shaped and reinforced with extra bone. The beak rests on a cushion of cartilage, and the muscles around the beak contract an instant before each impact to divert the force of the blow away from the brain and into the reinforced base of the skull. During each strike, the bird's eyelids close to keep its eyes from popping out. There is also a fan of delicate feathers covering the nostrils so that the bird doesn't inhale sawdust or wood chips when hammering. It uses a set of very stiff tail feathers to prop itself against the tree, and has an X-shaped, four-toed foot (two forward, two back) to securely grip the trunk.

Everywhere we look in nature, we see animals that *seem* beautifully designed to fit their environment, whether that environment be the physical circumstances of life, like temperature and humidity, or the other organisms—competitors, predators, and prey—that every species must deal with. It is no surprise that early naturalists believed that animals were the product of celestial design, created by God to do their jobs.

Darwin dispelled this notion in *The Origin*. In a single chapter, he completely replaced centuries of certainty about divine design with the notion of a mindless, materialistic process—natural selection—that could accomplish the same result. It is hard to overestimate the effect that this insight had not only on biology, but on people's worldview. Many have not yet recovered from the shock, and the idea of natural selection still arouses fierce and irrational opposition.

But natural selection posed a number of problems for biology as well. What is the evidence that it operates in nature? Can it really explain adaptations, including complex ones? Darwin relied largely on analogy to make his case: the well-known success of breeders in transforming animals and plants into organisms suitable for food, pets, and decoration. But at the time, he had little direct evidence for selection acting in natural populations. And because, as he proposed, selection was extremely slow, altering populations over thousands or millions of years, it would be hard to observe it acting during a single human lifetime.

Fortunately, thanks to the labors of field and laboratory biologists, we now have this evidence—lots of it. Natural selection, we find, is everywhere, scrutinizing individuals, culling the unfit and promoting the genes of the fitter. It can create intricate adaptations, sometimes in surprisingly little time.

Natural selection is the most misunderstood part of Darwinism. To see how it works, let's look at a simple adaptation: coat color in wild mice. Normal-colored, or "oldfield," mice (*Peromyscus polionotus*) have brown coats and burrow in dark soils. But on the pale sand dunes of Florida's Gulf Coast lives a light-colored race of the same species called "beach mice": these are nearly all white with only a faint brown stripe down the back. This pale color is an adaptation to camouflage the mice from predators, like hawks, owls, and herons, that hunt among the white dunes. How do we *know* this is an adaptation? A simple (albeit slightly gruesome) experiment by Donald Kaufman at Kansas State University showed that mice survive better when their fur matches the color of the soil in which they live. Kaufman built large outdoor enclosures, some with light soil and others with dark soil. In each cage he put equal numbers of mice with dark and light coat colors. He then released a very hungry owl into each cage, returning later to see which mice survived. As expected, mice whose coats contrasted most conspicuously with the soil were picked off more readily, showing that camouflaged mice really do survive better. This experiment also explains a general correlation that we see in nature: darker soils harbor darker mice.

Since white color is unique among beach mice, they presumably evolved from brown mainland mice, possibly as recently as six thousand years ago, when the barrier islands and their white dunes were first isolated from the mainland. This is where selection comes in. Oldfield mice vary in coat color, and among those that invaded the light beach sand, individuals with a lighter coat would have a higher chance of surviving than darker mice, who are easily spotted by predators. We also know that there is a genetic difference between light and dark mice: beach mice carry the "light" forms of several pigmentation genes that together give them their light-colored coats. Darker oldfield mice have the "dark" alternative form of the same genes. Over time, due to the differential predation, lighter mice would have left more copies of their light genes (they have a higher chance of surviving to reproduce) and, as this process continued for generation after generation, the population of beach mice would have evolved from dark to light.

What happened here? Natural selection, acting on coat color, has simply changed the genetic composition of a population, increasing the proportion of genetic variants (the light-color genes) that enhance survival and repro-duction. And while I said that natural selection *acts*, this is not really accu-rate. Selection is not a mechanism imposed on a population from outside. Rather, it is a *process*, a description of how genes that produce better adapta-tions become more frequent over time. When biologists say that selection is acting "on" a trait, they're merely using shorthand to say that the trait is under-going the process. In the same sense, species don't *try* to adapt to their envi-ronment. There is no will involved, no conscious striving. Adaptation to the environment is inevitable if a species has the right kind of genetic variation.

Three things are involved in creating an adaptation by natural selection. First, the starting population has to be *variable*: mice within a population have to show some difference in their coat colors. Otherwise this trait can-not evolve. In the case of mice, we know this is true because mice within mainland populations show some variability in coat color.

Second, some proportion of that variation has to come from changes in the forms of genes, that is, the variation has to have some genetic basis (called *heritability*). If there were no genetic difference between light and dark mice, the light ones would still survive better on the dunes, but the coat-color difference would not be passed on to the next generation, and there would be no evolutionary change. We know that the genetic require-ment is also satisfied in these mice. In fact, we know exactly which two genes have the largest effect on the dark/light color difference. One of them is called *Agouti*, the same gene whose mutations produce black color in domes-tic cats. The other is called *Mc1r*, and one of its mutant forms in humans, especially common in Irish populations, produces freckles and red hair.[28]

Where does this genetic variation come from? *Mutations*—accidental changes in the sequence of DNA that usually occur as errors when the molecule is copied during cell division. Genetic variation generated by mutation is widespread: mutant forms of genes, for example, explain variation in human eye color, blood type, and much of our—and other species'—variation in height, weight, biochemistry, and innumerable other traits.

On the basis of many laboratory experiments, scientists have concluded that mutations occur randomly. The term "random" here has a specific meaning that is often misunderstood, even by biologists. What this means is that *mutations occur regardless of whether they would be useful to the individual.* Mutations are simply errors in DNA replication. Most of them are harmful or neutral, but a few can turn out to be useful. The useful ones are the raw material for evolution. But there is no known biological way to jack up the probability that a mutation will meet the current adaptive needs of the organism. Although it's better for mice living on sand dunes to have lighter coats, their chance of getting such a useful mutation is no higher than for mice living on dark soil. Rather than calling mutations "random," then, it seems more accurate to call them "indifferent": the chance of a mutation arising is indifferent to whether it would be helpful or hurtful to the individual.

The third and last aspect of natural selection is that the genetic variation must affect an individual's probability of leaving offspring. In the case of mice, Kaufman's predation experiments showed that the most camouflaged mice would leave more copies of their genes. The white color of beach mice, then, meets all the criteria for having evolved as an adaptive trait.

Evolution by selection, then, is a combination of randomness and lawfulness. There is first a "random" (or "indifferent") process—the occurrence of mutations that generate an array of genetic variants, both good and bad (in the mouse example, a variety of new coat colors); and then a "lawful" process—natural selection—that orders this variation, keeping the good and winnowing the bad (on the dunes, light-color genes increase at the expense of dark-color ones).

This brings up what is surely the most widespread misunderstanding about Darwinism: the idea that, in evolution, "everything happens by chance" (also stated as "everything happens by accident"). This common claim is flatly wrong. No evolutionist—and certainly not Darwin—ever argued that natural selection is based on chance. Quite the opposite. Could a completely random process alone make the hammering woodpecker, the tricky bee orchid, or the camouflaged katydids and beach mice? Of course not. If suddenly evolution was forced to depend on random mutations alone, species would quickly degenerate and go extinct. Chance alone cannot explain the marvelous fit between individuals and their environment.

And it doesn't. True, the raw materials for evolution—the variations between individuals—are indeed produced by chance mutations. These mutations occur willy-nilly, regardless of whether they are good or bad for the individual. But it is the *filtering of that variation by natural selection* that produces adaptations, and natural selection is manifestly *not* random. It is a powerful molding force, accumulating genes that have a greater chance of being passed on than others, and in so doing making individuals ever better able to cope with their environment. It is, then, the unique combination of mutation and selection—chance and lawfulness—that tells us how organisms become adapted. Richard Dawkins provided the most concise definition of natural selection: it is "the non-random survival of random variants."

The theory of natural selection has a big job—the biggest in biology. Its task is to explain how *every* adaptation evolved, step by step, from traits that preceded it. This includes not just body form and color, but the molecular features that underlie everything. Selection must explain the evolution of complex physiological traits: the clotting of blood, the metabolic systems that transform food into energy, the marvelous immune system that can recognize and destroy thousands of foreign proteins. And what about the details of genetics itself? Why do pairs of chromosomes separate when eggs and sperm are formed? Why do we have sex at all, instead of budding off clones, as some species do? Selection has to explain behaviors, both cooperative and antagonistic. Why do lions hunt cooperatively in a pack, and yet when intruding males displace resident males from a social group, why do the intruders kill all the unweaned cubs?

And selection has to mold these features in a particular way. First, it has to create them—most often gradually—step by step from precursors. As we have seen, each newly evolved trait begins as a modification of an earlier feature. The legs of tetrapods, for example, are simply modified fins. And each step of the process, each elaboration of an adaptation, must confer a reproductive benefit on individuals possessing it. If this doesn't happen, selection won't work. What were the advantages of each step in the transition from a swimming fin to a walking leg? Or from an unfeathered dinosaur to one having both feathers and wings? There is no "going downhill" in the evolution of an adaptation, for selection by its very nature cannot create a step that doesn't benefit its possessor. In the world of adaptation, we never see the sign that's the bane of freeway drivers: "a temporary inconvenience— a permanent improvement."

If an "adaptive" trait evolved by natural selection instead of having been created, we can make some predictions. First, in principle we should be able to imagine a plausible step-by-step scenario for the evolution of that trait, with each step raising the *fitness* (that is, the average number of offspring) of its possessor. For some traits this is easy, like the gradual alteration of the skeleton that turned land animals into whales. For others it is harder, especially for the biochemical pathways that leave no trace in the fossil record. We may never have enough information to reconstruct the evolution of many traits, or even, in extinct species, to understand precisely how those traits functioned. (What were the bony plates on the back of the *Stegosaurus* really for?) It is telling, however, that biologists haven't found a single adaptation whose evolution absolutely *requires* an intermediate step that reduces the fitness of individuals.

Here's another requirement. An adaptation must evolve by increasing the *reproductive output of its possessor*. For it is reproduction, not survival, that determines which genes make it to the next generation and cause evolution. Of course, passing on a gene requires that you first survive to the age at which you can have offspring. On the other hand, a gene that knocks you off *after* reproductive age incurs no evolutionary disadvantage. It will remain in the gene pool. It follows that a gene will actually be favored if it helps you reproduce in your youth but kills you in your old age. The accumulation of such genes by natural selection, in fact, is widely thought to explain why we deteriorate in so many ways ("senesce") as we reach old age. The very genes that help you sow your wild oats when young may give you wrinkles and an enlarged prostate gland later in life.

Given how natural selection works, it shouldn't produce adaptations that help an individual survive without also promoting reproduction. One example would be a gene that helps human females survive after menopause. Nor do we expect to see adaptations in one species that benefit only members of another species.

We can test this last prediction by looking at traits of one species that are useful to members of a second species. If those features arose by selection, we'd predict that they'll also be useful for the first species. Take tropical acacia trees, which have swollen, hollow thorns that act as homes for colonies of fierce, stinging ants. The trees also secrete nectar and produce protein-rich bodies on their leaves that provide the ants with food. It looks as if the tree is housing and feeding the ants at its own expense. Does this violate our prediction? Not at all. In fact, harboring ants gives a tree huge benefits. First, herbivorous insects and mammals that stop by for a leafy treat are repelled by a furious ant horde—as I discovered to my chagrin when brushing up against an acacia in Costa Rica. The ants also cut down seedlings around the base of the tree—seedlings which, when larger, could compete with the tree for nutrients and light. It is easy to see how acacias that were able to enlist ants to defend them from both predators and competitors would produce more seeds than acacias lacking this ability. In every case, when one species does something to help another, it always helps itself. This is a direct prediction of evolution, and one that does not follow from the notion of special creation or intelligent design.

And adaptations always increase the fitness of the *individual*, not necessarily of the group or the species. The idea that natural selection acts "for the good of the species," though common, is misguided. In fact, evolution can produce features that, while helping an individual, harm the species as a whole. When a group of male lions displaces the resident males of a pride, this is often followed by a gruesome slaughter of the unweaned cubs. This behavior is bad for the species since it reduces the total number of lions, increasing their likelihood of extinction. But it's good for the invading lions, as they can quickly fertilize the females (who come back into estrus when they're not nursing) and replace the slaughtered cubs with their own offspring. It is easy—though unsettling—to see how a gene causing infanticide would spread at the expense of "nicer" genes, which would have the invading males simply babysit the unrelated cubs. As evolution predicts, we never see adaptations that benefit the species at the expense of the individual—something that we might have expected if organisms were designed by a beneficent creator.

Evolution Without Selection

LET'S TAKE A BRIEF DIGRESSION HERE, because it's important to appreciate that natural selection isn't the only process of evolutionary change. Most biologists define evolution as a change in the proportion of *alleles* (different forms of a gene) in a population. As the frequency of "light-color" forms of the *Agouti* gene increases in a mouse population, for example, the population and its coat color evolve. But such change can happen in other ways too. Every individual has two copies of each gene, which can be identical or different. Every time sexual reproduction occurs, one member of each pair of genes from a parent makes it into the offspring, along with one from the other parent. It's a toss-up which one of each parent's pair gets to the next generation. If you have an AB blood type, for example (one "A" allele and one "B" allele), and produce only one child, there's only a 50 percent chance it will get your A allele and a 50 percent chance it gets the B allele. In a one-child family, it's a certainty that one of your alleles will be lost. The upshot is that, every generation, the genes of parents take part in a lottery whose prize is representation in the next generation. Because the number of offspring is finite, the frequencies of the genes present in the offspring won't be present in exactly the same frequencies as in their parents. This "sampling" of genes is precisely like tossing a coin. Although there is a 50 percent chance of getting heads on any given toss, if you make only a few tosses there is a substantial chance that you'll deviate from this expectation (in four tosses, for example, you have a 12 percent chance of getting either all heads or all tails). And so, especially in small populations, the proportion of different alleles can change over time entirely by chance. And new mutations may enter the fray and themselves rise or fall in frequency due to this random sampling. Eventually the resulting "random walk" can even cause genes to become *fixed* in the population (that is, rise to 100 percent frequency) or, alternatively, get completely lost.

Such random change in the frequency of genes over time is called *genetic drift*. It is a legitimate type of evolution, since it involves changes in the frequencies of alleles over time, but it doesn't arise from natural selection. One example of evolution by drift may be the unusual frequencies of blood types (as in the ABO system) in the Old Order Amish and Dunker religious communities in America. These are small, isolated religious groups whose members intermarry—just the right circumstances for rapid evolution by genetic drift.

Accidents of sampling can also happen when a population is founded by just a few immigrants, as occurs when individuals colonize an island or a new area. The almost complete absence of genes producing the B blood type in Native American populations, for example, may reflect the loss of this gene in a small population of humans that colonized North America from Asia around twelve thousand years ago.

Both drift and natural selection produce the genetic change that we recognize as evolution. But there's an important difference. Drift is a random process, while selection is the antithesis of randomness. Genetic drift can change the frequencies of alleles regardless of how useful they are to their carrier. Selection, on the other hand, always gets rid of harmful alleles and raises the frequencies of beneficial ones.

As a purely random process, genetic drift can't cause the evolution of adaptations. It could never build a wing or an eye. That takes nonrandom natural selection. What drift *can* do is cause the evolution of features that are neither useful nor harmful to the organism. Ever prescient, Darwin himself broached this idea in *The Origin*:

> This preservation of favourable variations and the rejection of injurious variations, I call Natural Selection. Variations neither useful nor injurious would not be affected by natural selection, and would be left as a fluctuating element, as perhaps we see in the species called polymorphic.

In fact, genetic drift is not only powerless to create adaptations, but can actually *overpower* natural selection. Especially in small populations, the sampling effect can be so large that it raises the frequency of harmful genes even though selection is working in the opposite direction. This is almost certainly why we see a high incidence of genetically based diseases in isolated human communities, including Gaucher's disease in northern Swedes, Tay-Sachs in the Cajuns of Louisiana, and retinitis pigmentosa in the inhabitants of the island of Tristan da Cunha.

Because certain variations in DNA or protein sequence may be, as Darwin put it, "neither useful nor injurious" (or "neutral" as we now call them), such variants are especially liable to evolve by drift. For example, some mutations in a gene don't affect the sequence of the protein that it produces, and so don't change the fitness of its carrier. The same goes for mutations in nonfunctioning pseudogenes—old wrecks of genes still kicking around in the genome. Any mutations in these genes have no effect on the organism, and therefore can evolve only by genetic drift.

Many aspects of molecular evolution, then, such as certain changes in DNA sequence, may reflect drift rather then selection. It's also possible that many externally visible features of organisms could evolve via drift, especially if they don't affect reproduction. The diverse shapes of leaves of different tree species—like the differences between oak and maple leaves—were once suggested to be "neutral" traits that evolved by genetic drift. But it's hard to prove that a trait has absolutely *no* selective advantage. Even a tiny advantage, so small as to be unmeasurable or unobservable by biologists in real time, can lead to important evolutionary change over eons.

The relative importance of genetic drift versus selection in evolution remains a topic of hot debate among biologists. Every time we see an obvious adaptation, like the camel's hump, we clearly see evidence for selection. But features whose evolution we don't understand may reflect only our ignorance rather than genetic drift. Nevertheless, we know that genetic drift *must* occur, because in any population of finite size there are always sampling effects during reproduction. And drift has probably played a substantial role in the evolution of small populations, although we can't point to more than a few examples.

Animal and Plant Breeding

THE THEORY OF NATURAL SELECTION predicts what types of adaptations we'd expect to find and—more important—*not* find in nature. And these predictions have been fulfilled. But many people would like more: they'd like to *see* natural selection in action, and witness evolutionary change in their lifetime. It's not hard to accept the idea that natural selection could cause, say, the evolution of whales from land animals over millions of years, but somehow the idea of selection becomes more compelling when we see the process act before our eyes.

This demand to see selection and evolution in real time, while understandable, is curious. After all, we easily accept that the Grand Canyon resulted from millions of years of slow, imperceptible carving by the Colorado River, even though we can't see the canyon getting deeper over our lifetime. But for some people this ability to extrapolate time for geological forces doesn't apply to evolution. How, then, can we determine whether selection has been an important cause of evolution? Obviously, we can't replay the evolution of whales to see the reproductive advantage of each small step that took them back to the water. But if we can see selection causing small changes over just a few generations, then perhaps it becomes easier to accept that, over millions of years, similar types of selection could cause the big adaptive changes documented in fossils.

Evidence for selection comes from many areas. The most obvious is artificial selection—animal and plant breeding—which, as Darwin realized, is a good parallel to natural selection. We know that breeders have worked wonders in transforming wild plants and animals into completely different forms that are good to eat, or that satisfy our aesthetic needs. And we know that this has been done by selecting variation present in their wild ancestors. We also know that breeding has wrought huge changes in a remarkably short period of time, for animal and plant breeding has been practiced for only a few thousand years.

Take the domestic dog (*Canis lupus familiaris*), a single species that comes in all shapes, sizes, colors, and temperaments. Every single one, purebred or mutt, descends from a single ancestral species—most likely the Eurasian gray wolf—that humans began to select about ten thousand years ago. The American Kennel Club recognizes 150 different breeds, and you've seen many of them: the tiny, nervous Chihuahua, perhaps bred as a food animal by the Toltec of Mexico; the robust Saint Bernard, thick of fur and able to carry kegs of brandy to snow-stranded travelers; the greyhound, bred for racing with long legs and a streamlined shape; the elongated, short-legged dachshund, ideal for catching badgers in their holes; retrievers, bred to fetch game from the water; and the fluffy Pomeranian, bred as a comforting lap-dog. Breeders have virtually sculpted these dogs to their liking, changing the shade and thickness of their coats, the length and pointiness of their ears, the size and shape of their skeletons, the quirks of their behaviors and temperaments, and nearly everything else.

Think of the diversity you'd see if all these dogs were lined up together! If somehow the recognized breeds existed only as fossils, paleontologists would consider them not one species but many—certainly more than the thirty-six species of wild dogs that live in nature today.[29] In fact, the variation among domestic dogs far exceeds that among wild dog species. Take just one trait: weight. Domestic dogs range from the 2-pound Chihuahua to the 180-pound English mastiff, while the weight of wild dog species varies from 2 pounds to only about 60 pounds. And there is certainly no wild dog having the shape of a dachshund or the face of a pug.

The success of dog breeding validates two of the three requirements for evolution by selection. First, there was ample variation in color, size, shape, and behavior in the ancestral lineage of dogs to make possible the creation of all breeds. Second, some of that variation was produced by genetic mutations that could be inherited—for if it were not, breeders could make no progress. What is most astonishing about dog breeding is how fast it got results. All those breeds have been selected in less than ten thousand years, only 0.1 percent of the time that it took wild dog species to diversify from their common ancestor in nature. If *artificial* selection can produce such canine diversity so quickly, it becomes easier to accept that the lesser diversity of wild dogs arose by *natural* selection acting over a period a thousand times longer.

There's really only one difference between artificial and natural selection. In artificial selection it is the breeder rather than nature who sorts out which variants are "good" and "bad." In other words, the criterion of reproductive success is human desire rather than adaptation to a natural environment. Sometimes these criteria coincide. Look, for example, at the greyhound, which was selected for speed, and wound up shaped very much like a cheetah. This is an example of convergent evolution: similar selective pressures give similar outcomes.

The dog can stand for the success of other breeding programs. As Darwin noted in *The Origin*, "Breeders habitually speak of an animal's organization as something quite plastic, which they can model almost as they please." Cows, sheep, pigs, flowers, vegetables, and so on—all came from humans choosing variants present in wild ancestors, or variants that arose by mutation during domestication. Through selection, the svelte wild turkey has become our docile, meaty, and virtually tasteless Thanksgiving monster, with breasts so large that male domestic turkeys can no longer mount females, who must instead be artificially inseminated. Darwin himself bred pigeons, and described the huge variety of behaviors and appearance of different breeds, all selected from the ancestral rock dove. You wouldn't recognize the ancestor of our ear of corn, which was an inconspicuous grass. The ancestral tomato weighed only a few grams, but has now been bred into a two-pound behemoth (also tasteless) with a long shelf life. The wild cabbage has given rise to five different vegetables: broccoli, domestic cabbage, kohlrabi, Brussels sprouts, and cauliflower, each selected to modify a different part of the plant (broccoli, for example, is simply a tight, enlarged cluster of flowers). And the domestication of *all* wild crop plants occurred within the last twelve thousand years.

It's no surprise, then, that Darwin began *The Origin* not with a discussion of natural selection or evolution in the wild, but with a chapter called "Variation Under Domestication"—on animal and plant breeding. He knew that if people could accept artificial selection—and they had to, because its success was so obvious—then making the leap to *natural* selection was not so hard. As he argued:

Under domestication, it may be truly said that the whole organization becomes in some degree plastic. . . . Can it, then, be thought improbable, seeing that variations useful to man have undoubtedly occurred, that other variations useful in some way to each being in the great and complex battle of life, should sometimes occur in the course of thousands of generations?

Since domestication of wild species took place only in the relatively short period since humans became civilized, Darwin knew that it wouldn't be much of a stretch to accept that natural selection could create much greater diversity over a much longer time.

Evolution in the Test Tube

WE CAN GO A STEP FURTHER. Instead of breeders picking out favored variants, we can let this happen "naturally" in the laboratory, by exposing a captive population to new environmental challenges. This is easiest to do in microbes like bacteria, which can divide as often as once every twenty minutes, allowing us to observe evolutionary change over thousands of generations in real time. And this is *genuine* evolutionary change, demonstrating all three requirements of evolution via selection: variation, heritability, and the differential survival and reproduction of variants. Although the environmental challenge is created by humans, these sorts of experiments are more natural than artificial selection because humans don't choose which individuals get to reproduce.

Let's start with simple adaptations. Microbes can adapt to virtually anything that scientists throw at them in the lab: high or low temperature, antibiotics, toxins, starvation, new nutrients, and their natural enemies, viruses. Probably the longest-running study of this type has been carried out by Richard Lenski at Michigan State University. In 1988, Lenski put genetically identical strains of the common gut bacterium *E. coli* under conditions in which their food, the sugar glucose, was depleted each day and then renewed the next. This experiment was thus a test of the microbe's ability to adapt to a feast-and-famine environment. Over the next eighteen years (40,000 bacterial generations), the bacteria continued to accumulate new mutations adapting them to this new environment. Under the varying-food conditions, they now grow 70 percent faster than the original unselected strain. The bacteria continue to evolve, and Lenski and his colleagues have identified at least nine genes whose mutations result in adaptation.

But "laboratory" adaptations can also be more complex, involving the evolution of whole new biochemical systems. Perhaps the ultimate challenge is simply to take away a gene that a microbe needs to survive in a particular environment, and see how it responds. Can it evolve a way around this problem? The answer is usually yes. In a dramatic experiment, Barry Hall and his colleagues at the University of Rochester began a study by deleting a gene from *E. coli*. This gene produces an enzyme that allows the bacteria to break down the sugar lactose into subunits that can be used as food. The geneless bacteria were then put in an environment containing lactose as the only food source. Initially, of course, they lacked the enzyme and couldn't grow. But after only a short time, the function of the missing gene was taken over by another enzyme that, while previously unable to break down lactose, could now do so weakly because of a new mutation. Eventually, yet another adaptive mutation occurred: one that increased the *amount* of the new enzyme so that even more lactose could be used. Finally, a third mutation at a different gene allowed the bacteria to take up lactose from the environment more easily. All together, this experiment showed the evolution of a complex biochemical pathway that enabled bacteria to grow on a previously unusable food. Beyond demonstrating evolution, this experiment has two important lessons. First, natural selection can promote the evolution of complex, interconnected biochemical systems in which all the parts are codependent, despite the claims of creationists that this is impossible. Second, as we've seen repeatedly, selection does not create new traits out of thin air: it produces "new" adaptations by modifying preexisting features.

We can even see the origin of new, ecologically diverse bacterial species, all within a single laboratory flask. Paul Rainey and his colleagues at Oxford University placed a strain of the bacteria *Pseudomonas fluorescens* in a small vessel containing nutrient broth, and simply watched it. (It's surprising but true that such a vessel actually contains diverse environments. Oxygen concentration, for example, is highest on the top and lowest on the bottom.)

Within ten days—no more than a few hundred generations—the ancestral free-floating "smooth" bacterium had evolved into two additional forms occupying different parts of the beaker. One, called "wrinkly spreader," formed a mat on top of the broth. The other, called "fuzzy spreader," formed a carpet on the bottom. The smooth ancestral type persisted in the liquid environment in the middle. Each of the two new forms was genetically different from the ancestor, having evolved through mutation and natural selection to reproduce best in their respective environments. Here, then, is not only evolution but speciation occurring in the lab: the ancestral form produced, and coexisted with, two ecologically different descendants, and in bacteria such forms are considered distinct species. Over a very short time, natural selection on *Pseudomonas* yielded a small-scale "adaptive radiation," the equivalent of how animals or plants form species when they encounter new environments on an oceanic island.

Resistance to Drugs and Poisons

WHEN ANTIBIOTICS WERE FIRST INTRODUCED in the 1940s, everyone thought that they would finally solve the problem of infectious disease caused by bacteria. The drugs worked so well that nearly everyone with tuberculosis, strep throat, or pneumonia could be cured with a couple of simple injections or a vial of pills. But we forgot about natural selection. Given their huge population sizes and short generation times—features that make bacteria ideal for studies of evolution in the lab—the chance of a mutation producing antibiotic resistance is high. And those bacteria that are resistant to a drug will be those that survive, leaving behind genetically identical offspring that are also drug-resistant. Eventually the effectiveness of the drug wanes, and once again we have a medical problem. This has become a severe crisis for some diseases. There are now strains of tuberculosis bacteria, for example, that have evolved resistance to every drug doctors have used against them. After a long period of cures and medical optimism, TB is once again becoming a fatal disease.

This is natural selection, pure and simple. Everyone knows about drug resistance, but it's not often realized that this is about the best example we have of selection in action. (Had this phenomenon existed in Darwin's time, he would certainly have made it a centerpiece of *The Origin*.) It is a widespread belief that drug resistance occurs because somehow the patients themselves change in a way that makes the drug less effective. But this is wrong: resistance comes from evolution of the microbe, not habituation of patients to the drugs.

Another prime example of selection is resistance to penicillin. When it was introduced in the early 1940s, penicillin was a miracle drug, especially effective at curing infections caused by the bacterium *Staphylococcus aureus* ("staph"). In 1941, the drug could wipe out every strain of staph in the world. Now, seventy years later, more than 95 percent of staph strains are resistant to penicillin. What happened was that mutations occurred in individual bacteria that gave them the ability to destroy the drug, and of course these mutations spread worldwide. In response, the drug industry came up with a new antibiotic, methicillin, but even that is now becoming useless due to newer mutations. In both cases, scientists have identified the precise changes in the bacterial DNA that conferred drug resistance.

Viruses, the smallest form of evolvable life, have also evolved resistance to antiviral drugs, most notably AZT (azidothymidine), designed to prevent the HIV virus from replicating in an infected body. Evolution even occurs within the body of a single patient, since the virus mutates at a furious pace, eventually producing resistance and rendering AZT ineffective. Now we keep AIDS at bay with a daily three-drug cocktail, and if history is any guide, this too will eventually stop working.

The evolution of resistance creates an arms race between humans and microorganisms, in which the winners are not just bacteria but also the pharmaceutical industry, which constantly devises new drugs to overcome the waning effectiveness of old ones. But fortunately there are some spectacular cases of microorganisms that haven't succeeded in evolving resistance. (We must remember that the theory of evolution doesn't predict that everything will evolve: if the right mutations can't or don't arise, evolution won't happen.) One form of *Streptococcus*, for example, causes "strep throat," a common infection in children. These bacteria have failed to evolve even the slightest resistance to penicillin, which remains the treatment of choice. And, unlike the influenza virus, polio and measles viruses have not evolved resistance to the vaccines that have now been used for over fifty years.

Still other species have adapted via selection to human-caused changes in their environment. Insects have become resistant to DDT and other pesticides, plants have adapted to herbicides, and fungi, worms, and algae have evolved resistance to heavy metals that have polluted their environment. There almost always seem to be a few individuals with lucky mutations that allow them to survive and reproduce, quickly evolving a sensitive population into a resistant one. We can then make a reasonable inference: when a population encounters a stress that *doesn't* come from humans, such as a change in salinity, temperature, or rainfall, natural selection will often produce an adaptive response.

Selection in the Wild

THE RESPONSES WE'VE SEEN to human-imposed stress and chemicals constitute natural selection in any meaningful sense. Although the selective agents are devised by humans, the response is purely natural and, as we've seen, can be quite complex. But perhaps it would be even more convincing to see the whole process in action in nature—without human intervention. That is, we want to see a natural population meet a natural challenge, we want to know what that challenge is, and we want to see the population evolve to meet it before our eyes.

We can't expect this circumstance to be common. For one thing, natural selection in the wild is often incredibly slow. The evolution of feathers, for example, probably took hundreds of thousands of years. Even if feathers were evolving today, it would simply be impossible to watch this happening in real time, much less to measure whatever type of selection was acting to make feathers larger. If we are to see natural selection at all, it must be *strong* selection, causing rapid change, and we'd best look at animals or plants having short generation times so that the evolutionary change can be seen over several generations. And we have to do better than bacteria: people want to see selection in so-called "higher" plants and animals.

Further, we shouldn't expect to see more than small changes in one or a few features of a species—what is known as *microevolutionary* change. Given the gradual pace of evolution, it's unreasonable to expect to see selection transforming one "type" of plant or animal into another—so-called *macroevolution*—within a human lifetime. Though macroevolution is occurring today, we simply won't be around long enough to see it. Remember that the issue is not whether macroevolutionary change *happens*—we already know from the fossil record that it does—but whether it was caused by natural selection, and whether natural selection can build complex features and organisms.

Another factor making it hard to see real-time selection is that a very common type of natural selection doesn't cause species to change. Every species is pretty well adapted, which means that selection has already brought it into sync with its environment. Episodes of change that occur when a species meets a new environmental challenge are probably rare compared to periods when there's nothing new to adapt to. But that doesn't mean that selection is not occurring. If a species of birds, for example, has evolved the optimum body size for its environment, and that environment doesn't change, selection will act only to cull birds that are larger or smaller than the optimum. But this kind of selection, called *stabilizing selection*, won't change the average body size: if you look at the population from one generation to the next, nothing much will have changed (although genes for both large and small sizes will have been eliminated). We can see this, for example, for birth weight in human babies. Hospital statistics consistently show that babies having average birth weights, around 7.5 pounds in the United States and Europe, survive better than either lighter babies (born prematurely or from malnourished mothers) or heavier babies (who have difficulties being born).

If we want to see selection in action, then, we should look in species that have short generation times and are adapting to a new environment. This is most likely to happen when species either invade a new habitat or experience severe environmental change. And indeed, that is where the examples lie.

The most famous of these, which I won't belabor as it's been described in detail elsewhere (see, for example, Jonathan Weiner's superb book *The Beak of the Finch: A Story of Evolution in Our Time*), is the adaptation of a bird to an anomalous change in climate. The medium ground finch of the Galápagos Islands has been studied for several decades by Peter and Rosemary Grant of Princeton University and their colleagues. In 1977, a severe drought in the Galápagos drastically reduced the supply of seeds on the island of Daphne Major. This finch, which normally prefers small soft seeds, was forced to turn to larger and harder ones. Experiments showed that hard seeds are easily cracked only by larger birds, which have bigger and stouter beaks. The upshot was that only big-beaked individuals got adequate food, while those with smaller beaks starved to death or were too malnourished to reproduce. The large-beaked survivors left more offspring, and by the next generation natural selection had increased the average beak size by 10 percent (body size increased as well). This is a staggering rate of evolutionary change—far larger than anything we see in the fossil record. In comparison, brain size in the human lineage increased on average about 0.001 percent per generation. Everything we require of evolution by natural selection was amply documented by the Grants in other studies: individuals in the original population varied in beak depth, a large proportion of that variation was genetic, and individuals with different beaks left different numbers of off-spring *in the predicted direction.*

Given the importance of food to survival, the ability to gather, eat, and digest it efficiently is a strong selective force. Many insects are host-specific: they feed and lay their eggs on only one or a few species of plants. In such cases the insect needs adaptations for using the plants, including the right feeding apparatus to tap the plant's nutrients, a metabolism that detoxifies any plant poisons, and a reproductive cycle that produces young when there is available food (the plant's fruiting period). Since there are many closely related pairs of insects that use different host plants, there must have been many switches from one plant to another over evolutionary time. These switches, equivalent to colonizing a very different habitat, must have been accompanied by strong selection.

We have in fact seen this happen over the last few decades in the soapberry bug (*Jadera haematoloma*) of the New World. *Jadera* lives on two native plants in different parts of the United States: the soapberry bush in the south-central U.S. and the perennial balloon vine in southern Florida. With its long, needlelike beak, the bug penetrates the fruits of these plants and consumes the seeds within, liquefying their contents and sucking them up. But within the last fifty years, the bug has colonized three other plants introduced into its range. The fruits of these plants are very different in size from those of its native host: two are much larger and one much smaller.

Scott Carroll and his colleagues predicted that this host switch would cause natural selection for changes in beak size. Bugs colonizing the larger-fruited species should evolve larger beaks to penetrate the fruits and reach the seeds, while bugs colonizing the smaller-fruited species would evolve in the opposite direction. This is exactly what happened, with beak length changing by up to 25 percent in a few decades. This may not seem like much, but it is enormous by evolutionary standards, particularly over the short span of one hundred generations.[30] To put it in perspective, if this rate of beak evolution was sustained over only ten thousand generations (five thousand years), the beaks would increase in size by a factor of roughly *five billion*, becoming about eighteen hundred miles long, and able to skewer a fruit the size of the moon! This ludicrous and unrealistic figure is, of course, meant only to show the cumulative power of seemingly small changes.

Here's another prediction: under prolonged drought, natural selection will lead to the evolution of plants that flower earlier than their ancestors. This is because, during a drought, soils dry out quickly after the rains. If you're a plant that doesn't flower and produce seeds quickly in a drought, you leave no descendants. Under normal weather conditions, on the other hand, it pays to delay flowering so that you can grow larger and produce even more seeds.

This prediction was tested in a natural experiment involving the wild mustard plant (*Brassica rapa*), introduced to California about three hundred years ago. Beginning in 2000, Southern California suffered a severe five-year drought. Arthur Weis and his colleagues at the University of California measured the flowering time of mustards at the beginning and end of this period. Sure enough, natural selection had changed flowering time in precisely the predicted way: after the drought, plants began to flower a week earlier than their ancestors did.

There are many more examples, but they all demonstrate the same thing: we can directly witness natural selection leading to better adaptation. *Natural Selection in the Wild*, a book by the biologist John Endler, documents over 150 cases of observed evolution, and in roughly a third of these we have a good idea about how natural selection was acting. We see fruit flies adapting to extreme temperature, honeybees adapting to competitors, and guppies becoming less colorful to escape the notice of predators. How many more examples do we need?

Can Selection Build Complexity?

BUT EVEN IF WE AGREE that natural selection does work in nature, how much work can it *really* do? Sure, selection can change the beaks of birds, or the flowering period of plants, but can it build *complexity*? What about intricate traits like the tetrapod limb; or exquisite biochemical adaptations like blood clotting, which entails a precise sequence of steps involving many proteins; or perhaps the most complicated apparatus that ever evolved—the human brain?

We are at somewhat of a handicap here because, as we know, complex features take a long time to evolve, and most of them did so in the distant past when we weren't around to see how it happened. So how can we be sure that selection *was* involved? How do we know that creationists are wrong when they say that selection can make small changes in organisms but is powerless to make big ones?

But first we must ask: What's the alternative theory? We know of no other natural process that can build a complex adaptation. The most commonly suggested alternative takes us into the realm of the supernatural. This, of course, is creationism, known in its latest incarnation as "intelligent design". Advocates of ID suggest that a supernatural designer has intervened at various times during the history of life, either instantly calling into being the complex adaptations that natural selection supposedly can't make, or producing "miracle mutations" that can't occur by chance. (Some IDers go further: they are the extreme "young earth" creationists who believe that earth is about six thousand years old and that life has no evolutionary history at all.)

In the main, ID is unscientific, for it consists largely of untestable claims. How, for example, can we determine whether mutations were mere accidents in DNA replication or were willed into being by a creator? But we can still ask if there are adaptations *that could not have been built by selection*, and therefore require us to think of another mechanism. Advocates of ID have suggested several such adaptations, such as the bacterial flagellum (a small, hairlike apparatus with a complex molecular motor, used by some bacteria to propel themselves) and the mechanism of blood clotting. These are indeed complex features: the flagellum, for instance, is composed of dozens of separate proteins, all of which must work in concert for the hairlike "propeller" to move.

IDers argue that such traits, involving many parts that must cooperate for that trait to function at all, defy Darwinian explanation. Therefore, by default, they must have been designed by a supernatural agent. This is commonly called the "God of the gaps" argument, and it is an argument from ignorance. What it really says is that if we don't understand *everything* about how natural selection built a trait, that lack of understanding itself is evidence for supernatural creation.

You can probably see why this argument doesn't hold water. We'll never be able to reconstruct how selection created everything—evolution happened before we were on the scene, and some things will always be unknown. But evolutionary biology is like every science: it has mysteries, and many of them get solved, one after the other. We now know, for instance, where birds came from—they weren't created out of thin air (as creationists used to maintain), but evolved gradually from dinosaurs. And each time a mystery is solved, ID is forced to retreat. Since ID itself makes no testable scientific claims, but offers only half-baked criticisms of Darwinism, its credibility slowly melts away with each advance in our understanding. Further, ID's own explanation for complex features—the whim of a supernatural designer—can explain *any* conceivable observation about nature. It may even have been the creator's whim to make life look as though it evolved (apparently many creationists believe this, though few admit it). But if you can't think of an observation that could disprove a theory, that theory simply isn't scientific.

How, though, can we refute the ID claim that some traits simply defy *any* origin by natural selection? In such cases the onus is not on evolutionary biologists to sketch out a precise step-by-step scenario documenting exactly how a complex character evolved. That would require knowing everything about what happened when we were not around—an impossibility for most traits and for nearly all biochemical pathways. As the biochemists Ford Doolittle and Olga Zhaxybayeva argued when addressing the ID claim that flagella could not have evolved, "Evolutionists need not take on the impossible challenge of pinning down every detail of flagellar evolution. We need only show that such a development, involving processes and constituents not unlike those we already know and can agree upon, is feasible." And by "feasible," they mean that there must be evolutionary precursors of each new trait, and that evolution of that trait does not violate the Darwinian requirement that each step in building an adaptation benefits its possessor.

Indeed, we know of no adaptations whose origin could *not* have involved natural selection. How can we be sure? For anatomical traits, we can simply trace their evolution (when possible) in the fossil record, and see in what order different changes took place. We can then determine whether the sequences of changes at least conform to a step-by-step adaptive process. And in every case, we can find at least a feasible Darwinian explanation. We've seen this for the evolution of land animals from fish, of whales from land animals, and of birds from reptiles. It didn't have to be that way. The movement of nostrils to the top of the head in ancestral whales, for example, could have preceded the evolution of fins. That could be the providential act of a creator, but couldn't have evolved by natural selection. But we always see an evolutionary order that makes Darwinian sense.

Understanding the evolution of complex biochemical features and pathways is not as easy, since they leave no trace in the fossil record. Their evolution must be reconstructed in more speculative ways, trying to see how such pathways could be cobbled together from simpler biochemical precursors.

And we'd like to know the steps in this cobbling, to see if each new one could bring improved fitness.

Although advocates of ID claim a supernatural hand behind these pathways, dogged scientific research is beginning to give plausible (and testable) scenarios for how they could have evolved. Take the blood-clotting pathway of vertebrates. This involves a sequence of events that begins when one protein sticks to another in the vicinity of an open wound. That sets off a complicated cascade reaction, sixteen steps long, each involving an interaction between a different pair of proteins and culminating in the formation of the clot itself. Altogether more than twenty proteins are involved. How could this possibly have evolved?

We don't yet know for sure, but we have evidence that the system could have been built up in an adaptive way from simpler precursors. Many of the blood-clotting proteins are made by related genes that arose by duplication, a form of mutation in which an ancestral gene, and later its descendants, becomes duplicated in full along a strand of DNA because of a mistake during cell division. Once they arise, such duplicated genes can then evolve along separate pathways so that they eventually perform separate functions, as they now do in blood clotting. And we know that other proteins and enzymes in the pathway had different functions in groups that evolved before vertebrates. For example, a key protein in the clotting pathway is called fibrinogen, which is dissolved in blood plasma. In the last step of blood clotting, this protein gets cut by an enzyme, and the shorter proteins (called fibrins) stick together and become insoluble, forming the final clot. Since fibrinogen occurs in all vertebrates as a blood-clotting protein, it presumably evolved from a protein that had a different function in ancestral invertebrates, who were around earlier but lacked a clotting pathway. Although an intelligent designer could invent a suitable protein, evolution doesn't work that way. There must have been an ancestral protein from which fibrinogen evolved.

Russell Doolittle at the University of California predicted that we would find such a protein, and, sure enough, in 1990 he and his colleague Xun Xu discovered it in the sea cucumber, an invertebrate sometimes used in Chinese cooking. Sea cucumbers branched off from the vertebrate lineage at least 500 million years ago, yet they have a protein that, while clearly related to blood-clotting proteins of vertebrates, is not used to clot blood. This means that the common ancestor of sea cucumbers and vertebrates had a gene that was later co-opted in vertebrates for a new function, precisely as evolution predicts. Since then, both Doolittle and cell biologist Ken Miller have worked out a plausible and adaptive sequence for the evolution of the entire blood-clotting cascade from parts of precursor proteins. All of these precursors are found in invertebrates, where they have other, nonclotting functions, and were evolutionarily co-opted by vertebrates into a working clotting system. And the evolution of the bacterial flagellum, though not yet fully understood, is also known to involve many proteins co-opted from other biochemical pathways.[31]

Hard problems often yield before science, and though we still don't understand how every complex biochemical system evolved, we are learning more every day. After all, biochemical evolution is a field still in its infancy. If the history of science teaches us anything, it is that what conquers our ignorance is research, not giving up and attributing our ignorance to the miraculous work of a creator. When you hear someone claim otherwise, just remember these words of Darwin: "Ignorance more frequently begets confidence than does knowledge: it is those who know little, and not those who know much, who so positively assert that this or that problem will never be solved by science."

It appears, then, that in principle there's no real problem with evolution building complex biochemical systems. But what about *time*? Has there really been enough time for natural selection to create both complex adaptations as well as the diversity of living forms? Certainly we know that there was enough time for organisms to have evolved—the fossil record alone tells us that—but was natural selection strong enough to drive such change?

One approach is to compare the rates of evolution in the fossil record with those seen in laboratory experiments that used artificial selection, or with historical data on evolutionary change that occurred when species colonized new habitats in historical times. If evolution in the fossil record were much faster than in laboratory experiments or colonization events—both of which involve very strong selection—we might need to rethink whether selection could explain changes in fossils. But in fact the results are just the opposite. Philip Gingerich at the University of Michigan showed that rates of change in animal size and shape during laboratory and colonization studies are actually *much faster* than rates of fossil change: from five hundred times faster (selection during colonizations) to nearly a million times faster (laboratory selection experiments). And even the fastest rates of evolution in the fossil record are nowhere near as fast as the *slowest* rates seen when humans practice selection in the laboratory. Further, the *average* rates of evolution seen in colonization studies are large enough to turn a mouse into the size of an elephant in just ten thousand years!

The lesson, then, is that selection is perfectly adequate to explain changes that we see in the fossil record. One reason why people raise this question is because they don't (or can't) appreciate the immense spans of time that selection has had to work. After all, we evolved to deal with things that happen on the scale of our lifetime—probably around thirty years during most of our evolution. A span of ten million years is beyond our intuitive grasp.

Finally, is natural selection sufficient to explain a *really* complex organ, such as the eye? The "camera" eye of vertebrates (and mollusks like the squid and octopus) was once beloved by creationists. Noting its complex arrangement of the iris, lens, retina, cornea, and so on—all of which must work together to create an image—opponents of natural selection claimed that the eye could not have formed by gradual steps. How could "half an eye" be of any use?

Darwin brilliantly addressed, and rebutted, this argument in *The Origin*. He surveyed *existing* species to see if one could find functional but less complex eyes that not only were useful, but also could be strung together into a hypothetical sequence showing how a camera eye might evolve. If this could be done—and it can—then the argument that natural selection could never produce an eye collapses, for the eyes of existing species are obviously useful. Each improvement in the eye could confer obvious benefits, for it makes an individual better able to find food, avoid predators, and navigate around its environment.

A possible sequence of such changes begins with simple eyespots made of light-sensitive pigment, as seen in flatworms. The skin then folds in, forming a cup that protects the eyespot and allows it to better localize the light source. Limpets have eyes like this. In the chambered nautilus, we see a further narrowing of the cup's opening to produce an improved image, and in ragworms the cup is capped by a transparent cover to protect the opening. In abalones, part of the fluid in the eye has coagulated to form a lens, which helps focus light, and in many species, such as mammals, nearby muscles have been co-opted to move the lens and vary its focus. The evolution of a retina, an optic nerve, and so on follows by natural selection. Each step of this hypothetical transitional "series" confers increased adaptation on its possessor, because it enables the eye to gather more light or form better images, both of which aid survival and reproduction. And each step of this process is feasible because it is seen in the eyes of a different living species. At the end of the sequence we have the camera eye, whose adaptive evolution seems impossibly complex. But the complexity of the final eye can be broken down into a series of small, adaptive steps.

Yet we can do even better than just stringing together eyes of existing species in an adaptive sequence. We can, starting with a simple precursor, actually model the evolution of the eye and see whether selection can turn that precursor into a more complex eye in a reasonable amount of time. Dan-Eric Nilsson and Susanne Pelger of Lund University in Sweden made such a mathematical model, starting with a patch of light-sensitive cells backed by a pigment layer (a retina). They then allowed the tissues around this structure to deform themselves randomly, limiting the amount of change to only 1 percent of size or thickness at each step. To mimic natural selection, the model accepted only "mutations" that improved the visual acuity, and rejected those that degraded it.

Within an amazingly short time, the model yielded a complex eye, going through stages similar to the real-animal series described above. The eye folded inward to form a cup, the cup became capped with a transparent surface, and the interior of the cup gelled to form not only a lens, but a lens with dimensions that produced the best possible image.

Beginning with a flatwormlike eyespot, then, the model produced something like the complex eye of vertebrates, all through a series of tiny adaptive steps—1,829 of them, to be exact. But Nilsson and Pelger also calculated how long this process would take. To do this, they made some assumptions about how much genetic variation for eye shape existed in the population that began experiencing selection, and about how strongly selection would favor each useful step in eye size. These assumptions were deliberately conservative, assuming that there were reasonable but not large amounts of genetic variation and that natural selection was very weak. Nevertheless, the eye evolved very quickly: the entire process from rudimentary light-patch to camera eye took fewer than 400,000 years. Since the earliest animals with eyes date back 550 million years ago, there was, according to this model, enough time for complex eyes to have evolved more than fifteen hundred times over. In reality, eyes have evolved independently in at least forty groups of animals. As Nilsson and Pelger noted dryly in their paper, "It is obvious that the eye was never a real threat to Darwin's theory of evolution."

So where are we? We know that a process very like natural selection— animal and plant breeding—has taken the genetic variation present in wild species and from it created huge "evolutionary" transformations. We know that these transformations can be much larger, and faster, than real evolutionary change that took place in the past. We've seen that selection operates in the laboratory, in microorganisms that cause disease, and in the wild. We know of no adaptations that absolutely could not have been molded by natural selection, and in many cases we can plausibly infer how selection did mold them. And mathematical models show that natural selection can produce complex features easily and quickly. The obvious conclusion: we can provisionally assume that natural selection is the cause of all *adaptive* evolution—though not of *every* feature of evolution, since genetic drift can also play a role.

True, breeders haven't turned a cat into a dog, and laboratory studies haven't turned a bacterium into an amoeba (although, as we've seen, new bacterial species have arisen in the lab). But it is foolish to think that these are serious objections to natural selection. Big transformations take time— huge spans of it. To really see the power of selection, we must extrapolate the small changes that selection creates in our lifetime over the millions of years that it has really had to work in nature. We can't see the Grand Canyon getting deeper, either, but gazing into that great abyss, with the Colorado River carving away insensibly below, you learn the most important lesson of Darwinism: weak forces operating over long periods of time create large and dramatic change.

Chapter 6

How Sex Drives Evolution

*It cannot be supposed, for instance, that male birds
of paradise or peacocks should take such pains in erecting,
spreading, and vibrating their beautiful plumes before
the females for no purpose.*

—Charles Darwin

There are few animals in nature more resplendent than a male peacock in full display, with his iridescent blue-green tail, studded with eyespots, fanned out in full glory behind a shiny blue body. But the bird seems to violate every aspect of Darwinism, for the traits that make him beautiful are at the same time *maladaptive* for survival. That long tail produces aerodynamic problems in flight, as anyone knows who has ever seen a peacock struggle to become airborne. This surely makes it hard for the birds to get up to their nighttime roosts in the trees and to escape predators, especially during the monsoons when a wet tail is literally a drag. The sparkling colors too attract predators, especially compared to the females, who are short-tailed and camouflaged a drab greenish brown. And a lot of metabolic energy is diverted to the male's striking tail, which must be completely regrown each year.

Not only does the peacock's plumage seem pointless, but it's an impediment. How could it possibly be an adaptation? And if individuals with such plumage left more genes, as one would expect if the raiment evolved by natural selection, how come the females aren't equally resplendent? In a letter to the American biologist Asa Gray in 1860, Darwin griped about these questions: "I remember well the time when the thought of the eye made me cold all over, but I have got over this stage of complaint and now trifling particulars of structure often make me very uncomfortable. The sight of a feather in a peacock's tail, whenever I gaze at it, makes me sick!"

Enigmas like the peacock's tail abound. Take the extinct Irish elk (actually a misnomer, for it's neither exclusively Irish nor an elk; it is in fact the largest deer ever described, and lived throughout Europe and Asia). Males of this species, which disappeared only about ten thousand years ago, were the proud possessors of an enormous pair of antlers, spanning more than twelve feet from tip to tip! Together weighing about ninety pounds, they sat atop a paltry five-pound skull. Think of the stress that would cause. It's like walking around all day carrying a teenager on your head. And, like the peacock's tail, these antlers were completely regrown from scratch each year.

In addition to gaudy traits, there are strange behaviors seen in only one sex. Male túngara frogs of Central America use their inflatable vocal sacs to sing a long serenade each night. The songs attract the attention of females, but also of bats and bloodsucking flies, which prey on singing males far more often than on the noncalling females. In Australia, male bowerbirds build large and bizarre "bowers" out of sticks that, depending on the species, are shaped like tunnels, mushrooms, or tents. They are festooned with decorations: flowers, snail shells, berries, seed pods, and, where humans are nearby, bottle caps, pieces of glass, and tinfoil. These bowers take hours, sometimes days, to erect (some are nearly ten feet across and five feet tall), and yet they're not used as nests. Why do males go to all this trouble?

We don't have to just speculate, as Darwin did, that these traits reduce survival. In recent years scientists have actually shown how costly they can be. The male red-collared widowbird is shiny black, sporting a deep crimson necklace and head patch, and laden with immensely long tail feathers—

roughly twice as long as its body. Anybody seeing the male in flight, struggling through the air with its tail flopping behind, has to wonder what that tail is all about. Sarah Pryke and Steffan Andersson of Sweden's Göteborg University captured a group of males in South Africa and trimmed their tails, removing about an inch in one group and four inches in another. Recapturing the males over the breeding season, they found that longer-tailed males lost significantly more weight than shorter-tailed males. Clearly, those extended tails are a considerable handicap.

And so are bright colors, as demonstrated in a clever experiment on the collared lizard. In this footlong lizard that lives in the western United States, the sexes look very different: males sport a turquoise body, yellow head, black neck collars, and black-and-white spots, while the less gaudy females are grayish brown and only lightly spotted. To test the hypothesis that the male's bright color attracts more predators, Jerry Husak and his colleagues at Oklahoma State University put out in the desert clay models painted to look like male and female lizards. The soft clay would preserve the bite marks of any predators mistaking the models for real animals. After only a week, thirty-five of the forty garish male models showed bite marks, mostly by snakes and birds, while *none* of the forty drab female models were attacked.

Traits that differ between males and females of a species—such as tails, color, and songs—are called *sexual dimorphisms*, from the Greek for "two forms." (Figure 23 shows a few examples.) Over and over, biologists have found that sexually dimorphic traits in males seem to violate evolutionary theory, for they waste time and energy and reduce survival. Colorful male guppies are eaten more often than are the plainer females. The male black wheatear, a Mediterranean bird, laboriously erects large cairns of stones in various locations, piling up fifty times his own weight in pebbles over a period of two weeks. Male sage grouse perform elaborate displays, strutting up and down the prairie, flapping their wings, and making loud sounds from two large vocal sacs.[32] These shenanigans can use up a tremendous amount of energy for a bird: one day's display burns up the caloric equivalent of a banana split. If selection is responsible for these traits—and it should be, given their complexity—we need to explain how.

FIGURE 23. Examples of sexual dimorphisms, showing marked differences in the appearance of males and females. Top: the swordtail (*Xiphophorus helleri*); middle: King of Saxony Bird of Paradise (*Pteridophora alberti*), whose males have elaborate head ornaments that are sky blue on one side and brown on the other; bottom: the stag beetle *(Aegus formosae)*.

The Solutions

BEFORE DARWIN, sexual dimorphism was a mystery. Creationists then—as now—could not explain why a supernatural designer should produce features in one sex, and only one sex, that harm its survival. As the great explainer of nature's diversity, Darwin was naturally anxious to understand how these seemingly pointless traits evolved. He finally noticed the key to their explanation: if traits differ between males and females of a species, the elaborate behaviors, structures, and ornaments are nearly always restricted to males.

By now you might have guessed how these costly traits evolved. Remember that the currency of selection is not really survival, but successful reproduction. Having a fancy tail or a seductive song doesn't help you survive, but may increase your chances of having offspring—and that's how these flamboyant traits and behaviors arose. Darwin was the first to recognize this trade-off, and coined the name for the type of selection responsible for sexually dimorphic features: *sexual selection*. Sexual selection is simply selection that increases an individual's chance of getting a mate. It's really just a subset of natural selection, but one that deserves its own chapter because of the unique way it operates and the seemingly nonadaptive adaptations it produces.

Sexually selected traits evolve if they more than offset the male's diminished survival with an increase in his reproduction. Maybe widowbirds with longer tails don't evade predators very well, but females might prefer the longer-tailed males as mates. Deer with bigger antlers might struggle to survive under a metabolic burden, but perhaps they win jousting contests more frequently, thereby siring more offspring.

Sexual selection comes in two forms. One, exemplified by the Irish elk's huge antlers, is *direct competition between males* for access to females. The other, the one that produces the widowbird's long tail, is *female choosiness* among possible mates. Male-male competition (or, in Darwin's oft-pugnacious terminology, "the Law of Battle") is the easiest to understand. As Darwin noted, "It is certain that with almost all animals there is a struggle between the males for the possession of the female." When males of a species battle it out directly, be it through the clashing antlers of deer, the stabbing horns of the stag beetle, the head butting of stalk-eyed flies, or the bloody battles of massive elephant seals, they win access to females by driving off competitors. Selection will favor any trait that promotes such victories so long as the increased chance of getting mates more than offsets any reduced survival. This kind of selection produces armaments: stronger weapons, larger body size, or anything that helps a male win physical contests.

In contrast, features such as bright colors, ornaments, bowers, and mating displays are molded by the second type of sexual selection, mate choice. To female eyes, it seems, not all males are the same. They find some male traits and behaviors more attractive than others, so genes that produce those features accumulate in populations. There is also an element of competition between males in this scenario, but it is indirect: winning males have the loudest voices, the brightest colors, the most alluring pheromones, the sexiest displays, and so on. But in contrast to male-male competition, here the winner is decided by the females.

In both types of sexual selection, males compete for females. Why isn't it the other way around? We'll learn shortly that it all rests on the difference in size between two tiny cells: the sperm and the egg.

Is it really true, though, that males who win contests, or are more highly ornamented, or perform the best displays, actually get more mates? If they don't, the whole theory of sexual selection collapses.

In fact, the evidence strongly and consistently supports the theory. Let's start with contests. The northern elephant seal of North America's Pacific coast shows extreme sexual dimorphism for size. Females are roughly ten feet long and weigh about fifteen hundred pounds, while males are nearly twice as long and can weigh up to six thousand pounds—bigger than a Volkswagen and more than twice as heavy. They are also *polygynous*: that is, males mate with more than one female during the breeding season. About a third of the males guard harems of females with whom they couple (up to one hundred mates for an alpha male!), while the rest of the males are doomed to bachelorhood. Who wins and who loses the mating lottery is determined by fierce contests between males before the females even haul out on the beach. These contests get bloody, with the big bulls bashing their massive bodies together, inflicting deep neck wounds with their teeth, and setting up a dominance hierarchy that has the largest males at the top. When the females do arrive, the dominant males herd them into their harems and drive off approaching rivals. In a given year, most pups are sired by just a few of the largest males.

This is male competition, pure and simple, and the prize is reproduction. It is easy to see how, given this mating system, sexual selection promotes the evolution of large, fierce males: bigger males leave their genes to the next generation, smaller ones don't. (Females, who don't have to fight, are presumably close to their optimal weight for reproduction.) Sexual dimorphism of body size in many species—including our own—may be due to competition between males for access to females.

Male birds often compete fiercely over real estate. In many species, males attract females only by controlling a patch of land—one with good vegetation—that is suitable for nesting. Once they have their patch, males defend it with visual and vocal displays, as well as direct attacks on encroaching males. Many of the birdsongs that delight our ears are actually threats, warning other males to keep away.

The red-winged blackbird of North America defends territories in open habitats, usually freshwater marshes. Like elephant seals, this species is polygynous, with some males having as many as fifteen females nesting in their territory. Many other males, called "floaters," go unmated. Floaters constantly try to invade established territories to sneak copulations with females, keeping resident males busy driving them away. Up to a quarter of a male's time can be spent vigilantly protecting his turf. Besides direct patrolling, redwing males defend their territories by singing complex songs and making threat displays with their eponymous ornament, a bright red epaulet on the shoulder. (Females are brown, sometimes with a small, vestigial epaulet.) The epaulets aren't there to attract females—rather, they are used to threaten other males in the battle for territories. When experimenters effaced the epaulets of males by painting them black, 70 percent of males lost their territories, compared to only 10 percent of control males painted with a clear solvent. The epaulets probably keep intruders away by signaling that a territory is occupied. Song is also important. Muted males, temporarily deprived of their ability to sing, also lose territories.

In blackbirds, then, song and plumage help a male get more mates. In the studies described above, and many others as well, researchers have shown that sexual selection is acting because males with more elaborate features get a greater payoff in offspring. This conclusion seems simple but required hundreds of hours of tedious fieldwork by inquisitive biologists. Sequencing DNA in a gleaming lab may seem far more glamorous, but the only way a scientist can tell us how selection acts in nature is to get dirty in the field.

Sexual selection doesn't end with the sex act itself: males can continue to compete even after mating. In many species, females mate with more than one male over a short period of time. After a male inseminates a female, how can he prevent other males from fertilizing her and stealing his paternity? This *post-mating competition* has produced some of the most intriguing features built by sexual selection. Sometimes a male hangs around after mating, guarding his female against other suitors. When you see a pair of dragonflies attached to each other, it's likely that the male is simply guarding the female after having fertilized her, physically blocking access by other males. A Central American millipede has taken mate guarding to the extreme: after fertilizing a female, the male simply rides her for several days, preventing any competitor from claiming her eggs. Chemicals can also do this job. The ejaculate of some snakes and rodents contains substances that temporarily plug up a female's reproductive tract after mating, barricading out other probing males. In the group of fruit flies on which I work, the male injects the female with an antiaphrodisiac, a chemical in his semen that makes her unwilling to remate for several days.

Males use a variety of defensive weapons to guard their paternity. But they can be even more devious—many have *offensive* weapons to get rid of the sperm from previously mating males and replace it with their own. One of the cleverest devices is the "penis scoop" of some damselflies. When a male mates with an already mated female, he uses backward-pointing spines on his penis to scoop out the sperm of earlier-mating males. Only after she's despermed does he transfer his own sperm. In *Drosophila*, my own lab found that a male's ejaculate contains substances that inactivate the stored sperm of males who mated previously.

What about the second form of sexual selection: mate choice? Compared to male-male competition, we know a lot less about how this process works. That's because the significance of colors, plumage, and display is far less obvious than that of antlers and other weapons.

To figure out how mate choice evolves, let's begin with that pesky peacock tail that caused Darwin such angst. Much of the work on mate choice in the peacock has been done by Marion Petrie and her colleagues, who study a free-ranging population in Whipsnade Park, Bedfordshire, England. In this species males assemble at *leks*, areas where they all display together, giving females an opportunity to compare them directly. Not all males join the lek, but only the ones who do can win a female. One observational study of ten lekking males showed a strong correlation between the number of eyespots in a male's tail feathers and the number of matings he achieved: the most elaborate male, with 160 eyespots, garnered 36 percent of all copulations.

This suggests that more elaborate tails are preferred by females, but doesn't prove it. It's possible that some other aspect of male courtship— say, the vigor of his display—is really what females are choosing, and this just happens to be correlated with plumage. To rule this out, one can do experimental manipulations: change the number of eyespots on the tail of a peacock and see if this affects his ability to get mates. Remarkably, such an experiment was suggested in 1869 by Darwin's competitor, Alfred Russel Wallace. Although the two men agreed on many things, most notably natural selection, they parted ways when it came to sexual selection. The idea of male-male competition was no problem for either man, but Wallace frowned on the possibility of female choice. Nevertheless, he kept an open mind on this issue, and was way ahead of his time in suggesting how to test it:

> The part that remains to be played by ornament alone will be very small, even if it were proved, which it is not, that a slight superiority in ornament alone usually determines the choice of a mate.
>
> This, however, is a matter that admits of experiment, and I would suggest that either some Zoological Society or any person having the

means, should try such experiments. A dozen male birds of the same age—
domestic fowls, common pheasants, or gold pheasants, for instance—
should be chosen, all known to be acceptable to the hen birds. Half of
these should have one or two tail plumes cut off, or the neck plumes a
little shortened, just enough to produce such a difference as occurs by
variation in nature, but not enough to disfigure the bird, and then
observe whether the hens take any notice of the deficiency, and whether
they uniformly reject the less ornamented males. Such experiments,
carefully made and judiciously varied for a few seasons, would give most
valuable information on this interesting question.

In fact, such experiments weren't done until more than a century later.
But the results are now in, and female choice is common. In one experiment,
Marion Petrie and Tim Halliday cut twenty eyespots off the tail of every
male in a group of peacocks, and compared their mating success to that of a
control group that was handled but not clipped. Sure enough, in the next
breeding season the deornamented males each averaged 2.5 fewer matings
than the control males.

This experiment certainly suggests that females prefer males whose ornaments had not been reduced. But ideally, we'd also like to do the experiment
in the other direction: make the tails *more* elaborate and see if that enhances
mating success. While this is hard to do in peacocks, it's been done in the
territorial African long-tailed widowbird by the Swedish biologist Malte
Andersson. In this sexually dimorphic species, males have tails about twenty
inches long, females about three inches. By removing parts of the long male
tails and gluing some of these removed parts onto normal tails, Andersson
created males with abnormally short tails (six inches), normal "control" tails
(a piece cut off and then glued back on), and long tails (thirty inches). As
expected, short-tailed males acquired fewer females nesting on their territory compared to normal males. But males with the artificially long tails
gained a whopping increase in matings, attracting nearly twice as many
females as did normal males.

This raises a question: If males with thirty-inch tails won more females,
why haven't widowbirds evolved tails that long in the first place? We don't

know the answer, but it's likely that having tails that long would reduce a male's longevity more than they would increase his ability to get mates. Twenty inches is probably the length at which total reproductive output, averaged over a lifetime, is near its maximum.

And what do those male sage grouse gain from their arduous antics on the prairie? Again, the answer is mates. Like peacocks, male sage grouse form leks where they display en masse to inspecting females. It's been shown that only the most vigorous males—who "strut" about eight hundred times per day—win females, while the vast majority of males go unmated.

Sexual selection also explains the architectural feats of bowerbirds. Several studies have shown that the types of bower decorations, which differ in each species, are correlated with mating success. Satin bowerbirds, for example, get more mates if they put more blue feathers in their bowers. In spotted bowerbirds, the most success is achieved by displaying green *Solanum* berries (a species related to wild tomatoes). Joah Madden from Cambridge University stripped the decorations from spotted bowerbird bowers, and then offered the males a choice of sixty objects. Sure enough, they redecorated their bowers mainly with *Solanum* berries, placing them in the most conspicuous positions on the bower.

I've concentrated on birds because biologists have found it easiest to study mate choice in that group—birds are active during the day and easy to observe—but there are many examples of mate choice in other animals. Female túngara frogs prefer to mate with males who bellow the most complex calls. Female guppies like males with longer tails and more colored spots. Female spiders and fish often prefer larger males. In his exhaustive book *Sexual Selection*, Malte Andersson describes 232 experiments in 186 species showing that a huge variety of male traits are correlated with mating success, and the vast majority of these tests involve female choice. There is simply no doubt that female choice has driven the evolution of many sexual dimorphisms. Darwin was right after all.

So far we've neglected two important questions: Why do females get to do the choosing while males must woo or fight for them? And why do females choose at all? To answer these questions we must first understand why organisms bother to have sex.

Why Sex?

WHY SEX EVOLVED is in fact one of evolution's greatest mysteries. Any individual who reproduces sexually—that is, by making eggs or sperm that contain only half of its genes—sacrifices 50 percent of its genetic contribution to the next generation compared to an individual who reproduces asexually. Let's look at it this way. Suppose that there was a gene in humans whose normal form led to sexual reproduction but whose mutant form enabled a female to reproduce *parthenogenetically*—by producing eggs that develop without fertilization. (Some animals really do reproduce this way: it's been seen in aphids, fish, and lizards.) The first mutant woman would have only daughters, who themselves would produce more daughters. In contrast, nonmutant, sexually reproducing women would have to mate with males, producing half sons and half daughters. The proportion of women in the population would quickly begin to rise above 50 percent as the pool of females became increasingly full of mutants who produce only daughters. In the end, all the females would be produced by asexually reproducing mothers. Males would become superfluous and disappear: no mutant females would need to mate with them, and all females would give birth to only more females. The gene for parthenogenesis would have outcompeted the gene for sexual reproduction. You can show theoretically that in each generation the "asexual" gene would produce twice as many copies of itself as did the original "sexual" gene. Biologists call this situation the "twofold cost of sex." The bottom line is that under natural selection genes for parthenogenesis spread quickly, eliminating sexual reproduction.

But this hasn't happened. The vast majority of earth's species reproduce sexually, and that form of reproduction has been around for over a billion years.[33] Why hasn't the cost of sex led to its replacement by parthenogenesis? Clearly, sex must have some huge evolutionary advantage that outweighs its cost. Although we haven't yet figured out exactly what that advantage is, there's no shortage of theories. The key may well lie in the random shuffling of genes that occurs during sexual reproduction, which produces new combinations of genes in the offspring. By bringing together several favorable genes in one individual, sex might promote faster evolution to deal with aspects of the environment that are constantly changing—like the parasites that relentlessly evolve to counter our own evolving defenses. Or perhaps sex could purge bad genes from a species by recombining them together into one severely disadvantaged individual, a genetic scapegoat. Yet biologists still question whether any known advantage outweighs the twofold cost of sex.

Once sex has evolved, however, sexual selection follows inevitably if we can explain just two more things. First, why are there just two (rather than three or more) sexes that must mate and combine their genes to produce offspring? And second, why do the two sexes have different numbers and sizes of gametes (males produce a lot of small sperm, females fewer but larger eggs)? The question of the number of sexes is a messy theoretical issue that needn't detain us, except to note that theory shows that two sexes will evolutionarily replace mating systems involving three or more sexes; two sexes is the most robust and stable strategy.

The theory of why the two sexes have different numbers and sizes of gametes is equally messy. This condition presumably evolved from that in earlier sexually reproducing species in which the two sexes had gametes of equal size. Theoreticians have shown rather convincingly that natural selection will favor changing this ancestral state into a state in which one sex (the one we call "male") makes a lot of small gametes—sperm or pollen—and the other ("female") makes fewer but larger gametes, known as eggs.

It's this asymmetry in the size of gametes that sets the stage for all of sexual selection, for it causes the two sexes to evolve different mating strategies. Take males. A male can produce large quantities of sperm, and so can potentially father a huge number of offspring, limited only by the number of females he can attract and the competitive ability of his sperm. Things are different for females. Eggs are expensive and limited in number, and if a female mates many times over a short period, she does little—if anything—to increase her number of offspring.

A vivid demonstration of this difference can be seen by looking up the record number of children sired by a human female versus a male. If you were to guess the maximum number of children that a woman could produce in a lifetime, you might say around fifteen. Guess again. The *Guinness Book of World Records* gives the "official" record number of children for a woman as sixty-nine, produced by an eighteenth-century Russian peasant. In twenty-seven pregnancies between 1725 and 1745, she had sixteen pairs of twins, seven sets of triplets, and four sets of quadruplets. (She presumably had some physiological or genetic predisposition to multiple births.) One weeps for this belabored woman, but her record is far surpassed by that of a male, one Mulai Ismail (1646–1727), an emperor of Morocco. Ismail was reported by *Guinness* as having fathered "at least 342 daughters and 525 sons, and by 1721 he was reputed to have 700 male descendants." Even at these extremes, then, males outstrip females more than tenfold.

The evolutionary difference between males and females is a matter of differential *investment*—investment in expensive eggs versus cheap sperm, investment in pregnancy (when females retain and nourish the fertilized eggs), and investment in parental care in the many species in which females alone raise the young. For males, mating is cheap; for females it's expensive. For males, a mating costs only a small dose of sperm; for females it costs much more: the production of large, nutrient-rich eggs and often a huge expenditure of energy and time. In more than 90 percent of mammal species, a male's only investment in offspring is his sperm, for females provide all the parental care.

This asymmetry between males and females in potential numbers of mates and offspring leads to conflicting interests when it comes time to choose a mate. Males have little to lose by mating with a "substandard" female (say, one who is weak or sickly), because they can easily mate again, and repeatedly. Selection then favors genes that make a male promiscuous, relentlessly trying to mate with nearly any female. (Or any *thing* bearing the slightest resemblance to a female—male sage grouse, for instance, sometimes try to mate with piles of cow manure, and, as we learned earlier, some orchids get pollinated by luring randy male bees to copulate with their petals.)

Females are different. Because of their higher investment in eggs and offspring, their best tactic is to be picky rather than promiscuous. Females must make each opportunity count by choosing the best possible father to fertilize their limited number of eggs. They should therefore inspect potential mates very closely.

What this adds up to is that, in general, males must compete for females. Males should be promiscuous, females coy. The life of a male should be one of internecine conflict, constantly vying with his fellows for mates. The good males, either more attractive or more vigorous, will often secure a large number of mates (they will presumably be preferred by more females too), while substandard males go unmated. Almost all females, on the other hand, will eventually find mates. Since every male is competing for them, their distribution of mating success will be more even.

Biologists describe this difference by saying that the *variance* in mating success should be higher for males than females. Is it? Yes, we often see such a difference. In the red deer, for example, the variation among males in how many offspring they leave during their lifetime is three times higher than that of females. The disparity is even greater for elephant seals, in which fewer than 10 percent of all males leave *any* offspring over several breeding seasons, compared to more than half of the females.[34]

The difference between males and females in their potential number of offspring drives the evolution of both male-male competition and female choice. Males must compete to fertilize a limited number of eggs. That's why we see the "law of battle": the direct competition between males to leave their genes to the next generation. And that is also why males are colorful, or have displays, mating calls, bowers, and the like, for that is their way of saying "Pick me, pick me!" And it is ultimately female preference that drives the evolution of longer tails, more vigorous displays, and louder songs in males.

Now, the scenario I have just described is a generalization, and there are exceptions. Some species are monogamous, with both males and females providing parental care. Evolution can favor monogamy if males have more offspring by helping with child care than if they abandon their offspring to seek more matings. In many birds, for example, two full-time parents are required: when one goes off to forage, the other incubates the eggs. But monogamous species are not that common in the wild. Only 2 percent of all mammal species, for instance, have this type of mating system.

Further, there are explanations for sexual dimorphism in body size that do not involve sexual selection. In the fruit flies I study, for example, females may be larger simply because they need to produce large and costly eggs. Or males and females might be more efficient predators if they specialize on different food items. Natural selection for reduced competition between members of the two sexes could lead them to evolve differences in body size. This may explain a dimorphism in some lizards and hawks, in which females are larger than males and also catch larger prey.

Breaking the Rules

CURIOUSLY, we also see sexual dimorphisms in many "socially monoga-mous" species—those in which males and females pair up and rear young together. Since males don't seem to be competing for females, why have they evolved bright colors and ornaments? This seeming contradiction actually provides further support for sexual selection theory. It turns out that in these cases, appearances are deceiving. The species are socially monogamous but not *actually* monogamous.

One of these species is the splendid fairy wren of Australia, studied by my University of Chicago colleague Stephen Pruett-Jones. At first glance, this species looks like the paragon of monogamy. Males and females usually spend their entire adult lives socially bonded to each other, and they code-fend their territory and share parental care. Yet they show striking sexual dimorphism in plumage: males are a gorgeous iridescent blue and black, while females are a dull grayish brown. Why? Because adultery is rife. When it comes time to mate, females mate with *other* males more often than they do with their "social mate." (This is shown by DNA paternity analysis.) Males play the same game, actively seeking and soliciting "extra-pair" matings, but they still vary far more than females in their reproductive success. Sexual selection associated with these adulterous couplings almost certainly pro-duced the evolution of color differences between the sexes. This wren is not unique in its behavior. Although 90 percent of all bird species are socially monogamous, in fully three-quarters of these species males and females mate with individuals other than their social partner.

Sexual selection theory makes testable predictions. If only one sex has bright plumage or antlers, performs vigorous mating displays, or builds elaborate structures to lure females, you can bet that it is members of that sex who compete to mate with members of the other. And species showing less sexual dimorphism in behavior or appearance should be more monogamous: if males and females pair up and don't stray from their mates, there is no sexual competition and therefore no sexual selection. Indeed, biologists see strong correlations between mating systems and sexual dimorphism. Extreme dimorphisms in size, color, or behavior are found in those species, like the birds of paradise or elephant seals, in which males compete for females, and only a few males get most of the matings. Species in which males and females look similar—for instance, geese, penguins, pigeons, and parrots—tend to be truly monogamous, exemplars of animal fidelity. This correlation is another triumph for evolutionary theory, for it is predicted only by the idea of sexual selection and not by any creationist alternative. Why should there be a correlation between color and mating system unless evolution is true? Indeed, it is creationists rather than evolutionists who should become sick at the sight of a peacock's feather.[35]

So far we've talked about sexual selection as if the promiscuous sex is always male and the picky sex female. But sometimes, albeit rarely, it's the other way around. And when these behaviors switch between the sexes, so does the direction of dimorphism. We see this reversal in those most appealing of fish, seahorses, and their close relatives the pipefish. In some of these species the males rather than the females become pregnant! How can that happen? Although the female does produce eggs, after a male fertilizes them he places them in a specialized brood pouch on his belly or tail, and carries them about until they hatch. Males carry only one brood at a time, and their "gestation" period lasts longer than it takes a female to produce a fresh batch of eggs. Males, then, actually invest more in child-rearing than do females. Also, because there are more females carrying unfertilized eggs than males to accept them, females must compete for the rare "nonpregnant" males. Here, the male-female difference in reproductive strategy is reversed. And just as you might expect under sexual-selection theory, it is the females who are decorated with bright colors and body ornaments, while males are relatively drab.

The same goes for the phalaropes, three species of graceful shorebirds that breed in Europe and North America. These are among the few examples of a *polyandrous* ("one female and many male") mating system. (This rare mating system can also be found among a few human populations, including Tibetans.) Male phalaropes are entirely responsible for chick care, building the nests and feeding the brood while the female moves on to mate with other males. The male's investment in offspring, then, is greater than the female's, and females compete for males who will take care of their young. And, sure enough, in all three species females are colored much brighter than males.

Seahorses, pipefish, and phalaropes are the exceptions that prove the rule. Their "reverse" decoration is exactly what one would expect if the evolutionary explanation of sexual dimorphism is true, but doesn't make sense if these species were specially created.

Why Choose?

LET'S RETURN TO "NORMAL" MATE CHOICE, in which females are the choosy ones. What exactly are they looking for when they pick a male? This question inspired a famous disagreement in evolutionary biology. Alfred Russel Wallace, as we've seen, was dubious (and ultimately wrong) about whether females are even choosy. His own hypothesis was that females were less colorful than males because they needed to be camouflaged from predators, while the bright colors and ornaments of males were by-products of their physiology. He gave no explanation, though, why males shouldn't be camouflaged as well.

Darwin's hypothesis was a little better. He felt strongly that male calls, colors, and ornaments evolved via female choice. On what basis were females choosing? His answer was surprising: pure aesthetics. Darwin saw no reason why females should choose things like elaborate songs or long tails unless they found them intrinsically appealing. His pioneering study of sexual selection, *The Descent of Man, and Selection in Relation to Sex* (1871), is larded with quaint anthropomorphic descriptions of how female animals are "charmed" and "wooed" by various features of males. Yet, as Wallace noted, there was still a problem. Did animals, particularly simple ones like beetles and flies, really have an aesthetic sense like our own? Darwin punted on this one, pleading ignorance:

> Although we have some positive evidence that birds appreciate bright and beautiful objects, as with the bower-birds of Australia, and although they certainly appreciate the power of song, yet I fully admit that it is astonishing that the females of many birds and some mammals should be endowed with sufficient taste to appreciate ornaments, which we have reason to attribute to sexual selection; and this is even more astonishing in the case of reptiles, fish, and insects. But we really know little about the minds of the lower animals.

It turns out that Darwin, though he didn't have all the answers, was closer to the truth than was Wallace. Yes, females do choose, and that choice seems to explain sexual dimorphisms. But it doesn't make sense that female preference is based solely on aesthetics. Closely related species, like the New Guinea birds of paradise, have males with very different types of plumage and mating behavior. Is what is beautiful to one species so different from what is beautiful to its closest relatives?

In fact, we now have a lot of evidence that female preferences are themselves adaptive, because preferring certain types of males helps females spread their genes. Preferences aren't always a matter of random inborn taste, as Darwin supposed, but in many cases probably evolved by selection.

What does a female have to gain by choosing a particular male? There are two answers. She can benefit *directly*—that is, by picking a male who will help her produce more or healthier young *during the act of child care*. Or she can benefit *indirectly*, by choosing a male who has better genes than those of other males (that is, genes that will give her offspring a leg up in the next generation). Either way, the evolution of female preferences will be favored by selection—natural selection.

Take direct benefits. A gene that tells a female to mate with males holding better territories gives her offspring who are better nourished or occupy better nests. They will survive better and reproduce more than young who were not brought up in good territories. This means that the population of young will contain a higher proportion of females carrying the "preference gene" than it did in the previous generation. As generations pass and evolution continues, every female will eventually carry preference genes. And if there are other mutations that *increase* preference for better territories, those too will increase in frequency. Over time, the preference for males with better territories will evolve to be stronger and stronger. And this, in turn, selects on the males to compete more strongly for territories. The female preference evolves hand in hand with the male competition for real estate.

Genes that give *indirect* benefits to choosy females will also spread. Imagine that a male has genes that make him more resistant than other males to disease. A female who mates with such a male will have offspring that are also more disease-resistant. This gives her an evolutionary benefit in choosing that male. Now imagine as well that there is a gene that enables females to *identify* these healthier males as mates. If she mates with such a male, that mating will produce sons and daughters who carry both types of genes: those for disease resistance as well as those for *preferring* males with disease resistance. In each generation, the most disease-resistant individuals, who reproduce better, will also carry genes that tell females to choose the most resistant males. As those resistance genes spread by natural selection, the genes for female preference piggyback along with them. In this way both female preference and disease resistance increase thoughout a species.

Both of these scenarios explain why females prefer certain kinds of males, but not why they prefer certain *features* of those males, like bright colors or elaborate plumage. This probably happens because those particular features tell the female that a male will provide larger direct or indirect benefits. Let's look at a few examples of female choice.

The house finch of North America is sexually dimorphic for color: females are brown but males have bright colors on their head and breast. Males don't defend territories but do show parental care. Geoff Hill at the University of Michigan found that in one local population, males varied in color from pale yellow through orange to bright red. Wanting to see if color affected reproductive success, he used hair dyes to make males brighter or paler. Sure enough, brighter males obtained significantly more mates than paler ones. And among unmanipulated birds, females deserted the nests of lighter males more often than the nests of brighter males.

Why do female finches prefer brighter males? In the same population, Hill showed that brighter males feed their young more often than do lighter males. Females thus get a direct benefit, in the form of better provisioning of their offspring, by choosing brighter males. (Females mated to lighter males might abandon their nests because the young aren't adequately fed.) And why do brighter males bring more food? Probably because brightness is a sign of overall health. The red color of male finches comes entirely from carotenoid pigments in the seeds they eat—they can't make this pigment on their own. Brighter males are therefore better fed, and probably healthier in general. Females seem to choose bright males simply because the color tells them, "I'm a male who's better able to stock the family larder." Any genes that make females prefer brighter males gives those females a direct benefit, and so selection would increase that preference. And with the preference in place, any male who is better at converting seeds into bright plumage would also get an advantage, because he'll secure more mates. Over time, sexual selection will exaggerate a male's red color. The females stay drab because they gain no benefit from being bright; indeed, they could suffer by becoming more conspicuous to predators.

There are other direct benefits to choosing a healthy and vigorous male. Males can carry parasites or diseases that they can transmit to females, their young, or both, and it's to a female's advantage to avoid these males. A male's color, plumage, and behavior can be a clue to whether he's diseased or infested: only healthy males can sing a loud song, perform a vigorous display, or grow a bright, handsome set of feathers. If males of a species are normally bright blue, for example, you'd best avoid mating with a pale male.

Evolutionary theory shows that females should prefer *any* trait showing that a male will be a good father. All that's required is that there be some genes increasing the preference for that trait, and that variation in the expression of the trait gives a clue to the male's condition. The rest follows automatically. In sage grouse, parasitic lice produce spots of blood on the male's vocal sac, a feature prominently displayed as a swollen, translucent pouch while they're strutting on the lek. Males who have artificial blood spots painted on their vocal sacs get significantly fewer matings: the spots may tip off females that a male is infested and would literally be a lousy father. Selection will favor genes that promote not only the female preference for unspotted sacs, but also the male trait that indicates his condition. The male's vocal sac will get bigger, and the female's preference for the plain vocal sac will increase. This can lead to the evolution of highly exaggerated features in males, like the ludicrously long tail of the widowbird. The whole process stops only when the male trait becomes so exaggerated that any further increase reduces his survival more than it attracts females, so that his net production of offspring suffers.

What about female preferences that give *indirect* benefits? The most obvious such benefit is what a male always gives to his offspring—his genes. And the same type of traits that show a male is healthy could also show that he's genetically well endowed. Males with brighter colors, longer tails, or louder calls may be able to display these features only if they have genes that make them survive or reproduce better than their competitors. Likewise for males able to build elaborate bowers, or pile up large cairns of stones. You can imagine many features that could show a male has genes for greater survival, or a greater ability to reproduce. Evolutionary theory shows that in these cases, *three* types of genes will all increase in frequency together: genes for a male "indicator" trait reflecting that he has good genes, genes that make a female prefer that indicator trait, and of course the "good" genes whose presence is reflected by the indicator. This is a complex scenario, but most evolutionary biologists consider it the best explanation for elaborate male traits and behaviors.

But how can we test whether the "good-genes" model is really correct? Are females looking for direct or indirect benefits? A female might spurn a less vigorous or less showy male, but this might reflect not his poor genetic endowment but simply an environmentally caused debility, such as infection or malnutrition. Such complications make the causes of sexual selection in any given case hard to unravel.

Perhaps the best test of the good-genes model was done on gray tree frogs by Allison Welch and her colleagues at the University of Missouri. Male frogs attract females by giving loud calls, limning summer nights in the southern United States. Studies of captive frogs show that females strongly prefer males whose calls are longer. To test whether those males had better genes, researchers stripped eggs from different females, fertilizing half of each female's eggs in vitro with sperm from long-calling males, and the other half with sperm from short-calling males. The tadpoles from these crosses were then reared to maturity. The results were dramatic. Offspring from long-callers grew faster and survived better as tadpoles, were larger at metamorphosis (the time when tadpoles turn into frogs), and grew faster after metamorphosis. Since male gray tree frogs make no contribution to offspring except for sperm, females can get no *direct* benefits from choosing a long-calling male. This test strongly suggests that a long call is the sign of a healthy male with good genes, and that females who choose those males produce genetically superior offspring.

So what about those peacocks? We've seen that females prefer to mate with males who have more eyespots in their tails. And males make no contribution to raising their young. Working at Whipsnade Park, Marion Petrie showed that males with more eyespots produce young that not only grow faster but also survive better. It's likely that by choosing more elaborate tails, females are choosing good genes, for a genetically well-endowed male is more capable of growing an elaborate tail.

These two studies are all the evidence we have so far that females choose males with better genes. And a fair number of studies have found *no* association between mate preference and the genetic quality of offspring. Still, the good-genes model remains the favored explanation of sexual selection. This belief, in the face of relatively sparse evidence, may partly reflect a preference of evolutionists for strict Darwinian explanations—a belief that females must somehow be able to discriminate among the genes of males.

There is, however, a third explanation for sexual dimorphisms, and it's the simplest of all. It is based on what are called *sensory-bias* models. These models assume that the evolution of sexual dimorphisms is driven simply by preexisting biases in a female's nervous system. And those biases could be a by-product of natural selection for some function other than finding mates, like finding food. Suppose, for example, that members of a species had evolved a visual preference for red color because that preference helped them locate ripe fruits and berries. If a mutant male appeared with a patch of red on his breast, he might be preferred by females simply because of this preexisting preference. Red males would then have an advantage, and a color dimorphism could evolve. (We assume that red color is disadvantageous in females because it attracts predators.) Alternatively, females may also simply like novel features that somehow stimulate their nervous systems. They may, for example, prefer bigger males, males who hold their interest by doing more complex displays, or males who are shaped oddly because they have longer tails. Unlike the models I described earlier, in the sensory-bias model females derive neither direct nor indirect benefits from choosing a particular male.

You could test this theory by producing a truly novel trait in males and seeing if females like it. This was done in two species of Australian grass-finches by Nancy Burley and Richard Symanski at the University of California. They simply glued a single vertically pointing feather to the heads of males, forming an artificial crest, and then exposed these crested males, along with uncrested controls, to females. (Grassfinches don't have head crests, although some unrelated species, like cockatoos, do.) Females turned out to show a very strong preference for males sporting white artificial crests over males with either red or green crests, or normal uncrested males. We don't understand why females prefer white, but it may be because they line their nests with white feathers to camouflage their eggs from predators. Similar experiments in frogs and fish also show that females have preferences for traits to which they've never been exposed.[36] The sensory-bias model may be important, since natural selection may often create preexisting preferences that help animals survive and reproduce, and these preferences can be co-opted by sexual selection to create new male traits. Maybe Darwin's theory of animal aesthetics was partly correct, even if he did anthropomorphize female preferences as a "taste for the beautiful."

Conspicuously missing from this chapter has been any discussion of our own species. What about us? How far theories of sexual selection apply to humans is a complicated question, one that we'll pursue in chapter 9.

Chapter 7

The Origin of Species

Each species is a masterpiece of evolution that humanity could not possibly duplicate even if we somehow accomplish the creation of new organisms by genetic engineering.

—E. O. Wilson

In 1928, a young German zoologist named Ernst Mayr set off for the wilds of Dutch New Guinea to collect plants and animals. Fresh from graduate school, he lacked any field experience but did have three things going for him: a lifelong love of birds, tremendous enthusiasm, and, most important, the financial backing of the British banker and amateur naturalist Lord Walter Rothschild. Rothschild owned the world's largest private collection of bird specimens, and hoped that Mayr's efforts would add to it. Over the next two years, Mayr tramped through the mountains and jungles with his notebooks and collecting gear. Often alone, he was the victim of bad weather, treacherous paths, repeated illnesses (a serious matter in those preantibiotic days), and the xenophobia of the locals, many of whom had never seen a Westerner. Nevertheless, his one-man expedition was a great success: Mayr brought back many specimens new to science, including twenty-six species of birds and thirty-eight species of orchids. The New Guinea work launched his stellar career as an evolutionary biologist, culminating in a professorship at Harvard University, where as a graduate student I was honored to have him as a friend and mentor.

Mayr lived exactly one hundred years, producing a stream of books and papers up to the day of his death. Among these was his 1963 classic, *Animal Species and Evolution*, the very book that made me want to study evolution. In it Mayr recounted a striking fact. When he totaled up the names that the natives of New Guinea's Arfak Mountains applied to local birds, he found that they recognized 136 different types. Western zoologists, using traditional methods of taxonomy, recognized 137 species. In other words, both locals and scientists had distinguished the very same species of birds living in the wild. This concordance between two cultural groups with very different backgrounds convinced Mayr, as it should convince us, that the discontinuities of nature are not arbitrary, but an objective fact.[37]

Indeed, perhaps the most striking fact about nature is that it *is* discontinuous. When you look at animals and plants, each individual almost always falls into one of many discrete groups. When we look at a single wild cat, for example, we are immediately able to identify it as either a lion, a cougar, a snow leopard, and so on. All cats do not blur insensibly into one another through a series of feline intermediates. And although there is variation among individuals within a cluster (as all lion researchers know, each lion looks different from every other), the clusters nevertheless remain discrete in "organism space." We see clusters in all organisms that reproduce sexually.

These discrete clusters are known as *species*. And at first sight, their existence looks like a problem for evolutionary theory. Evolution is, after all, a continuous process, so how can it produce groups of animals and plants that are discrete and discontinuous, separated from others by gaps in appearance and behavior? How these groups arise is the problem of *speciation*—or the origin of species.

That, of course, is the title of Darwin's most famous book, a title implying that he had a lot to say about speciation. Even in the opening paragraph he claimed that the biogeography of South America would "throw some light on the origin of species—that mystery of mysteries, as it has been called by one of our greatest philosophers." (The "philosopher" was actually the British scientist John Herschel.) Yet Darwin's magnum opus was largely silent on the "mystery of mysteries," and what little it did say on this topic is seen by most modern evolutionists as muddled. Darwin apparently didn't see the discontinuities of nature as a problem to be solved, or thought that these discontinuities would somehow be favored by natural selection. Either way, he failed to explain nature's clusters in a coherent way.

A better title for *The Origin of Species*, then, would have been *The Origin of Adaptations*: while Darwin did figure out how and why a *single* species changes over time (largely by natural selection), he never explained how one species splits in two. Yet in many ways this problem of splitting is just as important as understanding how a single species evolves. After all, the diversity of nature encompasses millions of species, each with its own unique set of traits. And all of this diversity came from a single ancient ancestor. If we want to explain biodiversity, then, we have to do more than explain how new *traits* arise—we must also explain how new *species* arise. For if speciation didn't occur, there would be no biodiversity at all—only a single, long-evolved descendant of that very first species.

For years after publication of *The Origin*, biologists struggled, and failed, to explain how a continuous process of evolution produces the discrete groups known as species. The problem of speciation was in fact not seriously addressed until the mid-1930s. Today, well over a century after Darwin's death, we finally have a reasonably complete picture of what species are and how they arise. And we also have evidence for that process.

But before we can understand the origin of species, we need to figure out exactly what they represent. One obvious answer is based on how we recognize species: as a group of individuals that resemble one another more than they resemble members of other groups. According to this definition, known as the *morphological species concept*, the category "tiger" would be defined something like "that group including all Asian cats whose adults are more than five feet long and have vertical black stripes on an orange body, with white patches around the eyes and mouth." This is the way that you'll find species of animals and plants described in field guides, and it is the way that Linnaeus first classified species in 1735.

But this definition has some problems. In sexually dimorphic species, as we saw in the last chapter, males and females can look very different. In fact, early museum researchers working on birds and insects often misclassified males and females of a single species as members of two different species. It's easy to understand, if you are looking only at museum skins, how male and female peacocks could be classified this way. There is also the problem of variation *within* an interbreeding group. Humans, for example, could be classified into a few discrete groups based on eye color: those with blue eyes, brown eyes, and green eyes. These are almost unambiguously different, so why don't we consider them different species? The same goes for populations that look different in different places. Humans are again a prime example. The Inuit of Canada look different from the !Kung tribespeople of South Africa, and both look different from Finns. Do we classify all of these populations as different species? Somehow that strikes us as wrong—after all, members of all human populations can successfully interbreed. And what is true for humans is true for many plants and animals. The North American song sparrow, for example, has been classified into thirty-one geographic "races" (sometimes called "subspecies") based on small differences in plumage and song. Yet members of all these races can mate and produce fertile offspring. At what point are differences between populations large enough to make us call them different species? This concept makes the designation of species an arbitrary exercise, yet we know that species have an objective reality and are not simply arbitrary human constructs.

Conversely, some groups that biologists recognize as different species look either exactly alike or nearly alike. These "cryptic" species are found in most groups of organisms, including birds, mammals, plants, and insects. I study speciation in a group of fruit flies, *Drosophila*, that includes nine species. The females of all these species can't be told apart, even under the microscope, and males can be classified only by tiny differences in the shape of their genitals. Similarly, the malaria-carrying mosquito *Anopheles gambiae* is one of a group of seven species that look almost exactly alike, but differ in where they live and which hosts they bite. Some do not prey on humans and so carry no danger of malaria. If we are to combat the disease effectively, it is critical to be able to tell these species apart. Further, because humans are visual animals, we tend to overlook traits that can't easily be seen, like differences in pheromones that often distinguish species of similar-looking insects.

You might have asked yourself why, if these cryptic forms look so similar, we think that they're actually different species. The answer is that they coexist in the same location and yet never exchange genes: the members of one species simply don't hybridize with members of another. (You can test this in the laboratory by doing breeding experiments, or by looking at the genes directly to see if the groups are exchanging them.) The groups are thus *reproductively isolated* from one another: they constitute distinct "gene pools" that don't intermingle. It seems reasonable to assume that under any realistic view of what makes a group distinct in nature, these cryptic forms *are* distinct.

And when we think of why we feel that brown-eyed and blue-eyed humans, or Inuit and !Kung, are members of the same species, we realize that it's because they can mate with each other and produce offspring that contain combinations of their genes. In other words, they belong to the *same gene pool.* When you ponder cryptic species, and variation within humans, you arrive at the notion that species are distinct not merely because they *look* different, but because there are barriers between them that prevent interbreeding.

Ernst Mayr and the Russian geneticist Theodosius Dobzhansky were the first to realize this, and in 1942 Mayr proposed a definition of species that has become the gold standard for evolutionary biology. Using the reproductive criterion for species status, Mayr defined a species as *a group of interbreeding natural populations that are reproductively isolated from other such groups.* This definition is known as the *biological species concept,* or BSC. "Reproductively isolated" simply means that members of different species have traits—differences in appearance, behavior, or physiology—that prevent them from successfully interbreeding, while members of the same species can interbreed readily.

What keeps members of two related species from mating with each other? There are many different reproductive barriers. Species might not interbreed simply because their mating or flowering seasons don't overlap. Some corals, for example, reproduce only one night a year, spewing out masses of eggs and sperm into the sea over a several-hour period. Closely related species living in the same area remain distinct because their peak spawning periods are several hours apart, preventing eggs of one species from meeting sperm from another. Animal species often have different mating displays or pheromones, and don't find one another sexually attractive. Females in my *Drosophila* species have chemicals on their abdomens that males of other species find unappealing. Species can also be isolated by preferring different habitats, so they simply don't encounter one another. Many insects can feed and reproduce on only one single species of plant, and different species of insects are restricted to different species of plants. This keeps them from meeting others at mating time. Closely related species of plants can be kept apart because they use different pollinators. Two species of the monkeyflower *Mimulus*, for example, live in the same area of the Sierra Nevada, but rarely interbreed because one species is pollinated by bumblebees and the other by hummingbirds.

Isolating barriers can also act after mating. Pollen from one plant species might fail to germinate on the pistil of another. If fetuses are formed, they might die before birth; this is what happens when you cross a sheep with a goat. Or even if hybrids survive, they may be sterile: the classic example is the vigorous but sterile mule, the offspring of a female horse and a male donkey. Species that produce sterile hybrids certainly can't exchange genes.

And of course several of these barriers can act together. For much of the last ten years I've studied two species of fruit fly that live on the tropical volcanic island of São Tomé, off the west coast of Africa. The species are somewhat isolated by habitat: one lives on the upper part of the volcano, the other at the bottom, though there is some overlap in their distributions. But they also differ in courtship displays, so even when they do meet, members of the two species rarely mate. When they do succeed at mating, the sperm of one species is poor at fertilizing the eggs of the other, so that relatively few offspring are produced. And half of these hybrid offspring—all of the males—are sterile. Putting all these barriers together, we conclude that the species exchange virtually no genes in nature, and we have confirmed this result by sequencing their DNA. These, then, can be considered good biological species.

The advantage of the BSC is that it takes care of many problems that appearance-based species concepts can't handle. What are those cryptic groups of mosquitoes? They are different species because they don't exchange genes. What about Inuit and !Kung? These populations may not mate directly with each other (I doubt that such a union has ever occurred), but there is *potential* gene flow from one population to the other through intermediate geographical areas, and little doubt that if they did mate they'd produce fertile offspring. And males and females are members of the same species because their genes unite at reproduction.

According to the BSC, then, a species is a reproductive community—a gene pool. And this means that a species is also an *evolutionary* community. If a "good mutation" crops up within a species, say a mutation in tigers that boosts a female's output of cubs by 10 percent, then the gene containing that mutation will spread throughout the tiger species. But it won't go any further, for tigers don't exchange genes with other species. The biological species, then, is the unit of evolution—it is, to a large extent, *the thing that evolves*. This is why members of all species generally look and behave pretty much alike: because they all share genes, they respond in the same way to evolutionary forces. And it is the lack of interbreeding between species living in the same area that not only maintains species' differences in appearance and behavior, but also allows them to continue diverging without limits.

But the BSC isn't a foolproof concept. What about organisms that are extinct? They can hardly be tested for reproductive compatibility. So museum curators and paleontologists must resort to traditional appearance-based species concepts, and classify fossils and specimens by their overall similarity. And organisms that don't reproduce sexually, such as bacteria and some fungi, don't fit the criteria of the BSC either. The question of what constitutes a species in such groups is complicated, and we're not even sure that asexual organisms form discrete clusters in the way that sexual ones do.

But despite these problems, the biological species concept is still the one that evolutionists prefer when studying speciation, because it gets to the heart of the evolutionary question. Under the BSC, if you can explain how reproductive barriers evolve, you've explained the origin of species.

Exactly how these barriers arise puzzled biologists for a long time. Finally, around 1935, biologists began to make headway in both the field and laboratory. One of the most important observations was made by naturalists, who noticed that so-called "sister species"—species that are each other's closest relatives—were often separated in nature by geographical barriers. Sister species of sea urchins, for example, were found on opposite sides of the Isthmus of Panama. Sister species of freshwater fish often inhabited separated river drainages. Could this geographic separation have something to do with how these species arose from a common ancestor?

Yes, said the geneticists and naturalists, and they eventually proposed how the combined effects of evolution and geography could make this happen. How do you get one species to divide into two, separated by reproductive barriers? Mayr argued that these barriers were merely the by-products of natural or sexual selection that caused geographically isolated populations to evolve in different directions.

Suppose, for example, that an ancestral species of flowering plant was split into two portions by a geographic barrier, like a mountain range. The species may, for example, have been dispersed over the mountains in the stomachs of birds. Now imagine that one population lives in a place having a lot of hummingbirds but only a few bees. In that area, the flowers will evolve to attract hummingbirds as pollinators: typically the flowers would become red (a color that the birds find attractive), produce copious nectar (which rewards birds), and have deep tubes (to accommodate hummingbirds' long bills and tongues). The population on the other side of the mountain may find its pollinator situation reversed: few hummingbirds but many bees. There the flowers will evolve to attract bees; they may become pink (a color bees favor), and evolve shallow nectar tubes with less nectar (bees have short tongues and don't require a large nectar reward) as well as flatter flowers whose petals form a landing platform (unlike hovering hummingbirds, bees usually land to collect nectar). Eventually, the two populations would diverge in the form of their flowers and amount of their nectar, and each would be specialized for pollination by only a single type of animal. Now imagine that the geographic barrier disappeared, and the newly diverged populations found themselves back in the *same* area—an area containing both bees and hummingbirds. They would now be reproductively isolated: each type of flower would be served by a different pollinator, so their genes would not mix via cross-pollination. They would have become two different species. This is in fact the likely way that the monkeyflowers we considered earlier *did* diverge from their common ancestor.

This is just one way that a reproductive barrier can evolve by "divergent" selection—that is, selection that drives different populations in different evolutionary directions. You can imagine other scenarios in which geographically isolated populations diverge so that later they could not interbreed. Different mutations affecting male behaviors or traits could appear in different places—say, longer tail feathers in one population and orange color in another—and sexual selection might then drive the populations in different directions. Eventually, females in one population would prefer long-tailed males, and females in the other, orange males. If the two populations later encountered each other, their mating preferences would prevent them from mixing genes, and they would be considered different species.

What about the sterility and inviability of hybrids? This was a big problem for early evolutionists, who had trouble seeing how natural selection could yield such palpably maladaptive and wasteful features. But suppose that these features were not selected directly, but were simply accidental by-products of genetic divergence, divergence caused by natural selection or genetic drift. If two geographically isolated populations evolve along different pathways long enough, their genomes can become so different that, when they're put together in a hybrid, they just don't work well together. This can disrupt development, causing hybrids to either die prematurely or, if they live, turn out to be sterile.

It's important to realize that species don't arise, as Darwin thought, for the purpose of filling up empty niches in nature. We don't have different species because nature somehow needs them. Far from it. The study of speciation tells us that *species are evolutionary accidents*. The "clusters" so important for biodiversity don't evolve because they increase that diversity, nor do they evolve to provide balanced ecosystems. They are simply the inevitable result of genetic barriers that arise when spatially isolated populations evolve in different directions.

In many ways biological speciation resembles the "speciation" of two closely related languages from a common ancestor (an example is German and English, two "sister tongues"). Like species, languages can diverge in isolated populations that once shared an ancestral tongue. And languages change more rapidly when there is less mixing of individuals from different populations. While populations change genetically via natural selection (and sometimes genetic drift), human languages change by linguistic selection (appealing or useful new words get invented) and linguistic drift (pronunciations change due to imitation and cultural transmission). During biological speciation, populations change genetically to the extent that their members no longer recognize each other as mates, or their genes can't cooperate to produce a fertile individual. Likewise, languages can diverge to the extent that they become mutually unintelligible: English speakers don't automatically understand German, and vice versa. Languages are like biological species in that they occur in discrete groups rather than as a continuum: the speech of any given person can usually be placed unambiguously in one of the several thousand human languages.

The parallel goes even further. The evolution of languages can be traced back to the distant past, and a family tree drawn up, by cataloging the similarities of words and grammar. This is very like reconstructing an evolutionary tree of organisms from reading the DNA code of their genes. We can also reconstruct protolanguages, or ancestral tongues, by looking at the features that descendant languages have in common. This is precisely the way biologists predict what missing links or ancestral genes should look like. And the origin of languages is accidental: people don't start to speak in different tongues just to be different. New languages, like new species, form as a by-product of other processes, as in the transformation of Latin to Italian in Italy. The analogies between speciation and languages were first drawn by—who else?—Darwin, in *The Origin*.

But we shouldn't push this analogy too far. Unlike species, languages can "cross-fertilize," adopting phrases from each other, like the English use of the German *angst* and *kindergarten*. Steven Pinker describes other striking similarities and differences between the diversification of languages and species in his engrossing book *The Language Instinct*.

The idea that geographic isolation is the first step in the origin of species is called the *theory of geographic speciation*. The theory can be stated simply: the evolution of genetic isolation between populations requires that they first be geographically isolated. Why is geographic isolation so important? Why can't two new species just arise in the same location as their ancestor? The theory of population genetics—and a lot of lab experiments—tell us that splitting a single population into two genetically isolated parts is very difficult if they retain the opportunity to interbreed. Without isolation, selection that could drive populations apart has to work against the interbreeding that constantly brings individuals together and mixes up their genes. Imagine an insect living in a patch of woods that harbors two types of plants on which it can feed. Each plant requires a different set of adaptations to use it, for they have different toxins, different nutrients, and different odors. But as each group of insects within the area begins adapting to one plant, it also mates with insects adapting to the other plant. This constant intermixing will keep the gene pool from splitting into two species. What you will probably wind up with is just a single "generalist" species that uses both plants. Speciation is like separating oil and vinegar: though striving to pull apart, they won't do so if they're constantly being mixed.

What is the evidence for geographic speciation? What we're asking about here is not *whether* speciation happens, but *how*. We already know from the fossil record, embryology, and other data that species diverged from common ancestors. What we really want to see is geographically separated populations turning into new species. This is no easy task. First of all, speciation in organisms other than bacteria is usually slow—much slower than the splitting of languages. My colleague Allen Orr and I calculated that, starting with one ancestor, it takes roughly between 100,000 and five million years to evolve two reproductively isolated descendants. The glacial pace of speciation means that, with a few exceptions, we can't expect to witness the whole process, or even a small part of it, over a human lifetime. To study how species form we must resort to indirect methods, testing predictions derived from the theory of geographic speciation.

The first prediction is that if speciation depends largely on geographical isolation, there must have been lots of opportunities during the history of life for populations to experience that isolation. After all, there are millions of species on earth today. But geographic isolation is common. Mountain ranges rise, glaciers spread, deserts form, continents drift, and drought divides a continuous forest into patches separated by grassland. Each time this happens, there is a chance for a species to be sundered into two or more populations. When the Isthmus of Panama was formed about three million years ago, the emerging land separated populations of marine organisms on either side, organisms that originally belonged to the same species. Even a river can serve as a geographical barrier for many birds that don't like to fly over water.

But populations don't have to become isolated by the formation of geographic barriers. They might simply become separated by accidental long-distance dispersal. Suppose that a few wayward individuals, or even a single pregnant female, go astray and end up colonizing a distant shore. The colony will thereafter evolve in isolation from its mainland ancestors. This is just what happens on oceanic islands. The chances for this kind of isolation through dispersal are even greater on archipelagoes, where individuals can occasionally move back and forth between neighboring islands, each time becoming geographically isolated. Each round of isolation provides another chance for speciation. This is why archipelagoes harbor the famous "radiations" of closely related species, such as the fruit flies of Hawaii, the *Anolis* lizards of the Caribbean, and the finches of the Galápagos.

There's been ample opportunity for geographic speciation, then, but has there been enough time? That too is not a problem. Speciation is a splitting event, in which each ancestral branch splits into two twigs, which themselves split later, and so on as the tree of life ramifies. This means that the number of species builds up exponentially, although some branches are pruned through extinction. How fast would speciation need to be to explain the present diversity of life? It's been estimated that there are 10 million species on earth today. Let's raise that to 100 million to take into account undiscovered species. It turns out that if you started with a single species 3.5 billion years ago, you could get 100 million species living today even if each ancestral species split into two descendants only once every *130 million years*. As we've seen, real speciation happens a lot faster than that, so even if we account for the many species that evolved but went extinct, time is simply not a problem.[38]

What about the critical idea that reproductive barriers are the by-product of evolutionary change? That, at least, can be tested in the laboratory. Biologists do this by performing selection experiments, forcing animals or plants to adapt through evolution to different environments. This is a model of what happens when isolated natural populations encounter different habitats. After a period of adaptation, the different "populations" are tested in the lab to see if they've evolved reproductive barriers. Since these experiments take place over tens to dozens of generations, while speciation in the wild takes thousands of generations, we can't expect to see the origin of full species. But we should occasionally see the beginnings of reproductive isolation.

Surprisingly, even these short-duration experiments quite often produce genetic barriers. More than half of these studies (there are about twenty of them, all done on flies because of their short generation time) give a positive result, often showing reproductive isolation between populations within a year after selection begins. Most often, adaptation to different "environments" (different types of food, for example, or the ability to move up versus down in a vertical maze) results in mating discrimination between the populations. We're not sure exactly what traits the populations use to discriminate against each other, but the evolution of genetic barriers in such a short time confirms a key prediction of geographic speciation.

The second prediction of the theory involves geography itself. If populations must usually be physically isolated from one another to become species, then we should find the most recently formed species in different but nearby areas. You can get a rough idea of how long ago species arose by looking at the amount of difference between their DNA sequences, which is roughly proportional to the time elapsed since they split from a common ancestor. We can then look for "sister" species in a group who will have the greatest similarity in their DNA (and are thus most closely related), and see if they're geographically isolated.

This prediction too is fulfilled: we see many sister species divided by a geographic barrier. Each side of the Isthmus of Panama, for example, harbors seven species of snapping shrimp in shallow waters. The closest relative of each species is another species on the *other* side. What must have happened is that seven ancestral species of shrimp were divided when the isthmus arose from beneath the sea three million years ago. Each ancestor formed an Atlantic and a Pacific species. (Snapping shrimp, by the way, are a biological marvel. Their name comes from the way they kill. The shrimp doesn't touch its prey but, by snapping together its single oversized claw, creates a high-pressure sonic blast that stuns its victim. Large groups of these shrimp can be so noisy that they confuse the sonar of submarines.)

It's the same with plants. You can find pairs of sister species of flowering plants in eastern Asia and eastern North America. All botanists know that these areas have similar flora, including skunk cabbage, tulip trees, and magnolias. One survey of plants uncovered nine pairs of sister species, including trumpetvines, dogwoods, and mayapples, with each pair having one species in Asia and its closest relative in North America. Botanists theorized that each of the nine pairs used to be a single species continuously distributed across both continents, but these became geographically isolated (and began to evolve separately) when the climate became cooler and dryer about five million years ago, wiping out the intervening forest. Sure enough, DNA-based dating of these nine pairs puts their divergence times at around five million years.

Archipelagoes are a good place to find out whether speciation requires physical isolation. If a group has produced species within a cluster of islands, then we should find that the closest relatives live on different islands rather than the same one. (Single islands are often too small to allow the geographic separation of populations that is the first step in speciation. Different islands, on the other hand, are isolated by water, and should allow new species to arise easily.) This prediction also turns out to be generally true. In Hawaii, for instance, sister species of *Drosophila* flies usually occupy different islands; this is also true of the lesser-known but still dramatic radiations of flightless crickets and lobelia plants. What's more, the dates of the speciation events in *Drosophila* have been determined using the flies' DNA, and we find, exactly as predicted, that the oldest species are found on the oldest islands.

Still another prediction of the geographic-speciation model rests on the reasonable assumption that geographic speciation is still occurring in nature.

If that's so, we should be able to find isolated populations of a single species that are beginning to speciate, and show small amounts of reproductive isolation from other populations. And sure enough, there are many examples. One is the orchid *Satyrium hallackii*, which lives in South Africa. In the northern and eastern parts of the country it is pollinated by hawkmoths and long-tongued flies. To attract these pollinators, the orchid has evolved long nectar tubes in its flowers; pollination can occur only when the long-tongued moths and flies get close enough to the flower to stick their tongues into the tubes. But in coastal regions, the only pollinators are short-tongued bees, and here the orchid has evolved much shorter nectar tubes. If the populations were to live in an area containing all three types of pollinators, the long- and short-tubed flowers would undoubtedly show some genetic isolation, for long-tongued species can't easily pollinate short-tubed flowers, and vice versa. And there are many examples of animal species in which individuals from different populations mate less readily than do individuals from the same population.

There's a final prediction we can make to test geographic speciation: we should find that reproductive isolation between a pair of physically isolated populations increases slowly with time. My colleague Allen Orr and I tested this by looking at many pairs of *Drosophila* species, each pair having diverged from its own common ancestor at various times in the past. (With the molecular-clock method described in chapter 4, we could estimate the time when a pair of species began diverging by counting the number of differences in their DNA sequences.) We measured three types of reproductive barriers in the laboratory: mating discrimination between the pairs, and the sterility and inviability of their hybrids. Just as predicted, we found that the reproductive isolation between species increased steadily with time. Genetic barriers between groups became strong enough to completely prevent interbreeding after about 2.7 million years of divergence. That's a long time. It's clear that, at least in fruit flies, the origin of new species is a slow process.

The way we discovered how species arise resembles the way astronomers discovered how stars "evolve" over time. Both processes occur too slowly for us to see them happening over our lifetime. But we can still understand how they work by finding snapshots of the process at different evolutionary stages and putting these snapshots together into a conceptual movie. For stars, astronomers saw dispersed clouds of matter ("star nurseries") in galaxies. Elsewhere they saw those clouds condensing into protostars. And in other places they saw protostars becoming full stars, condensing further and then generating light as their core temperature became high enough to fuse hydrogen atoms into helium. Other stars were large "red giants" like Betelgeuse; some showed signs of throwing off their outer layers into space; and others still were small, dense white dwarfs. By assembling all these stages into a logical sequence, based on what we know of their physical and chemical structure and behavior, we've been able to piece together how stars form, persist, and die. From this picture of stellar evolution, we can make predictions. We know, for example, that stars about the size of our sun shine steadily for about ten billion years before bulging out to form red giants. Since the sun is about 4.6 billion years old, we know that we're roughly halfway through our tenure as a planet before we'll finally be swallowed up by the sun's expansion.

And so it is with speciation. We see geographically isolated populations running the gamut from those showing no reproductive isolation, through those having increasing degrees of reproductive isolation (as the populations become isolated for longer periods), and, finally, to complete speciation. We see young species, descended from a common ancestor, on either side of geographic barriers like rivers or the Isthmus of Panama, and on different islands of an archipelago. Putting all this together, we conclude that isolated populations diverge, and that when that divergence has gone on for a sufficiently long time, reproductive barriers develop as a by-product of evolution.

Creationists often claim that if we can't see a new species evolve during our lifetime, then speciation doesn't occur. But this argument is fatuous: it's like saying that because we haven't seen a single star go through its complete life cycle, stars don't evolve, or because we haven't seen a new language arise, languages don't evolve. Historical reconstruction of a process is a perfectly valid way to study that process, and can produce testable predictions.[39] We can predict that the sun will begin to burn out in about five billion years, just as we can predict that laboratory populations artificially selected in different directions will become genetically isolated.

Most evolutionists accept that geographic isolation of populations is the most common way that speciation takes place. This means that when closely related species live in the same area—a common situation—they actually diverged from each other during an earlier time when their ancestors were geographically isolated. But some biologists think that new species can arise without the need for any geographic separation. In *The Origin*, for example, Darwin repeatedly suggested that new species, especially plants, could arise within a very small, circumscribed area. And since Darwin's time, biologists have argued fiercely about the likelihood that speciation could occur without geographic barriers (this is called *sympatric* speciation, from the Greek for "same place"). The problem with this, as I mentioned before, is that it's hard to split one gene pool in two while its members remain in the same area, because interbreeding between the diverging forms will constantly be pulling them back into a single species. Mathematical theories show that sympatric speciation is possible, but only under restrictive conditions that may be uncommon in nature.

It's relatively easy to find evidence for geographic speciation, but it's much harder for sympatric speciation. If you see two related species living in one area, that doesn't necessarily mean that they arose in that area. Species constantly shift their ranges as their habitats expand and contract during long-term changes in climate, episodes of glaciation, and so on. Related species living in the same place may have arisen elsewhere and come into contact with each other only later. How can we be sure, then, that two related species living in one place actually *arose* in that place?

Here's one way to do it. We can look at habitat islands: small patches of isolated terrain (like oceanic islands) or water (like tiny lakes) that are generally too small to contain any geographic barriers. If we see closely related species in these habitats, we could conclude that they formed sympatrically, since the possibility of geographic isolation is remote.

There are only a few examples. The best involves cichlid fish in two tiny lakes in Cameroon. These isolated African lakes, filling the craters of volcanoes, are too small to permit populations within them to become spatially separated (their areas are 0.2 and 1.6 square miles, respectively). Nevertheless, each lake contains a different miniradiation of species, each recently descended from a common ancestor: one lake has eleven species, the other nine. This is perhaps the best evidence we have for sympatric speciation, although we don't know how and why it happened.

Another case involves palm trees on Lord Howe, an oceanic island lying in the Tasman Sea about 350 miles off the east coast of Australia. Although the island is small—about five square miles—it contains two native species of palms, the kentia and curly palms, which happen to be each other's closest relatives. (The kentia palm may be familiar—it's a popular houseplant throughout the world.) These appear to have arisen from an ancestral palm that lived on the island about five million years ago. The chance that this speciation involved geographic isolation appears quite small, especially because the palms are pollinated by wind, which can spread pollen over a large area.

There are a few more examples of sympatric speciation, though they're not quite as convincing as these. What is most surprising, however, is the number of times that sympatric speciation has *not* occurred given the opportunity. There are many habitat islands that contain a fair number of species, but none of these are each other's closest relatives. Obviously, sympatric speciation has not occurred on those islands. My colleague Trevor Price and I surveyed bird species on isolated oceanic islands, looking for the presence of close relatives that might indicate speciation. Of forty-six islands we examined, not a single one contained endemic bird species that were each other's closest relatives. A similar result was seen for *Anolis* lizards, the small green animals often sold in pet shops. Closely related *Anolis* species simply aren't found on islands smaller than Jamaica, which is large, mountainous, and varied enough to allow geographic speciation. The absence of sister species on these islands shows that sympatric speciation can't be common in these groups. It also counts as evidence against creationism. After all, there's no obvious reason why a creator would produce similar species of birds or lizards on continents but not on isolated islands. (By "similar," I mean so similar that evolutionists would regard them as close relatives. Most creationists do not accept species as "relatives," since that presupposes evolution.) The rarity of sympatric speciation is precisely what evolutionary theory predicts, and is further support for that theory.

There are, however, two special forms of sympatric speciation that are not only common in plants, but also give us our only cases of "speciation in action": species actually forming during a human lifetime. One of them is called *allopolyploid speciation*. The curious thing about this form of speciation is that instead of beginning with isolated populations of the same species, it starts with the hybridization of two *different* species that live in the same area. And it usually requires that those two different species also have different numbers or types of chromosomes. Because of this difference, a hybrid between the species won't undergo proper pairing of chromosomes when it tries to make pollen or ovules, and it will be sterile. However, if there was a way to double every chromosome in that hybrid, each chromosome would now have a pairing partner, and the doubled-chromosome hybrid would be fertile. And it would also be a new species, because while interfertile with other similar hybrids, it would be unable to interbreed with either of the original two parent species, for such a mating would yield sterile offspring with odd numbers of chromosomes. In fact, such "doubled-chromosome" allopolyploids occur with regularity, giving rise to new species.[40]

Polyploid speciation doesn't always require hybridization. A polyploid can arise simply by doubling all of the chromosomes of a single species—a process called *autopolyploidy*. This too results in a new species, for each autopolyploid is able to produce fertile hybrids when mating with other autopolyploids, but produces only sterile hybrids when mating with the original parental species.[41]

To get either type of polyploid speciation, you need a rare event to occur in two successive generations: the formation and union of sperm and eggs with abnormally high numbers of chromosomes. Because of this, you might have thought that such speciation would be very rare indeed. But it isn't. Given that a single plant can produce millions of eggs and pollen grains, an improbable event eventually becomes probable. Estimates vary, but in well-studied areas of the world it's been estimated that as many as a quarter of all species of flowering plants were formed via polyploidy. The fraction of existing species that had a polyploidy event occurring *somewhere* in their ancestry, on the other hand, could be as high as 70 percent. This is obviously a common way that new plant species arise. What's more, we find polyploid species in nearly all groups of plants (a notable exception is trees). And many plants used for food or decoration are polyploids or sterile hybrids that had a polyploid parent, including wheat, cotton, cabbage, chrysanthemums, and bananas. This is because humans recognized the hybrids in nature as having useful traits from both parental species, or they deliberately produced the polyploids to create desirable gene combinations. Two everyday examples from your kitchen show this. Many forms of wheat have six sets of chromosomes, arising from a complicated series of crosses, involving three different species, that were made by our ancestors. Commercial bananas are sterile hybrids between two wild species, having two sets of chromosomes from one species and one set from the other. Those black specks in the middle of your banana are, in fact, aborted plant ovules that don't become seeds because their chromosomes can't pair properly. Since banana plants are sterile, they must be propagated from cuttings.

Polyploidy is much rarer in animals, appearing only occasionally in fish, insects, worms, and reptiles. Most of these forms reproduce asexually, but there is one sexually reproducing polyploid mammal, the curious red viscacha rat of Argentina. Its 112 chromosomes are the most seen in any mammal. We don't understand why animal polyploids are so rare. It may have something to do with polyploidy disrupting the mechanism of X/Y sex determination, or with the inability of animals to self-fertilize. In contrast, many plants do have the ability to self-fertilize, which allows a single new polyploid individual to produce many related individuals that are all members of its new species.

Polyploid speciation differs from other types of speciation because it involves changes in chromosome number rather than changes in the genes themselves. It is also immensely faster than "normal" geographic speciation, for a new polyploid species can arise in just two generations. That is nearly instantaneous in geologic time. And it gives us the unprecedented chance to see a new species appear in "real time," satisfying the demand to view speciation in action. We know of at least five new plant species that arose this way.

One is the Welsh groundsel (*Senecio cambrensis*), a flowering plant in the daisy family. It was first observed in North Wales in 1958. Recent studies have shown that it is in fact a polyploid hybrid between two other species, one of them the common groundsel (*Senecio vulgaris*), native to the United Kingdom, and the other the Oxford ragwort (*Senecio squalidus*), introduced to the UK in 1792. The ragwort didn't appear in Wales until about 1910. This means that, given the British penchant for botanizing—which produces a continuous inventory of local plants—the hybrid Welsh groundsel must have arisen between 1910 and 1958. The evidence that it is indeed a hybrid, and arose via polyploidy, comes from several fronts. For a start, it *looks* like a hybrid, since it has features of both the common groundsel and the Oxford ragwort. Moreover, it has exactly the chromosome number (sixty) predicted for a polyploid hybrid with those two parents. (One parent has forty chromosomes, the other twenty.) Genetic studies have shown that the genes and chromosomes of the hybrid are combinations of those seen in the parental species. The final proof came from Jacqueline Weir and Ruth Ingram of St. Andrews University in Scotland, who completely synthesized the hybrid species in the laboratory by making various crosses between its two parental species. The artificially produced hybrid looks precisely like the Welsh groundsel seen in the wild. (Wild hybrid species are often resynthesized in this way to check their ancestry.) There is little doubt, then, that the Welsh groundsel represents a new species that arose in the last hundred years.

The other four cases of real-time speciation are similar. All involve hybrids between a native species and an introduced one. Although this involves some artificiality, in the form of humans moving plants around, it's almost necessary to have this happen if we want to see new species form before our eyes. It seems that polyploid speciation occurs very quickly when the appropriate parental species live in the same place. To see an allopolyploid species arising in nature, then, we must be on the scene soon after its two ancestral species come into close proximity. And this will happen only after a recent biological invasion.

But polyploid speciation has occurred, unwitnessed, many times during the course of evolution. We know this because scientists have synthesized polyploid hybrids in the greenhouse that are virtually identical to those that formed in nature long before we were around. And the artificially produced polyploids are interfertile with the ones in the wild. All this is good evidence that we've reconstructed the origin of a naturally formed species.

These cases of polyploid speciation should satisfy those critics who won't accept evolution unless it happens before their eyes.[42] But even without polyploidy, we still have plenty of evidence for speciation. We see lineages splitting in the fossil record. We see closely related species separated by geographic barriers. And we see new species beginning to arise as populations evolve incipient reproductive barriers—barriers that are the foundation of speciation. No doubt Mr. Darwin, were he to awaken today, would be delighted to find that the origin of species is no longer a "mystery of mysteries."

Chapter 8

What About Us?

Darwinian Man, though well behaved,
At best is only a monkey shaved.

—William S. Gilbert and Arthur Sullivan, *Princess Ida*

I n 1924, while dressing for a wedding, Raymond Dart was literally handed what would become the greatest fossil find of the twentieth century. Dart was not only a young professor of anatomy at the University of Witwatersrand in South Africa, but also an amateur anthropologist, and had spread the word that he was looking for "interesting finds" to fill a new anatomy museum. As Dart was donning his tuxedo, the postman brought him two boxes of rocks containing bone fragments excavated from a limestone quarry near Taungs, in the Transvaal region. In his memoir, *Adventures with the Missing Link*, Dart describes the moment:

> As soon as I removed the lid a thrill of excitement shot through me. On the very top of the rock heap was what was undoubtedly an endocranial cast or mold of the interior of the skull. Had it been only the fossilised brain cast of any species of ape it would have ranked as a great discovery, for such a thing had never before been reported. But I knew at a glance that what lay in my hands was no ordinary anthropoidal brain. Here in lime-consolidated sand was the replica of a brain three times as large as that of a baboon and considerably bigger than that of an adult chimpan-

zee. The startling image of the convolutions and furrows of the brain and
the blood vessels of the skull were plainly visible.

It was not big enough for primitive man, but even for an ape it was a
big bulging brain and, most important, the forebrain was so big and had
grown so far backward that it completely covered the hindbrain.

Was there, anywhere among this pile of rocks, a face to fit the brain?
I ransacked feverishly through the boxes. My search was rewarded, for I
found a large stone with a depression into which the cast fitted perfectly.
There was faintly visible in the stone the outline of a broken part of the
skull and even the back of the lower jaw and a tooth socket which showed
that the face must be somewhere there in the block. . . .

I stood in the shade holding the brain as greedily as any miser hugs
his gold, my mind racing ahead. Here I was certain was one of the most
significant finds ever made in the history of anthropology.

Darwin's largely discredited theory that man's early progenitors
probably lived in Africa came back to me. Was I to be the instrument by
which his "missing link" was found?

These pleasant daydreams were interrupted by the bridegroom himself tugging at my sleeve.

"My God, Ray," he said, striving to keep the nervous urgency out of
his voice. "You've got to finish dressing immediately—or I'll have to find
another best man. The bridal car should be here any moment."

The groom's concern is understandable. Nobody wants to discover on their
wedding day that their best man is more interested in a box of dusty rocks
than in the impending nuptials. Yet it's difficult not to sympathize with Dart as
well. In *The Descent of Man*, Darwin had conjectured that our species had
originated in Africa because our closest relatives, gorillas and chimpanzees,
are both found there. But this was little more than a hunch. There were no fossils to back it up. And there was manifestly something of an evolutionary gulf
between us and the common ancestor we must have shared with other great
apes—an ancestor that was surely more apelike than human. On that day in
1924, the first stepping stone was uncovered, showing that the gulf would
eventually be crossed: there it was, in Dart's trembling hands, a direct glimpse

of what had long before been simplistically dubbed the "missing link." One wonders how he could have concentrated on his duties at the wedding.

What Dart found in that box was the first specimen of what he later named *Australopithecus africanus* ("Southern ape-man"). In the next three months, Dart's meticulous dissection of the rock, using sharpened knitting needles purloined from his wife, revealed the full face. It was the face of an infant, now known as the "Taungs child," complete with milk teeth and erupting molars. Its mixture of human and apelike traits clearly confirmed Dart's idea that he had indeed stumbled upon the dawn of human ancestry.

Since Dart's time, paleoanthropologists, geneticists, and molecular biologists have used fossils and DNA sequences to establish our place in the tree of evolution. We are apes descended from other apes, and our closest cousin is the chimpanzee, whose ancestors diverged from our own several million years ago in Africa. These are indisputable facts. And rather than diminishing our humanity, they should produce satisfaction and wonder, for they connect us to all organisms, the living and the dead.

But not everyone sees it that way. Among those reluctant to accept Darwinism, human evolution forms the core of their resistance. It doesn't seem so hard to accept that mammals evolved from reptiles, or land animals from fish. We just can't bring ourselves to acknowledge that, just like every other species, we too evolved from an ancestor that was very different. We've always perceived ourselves as somehow standing apart from the rest of nature. Encouraged by the religious belief that humans were the special object of creation, as well as by a natural solipsism that accompanies a self-conscious brain, we resist the evolutionary lesson that, like other animals, we are contingent products of the blind and mindless process of natural selection. And because of the hegemony of fundamentalist religion in the United States, this country has been among the most resistant to the fact of human evolution.

In the famous "Monkey Trial" of 1925, high school teacher John Scopes went on trial in Dayton, Tennessee—and was convicted—for violating Tennessee's Butler Act. Tellingly, this law didn't proscribe the teaching of evolution in general, but only the idea that *humans* had evolved:

Be it enacted by the General Assembly of the State of Tennessee, That it shall be unlawful for any teacher in any of the Universities, Normals and all other public schools of the State which are supported in whole or in part by the public school funds of the State, to teach any theory that denies the story of the Divine Creation of man as taught in the Bible, and to teach instead that man has descended from a lower order of animals.

While more liberal creationists admit that some species could have evolved from others, *all* creationists draw the line at humans. The gap between us and other primates, they say, was unbridgeable by evolution, and must therefore have involved an act of special creation.

The idea that humans are part of nature has been anathema over most of the history of biology. In 1735, the Swedish botanist Carl Linnaeus, who established biological classification, lumped humans, whom he named *Homo sapiens* ("man the wise"), with monkeys and apes based on anatomical similarity. Linnaeus didn't suggest an evolutionary relationship between these species—his intention was explicitly to reveal the order behind God's creation—but his decision was still controversial, and he incurred the wrath of his archbishop.

A century later, Darwin knew full well the ire he would face by suggesting, as he firmly believed, that humans had evolved from other species. In *The Origin* he pussyfooted around the issue, sneaking in one oblique sentence at the end of the book: "Light will be thrown on the origin of man and his history." Darwin didn't come to grips with the issue until more than a decade later in *The Descent of Man* (1871). Emboldened by his growing insight and conviction, and by the confidence gained from the rapid acceptance of his ideas, he finally made his views explicit. Mustering evidence from anatomy and behavior, Darwin asserted not only that humans had evolved from apelike creatures, but did so in Africa:

We thus learn that man is descended from a hairy quadruped, furnished with a tail and pointed ears, probably arboreal in its habits, and an inhabitant of the Old World.

Imagine the effect of that sentence on Victorian ears. To think that our ancestors lived in trees! And were *furnished* with tails and pointed ears! In his last chapter, Darwin finally dealt head-on with the religious objections:

I am aware that the conclusions arrived at in this work will be denounced by some as highly irreligious; but he who denounces them is bound to shew why it is more irreligious to explain the origin of man as a distinct species by descent from some lower form, through the laws of variation and natural selection, than to explain the birth of the individual through the laws of ordinary reproduction [the pattern of development].

Nevertheless, he didn't convince all of his colleagues. Alfred Russel Wallace and Charles Lyell—Darwin's competitor and mentor, respectively—both signed on to the idea of evolution but remained unconvinced that natural selection could explain the higher mental faculties of humans. It took fossils to finally convince the skeptics that humans had indeed evolved.

Fossil Ancestors

IN 1871, the human fossil record comprised only a few bones of the late-appearing Neanderthals—too humanlike to count as a missing link between ourselves and apes. They were regarded instead as an aberrant population of *Homo sapiens*. In 1891, the Dutch physician Eugene Dubois turned up a skull-cap, some teeth, and a thighbone in Java that filled the bill: the skull was somewhat more robust than that of modern humans, and the brain size smaller. But distressed by the religious and scientific opposition to his ideas, Dubois reburied the bones of *Pithecanthropus erectus* (now called *Homo erectus*) beneath his house, hiding them from scientific scrutiny for three decades.

Dart's 1924 discovery of the Taungs child set off a hunt for human ancestors in Africa, eventually leading to the famous excavations of the Leakeys at Olduvai Gorge beginning in the 1930s, the discovery of "Lucy" by Donald Johanson in 1974, and a host of other finds. We now have a reasonable fossil record of our evolution, although one that's far from complete. There are, as we'll see, many mysteries, and more than a few surprises.

But even without fossils we'd still know something about our place on the tree of evolution. As Linnaeus proposed, our anatomy places us in the order Primates along with monkeys, apes, and lemurs, all sharing traits such as forward-facing eyes, fingernails, color vision, and opposable thumbs. Other features put us in the smaller superfamily Hominoidea along with the "lesser apes" (gibbons) and "great apes" (chimpanzees, gorillas, orangutans, and ourselves). And within the Hominoidea we are grouped with the great apes in the family Hominidae, sharing unique features like flattened fingernails, thirty-two teeth, enlarged ovaries, and prolonged parental care. These shared characters show that our common ancestor with the great apes lived more recently than our common ancestor with any other mammal.

Molecular data derived from DNA and protein sequences confirms these relationships, and also tells us roughly when we diverged from our relatives. We are most closely related to the chimpanzees—equally to the common chimp and the bonobo—and we diverged from our joint common ancestor about seven million years ago. The gorilla is a slightly more distant relative, and orangutans more distant yet (12 million years since the common ancestor).

Yet to many, fossil evidence is psychologically more convincing than molecular data. It's one thing to learn that we share 98.5 percent of our DNA sequence with chimps, but another entirely to see the skeleton of an australopithecine, with its small, apelike skull perched atop a skeleton nearly identical to that of modern humans. But before we look at the fossils, we can make some predictions about what we'd expect to find if humans evolved from apes.

What should our "missing link" with apes look like? Remember that the "missing link" is the *single ancestral species* that gave rise to modern humans on the one hand and chimpanzees on the other. It's not reasonable to expect the discovery of that critical single species, for its identification would require a complete series of ancestor-descendant fossils on both the chimp and human lineages, series that we could trace back until they intersect at the ancestor. Except for a few marine microorganisms, such complete fossil sequences don't exist. And our early human ancestors were large, relatively few in number compared to grazers like antelopes, and inhabited a small part of Africa under dry conditions not conducive to fossilization. Their fossils, like those of all apes and monkeys, are scarce. This resembles our problem with the evolution of birds, for whom transitional fossils are also rare. We can certainly trace the evolution of birds from feathered reptiles, but we're not sure exactly which fossil species were the direct ancestors of modern birds.

Given all this, we can't expect to find the single particular species that represents the "missing link" between humans and other apes. We can hope only to find its evolutionary cousins. Remember also that this common ancestor was not a chimpanzee, and probably didn't look like either modern chimps or humans. Nevertheless, it's likely that the "missing link" was closer in appearance to modern chimps than to modern humans. We are the odd man out in the evolution of modern apes, who all resemble one another far more than they resemble us. Gorillas are our distant cousins, and yet they share with chimps features like relatively small brains, hairiness, knuckle-walking, and large, pointed canine teeth. Gorillas and chimps also have a "rectangular dental arcade": when viewed from above, the bottom row of their teeth looks like three sides of a rectangle (see figure 27). Humans are the one species that has diverged from the ape ground plan: we have uniquely flexible thumbs, very little hair, smaller and blunter canine teeth, and we walk erect. Our tooth row is not rectangular, but parabolic, as you can see by inspecting your lower teeth in the mirror. Most striking, we have a much larger brain than any ape: the adult chimp's brain has a volume of about 450 cubic centimeters, that of a modern human about 1,450 cubic centimeters. When we compare the similarities of chimps, gorillas, and orangutans to the divergent features of humans, we can conclude that, relative to our common ancestor, we have changed more than have modern apes.

Around five to seven million years ago, then, we expect to find fossil ancestors having traits shared by chimpanzees, orangutans, and gorillas (these traits are shared because they were present in the common ancestor), but with some human features too. As the fossils become more and more recent, we should see brains getting relatively larger, canine teeth becoming smaller, the tooth row becoming less rectangular and more curved, and the posture becoming more erect. And this is exactly what we see. Although far from complete, the record of human evolution is one of the best confirmations we have of an evolutionary prediction, and is especially gratifying because the prediction was Darwin's.

But first a few caveats. We don't (and can't expect to) have a continuous fossil record of human ancestry. Instead, we see a tangled bush of many different species. Most of them went extinct without leaving descendants, and only one genetic lineage threaded its way through time to become modern humans. We're not yet sure which fossil species lie along that particular thread, and which were evolutionary dead ends. The most surprising thing we've learned about our history is that we've had many close evolutionary cousins who died out without leaving descendants. It's even possible that as many as four humanlike species lived in Africa at the same time, and maybe in the same place. Imagine the encounters that might have taken place! Did they kill one another, or try to interbreed?

And the names of ancestral human fossils can't be taken too seriously. Like theology, paleoanthropology is a field in which the students far outnumber the objects of study. There are lively—and sometimes acrimonious—debates about whether a given fossil is really something new, or merely a variant of an already named species. These arguments about scientific names often mean very little. Whether a humanlike fossil is named as one species or another can turn on matters as small as half a millimeter in the diameter of a tooth, or slight differences in the shape of the thighbone. The problem is that there are simply too few specimens, spread out over too large a geographic area, to make these decisions with any confidence. New finds and revisions of old conclusions occur constantly. What we must keep in sight is the general trend of the fossils over time, which clearly shows a change from apelike to humanlike features.

On to the bones. Anthropologists apply the term *hominin* to all the species on the "human" side of our family tree after it split from the branch that became modern chimps.[43] Twenty types of hominins have been named as separate species; fifteen of these are shown in rough order of appearance in figure 24.

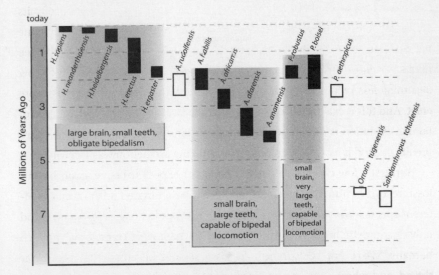

FIGURE 24. Fifteen hominin species, the periods over which they occur as fossils, and the nature of their brain, teeth, and locomotion. Fossils designated by open boxes are too fragmentary to draw conclusions about locomotion and brain size.

I show the skulls of a few representative hominins in figure 25, along with those of a modern chimp and human for comparison.

Our main question is, of course, how to determine the *pattern* of human evolution. When do we see the earliest fossils that might represent our ancestors who had already diverged from other apes? Which of our hominin relatives went extinct, and which were our direct ancestors? How did the features of the ancestral ape become those of modern humans? Did our big brain evolve first, or our upright posture? We know that humans *began* evolving in Africa, but what part of our evolution happened elsewhere?

Homo sapiens	Homo habilis	Australopithecus afarensis

Sahelanthropus tchadensis	Paranthropus boisei	Pan troglodytes (chimp)

FIGURE 25. Skulls of modern humans (*Homo sapiens*), earlier hominins, and a chimpanzee (*Pan troglodytes*).

Except for some bone fragments whose classification is unclear, until recently the hominin fossil record didn't go back beyond four million years. But in 2002, Michel Brunet and his colleagues announced the astounding discovery of an older possible hominin, *Sahelanthropus tchadensis,* from the Central African deserts of Chad, the region known as the Sahel. The most surprising thing about this find is its date: between six and seven million years ago, right when molecular evidence tells us that our lineage diverged from that of chimps. *Sahelanthropus* might well represent the earliest human ancestor—or it could be a side branch that went extinct. But its mix of traits certainly seems to place it on the human side of the human/chimp divide. What we have here is a nearly complete skull (albeit a bit squashed during fossilization), but one that is a *mosaic,* showing a curious mixture of homininlike and apelike traits. Like apes, it had a long cranium with a small, chimp-sized brain, but like later hominins, it had a flat face, small teeth, and brow ridges (figure 25).

Lacking the rest of the skeleton, we can't tell if *Sahelanthropus* had the critical ability to walk upright, but there is a tantalizing hint that it could. In knuckle walkers like gorillas and chimps, the animal's usual posture is horizontal, so its spinal cord enters the skull from the rear. In erect humans, however, the skull sits directly atop the spinal cord. You can see this difference in the position of the opening in the skull through which the spinal cord passes (the *foramen magnum,* Latin for "big hole"): this hole is set farther forward in humans. In *Sahelanthropus,* the hole is farther forward than in knuckle-walking apes. This is exciting, for if this species really was on the hominin side of the divide, it suggests that bipedal walking was one of the first evolutionary innovations to distinguish us from other apes.[44]

After *Sahelanthropus,* we have a few six-million-year-old fragments from another species, *Orrorin tugenensis,* including a single leg bone that has been interpreted as evidence of bipedality. But then there is a two-million-year gap with no substantive hominin fossils. This is where, one day, we'll find crucial information about when we began to walk upright. But, beginning about four million years ago, the fossils reappear, and from them we see branches beginning to sprout from the hominin tree. In fact, several species might have lived at the same time. Among these are the "gracile" (slender and graceful) australopithecines, which again show mixtures of apelike and humanlike traits. On the ape side, their brains are roughly chimp-sized, and their skulls are more apelike than humanlike. But the teeth are relatively small, and set in rows midway between the rectangular shape of apes and the parabolic palate of humans. And they were definitely bipedal.

An early set of fossils from Kenya, grouped together as *Australopithecus anamensis*, shows tantalizing hints of bipedality from a single fossilized leg bone. But the decisive find was made by Donald Johanson, an American paleoanthropologist prospecting for fossils in the Afar region of Ethiopia. On the morning of November 30, 1974, Johanson awoke feeling lucky, and made a note to that effect in his field diary. But he had no idea how lucky he'd be. After searching vainly all morning in a dry gulley, Johanson and Tom Gray, a graduate student, were about to give up and head back to camp. Suddenly Johanson spotted a hominid bone on the ground, and then another, and another. Remarkably, they had stumbled on the bones of a single individual, later formally designated AL 288-1, but more famously known as "Lucy," after the Beatles' song "Lucy in the Sky with Diamonds," played repeatedly in camp to celebrate the find.

When Lucy's hundreds of fragments were assembled, she turned out to be a female of a new species, *Australopithecus afarensis*, dating back 3.2 million years. She was between twenty and thirty years old, three and a half feet tall, weighing a scant sixty pounds, and possibly afflicted with arthritis. But most important, she walked on two legs.

How can we tell? From the way that the femur (thighbone) connects to the pelvis at one end and to the knee at its other (figure 26). In a bipedally walking primate like ourselves, the femurs angle in toward each other from the hips so that the center of gravity stays in one place while walking, allowing an efficient fore-and-aft bipedal stride. In knuckle-walking apes, the femurs are slightly splayed out, making them bowlegged. When they try to walk upright, they waddle awkwardly, like Charlie Chaplin's little tramp.[45] If you take a primate fossil, then, and look at how the femur fits together with the pelvis, you can tell whether the creature walked on two legs or four. If the femurs angle toward the middle, it's bipedal. And Lucy's angle in—at almost the same angle as that of modern humans. She walked

Homo sapiens

Australopithecus afarensis

Pan troglodytes
(chimp)

FIGURE 26. The attachment of the femur (long leg bone) to the pelvis in modern humans, chimps, and *Australopithecus afarensis*. The pelvis of *A. afarensis* is intermediate to the other two, but its inward-pointing femur—a sign of upright walking—resembles that of humans and contrasts with the splayed femur of the knuckle-walking chimp.

upright. Her pelvis too resembles that of modern humans far more than that of modern chimps.

A team of paleoanthropologists led by Mary Leakey confirmed the bipedality of *A. afarensis* with another remarkable find in Tanzania: the famous "Laetoli footprints." In 1976, Andrew Hill and another member of the team were taking a break by indulging in a favorite field pastime: pelting each other with chunks of dried elephant dung. Looking for ammunition in a dry stream bed, Hill stumbled upon a line of fossilized footprints. After careful excavation, the footprints turned out to be an eighty-foot trail made by two hominins who had clearly been walking on two legs (there were no impressions of knuckles) during an ash storm from an erupting volcano. That storm was followed by a rain, which turned the ash into a cementlike layer that was later sealed in by another layer of dry ash, preserving the footprints.

The Laetoli footprints are virtually identical to those made by modern humans walking on soft ground. And the feet were almost certainly from Lucy's kin: the tracks are the right size, and the trail dates from around 3.6 million years ago, a time when *A. afarensis* was the only hominin of record. What we have here is that rarest of finds—fossilized human behavior.[46] One of the tracks is larger than the other, so they were probably made by a male and female (other *afarensis* fossils have shown sexual dimorphism in size). The female's footprints seem a bit deeper on one side than on the other, so she may have been carrying an infant on her hip. The trail evokes visions of a small, hairy couple making their way across the plain during a volcanic eruption. Were they frightened, and holding hands?

Like other australopithecines, Lucy had a very apelike head with a chimp-sized braincase. But her skull shows more humanlike traces too, such as a semiparabolic tooth row and reduced canine teeth (figures 25 and 27). Between the head and pelvis she had a mixture of apelike and humanlike traits: the arms were relatively longer than those of modern humans, but shorter than those of chimps, and the finger bones were somewhat curved, like those of apes. This has led to the suggestion that *afarensis* might have spent at least some time in the trees.

One could not ask for a better transitional form between humans and ancient apes than Lucy. From the neck up, she's apelike; in the middle, she's a mixture; and from the waist down, she's almost a modern human. And she tells us a critical fact about our evolution: our upright posture evolved long before our big brain. When this was discovered, it went against the conventional wisdom that larger brains evolved first, and made us rethink the way that natural selection may have shaped modern humans.

After *A. afarensis*, the fossil record shows a confusing mélange of gracile australopithecine species lasting up to about two million years ago. Viewed chronologically, they show a progression to a more modern human form: the tooth row gets more parabolic, the brain gets larger, and the skeleton loses its apelike features.

FIGURE 27. The skeletons and dental arcades of modern *Homo sapiens*,
Australopithecus afarensis ("Lucy"), and a chimpanzee. While chimps
are not the ancestors of the human lineage, they probably resemble the
common ancestor more than do humans. In many respects *A. afarensis*
is intermediate between the apelike and human morphology.

Then things get even messier, for two million years ago marks the border-
line between fossils placed in the genus *Australopithecus* and those placed in
the more modern genus *Homo*. We shouldn't think, though, that this change
of names means that something momentous happened—that "real humans"
suddenly evolved. Whether a fossil is called one name or another depends on
whether it has a larger (*Homo*) or smaller (*Australopithecus*) brain, usually

with a somewhat arbitrary cutoff of around 600 cubic centimeters. Some australopithecine fossils, like *A. rudolfensis*, appear so intermediate in brain size that scientists argue hotly about whether they should be called *Homo* or *Australopithecus*. This naming problem is compounded by the fact that even within a single species we see considerable variation in brain size. (Modern humans, for example, span a very wide range: between 1,000 and 2,000 cubic centimeters, which doesn't, by the way, correlate with intelligence.) But the semantic difficulties shouldn't distract us from realizing that the late australopithecines, already bipedal, were beginning to show changes in teeth, skull, and brain that presage modern humans. It is very likely that the lineage that gave rise to modern humans included at least one of these species.

Another great leap forward in human evolution was the ability to make and use tools. Although chimpanzees use simple tools, including sticks to extract termites from their mounds, using more elaborate tools probably required more flexible thumbs and an erect posture that freed the hands. The first unequivocally tool-using human was *Homo habilis* (figure 25), whose remains first appear about 2.5 million years ago. *H. habilis* means "handy man," and his fossils are associated with a variety of flaked stone tools used for chopping, scraping, and butchering. We're not sure if this species was a direct ancestor of *H. sapiens*, but *habilis* does show changes toward a more humanlike condition, including reduced back teeth and a brain larger than that of the australopithecines. A cast of one brain shows distinct swellings corresponding to Broca's area and Wernicke's area, parts of the brain's left lobe associated with speech production and comprehension. These bumps raise the possibility—still far from certain—that *habilis* was the first species with spoken language.

We do know that *H. habilis* coexisted—in time if not in space—with a whole host of other hominins. The most famous are the East African "robust" (as opposed to gracile) hominins. There were at least three of these—*Paranthropus* (or *Australopithecus*) *boisei* (figure 25), *P. robustus*, and *P. aethiopicus*, all with massive skulls, heavy chewing teeth (some of the molars were nearly an inch across), sturdy bones, and relatively small brains. They also sported sagittal crests: a ridge of bone atop the skull that anchored large chewing muscles. Such robust species probably subsisted on coarse food like roots, nuts, and tubers (*P. boisei*, discovered by Louis Leakey, was nick-named "Nutcracker man"). All three species went extinct by 1.1 million years ago, leaving no descendants.

But *H. habilis* may have lived alongside three species of *Homo* as well: *H. ergaster*, *H. rudolfensis*, and *H. erectus*, although each of these species shows considerable variation and their relationships are disputed. *H. erectus* ("upright man") holds the distinction of being the first hominin to leave Africa: its remains have been found in China ("Peking man"), Indonesia ("Java man"), Europe, and the Middle East. It is likely that as its populations in Africa expanded, *erectus* simply sought new places to live.

By the time of this diaspora, the brain size of *erectus* was nearly equal to that of modern humans. Their skeletons were also nearly identical to ours, though they still had a flattened, chinless face (the chin is a hallmark of modern *H. sapiens*). Their tools were complex, particularly those of late *erectus*, who fashioned complex stone axes and scrapers with intricate flaking. The species also seems responsible for one of the most momentous events in human cultural history: the control of fire. In a cave at Swartkrans, in South Africa, scientists found *erectus* remains alongside burned bones—bones heated at a temperature too high to have come from a brushfire. These could be the remains of animals cooked over a campfire or hearth.

H. erectus was a highly successful species, not only in population size but in longevity. It was around for one and a half million years, disappearing from the fossil record about 300,000 years ago. It may, though, have left two famous descendants: *H. heidelbergensis* and *H. neanderthalensis*, known respectively as "archaic *H. sapiens*" and the famous "Neanderthal man." Both of these are sometimes classified as subspecies (differentiated but inter-breeding populations) of *H. sapiens*, though we have no idea whether either contributed to the gene pool of modern humans.

Living in what is now Germany, Greece, and France, as well as Africa, *H. heidelbergensis* first appears half a million years ago, showing a mixture of modern human and *H. erectus* features. Neanderthals show up a bit later— 230,000 years ago—and lived all over Europe and the Middle East. They had large brains—even bigger than those of modern humans—and were excel-lent toolmakers, as well as adept hunters. Some skeletons bear traces of the pigment ochre, and are accompanied by "grave goods" such as animal bones and tools. This suggests that Neanderthals ceremonially buried their dead: perhaps the first inkling of human religion.

But around 28,000 years ago, the Neanderthal fossils vanish. When I was a student, I was taught that they simply evolved into modern humans. This idea now seems incorrect. What really happened to them is arguably the biggest unknown about human evolution. Their disappearance may have been associated with the spread of another form originating in Africa: *Homo sapiens*. As we learned, by about 1.5 million years ago *H. erectus* had spread all the way from Africa to Indonesia. And within this species there were different "races," that is, populations that differed in some of their traits. (*H. erectus* from China, for example, had shovel-shaped incisor teeth not seen in other populations.) Then, about 300,000 years ago, every *H. erectus* population suddenly vanished and was replaced by fossils of "anatomically modern" *H. sapiens*, who had skeletons nearly identical to those of living humans. Neanderthals hung on awhile longer, but then, after finding a last redoubt in caves overlooking the Strait of Gibraltar, they too gave way to modern *H. sapiens*. In other words, *Homo sapiens* apparently elbowed out every other hominin on earth.

What happened? There are two theories. The first, called the "multiregional" theory, proposes an *evolutionary* replacement: *H. erectus* (and perhaps *H. neanderthalensis*) simply evolved into *H. sapiens independently in several areas*, perhaps because natural selection was acting in the same way all over Asia, Europe, and Africa.

The second idea, dubbed the "out of Africa" theory,[47] proposes that modern *H. sapiens* originated in Africa and spread, *physically* replacing *H. erectus* and the Neanderthals, perhaps by outcompeting them for food or killing them.

Genetic and fossil evidence supports the "out of Africa" theory, but the debate continues. Why? Probably because it boils down to the significance of race. The longer human populations have been separated, the more genetic differences they will have accumulated. The multiregional hypothesis, with its splitting of populations over a million years ago, would predict fifteen times more genetic difference between races than if our human ancestors left Africa only 60,000 years ago. But more about race later.

One population of earlier hominins may have survived the worldwide extinction of *H. erectus*, and it is perhaps the most bizarre twig on the human family tree. Discovered in 2003 on the island of Flores in Indonesia, individuals of *Homo floresiensis* were promptly dubbed "hobbits," for their adult height was a scant one meter (thirty-nine inches), and they weighed only fifty pounds—roughly the size of a five-year-old child. Their brains were also proportionately small—about australopithecine size—but their teeth and skeletons were indisputably those of *Homo*. They used stone tools and may have preyed on the Komodo dragons and dwarf elephants that populated the island. Amazingly, *floresiensis* fossils date to a mere 18,000 years ago, well after Neanderthals disappeared and twenty-five centuries after modern *H. sapiens* had already reached Australia. The best guess is that *floresiensis* represents an isolated population of *H. erectus* that colonized Flores and was somehow bypassed by the spread of modern *H. sapiens*. Although *floresiensis* was probably an evolutionary dead end, it is hard not to be charmed by the idea of a recent population of tiny humans who hunted dwarf elephants with miniature spears; and the hobbits have drawn wide public interest.

But the nature of the *floresiensis* fossils is disputed. Some contend that the tiny size of the one well-preserved skull may simply represent a diseased individual of modern *Homo sapiens*—perhaps one suffering from hypothyroid cretinism, a condition producing abnormally small skulls and brains. Recent analysis of fossil wrist bones, however, do support *H. floresiensis* as a genuine species of hominin, but questions remain.

Looking at the whole array of bones, then, what do we have? Clearly, indisputable evidence for human evolution from apelike ancestors. Granted, we can't yet trace out a continuous lineage from an apelike early hominin to modern *Homo sapiens*. The fossils are scattered in time and space, a series of dots yet to be genealogically connected. And we may never have enough fossils to join them. But if you put those dots in chronological order, as in figure 24, you see exactly what Darwin predicted: fossils that start off apelike and become more and more like modern humans as time passes. It's a fact that our divergence from the ancestor of chimps occurred in East or Central Africa about seven million years ago, and that bipedal walking evolved well before the evolution of large brains. We know that during much of hominin evolution, several species existed at the same time, sometimes at the same place. Given the small population size of humans and the improbability of their fossilization (remember, this usually requires that a body find its way into water and be quickly covered with sediment), it's amazing that we have as good a record as we do. It seems impossible to survey the fossils we have, or look at figure 25, and deny that humans have evolved.

Yet some still do. When dealing with the human fossil record, creationists go through extreme, indeed almost humorous, contortions to avoid admitting the obvious. In fact, they'd prefer to steer clear of the issue. But when forced to confront it, they simply sort hominin fossils into what they see as two discrete groups—humans and apes—and assert that these groups are separated by a large and unbridgeable gap. This reflects their religiously based view that although some species may have evolved from others, humans did not, but were the object of a special act of creation. But the whole folly is exposed by the fact that creationists can't agree on exactly which fossils are "human" and which are "ape." Specimens of *H. habilis* and *H. erectus*, for example, are classified as "apes" by some creationists and "humans" by others. One author has even described a *H. erectus* specimen as an ape in one of his books and a human in another![48] Nothing shows the intermediacy of these fossils better than the inability of creationists to classify them consistently.

What, then, propelled the evolution of humans? It's always easier to document evolutionary change than to understand the forces behind it. What we see in the human fossil record is the appearance of complex adaptations such as erect posture and remodeled skulls, both of which involve many coordinated changes in anatomy, so there's no doubt that natural selection was involved. But what sort of selection? What were the precise reproductive advantages of larger brains, erect posture, and smaller teeth? We'll probably never know for sure, and can only make more or less plausible guesses. We can, however, inform these guesses by learning something about the environment in which humans evolved. Between ten million and three million years ago, the most profound environmental change in East and Central Africa was drought. During this critical period of hominin evolution, the climate gradually became dryer, and was later followed by alternating and erratic periods of drought and rainfall. (This information comes from pollen and African dust blown into the ocean and preserved in sediments.) During the dry periods, the rainforests gave way to more open habitat, including savanna, grassland, open forest, and even desert scrub. This is the stage on which the first act of human evolution played out.

Many biologists feel that these changes in climate and environment had something to do with the first significant hominin trait to evolve: bipedality. The classic explanation is that walking on two legs allowed humans to travel more efficiently from one patch of forest to another across newly open habitat. But this seems unlikely, because studies of knuckle-walking and bipedality show that these forms of locomotion don't use significantly different amounts of energy. Still, there are a host of other reasons why walking erect may have had a selective advantage. It could, for instance, have freed the hands to gather and carry newly available types of food, including meat and tubers (this could also explain our smaller teeth and increased manual dexterity). Walking erect could also have helped us deal with high temperature by raising our body off the ground, reducing the surface area exposed to the sun. We have far more sweat glands than any other ape, and since hair interferes with the cooling evaporation of sweat, this may explain our unique status as "naked apes." There is even an improbable "aquatic ape" theory, arguing that early hominins spent much of their time foraging for food in the water, with erect posture evolving to keep our heads above the surface. Jonathan Kingdon's book on bipedality, *Lowly Origin*, describes still more theories. And of course these evolutionary forces are not mutually exclusive: several might have been operating together. Unfortunately, we can't yet distinguish among them.

The same goes for the evolution of increased brain size. The classic adaptive story is that once our hands were freed by the evolution of two-legged walking, hominins were able to fashion tools, leading to selection for bigger brains that allowed us to envision and fashion more complex tools. This theory has the advantage that the first tool appeared around the time that brains started getting larger. But it ignores other selective pressures for bigger and more complex brains, including the development of language, negotiating the psychological intricacies of primitive society, planning for the future, and so on.

These mysteries about *how* we evolved should not distract us from the indisputable fact that we *did* evolve. Even without fossils, we have evidence of human evolution from comparative anatomy, embryology, our vestigial traits, and even biogeography. We've learned of our fishlike embryos, our dead genes, our transitory fetal coat of hair, and our poor design, all testifying to our origins. The fossil record is really the icing on the cake.

Our Genetic Heritage

IF WE DON'T YET UNDERSTAND why selection made us different from other apes, can we at least find out how many and what sort of *genes* differentiate us? "Humanness" genes have become almost a Holy Grail of evolutionary biology, with many laboratories engaged in the search. The first attempt to find them was made in 1975 by Allan Wilson and Mary-Claire King at the University of California. Their results were surprising. Looking at protein sequences taken from humans and chimps, they found that they differed on average by only about 1 percent. (More recent work hasn't changed this figure much: the difference has risen to about 1.5 percent.) King and Wilson concluded that there was a remarkable genetic similarity between us and our closest relatives. They speculated that perhaps changes in just a very few genes produced the striking evolutionary differences between humans and chimps. This result garnered tremendous publicity in both the popular and scientific press, for it seemed to imply that "humanness" rested on just a handful of key mutations.

But recent work shows that our genetic resemblance to our evolutionary cousins is not quite as close as we thought. Consider this. A 1.5 percent difference in protein sequence means that when we line up the same protein (say, hemoglobin) of humans and chimps, on average we'll see a difference at just one out of every hundred amino acids. But proteins are typically composed of *several hundred* amino acids. So a 1.5 percent difference in a protein three hundred amino acids long translates into about four differences in the total protein sequence. (To use an analogy, if you change only 1 percent of the letters on this page, you will alter far more than 1 percent of the sentences.) That oft-quoted 1.5 percent difference between ourselves and chimps, then, is really larger than it looks: a lot more than 1.5 percent of our proteins will differ by *at least one amino acid* from the sequence in chimps.

And since proteins are essential for building and maintaining our bodies, a single difference can have substantial effects.

Now that we've finally sequenced the genomes of both chimp and human, we can see directly that more than 80 percent of all the proteins shared by the two species differ in at least one amino acid. Since our genomes have about 25,000 protein-making genes, that translates to a difference in the sequence of more than 20,000 of them. That's not a trivial divergence. Obviously, more than a few genes distinguish us. And molecular evolutionists have recently found that humans and chimps differ not only in the *sequence* of genes, but also in the *presence* of genes. More than 6 percent of genes found in humans simply aren't found *in any form* in chimpanzees. There are over fourteen hundred novel genes expressed in humans but not in chimps. We also differ from chimps in the *number of copies* of many genes that we do share. The salivary enzyme amylase, for example, acts in the mouth to break down starch into digestible sugar. Chimps have but a single copy of the gene, while individual humans have between two and sixteen, with an average of six copies. This difference probably resulted from natural selection to help us digest our food, as the ancestral human diet was probably much richer in starch than that of fruit-eating apes.

Putting this together, we see that the genetic divergence between ourselves and chimpanzees comes in several forms—changes not only in the proteins produced by genes, but also in the presence or absence of genes, the number of gene copies, and when and where genes are expressed during development. We can no longer claim that "humanness" rests on only one type of mutation, or changes in only a few key genes. But this is not really surprising if you think about the many traits that distinguish us from our closest relatives. There are differences not only in anatomy, but also in physiology (we are the sweatiest of apes, and the only ape whose females have concealed ovulation),[49] behavior (humans pair-bond and other apes do not), language, and brain size and configuration (surely there must be many differences in how the neurons in our brains are hooked up). Despite our general resemblance to our primate cousins, then, evolving a human from an apelike ancestor probably required substantial genetic change.

Can we say anything about the specific genes that did make us human?

Right now, not very much. Using genomic "scans" that compare the entire DNA sequence of chimps and humans, we can pick out *classes* of genes that have evolved rapidly on the human branch of our divergence. These happen to include genes involved in the immune system, gamete formation, cell death, and, most intriguingly, sensory perception and nerve formation. But it's a different matter entirely to zero in on a single gene and demonstrate that mutations in that gene actually *produced* human/chimp differences. There are "candidate" genes of this sort, including one (*FOXP2*) that might have been involved in the appearance of human speech,[50] but the evidence is inconclusive. And it might always remain so. Conclusive proof that a given gene causes human/chimp differences requires moving the gene from one species to another and seeing what difference it makes, and that's not the kind of experiment anyone would want to try.[51]

The Sticky Question of Race

TRAVELING AROUND THE GLOBE, you quickly see that humans from different places look different. Nobody, for example, would mistake a Japanese for a Bantu. The existence of visibly different human types is obvious, but there's no bigger minefield in human biology than the question of race. Most biologists stay as far away from it as they can. A look at the history of science tells us why. From the beginning of modern biology, racial classification has gone hand in hand with racial prejudice. In his eighteenth-century classification of animals, Carl Linnaeus noted that Europeans are "governed by laws," Asians "governed by opinions," and Africans "governed by caprice." In his superb book *The Mismeasure of Man*, Stephen Jay Gould documents the unholy connection between biologists and race in the last century.

In response to these distasteful episodes of racism, some scientists have overreacted, arguing that human races have no biological reality and are merely sociopolitical "constructs" that don't merit scientific study. But to biologists, race—so long as it doesn't apply to humans!—has always been a perfectly respectable term. Races (also called "subspecies" or "ecotypes") are simply populations of a species that are both geographically separated and differ genetically in one or more traits. There are plenty of animal and plant races, including those mouse populations that differ only in coat color, sparrow populations that differ in size and song, and plant races that differ in the shape of their leaves. Following this definition, *Homo sapiens* clearly *does* have races. And the fact that we do is just another indication that we don't differ from other evolved species.

The existence of different races in humans shows that our populations were geographically separated long enough to allow some genetic divergence to occur. But how much divergence, and does it fit with what the fossils indicate about our spread from Africa? And what kind of selection drove those differences?

As we would expect from evolution, human physical variation occurs in nested groups, and in spite of valiant efforts by some to create formal divisions of races, exactly where one draws the line to demarcate a particular race is completely arbitrary. There are no sharp boundaries: the number of races recognized by anthropologists has ranged from three to more than thirty. Looking at genes shows even more clearly the lack of sharp differences between races: virtually all the genetic variation uncovered by modern molecular techniques correlates only weakly with the classical combinations of physical traits such as skin color and hair type commonly used to determine race.

Direct genetic evidence, accumulated over the last three decades, shows that only about 10 to 15 percent of all genetic variation in humans is represented by differences *between* "races" that are recognized by differences in physical appearance. The remainder of the genetic variation, 85 to 90 percent, occurs *among individuals within races*.

What this means is that races don't show all-or-none differences in the forms of genes (alleles) that they carry. Instead, they usually have the same alleles, but in different frequencies. The ABO blood group gene, for example, has three alleles: A, B, and O. Almost all human populations have these three forms, but they are present in different frequencies in different groups. The O allele, for example, has a frequency of 54 percent in Japanese, 64 percent in Finns, 74 percent in South African !Kung, and 85 percent in Navajos. This is typical of the kind of differences we see in DNA: you can't diagnose a person's origin from a single gene alone, but must do so from looking at a combination of many genes.

At the genetic level, then, human beings are a remarkably similar lot. That is just what we would expect if modern humans left Africa a mere 60,000 or 100,000 years ago. There has been little time for genetic divergence, although we have spread to all corners of the world, breaking up into various far-flung populations that were genetically isolated until recent decades.

So does this mean that we can ignore human race? No. These conclusions don't mean that races are merely mental constructs or that the small genetic differences between them are uninteresting. Some racial differences give us clear evidence of evolutionary pressures that acted in different areas, and can be useful in medicine. Sickle-cell anemia, for example, is most common in blacks whose ancestors came from equatorial Africa. Because carriers of the sickle-cell mutation have some resistance to falciparium malaria (the deadliest form of the disease), it's likely that the high frequency of this mutation in African and African-derived populations resulted from natural selection in response to malaria. Tay-Sachs disease is a fatal genetic disorder that is common among both Ashkenazi Jews and the Cajuns of Louisiana, probably reaching high frequencies via genetic drift in small ancestral populations. Knowing one's ethnicity is a tremendous help in diagnosing these and other genetically based diseases. Moreover, the differences in allele frequencies between racial groups mean that finding appropriate organ donors, which requires a match between several "compatibility genes," should take race into account.

Most of the genetic differences between races are trivial. And yet others, like those physical differences between a Japanese individual and a Finn, a Masai and an Inuit, are striking. We have the interesting situation, then, that the overall differences in gene sequences between peoples are minor, yet those same groups show dramatic differences in a range of visually apparent traits, such as skin color, hair color, body form, and nose shape. These obvious physical differences are not characteristic of the genome as a whole. So why has the small amount of divergence that has occurred between human populations become focused on such visually striking traits?

Some of these differences make sense as adaptations to the different environments in which early humans found themselves. The darker skin of tropical groups probably provides protection from intense ultraviolet light that produces lethal melanomas, while the pale skin of higher-latitude groups allows penetration of light necessary for the synthesis of essential vitamin D, which helps prevent rickets and tuberculosis.[52] But what about the eye folds of Asians, or the longer noses of Caucasians? These don't have any obvious connection to the environment. For some biologists, the existence of greater variation between races in genes that affect physical appearance, something easily assessed by potential mates, points to one thing: *sexual selection.*

Apart from the characteristic pattern of genetic variation, there are other grounds for considering sexual selection as a strong driving force for the evolution of races. We are unique among species for having developed complex cultures. Language has given us a remarkable ability to disseminate ideas and opinions. A group of humans can change their culture much faster than they can evolve genetically. But the cultural change can also *produce* genetic change. Imagine that a spreading idea or fad involves the preferred appearance of one's mate. An empress in Asia, for example, might have a penchant for men with straight black hair and almond-shaped eyes. By creating a fashion, her preference spreads culturally to all her female subjects, and, lo and behold, over time the curly-haired and round-eyed individuals will be largely replaced by individuals with straight black hair and almond-shaped eyes. It is this "gene-culture cocvolution"—the idea that a change in cultural environment leads to new types of selection on genes—that makes the idea of sexual selection for physical differences especially appealing.

Moreover, sexual selection can often act incredibly fast, making it an ideal candidate for driving the rapid evolutionary differentiation of physical traits that occurred since the most recent migration of our ancestors from Africa. Of course, all this is just speculation, and nearly impossible to test, but it potentially explains certain puzzling differences between groups.

Nevertheless, most controversy about race centers not on physical differences between populations, but behavioral ones. Has evolution caused certain races to become smarter, more athletic, or cannier than others? We have to be especially careful here, because unsubstantiated claims in this area can give racism a scientific cachet. So what do the scientific data say? Almost nothing. Although different populations may have different behaviors, different IQs, and different abilities, it's hard to rule out the possibility that these differences are a nongenetic product of environmental or cultural differences. If we want to determine whether certain differences between races are based on genes, we must rule out these influences. Such studies require controlled experiments: removing infants of different ethnicity from their parents and bringing them up in identical (or randomized) environments. What behavioral differences remain would be genetic. Because these experiments are unethical, they haven't been done systematically, but cross-cultural adoptions anecdotally show that cultural influences on behavior are strong. As the psychologist Steven Pinker noted, "If you adopt children from a technologically undeveloped part of the world, they will fit in to modern society just fine." That suggests, at least, that races don't show big innate differences in behavior.

My guess—and this is just informed speculation—is that human races are too young to have evolved important differences in intellect and behavior. Nor is there any reason to think that natural or sexual selection has favored this sort of difference. In the next chapter we'll learn about the many "universal" behaviors seen in all human societies—behaviors like symbolic language, childhood fear of strangers, envy, gossip, and gift-giving. If these universals have any genetic basis, their presence in every society adds additional weight to the view that evolution hasn't produced substantial psychological divergence among human groups.

Although certain traits like skin color and hair type have diverged among populations, these appear to be special cases, driven by environmental differences between localities or by sexual selection for external appearance. The DNA data shows that, overall, genetic differences among human populations are minor. It's more than a soothing platitude to say that we're all brothers and sisters under the skin. And that's just what we'd expect given the brief evolutionary span since our most recent origin in Africa.

What About Now?

ALTHOUGH SELECTION doesn't seem to have produced major differences between races, it has produced some intriguing differences between *popula-*

tions within ethnic groups. Since these populations are quite young, it is clear evidence that selection has acted in humans within recent times.

One case involves our ability to digest lactose, a sugar found in milk. An enzyme called lactase breaks down this sugar into the more easily absorbed sugars glucose and galactose. We are born with the ability to digest milk, of course, for that's always been the main food of infants. But after we're weaned, we gradually stop producing lactase. Eventually, many of us entirely lose our ability to digest lactose, becoming "lactose intolerant" and prone to diarrhea, bloating, and cramps after eating dairy products. The disappearance of lactase after weaning is probably the result of natural selection: Our ancient ancestors had no source of milk after weaning, so why produce a costly enzyme when it's not needed?

But in some human populations, individuals continue to produce lactase throughout adulthood, giving them a rich source of nutrition unavailable to others. It turns out that lactase persistence is found mainly in populations that were, or still are, "pastoralists"—that is, populations who raise cows. These include some European and Middle Eastern populations, as well as Africans such as Masai and Tutsi. Genetic analysis shows that the persistence of lactase in these populations depends on a simple change in the DNA that regulates the enzyme, keeping it turned on beyond infancy. There are two alleles of the gene—the "tolerant" (on) and "intolerant" (off) form—and they differ in only a single letter of their DNA code. The frequency of the tolerant allele correlates well with whether populations use cows: it's high (50 to 90 percent) in pastoralist populations of Europe, the Middle East, and Africa, and very low (1 to 20 percent) in Asian and African populations that depend on agriculture rather than milk.

Archaeological evidence shows that humans began domesticating cows between 7,000 and 9,000 years ago in Sudan, and the practice spread into sub-Saharan Africa and Europe a few thousand years later. The nice part of this story is that we can, from DNA sequencing, determine when the "tolerant" allele arose by mutation. That time, between 3,000 and 8,000 years ago, fits remarkably well with the rise of pastoralism. What's even nicer is that DNA extracted from 7,000-year-old European skeletons showed that they were lactose-intolerant, as we'd expect if they weren't yet pastoral.

The evolution of lactose tolerance is another splendid example of gene-culture coevolution. A purely cultural change (the raising of cows, perhaps for meat) produced a new evolutionary opportunity: the ability to use those cows for milk. Given the sudden availability of a rich new source of food, ancestors possessing the tolerance gene must have had a substantial reproductive advantage over those carrying the intolerant gene. In fact, we can calculate this advantage by observing how fast the tolerance gene increased to the frequencies seen in modern populations. It turns out that tolerant individuals must have produced, on average, 4 to 10 percent more offspring than those who were intolerant. That is pretty strong selection.[53]

Anybody who teaches human evolution is inevitably asked: Are we still evolving? The examples of lactose tolerance and duplication of the amylase gene show that selection has certainly acted within the last few thousand years. But what about right now? It's hard to give a good answer. Certainly many types of selection that challenged our ancestors no longer apply: improvements in nutrition, sanitation, and medical care have done away with many diseases and conditions that killed our ancestors and removed previously potent sources of natural selection. As the British geneticist Steve Jones notes, five hundred years ago a British infant had only a 50 percent chance of surviving to reproductive age, a figure that has now risen to 99 percent. And for those who do survive, medical intervention has allowed many to lead normal lives who would have been ruthlessly culled by selection over most of our evolutionary history. How many people with bad eyes, or bad teeth, unable to hunt or chew, would have perished on the African savanna? (I would certainly have been among the unfit.) How many of us have had infections that, without antibiotics, would have killed us? It's likely that, due to cultural change, we are going downhill genetically in many ways. That is, genes that once were detrimental are no longer so bad (we can compensate for "bad" genes with a simple pair of eyeglasses or a good dentist), and these genes can persist in populations.

Conversely, genes that were once useful may, due to cultural change, now have destructive effects. Our love of sweets and fats, for example, may well have been adaptive in our ancestors, for whom such treats were a valuable but rare source of energy.[54] But these once rare foods are now readily available, and so our genetic heritage brings us tooth decay, obesity, and heart problems. Too, our tendency to lay on fat from rich food may also have been adaptive during times when variation in local food abundance produced a feast-or-famine situation, giving a selective advantage to those who were able to store up calories for lean times.

Does this mean that we're really *de*-evolving? To some degree, yes, but we're probably also becoming more adapted to modern environments that create new types of selection. We should remember that so long as people die before they've stopped reproducing, and so long as some people leave more offspring than others, there is an opportunity for natural selection to improve us. And if there's genetic variation that affects our ability to survive and leave children, it will promote evolutionary change. That is certainly happening now. Although pre-reproductive mortality is low in some Western populations, it's high in many other places, especially Africa, where child mortality can exceed 25 percent. And that mortality is often caused by infectious diseases such as cholera, typhoid fever, and tuberculosis. Other diseases, like malaria and AIDS, continue to kill many children and adults of reproductive age.

The sources of mortality are there, and so are the genes that alleviate them. Variant alleles of some enzymes, for example hemoglobin (notably the sickle-cell allele), confer resistance to malaria. And there is one mutant gene—an allele called *CCR5-Δ32*—that provides its carriers with strong protection against infection with the AIDS virus. We can predict that if AIDS continues as a significant source of mortality, the frequency of this allele will rise in affected populations. That's evolution, as surely as is antibiotic resistance in bacteria. And there are undoubtedly other sources of mortality that we don't fully understand: toxins, pollution, stress, and the like. If we've learned anything from breeding experiments, it is that nearly every species has genetic variation to respond to nearly any form of selection. Slowly, inexorably, and invisibly, our genome adapts to many new sources of mortality. But not every source. Conditions that have both genetic and environmental causes, including obesity, diabetes, and heart disease, may not respond to selection because the mortality they produce occurs mostly after their victims have stopped reproducing. Survival of the fittest is accompanied by survival of the fattest.

But people don't care that much about disease resistance, important as it is. They want to know whether humans are getting stronger, smarter, or prettier. That, of course, depends on whether these traits are associated with differential reproduction, and this we just don't know. Nor does it much matter. In our rapidly changing culture, social improvements enhance our abilities far more than any changes in our genes—unless, that is, we decide to tinker with our evolution through genetic manipulations like preselecting favorable sperm and eggs.

The lesson from the human fossil record, then, combined with more recent discoveries in human genetics, confirms that we are evolved mammals— proud and accomplished ones, to be sure, but mammals built by the same processes that transformed every form of life over the past few billion years. Like all species, we are not an end product of evolution, but a work in progress, though our own genetic progress may be slow. And though we have come a long way from ancestral apes, the marks of our heritage still betray us. Gilbert and Sullivan joked that we are just depilated monkeys; Darwin was not as funny but far more lyrical—and truthful:

> I have given the evidence to the best of my ability; and we must acknowl-
> edge, as it seems to me, that man with all his noble qualities, with sym-
> pathy which feels for the most debased, with benevolence which extends
> not only to other men but to the humblest living creature, with his god-
> like intellect which has penetrated into the movements and constitution
> of the solar system—with all these exalted powers—Man still bears in
> his bodily frame the indelible stamp of his lowly origin.

Chapter 9

Evolution Redux

After sleeping through a hundred million centuries
we have finally opened our eyes on a sumptuous planet,
sparkling with color, bountiful with life. Within decades we
must close our eyes again. Isn't it a noble, an enlightened way
of spending our brief time in the sun, to work at understanding
the universe and how we have come to wake up in it?
This is how I answer when I am asked—as I am surprisingly
often—why I bother to get up in the mornings.

—Richard Dawkins

A few years ago, a group of businessmen in a ritzy suburb of Chicago asked me to speak on the topic of evolution versus intelligent design. To their credit, they were intellectually curious enough to want to learn more about the supposed "controversy." I laid out the evidence for evolution and then explained why intelligent design was a religious rather than a scientific explanation of life. After the talk, a member of the audience approached me and said, "I found your evidence for evolution very convincing—but I still don't believe it."

This statement encapsulates a deep and widespread ambiguity that many feel about evolutionary biology. The evidence is convincing, but they're not convinced. How can that be? Other areas of science aren't plagued by such problems. We don't doubt the existence of electrons or black holes, despite the fact that these phenomena are much further removed from everyday experience than is evolution. After all, you can see fossils in any natural history museum, and we read constantly about how bacteria and viruses are evolving resistance to drugs. So what's the problem with evolution?

What's *not* a problem is the lack of evidence. Since you've read this far, I hope you're convinced that evolution is far more than a scientific theory: it is a scientific fact. We've looked at evidence from many areas—the fossil record, biogeography, embryology, vestigial structures, suboptimal design, and so on—all of that evidence showing, without a scintilla of doubt, that organisms have evolved. And it's not just small "microevolutionary" changes, either: we've seen new species form, both in real time and in the fossil record, and we've found transitional forms between major groups, such as whales and land animals. We've observed natural selection in action, and have every reason to think that it can produce complex organisms and features.

We've also seen that evolutionary biology makes testable predictions, though not of course in the sense of predicting how a particular species will evolve, for that depends on a myriad of uncertain factors such as which mutations crop up and how environments may change. But we *can* predict where fossils will be found (take Darwin's prediction that human ancestors would be found in Africa), we can predict *when* common ancestors would appear (for example, the discovery of the "fishapod" *Tiktaalik* in 370-million-year-old rocks, described in chapter 2), and we can predict what those ancestors should look like before we find them (one is the remarkable "missing link" between ants and wasps, also shown in chapter 2). Scientists predicted that they would find fossils of marsupials in Antarctica—and they did. And we can predict that if we find an animal species in which males are brightly colored and females are not, that species will have a polygynous mating system.

Every day, hundreds of observations and experiments pour into the hopper of the scientific literature. Many of them don't have much to do with evolution—they're observations about details of physiology, biochemistry, development, and so on—but many of them do. And every fact that has something to do with evolution confirms its truth. Every fossil that we find, every DNA molecule that we sequence, every organ system that we dissect supports the idea that species evolved from common ancestors. Despite innumerable *possible* observations that could prove evolution untrue, we don't have a single one. We don't find mammals in Precambrian rocks, humans in the same layers as dinosaurs, or any other fossils out of evolutionary order. DNA sequencing supports the evolutionary relationships of species originally deduced from the fossil record. And, as natural selection predicts, we find no species with adaptations that benefit only a different species. We do find dead genes and vestigial organs, incomprehensible under the idea of special creation. Despite a million chances to be wrong, evolution always comes up right. That is as close as we can get to a scientific truth.

Now, when we say that "evolution is true," what we mean is that the major tenets of Darwinism have been verified. Organisms evolved, they did so gradually, lineages split into different species from common ancestors, and natural selection is the major engine of adaptation. No serious biologist doubts these propositions. But this doesn't mean that Darwinism is scientifically exhausted, with nothing left to understand. Far from it. Evolutionary biology is teeming with questions and controversies. How exactly does sexual selection work? Do females select males with good genes? How much of a role does genetic drift (as opposed to natural or sexual selection) play in the evolution of DNA sequences or the features of organisms? Which fossil hominins are on the direct line to *Homo sapiens*? What caused the Cambrian "explosion" of life, in which many new types of animals appeared within only a few million years?

Critics of evolution seize upon these controversies, arguing that they show that something is wrong with the theory of evolution itself. But this is specious. There is no dissent among serious biologists about the major claims of evolutionary theory—only about the details of how evolution occurred, and about the relative roles of various evolutionary mechanisms. Far from discrediting evolution, the "controversies" are in fact the sign of a vibrant, thriving field. What moves science forward is ignorance, debate, and the testing of alternative theories with observations and experiments. A science without controversy is a science without progress.

At this point I could simply say, "I've given the evidence, and it shows that evolution is true. Q.E.D." But I'd be remiss if I did that, because, like the businessman I encountered after my lecture, many people require more than just evidence before they'll accept evolution. To these folks, evolution raises such profound questions of purpose, morality, and meaning that they just can't accept it no matter how much evidence they see. It's not that we evolved from apes that bothers them so much; it's the emotional *consequences* of facing that fact. And unless we address those concerns, we won't progress in making evolution a universally acknowledged truth. As the American philosopher Michael Ruse noted, "Nobody lies awake worrying about gaps in the fossil record. Many people lie awake worrying about abortion and drugs and the decline of the family and gay marriage and all of the other things that are opposed to so-called 'moral values.'"

Nancy Pearcey, a conservative American philosopher and advocate of intelligent design, expressed this common fear:

Why does the public care so passionately about a theory of biology? Because people sense intuitively that there's much more at stake than a scientific theory. They know that when naturalistic evolution is taught in the science classroom, then a naturalistic view of ethics will be taught down the hallway in the history classroom, the sociology classroom, the family life classroom, and in all areas of the curriculum.

Pearcey argues (and many American creationists agree) that all the perceived evils of evolution come from two worldviews that are part of science: naturalism and materialism. Naturalism is the view that the only way to understand our universe is through the scientific method. Materialism is the idea that the only reality is the physical matter of the universe, and that everything else, including thoughts, will, and emotions, comes from physical laws acting on that matter. The message of evolution, and all of science, is one of naturalistic materialism. Darwinism tells us that, like all species, human beings arose from the working of blind, purposeless forces over eons of time. As far as we can determine, the same forces that gave rise to ferns, mushrooms, lizards, and squirrels also produced us. Now, science cannot completely exclude the possibility of supernatural explanation. It is possible—

though very unlikely—that our whole world is controlled by elves. But supernatural explanations like these are simply never needed: we manage to understand the natural world just fine using reason and materialism. Furthermore, supernatural explanations always mean the end of inquiry: that's the way God wants it, end of story. Science, on the other hand, is never satisfied: our studies of the universe will continue until humans go extinct.

But Pearcey's notion that these lessons of evolution will inevitably spill over into the study of ethics, history, and "family life" is unnecessarily alarmist. How can you derive meaning, purpose, or ethics from evolution? You can't. Evolution is simply a theory about the process and patterns of life's diversification, not a grand philosophical scheme about the meaning of life. It can't tell us what to do, or how we should behave. And this is the big problem for many believers, who want to find in the story of our origins a reason for our existence, and a sense of how to behave.

Most of us *do* need meaning, purpose, and moral guidance in our lives. How do we find them if we accept that evolution is the real story of our origin? That question is outside the domain of science. But evolution can still shed some light on whether our morality is constrained by our genetics. If our bodies are the product of evolution, what about our behavior? Do we carry the psychological baggage of our millions of years on the African savanna? If so, how far can we overcome it?

The Beast Within

A COMMON BELIEF about evolution is that if we recognize that we are only evolved mammals, there will be nothing to prevent us from acting like beasts. Morality will be out the window, and the law of the jungle will prevail. This is the "naturalistic view of ethics" that Nancy Pearcey fears will pervade our schools. As the old Cole Porter song goes:

> *They say that bears have love affairs*
> *And even camels*
> *We're men and mammals—let's misbehave!*

A more recent version of this notion was furnished by former congress-man Tom DeLay in 1999. Implying that the Columbine High School massa-cre in Colorado might have Darwinian roots, DeLay read out loud on the floor of the U.S. Congress a letter from a Texas newspaper suggesting—sarcastically—that "it [the massacre] couldn't have been because our school systems teach the children that they are nothing but glorified apes who have evolutionized out of some primordial soup of mud." In her best-selling book *Godless: The Church of Liberalism*, conservative pundit Ann Coulter is even more explicit, claiming that, for liberals, evolution "lets them off the hook morally. Do whatever you feel like doing—screw your secretary, kill Grandma, abort your defective child—Darwin says it will benefit humanity!" Darwin, of course, never said anything of the sort.

But does modern evolutionary biology even *claim* that we're genetically hardwired to behave like our supposedly beastly forebears? To many, this impression came from the evolutionist Richard Dawkins's immensely popu-lar book *The Selfish Gene*—or rather from its title. This seemed to imply that evolution makes us behave selfishly, caring only for ourselves. Who wants to live in a world like that? But the book says nothing of the kind. As Dawkins shows clearly, the "selfish" gene is a metaphor for how natural selection works. Genes act *as if* they're selfish molecules: those that produce better adaptations act as if they're elbowing out other genes in the battle for future existence. And, to be sure, selfish genes can produce selfish behaviors. But there is also a huge scientific literature on how evolution can favor genes that lead to cooperation, altruism, and even morality. Our forebears may not have been entirely beastly after all, and in any case, the jungle, with its vari-ety of animals, many of which live in quite complex and cooperative societ-ies, is not as lawless as the saying implies.

So if our evolution as social apes has left its imprint on our brains, what sorts of human behavior might be "hardwired"? Dawkins himself has said that *The Selfish Gene* could equally well have been called *The Cooperative Gene*. Are we hardwired to be selfish, cooperative, or both?

In recent years a new academic discipline has arisen that tries to answer this question, interpreting human behavior in the light of evolution. *Evolu-tionary psychology* traces its origin to E. O. Wilson's book *Sociobiology*, a sweeping evolutionary synthesis of animal behavior that suggested, in its last chapter, that human behavior could also have evolutionary explanations. Much of evolutionary psychology seeks to explain modern human behaviors as adaptive results of natural selection acting on our ancestors. If we take the beginning of "civilization" at about 4000 BC, when there were complex societies both urban and agricultural, then only six thousand years have passed until now. This represents only one-thousandth of the total time that the human lineage has been isolated from that of chimpanzees. Like icing on a cake, roughly 250 generations of civilized society lie atop 300,000 generations during which we may have been hunter-gatherers living in small social groups. And selection would have had many eons to adapt us to such a lifestyle. Evolutionary psychologists call the physical and social environment to which we adapted during this long period the "Environment of Evolutionary Adaptedness," or EEA.[55] Surely, as evolutionary psychologists say, we must retain many behaviors that evolved in the EEA, even if they are no longer adaptive—or even maladaptive. After all, there's been relatively little time for evolutionary change since the rise of modern civilization.

Indeed, all human societies seem to share a number of widely recognized "human universals." Donald Brown listed dozens of such traits in his book by that name, including the use of symbolic language (in which words are abstract symbols for actions, objects, and thoughts), the division of labor between the sexes, male dominance, religious or supernatural belief, mourning for the dead, favoring relatives over nonrelatives, decorative art and fashion, dance and music, gossip, body adornment, and a love of sweets. Because most of these behaviors distinguish humans from other animals, they can be seen as aspects of "human nature."

But we shouldn't always assume that widespread behaviors reflect genetically based adaptations. One problem is that it is all too easy to make up an evolutionary reason why many modern human behaviors should have been adaptive in the EEA. For example, art and literature might be the equivalent to the peacock's tail, with artists and writers leaving more genes because their productions appealed to women. Rape? It's a way for men who can't find mates to father offspring; such men were then selected in the EEA for a propensity to overpower and forcibly copulate with women. Depression? No problem: it could be a way of withdrawing adaptively from stressful situations, mustering your mental resources so that you can cope with life. Or it could represent a ritualized form of social defeat, enabling you to withdraw from competition, recoup, and come back to struggle another day. Homosexuality? Even though this behavior seems the very opposite of what natural selection would foster (genes for gay behavior, which don't get passed on, would quickly disappear from populations), one can save the day by assuming that, in the EEA, homosexual males stayed home and helped their mothers produce other offspring. In this circumstance, "gayness" genes could be passed on by homosexuals producing more brothers and sisters, individuals who share those genes. None of these explanations, by the way, are mine. All of them have actually appeared in the published scientific literature.

There is an increasing (and disturbing) tendency of psychologists, biologists, and philosophers to Darwinize every aspect of human behavior, turning its study into a scientific parlor game. But imaginative reconstructions of how things might have evolved are not science; they are stories. Stephen Jay Gould satirized them as "Just-So Stories," after Kipling's eponymous book that gave delightful but fanciful explanations for various traits of animals ("How the Leopard Got His Spots," and so on).

Yet we can't dismiss *all* behaviors as having no evolutionary basis. Surely some of them do. These include behaviors that are almost certainly adaptations because they're widely shared among animals and whose importance in survival and reproduction is obvious. Behaviors that come to mind are eating, sleeping (though we don't know yet why we need to sleep, a resting period of the brain is widespread in animals), a sex drive, parental care, and favoring relatives over nonrelatives.

A second category of behaviors includes those very likely to have evolved by selection, but whose adaptive significance is not quite as clear as, say, parental care. Sexual behavior is the most obvious. In parallel with many animals, human males are largely promiscuous and females choosy (this despite the socially enforced monogamy that prevails in many societies). Males are larger and stronger than females and have higher levels of testosterone, a hormone associated with aggression. In societies where reproductive success has been measured, its variation among males is invariably higher than among females. Statistical surveys of personal ads in newspapers—granted, not the most rigorous form of scientific investigation—have shown that while men search for younger women with bodies suited to childbearing, women prefer somewhat older males who have wealth, status, and a willingness to invest in their relationships. All of these features make sense in light of what we know about sexual selection in animals. While this doesn't make us quite the equivalent of elephant seals, the parallels strongly imply that features of our body and behavior were molded by sexual selection.

But we must again take care when extrapolating from other animals. Men might be larger not because they compete for women, but because of the evolutionary outcome of a division of labor: in the EEA, men might have hunted while women, the childbearers, took care of children and foraged for food. (Note that this is still an evolutionary explanation, but one that involves natural rather than sexual selection.) And it takes some mental contortions to try to explain *every* facet of human sexuality by evolution. In modern Western societies, for example, women adorn themselves much more elaborately than males, wearing makeup, diverse and fancy dress, and so on. This is very different from most sexually selected animals like the birds of paradise, in which it is males who have evolved elaborate displays, body colors, and ornaments. And there is always a temptation to look at behavior in our immediate surroundings, in our society, and forget that behaviors are often variable over time and space. Being homosexual may not be the same thing in San Francisco today as it was in Athens twenty-five hundred years ago. Few behaviors are as absolute, or inflexible, as language or sleeping. Nevertheless, we can be fairly confident that some aspects of sexual behavior, the universal love of fats and sweets, and our tendency to lay on fat reserves are traits that were adaptive in our ancestors—but not necessarily today. And linguists like Noam Chomsky and Steven Pinker have argued convincingly that the use of symbolic language is likely a genetic adaptation, with aspects of syntax and grammar somehow coded in our brains.

Finally, there is the very large category of behaviors sometimes seen as adaptations, but about whose evolution we know virtually nothing. This includes many of the most interesting human universals, including moral codes, religion, and music. There is no end of theories (and books) about how such features may have evolved. Some modern thinkers have constructed elaborate scenarios about how our sense of morality, and many moral tenets, might be the products of natural selection working on the inherited mind-set of a social primate, just as language enabled the building of a complex society and culture. But in the end these ideas come down to untested—and probably untestable—speculations. It's almost impossible to reconstruct how these features evolved (or even if they *are* evolved genetic traits) and whether they are direct adaptations or, like making fire, merely by-products of a complex brain that evolved behavioral flexibility to take care of its body. We should be deeply suspicious of speculations that come unaccompanied by hard evidence. My own view is that conclusions about the evolution of human behavior should be based on research at least as rigorous as that used in studying nonhuman animals. And if you read the animal-behavior journals, you'll see that this requirement sets the bar pretty high, so that many assertions about evolutionary psychology sink without a trace.

There is no reason, then, to see ourselves as marionettes dancing on the strings of evolution. Yes, certain parts of our behavior may be genetically encoded, instilled by natural selection in our savanna-dwelling ancestors. But genes aren't destiny. One lesson that all geneticists know, but which doesn't seem to have permeated the consciousness of nonscientists, is that "genetic" does not mean "unchangeable." All sorts of environmental factors can affect the expression of genes. Juvenile diabetes, for example, is a genetic disease, but its harmful effects can be largely eliminated by small doses of insulin: an environmental intervention. My poor eyesight, which runs in the family, is no encumbrance thanks to glasses. Likewise, we can curtail our voracious appetites for chocolate and meat with some willpower and the help of Weight Watchers meetings, and the institution of marriage has gone a long way toward curbing the promiscuous behavior of men.

The world still teems with selfishness, immorality, and injustice. But look elsewhere and you'll also find innumerable acts of kindness and altruism. There may be elements of both behaviors that come from our evolutionary heritage, but these acts are largely matters of choice, not of genes. Giving to charity, volunteering to eradicate disease in poor countries, fighting fires at immense personal risk—none of these acts could have been instilled in us directly by evolution. And as the years pass, although horrors like "ethnic cleansing" in Rwanda and the Balkans are still with us, we see an increasing sense of justice sweeping through the world. In Roman times, some of the most sophisticated minds that ever existed found it an excellent afternoon's entertainment to sit down and watch humans literally fighting for their lives against each other, or against wild animals. There is now no culture on the planet that would not think this barbaric. Similarly, human sacrifice was once an important part of many societies. That too has thankfully disappeared. In many countries, the equality of men and women is now taken for granted. Richer nations are becoming aware of their obligations to help, rather than exploit, poorer ones. We worry more about how we treat animals. None of this has anything to do with evolution, for the change is happening far too fast to be caused by our genes. It is clear, then, that whatever genetic heritage we have, it is not a straitjacket that traps us forever in the "beastly" ways of our forebears. Evolution tells us where we came from, not where we can go.

And although evolution operates in a purposeless, materialistic way, that doesn't mean that our lives have no purpose. Whether through religious or secular thought, we make our own purposes, meaning, and morality. Many of us find meaning in our work, our families, and our avocations. There is solace, and food for the brain, in music, art, literature, and philosophy.

Many scientists have found profound spiritual satisfaction in contemplating the wonders of the universe and our ability to make sense of them. Albert Einstein, often mistakenly described as conventionally religious, nevertheless saw the study of nature as a spiritual experience:

> The fairest thing we can experience is the mysterious. It is the fundamental emotion which stands at the cradle of true art and true science. He who knows it not and can no longer wonder, no longer feel amazement, is as good as dead, a snuffed-out candle. It was the experience of mystery—even if mixed with fear—that engendered religion. A knowledge of the existence of something we cannot penetrate, of the manifestations

of the profoundest reason and the most radiant beauty, which are only accessible to our reason in their most elementary forms—it is this knowledge and this emotion that constitute the truly religious attitude; in this sense, and in this alone, I am a deeply religious man. . . . Enough for me the mystery of the eternity of life, and the inkling of the marvelous structure of reality, together with the single-hearted endeavour to comprehend a portion, be it ever so tiny, of the reason that manifests itself in nature.

Deriving your spirituality from science also means accepting an attendant sense of humility before the universe and the likelihood that we'll never have all the answers. The physicist Richard Feynman was one of these stalwarts:

I don't have to know an answer. I don't feel frightened by not knowing things, by being lost in a mysterious universe without any purpose, which is the way it really is as far as I can tell, possibly. It doesn't frighten me.

But it's too much to expect everyone to feel like that, or to assume that *The Origin of Species* can supplant the Bible. Only relatively few people can find abiding consolation and sustenance in the wonders of nature; even fewer are granted the privilege of adding to those wonders through their own research. The British novelist Ian McEwan laments the failure of science to replace conventional religion:

Our secular and scientific culture has not replaced or even challenged these mutually incompatible, supernatural thought systems. Scientific method, skepticism, or rationality in general, has yet to find an overarching narrative of sufficient power, simplicity, and wide appeal to compete with the old stories that give meaning to people's lives. Natural selection is a powerful, elegant, and economic explicator of life on earth in all its diversity, and perhaps it contains the seeds of a rival creation myth that would have the added power of being true—but it awaits its inspired synthesizer, its poet, its Milton. . . . Reason and myth remain uneasy bedfellows.

I certainly make no claim to be the Milton of Darwinism. But I can at least try to dispel the misconceptions that frighten people away from evolution and from the amazing derivation of life's staggering diversity from a single naked replicating molecule. The biggest of these misconceptions is that accepting evolution will somehow sunder our society, wreck our morality, impel us to behave like beasts, and spawn a new generation of Hitlers and Stalins.

That just won't happen, as we know from the many European countries whose residents wholly embrace evolution yet manage to remain civilized. Evolution is neither moral nor immoral. It just is, and we make of it what we will. I have tried to show that two things we *can* make of it are that it's simple and it's marvelous. And far from constricting our actions, the study of evolution can liberate our minds. Human beings may be only one small twig on the vast branching tree of evolution, but we're a very special animal. As natural selection forged our brains, it opened up for us whole new worlds. We have learned how to improve our lives immeasurably over those of our ancestors, who were plagued with disease, discomfort, and a constant search for food. We can fly above the tallest mountains, dive deep below the sea, and even travel to other planets. We make symphonies, poems, and books to fulfill our aesthetic passions and emotional needs. No other species has accomplished anything remotely similar.

But there is something even more wondrous. We are the one creature to whom natural selection has bequeathed a brain complex enough to comprehend the laws that govern the universe. And we should be proud that we are the only species that has figured out how we came to be.

Notes

1. The modern theory of evolution is still called "Darwinism," despite having gone well beyond what Darwin first proposed (he knew nothing, for example, about DNA or mutations). This kind of eponymy is unusual in science: we don't call classical physics "Newtonism" or relativity "Einsteinism." Yet Darwin was so correct, and accomplished so much in *The Origin*, that for many people evolutionary biology has become synonymous with his name. I'll sometimes use the term "Darwinism" throughout this book, but keep in mind that what I mean is "modern evolutionary theory."

2. Unlike matchbooks, human languages *do* fall into a nested hierarchy, with some (like English and German) resembling each other far more than they do others (e.g., Chinese). You can, in fact, construct an evolutionary tree of languages based on the similarity of words and grammar. The reason languages can be so arranged is because they underwent their own form of evolution, changing gradually through time and diverging as people moved to new regions and lost contact with one another. Like species, languages have speciation and common ancestry. It was Darwin who first noticed this analogy.

3. Wooly mammoths died out about ten thousand years ago, probably hunted to extinction by our ancestors. At least one ancient specimen was so well preserved by freezing that in 1951 it furnished meat for an Explorer's Club dinner in New York.

4. It's likely that ancestral mammals retained their adult testes in the abdomen (some mammals, like the platypus and elephant, still do), which makes us ask why evolution favored the movement of testes into an easily injured position outside the body. We don't yet know the answer, but a clue is that the enzymes involved in making sperm simply don't function well at core body temperature (that's why doctors tell potential fathers to avoid warm baths before sex). It's possible that as warm-bloodedness evolved in mammals, the testes of some

groups were forced to descend to remain cool. But perhaps external testes evolved for other reasons, and the enzymes involved in making sperm simply lost their ability to function at higher temperatures.

5. Opponents of evolution often claim that the theory of evolution must also explain how life originated, and that Darwinism fails because we don't yet have the answer. This objection is misguided. Evolutionary theory deals only with what happens *after* life (which I'll define as self-reproducing organisms or molecules) came into being. The origin of life itself is the remit not of evolutionary biology, but of abiogenesis, a scientific field that encompasses chemistry, geology, and molecular biology. Because this field is in its infancy, and has yet given few answers, I've omitted from this book any discussion of how life on earth began. For an overview of the many competing theories, see Robert Hazen's *Gen*e*sis: The Scientific Quest for Life's Origin.*

6. Note that for the first half of life's history the only species were bacteria. Complex multicellular organisms don't show up until the last 15 percent of the history of life. To see an evolutionary timeline in true scale, showing how recently many familiar forms arose, go to http://andabien.com/html/evolution-timeline.htm, and keep scrolling.

7. Creationists often use the biblical concept of "kinds" to refer to those groups that were specially created (see Genesis 1:12–25), but within which some evolution is allowed. Explaining "kinds," one creationist Web site claims, "For example, there may be many species of doves, but they are all still doves. Therefore, doves would be a 'kind' of animal (bird, actually)." Thus, microevolution is allowed within "kinds," but macroevolution *between* kinds could not, and did not, occur. In other words, members of a kind have a common ancestor; members of different kinds do not. The problem is that creationists give no criterion for identifying "kinds" (do they correspond to the biological genus? The family? Are all flies members of one kind, or of different kinds?), so we cannot judge what they see as the limits to evolutionary change. But creationists all agree on one thing: *Homo sapiens* is a "kind" by itself, and therefore must have been created. Yet there is nothing in either the theory or data from evolution implying that evolutionary change could be limited: as far as we can see, macroevolution is simply microevolution extended over a long period of time. (See http://www.clarifyingchristianity.com/creation.shtml and http://www.nwcreation.net/biblicalkinds.html for the creationist view of "kinds," and http://www.geocities.com/CapeCanaveral/Hangar/2437/kinds.htm for a rebuttal.)

8. Paleontologists now think that all theropods—and that includes the famous *Tyrannosaurus rex*—were covered with some form of feathers. These aren't usually shown in museum reconstructions, or in movies like *Jurassic Park*. It wouldn't bolster the fearsome reputation of *T. rex* to show it covered with fluff!

9. For an engrossing description of how "Dave," the first *Sinornithosaurus* specimen, was found and prepared, see http://www.amnh.org/learn/pd/dinos/markmeetsdave.html.

10. *NOVA* made a brilliant television program documenting the finding of *Microraptor gui* and the subsequent controversy about whether it flew. "The Four-Winged Dinosaur" can be seen online at http://www.pbs.org/wgbh/nova/microraptor/program.html.

11. In a stunning recent achievement, scientists have managed to obtain fragments of the protein collagen from a 68 million-year-old fossil of *T. rex*, and determined the amino acid sequence of these fragments. The analysis shows that *T. rex* is more closely related to living birds (chickens and ostriches) than to any other living vertebrates. The pattern confirms what scientists have long suspected: all the dinosaurs went extinct except for the one lineage that gave rise to birds. Increasingly, biologists recognize that birds are simply highly modified dinosaurs. Indeed, birds are often *classified* as dinosaurs.

12. The sequence of whale DNA and protein shows that among mammals they are most closely related to the artiodactyls, a finding completely consistent with the fossil evidence.

13. To see a water chevrotain taking to the water to escape an eagle, go to http://www.youtube.com/watch?v=13GQbT2ljxs.

14. The paper was published, however, and showed that despite their different styles of running, ostriches and horses use similar amounts of energy to cover the same distance: M. A. Fedak and H. J. Seeherman. 1981. A reappraisal of the energetics of locomotion shows identical costs in bipeds and quadrupeds including the ostrich and the horse. *Nature* 282:713–716.

15. This video shows how wings are used in mating: http://revver.com/video/213669/masai-ostrich-mating/.

16. Whales, which lack external ears, also have nonfunctional ear muscles (and sometimes tiny, useless ear openings) inherited from their land-mammal ancestors.

17. Pseudogenes are, to my knowledge, never resurrected. Once a gene experi-

ences a mutation that inactivates it, it quickly accumulates others that further degrade the information for making its protein. The chance of all those mutations reversing themselves to reawaken the gene is nearly zero.

18. Predictably, marine mammals that spend part of their time on land, like sea lions, have more active OR genes than do whales or dolphins, presumably because they still need to detect airborne odors.

19. Creationists often cite Haeckel's "fudged" drawings as a tool for attacking evolution in general: evolutionists, they claim, will distort the facts to support a misguided Darwinism. But the Haeckel story is not so simple. Haeckel may not have been guilty of malfeasance, but only of sloppiness: his "fraud" consisted solely of illustrating three different embryos using the same woodcut. When called to account, he admitted the error and corrected it. There's simply no evidence that he consciously distorted the appearance of embryos to make them look more similar than they were. R. J. Richards (2008, chapter 8) tells the full story.

20. Our ancestry has left us with many other physical woes. Hemorrhoids, bad backs, hiccups, and inflamed appendixes—all of these conditions are the legacy of our evolution. Neil Shubin describes these and many others in his book *Your Inner Fish*.

21. It also inspired William Cowper's poem "The Solitude of Alexander Selkirk," with its famous first line:

> *I am monarch of all I survey;*
> *My right there is none to dispute;*
> *From the centre all round to the sea*
> *I am lord of the fowl and the brute.*

22. For an animation of continental drift over the last 150 million years, see http://mulinet6.li.mahidol.ac.th/cd-rom/cd-rom0309t/Evolution_files/platereconanim.gif. More comprehensive animations over earth's entire history are at http://www.scotese.com/.

23. This phrase, surely Tennyson's most famous, comes from his poem "In Memoriam A.H.H." (1850):

> *[Man,] Who trusted God was love indeed*
> *And love Creation's final law—*
> *Tho' Nature, red in tooth and claw*
> *With ravine, shrieked against his creed.*

24. A graphic video of Japanese hornets preying on introduced honeybees, and being cooked to death by defending Japanese honeybees, can be seen at http://www.youtube.com/watch?v=DcZCttPGyJ0. Scientists have recently found yet another way that bees kill hornets—through suffocation. In Cyprus, local honeybees also form a ball around intruding hornets. Wasps breathe by expanding and contracting their abdomen, pumping air into their bodies through tiny passages. The tight bee-ball prevents the wasps from moving their abdomens, depriving them of air.

25. Carl Zimmer's *Parasite Rex* recounts many other fascinating (and horrifying) ways that parasites have evolved to manipulate their hosts.

26. There's another aspect of this story that is almost as amazing: the ants, which spend a lot of time in trees, have evolved the ability to glide. When they fall off a branch, they can maneuver in the air so that, instead of landing on the hostile forest floor, they swoop back to the safety of the tree trunk. It's not yet known how a falling ant can control the direction of its glide, but you can see videos of this remarkable behavior at http://www.canopyants.com/video1.html.

27. Creationists sometimes cite this tongue as an example of a trait that could not have evolved, since the intermediate stages of evolution from short to long tongues were supposedly maladaptive. This assertion is baseless. For a description of the long tongue and how it probably evolved by natural selection, see http://www.talkorigins.org/faqs/woodpecker/woodpecker.html.

28. As I write, a report has just appeared showing that DNA extracted from the bones of Neanderthals contains another light-color form of the gene. It's likely, then, that some Neanderthals had red hair.

29. Different breeds are all considered to fall under the species *Canis lupus familiaris* because they can successfully hybridize. If they occurred only as fossils, their substantial differences would lead us to conclude that there is some genetic barrier preventing them from hybridizing, ergo they must represent different species.

30. The insects also adapted to the different chemistry of the plant species, so that each new form of the bug now thrives best on the introduced plant it inhabits rather than the old soapberry bush.

31. For descriptions of how blood clotting and the flagellum might have evolved through selection, see Kenneth Miller's book *Only a Theory*, as well as M. J. Pallen and N. J. Matzke (2006).

32. To see sage grouse strutting on the lek before females, go to http://www.youtube.com/watch?v=qcWx2VbT_j8.

33. The earliest sexually reproducing species so far identified is a red alga aptly named *Bangiomorpha pubescens*. Two sexes are clearly visible in its fossils from 1.2 billion years ago.

34. It's important to remember that we're talking about the difference between males and females in the *variance* of mating success. In contrast, the *average* mating success of males and females must be equal, because each offspring must have one father and one mother. In males, this average is attained by a few of them siring most of the offspring while the rest have none. Each female, on the other hand, has roughly the same number of offspring.

35. When pressed, creationists explain sexual dimorphisms by resorting to the mysterious whims of the creator. In his book *Darwin on Trial*, intelligent design advocate Phillip Johnson responds to evolutionist Douglas Futuyma's query: "Do the creation scientists really suppose their Creator saw fit to create a bird that couldn't reproduce without six feet of bulky feathers that make it easy prey for leopards?" Johnson replies: "I don't know what creation-scientists may suppose, but it seems to me that the peacock and peahen are just the kind of creatures a whimsical Creator might favor, but that an 'uncaring mechanical process' like natural selection would never permit to develop." But a well-understood and *testable* hypothesis like sexual selection surely trumps an untestable appeal to the inscrutable caprices of a creator.

36. You may ask why, if females have a preference for unexpressed traits, those traits never evolve in males? One explanation is simply that the right mutations didn't occur. Another is that the right mutations *did* occur, but reduced the male's survival more than it enhanced his ability to attract mates.

37. You might object that this concordance shows only that all human brains are neurologically wired to divide up what is really a continuum of birds at the same arbitrary points. But this objection loses force when you remember that *the birds themselves* recognize the same clusters. When it comes time to reproduce, a male robin courts only female robins, not female sparrows, starlings, or crows. Birds, like other animals, are good at recognizing different species!

38. For example, if 99 percent of all species produced went extinct, we still need a speciation rate of only one new species arising per hundred million years to produce 100 million living species.

39. For a lucid presentation of how science reconstructs ancient events in geology, biology, and astronomy, see C. Turney. 2006. *Bones, Rocks and Stars: The Science of When Things Happened*. Macmillan, New York.

40. Here's a more detailed description of how a new allopolyploid species arises. Bear with me, for although understanding the process isn't hard, it requires keeping track of a few numbers. Every species, except for bacteria and viruses, carries two copies of each chromosome. We humans, for example, have forty-six chromosomes, comprising twenty-two pairs, or *homologs*, plus the two sex chromosomes: XX in females and XY in males. One member of each chromosome pair is inherited through the father, the other through the mother. When individuals of a species make gametes (sperm and eggs in animals, pollen and eggs in plants), the homologs get separated from one another, and only one member of each pair goes into a sperm, egg, or pollen grain. But before that, the homologs must line up and pair with each other so that they can be properly divided. If the chromosomes can't pair up properly, the individual can't produce gametes and is sterile.

This failure to pair is the basis of allopolyploid speciation. Suppose, for example, that a plant species (let's be imaginative and call it A) has six chromosomes, three pairs of homologs. Suppose further that it has a relative, species B, with ten chromosomes (five pairs). A hybrid between the two species will have eight chromosomes, getting three from species A and five from species B (remember that the gametes of each species carry only half of its chromosomes). This hybrid may be viable and vigorous, but when it tries to form pollen or eggs, it runs into trouble. Five chromosomes from one species try to pair with three from the other, creating a mess. Gamete formation is aborted, and the hybrid is sterile.

But suppose that somehow the hybrid could simply duplicate *all* of its chromosomes, raising the number from eight to sixteen. This new super-hybrid will be able to undergo proper chromosome pairing: each of the six chromosomes from species A will find its homolog, and likewise the ten chromosomes from species B. Because pairing occurs properly, the super-hybrid will be fertile, producing pollen or eggs carrying eight chromosomes. The super-hybrid is technically known as a *allopolyploid*, from the Greek for "different" and "many-fold." In its sixteen chromosomes, it carries the complete genetic material of both parental species, A and B. We would expect it to look somewhat like an intermediate between the two parents. And its new combination of traits might enable it to live in a novel ecological niche.

The AB polyploid is not only fertile, but will produce offspring if it is fertilized by another similar polyploid. Each parent contributes eight chromosomes to the seed, which will grow into another sixteen-chromosome AB plant, just like its parents. A group of such polyploids makes up a self-perpetuating, inter-breeding population.

And it will also be a new species. Why? Because the AB polyploid is repro-ductively isolated from both parental species. When they hybridize with either species A or species B, the offspring are sterile. Suppose it hybridizes with spe-cies A. The polyploid will produce gametes having eight chromosomes, three originally from species A and five from species B. These will fuse with the gametes from species A, which contain three chromosomes. The plant arising from this union will have eleven chromosomes. And it will be sterile, for while each A chromosome has a pairing partner, none of the B chromosomes do. A similar situation arises when the AB polyploid mates with species B: the off-spring will have thirteen chromosomes, and the five A chromosomes can't pair during gamete formation.

The new polyploid, then, produces only sterile hybrids when it mates with either of the two species that gave rise to it. Yet when the polyploids mate with each other, the offspring will be fertile, having all sixteen chromosomes of their parents. In other words, the polyploids form an interbreeding group that is reproductively isolated from other groups—and that's just what defines a distinct biological species. And this species has arisen without geographical isolation—that's necessary because if two species are to form hybrids, they must live in the same place.

How does the polyploid species form in the first place? We needn't go into the messy details here except to say that it involves the formation of a hybrid between the two parental species followed by a series of steps in which those hybrids produce rare pollen or eggs carrying double sets of chromosomes (these are called *unreduced gametes*). Fusion of these gametes produces a poly-ploid individual in only two generations. And all of these steps have been doc-umented in both the greenhouse and in nature.

41. As an example of autopolyploidy, let's assume that members of a plant species have fourteen chromosomes, or seven pairs. An individual might occasionally produce unreduced gametes containing all fourteen chromosomes instead of seven. If this gamete fused with a normal, seven-chromosome gamete from another individual of the same species, we would get a semisterile plant having twenty-one chromosomes: it's mostly sterile because during gamete forma-tion, three homologous chromosomes try to pair instead of the normal two,

and this doesn't work well. But if this individual again produces a few unreduced twenty-one-chromosome gametes that fuse with normal gametes from the same species, we get a twenty-eight-chromosome autopolyploid individual. It carries two complete copies of the parental genome. A population of such individuals can be considered a new species, for they can interbreed with other similar autopolyploids but will produce largely sterile twenty-one-chromosome individuals when they try to mate with the parental species. This autopolyploid species has exactly the same genes as members of the single parental species, but in quadruple rather than double dose.

Since a newly formed autopolyploid has the same genes as its parental species, it often resembles it closely. Members of the new species can sometimes be identified only by counting their chromosomes under the microscope and seeing that they have twice as many chromosomes as individuals of the parental species. Because they resemble their parents, many autopolyploid species surely exist in nature that haven't yet been identified.

42. Although cases of nonpolyploid speciation occurring in "real time" are rare, there is at least one that seems plausible. This involves two groups of mosquitoes in London, which are usually named as subspecies but show substantial reproductive isolation. *Culex pipiens pipiens* is one of the most common urban mosquitoes. Its most frequent victims are birds, and, as in many species of mosquitoes, females lay eggs only after they've had a blood meal. During winter, males die but females enter a hibernation-like state called "diapause." When mating, *pipiens* form large swarms in which males and females copulate en masse.

Fifty feet below, within the tunnels of the London Underground, lives a closely related subspecies: *Culex pipiens molestus*, so called because it prefers to bite mammals, especially ones that ride the Tube. (It became a real annoyance during the Blitz of World War II, when thousands of Londoners were forced to sleep in Underground stations during air raids.) Besides preying on rats and humans, *molestus* doesn't need a blood meal to lay eggs, and, as one might expect for inhabitants of mild-temperature tunnels, prefers to mate in confined spaces and doesn't diapause during winter.

The difference in the way these two subspecies mate leads to strong sexual isolation between the forms in both nature and the laboratory. That, coupled with the substantial genetic divergence between the forms, indicates that they are on their way to becoming different species. Indeed, some entomologists already classify them this way—as *Culex pipiens* and *Culex molestus*. Since construction of the Underground was not begun until the 1860s, and many of the lines are less than a hundred years old, this "speciation" event may have occurred within recent memory. The reason the story is not airtight, though, is that there is a similar pair of species in New York: one above ground and the other in the subway tunnels. It is possible that both pairs of species are representatives of a similar and longer-diverged pair that lives elsewhere in the world, each of which migrated to its respective habitat in London and New York. What we need to attack this problem, and don't yet have, is a good DNA-based family tree of these mosquitoes.

43. This group used to be called *hominids*, but that term is now reserved for all modern and extinct great apes, including humans, chimpanzees, gorillas, orangutans, and all of their ancestors.

44. A sidelight on the competitive nature of paleoanthropology is the number of people sharing credit for the discovery, preparation, and description of *Sahelanthropus*: the paper announcing it has thirty-eight authors—all for a single skull!

45. http://www.youtube.com/watch?v=V9DIMhKotWU&NR=1 shows a chimp walking awkwardly on two legs.

46. See http://www.pbs.org/wgbh/evolution/library/07/1/l_071_03.html for a video clip of the footprints and how they were made.

47. Note that this would actually be the *second* time that the human lineage had migrated out of Africa, the first being the spread of *Homo erectus*.

48. See http://www.talkorigins.org/faqs/homs/compare.html for a discussion of how creationists treat the human fossil record.

49. Unlike most primates, human females show no visible signs when ovulating. (The genitals of female baboons, for example, swell up and turn red when they're fertile.) There are more than a dozen theories about why human females evolved to conceal their periods of fertility. The most famous is that this is a female strategy to keep their mates around for sustenance and child care. If a man doesn't know when his wife is fertile, and wants to father children, he should hang around and copulate with her frequently.

50. The idea that *FOXP2* is a language gene comes from observing that it has evolved extremely fast in the human lineage, that mutant forms of the gene affect people's ability to produce and comprehend speech, and that similar mutations in mice make the babies unable to squeak.

51. Actually, it has been tried at least once. In 1927, Ilya Ivanovich Ivanov, an eccentric Russian biologist whose forte was making animal hybrids through artificial insemination, used that technique to try to create human/chimpanzee hybrids (dubbed "humanzees" or "chumans"). At a field station in French Guinea, he inseminated three female chimps with human sperm. Fortunately, there were no pregnancies, and his later plans to do the reverse experiment were thwarted.

52. Biologists have identified at least two genes responsible for much of the difference in skin pigmentation between European and African populations. Curiously, they were both discovered because they affect the pigmentation of fish.

53. A similar case was recently described for *amylase-1*, the salivary enzyme that breaks down starch into simple sugars. Human populations with a lot of starch in their diets, such as Japanese and Europeans, have more copies of the gene than populations who subsist on low-starch diets, such as fishermen or rainforest hunter-gatherers. In contrast to the lactase enzyme, natural selection increased the expression of *amylase-1* by favoring the duplication of genes that produce it.

54. Remember that no food has an inherent flavor—how it "tastes" to individuals depends on their evolved interactions between taste receptors and neurons stimulated in the brain. It's almost certain that natural selection shaped our brains and taste buds so that we'd find the flavors of sweet and fatty foods appealing, prompting us to seek them out. Rotten meat is probably as delicious to a hyena as an ice cream sundae is to us.

55. Most evolutionary psychologists feel that the EEA was a reality—that over the millions of years of human evolution, the environment, both physical and social, was relatively constant. But of course we know no such thing. After all, during seven million years of evolution our ancestors lived in different climates, interacted with diverse species (including other hominins), interacted in various types of societies, and spread out over the whole planet. The very idea that there was some "ancestral environment" that we can invoke to explain modern human behavior is an intellectual conceit, an assumption made because, in the end, it is all we can do.

Glossary

Note: For some terms, like "gene," scientists have several definitions, often technical and sometimes at odds with one another. In such cases I provide what I think is the most common working definition.

adaptation: A feature of an organism that evolved by natural selection because it performed a certain function better than its antecedents. The flowers of plants, for example, are adaptations to attract pollinators.

adaptive radiation: The production of several or many new species from a common ancestor, usually when the ancestor invades a new and empty habitat such as an archipelago. The radiation is "adaptive" because the genetic barriers between species arise as by-products of natural selection adapting populations to their environments. An example is the profuse speciation of honeycreepers in Hawaii.

allele: A particular form of a given gene produced by mutation. For example, there are three alleles at the protein-coding gene that produces our blood type: the A, B, and O alleles. All are mutant forms of a single gene that differ only slightly in their DNA sequence.

allopolyploid speciation: The origin of a new species of plant beginning with the hybridization of two different species, followed by a doubling of the chromosome number of that hybrid.

atavism: The occasional expression in a living species of a trait that was once present in an ancestral species but has since disappeared. An example is the sporadic appearance of a tail in human infants.

autopolyploid speciation: The origin of a new species of plant that occurs when the entire set of chromosomes of an ancestral species is doubled.

biogeography: The study of the distribution of plants and animals on the surface of the earth.

continental islands: Islands, like Great Britain and Madagascar, that were once part of continents but became separated from them by continental drift or rising sea levels.

ecological niche: The set of physical and biological conditions, including climate, food, predators, prey, etc., encountered by a particular species in nature.

endemic: An adjective referring to a species confined to a particular region and found nowhere else, such as the endemic finches of the Galápagos Islands. The word can also be used as a noun.

evolution: Genetic change in populations, often producing changes in observable traits of organisms over time.

fitness: In evolutionary biology, a technical term that denotes the relative number of offspring produced by carriers of one allele versus another. The more offspring, the higher the fitness. But "fitness" can also be used more casually, referring to how well an organism is adapted to its environment and way of life.

gametes: Reproductive cells, including the sperm and eggs of animals, and the pollen and eggs of plants.

gene: A segment of DNA that produces a protein or an RNA product.

genetic drift: Evolutionary change that occurs by random sampling of different alleles from one generation to the next. This causes nonadaptive evolutionary change.

genome: The entire genetic complement of an organism, comprising all of its genes and DNA.

geographic speciation: Speciation that begins with the geographic isolation of two or more populations, which subsequently develop genetically based reproductive isolating barriers.

heritability: The proportion of observable variation in a trait that is explained by variation among the genes of individuals. Varying from zero (all variation due to the environment) to one (all variation due to genes), heritability gives an idea of how readily a trait will respond to natural or artificial selection. The heritability of human height, for example, ranges from 0.6 to 0.85, depending on the population tested.

hominin: All species, living or extinct, on the "human" side of the evolutionary tree after our common ancestor with chimpanzees divided into the two lineages that would produce modern humans and modern chimpanzees.

homologs: A pair of chromosomes that contain the same genes, though they may have different *forms* of those genes.

lek: An area where males of a species gather to perform courtship displays.

macroevolution: "Major" evolutionary change, usually thought of as large changes in body form or the evolution of one type of plant or animal from another type. The change from our primate ancestor to modern humans, or from early reptiles to birds, would be considered macroevolution.

microevolution: "Minor" evolutionary change, such as the change in size or color of a species. One example is the evolution of different skin colors or hair types among human populations; another is the evolution of antibiotic resistance in bacteria.

mutation: A small change in the DNA, usually changing only a single nucleotide base in the sequence of bases that forms an organism's genetic code. Mutations often arise as errors during the copying of DNA molecules that accompanies cell division.

natural selection: The nonrandom, differential reproduction of alleles from one generation to the next. This usually results from the carriers of some alleles being better able to survive or reproduce in their environments than the carriers of alternative alleles.

oceanic island: An island that was never connected to a continent, but, like the islands of Hawaii and the Galápagos, was formed by volcanoes or other forces producing new land from beneath the sea.

parthenogenesis: A form of asexual reproduction in which individuals form eggs that develop into adults without fertilization.

polyandry: A mating system in which females mate with more than one male.

polygyny: A mating system in which males mate with more than one female.

polyploidy: A form of speciation involving hybridization in which the new species has an increased number of chromosomes. This can involve either autopolyploidy or allopolyploidy (see above).

pseudogene: An inactive gene that does not produce a protein product.

race: A geographically distinct population of a species that differs from other populations in one or more traits. Biologists sometimes call races "ecotypes" or "subspecies."

reproductive isolating barriers: Genetically based features of a species that prevent it from forming fertile hybrids with another species—for example, differences in courtship rituals that prevent cross-mating.

sexual dimorphism: A trait that differs between males and females of a species, such as size or presence of body hair in humans.

sexual selection: The nonrandom, differential reproduction of alleles that gives their carriers different success at obtaining mates. This is one form of natural selection.

sister species: Two species that are each other's closest relatives; that is, those that are more closely related to each other than to any other species. Humans and chimps are one such pair.

speciation: The evolution of new populations that are reproductively isolated from other populations.

species: A group of interbreeding natural populations that are reproductively isolated from other such groups. This is the definition of "species" preferred by most biologists, and is also called the "biological species concept."

stabilizing selection: Natural selection that favors "average" individuals in a population over those at the extremes. One example is the higher survival of human babies having average birth weight than those born either heavier or lighter.

sympatric speciation: Speciation that takes place without the existence of any geographic barriers that physically isolate populations from one another.

systematics: The branch of evolutionary biology involved in discerning the evolutionary relationships between species and in constructing evolutionary trees that portray those relationships.

tetrapod: A vertebrate animal with four limbs.

vestigial trait: A trait that is the evolutionary remnant of a feature once useful in an ancestral species but that is no longer useful in the same way. Vestigial traits can be either nonfunctional (the wings of the kiwi) or co-opted for new uses (the wings of the ostrich).

Suggestions for Further Reading

Note: I give references using the conventional format for scientific literature. Each reference shows, in order, the last name and first initials of the author, names of other authors, year of publication, title of the book or article, and, when the article is from a scientific journal, the name of that journal followed by the volume and page numbers.

General

Browne, J. 1996. *Charles Darwin: Voyaging.* 2002. *Charles Darwin: The Power of Place.* Knopf, New York. (Issued in 2003 as a set by Princeton University Press.) Janet Browne's two-volume biography of Darwin is a magisterial and beautifully written treatment of the man, his milieu, and his ideas. By far the best of the many Darwin biographies.

Carroll, S. B. 2005. *Endless Forms Most Beautiful.* W. W. Norton, New York. A lively discussion of the interface between evolution and developmental biology by one of the foremost practitioners of "evo devo."

Chiappe, L. M. 2007. *Glorified Dinosaurs: The Origin and Early Evolution of Birds.* Wiley, Hoboken, NJ. A clearly written and up-to-date account of the origin of birds from feathered dinosaurs.

Cronin, H. 1992. *The Ant and the Peacock: Sexual Selection from Darwin to Today.* Cambridge University Press, Cambridge, UK. An introduction to sexual selection for the general reader.

Darwin, C. 1859. *On the Origin of Species.* Murray, London. The book that started it all; a world classic. The best popular science book of all time (it was, after all, written for the English public), and the science book anyone *must* have read to be truly educated. Although the Victorian prose puts off some people, there are beautiful stretches, and the arguments trump everything.

Dawkins, R. 1982. *The Extended Phenotype: The Long Reach of the Gene.* Oxford University Press, Oxford, UK. One of Dawkins's best—a discussion of how selection on one species can produce a diversity of traits, including alterations in the environment and the behavior of other species.

——. 1996. *The Blind Watchmaker: Why the Evidence of Evolution Reveals a Universe Without Design.* W. W. Norton, New York. Dawkins's paean to the power and beauty of natural selection. An engrossing read by our best science writer.

——. 2004. *The Ancestor's Tale: A Pilgrimage to the Dawn of Evolution.* Weidenfeld & Nicolson. New York. A large, lavishly illustrated account of evolution, starting with humans and working its way back to our common ancestors with all other species.

——. 2006. *The Selfish Gene: 30th Anniversary Edition.* (First published 1976). Oxford University Press, Oxford, UK. Another classic—perhaps the best book written about modern evolutionary theory, essential for anyone who wants to understand natural selection.

Dunbar, R., L. Barrett, and J. Lycett. 2005. *Evolutionary Psychology: A Beginner's Guide.* Oneworld, Oxford, UK. A short but valuable guide to this growing field.

Futuyma, D. J. 2005. *Evolution.* Sinauer Associates, Sunderland, MA. The best academic textbook on evolutionary biology. Unless you're studying biology, this may be too technical for a straight read-through, but is well worth consulting as a reference.

Gibbons, A. 2006. *The First Human: The Race to Discover Our Earliest Ancestors.* Doubleday, New York. A fine account of recent discoveries in paleoanthropology, dealing not only with the science but also with the strong, competitive personalities involved in the search for our origins.

Gould, S. J. 2007. *The Richness of Life: The Essential Stephen Jay Gould* (S. Rose, ed.). W. W. Norton, New York. This one book must stand for many, as all of Gould's books and essays are worth reading. This posthumous collection includes forty-four essays by the most eloquent exponent and defender of evolution.

Johanson, D., and B. Edgar. 2006. *From Lucy to Language* (rev. ed.). Simon & Schuster, New York. Perhaps the best general account of human evolution in nearly all its aspects, written by one of the finders of the "Lucy" specimen of *Australopithecus afarensis.*

Kitcher, P. 1987. *Vaulting Ambition: Sociobiology and the Quest for Human Nature.*

MIT Press, Cambridge, MA. A clear and strongly argued critique of sociobiology.

Mayr, E. 2002. *What Evolution Is.* Basic Books, New York. A popular summary of modern evolutionary theory by one of the greatest evolutionary biologists of our time.

Mindell, David. 2007. *The Evolving World: Evolution in Everyday Life.* Harvard University Press, Cambridge, MA. A discussion of the practical value of evolutionary biology, including its applications in agriculture and medicine.

Pinker, S. 2002. *The Blank Slate: The Modern Denial of Human Nature.* Viking, New York. A readable and forceful argument for the "nature" side of the nature-versus-nurture debate.

Prothero, D. R. 2007. *Evolution: What the Fossils Say and Why It Matters.* Columbia University Press, New York. The best popular treatment of the fossil record, this includes extensive discussion of fossil evidence for evolution, including transitional forms, and a critique of how creationists distort that evidence.

Quammen, D. 1997. *The Song of the Dodo: Island Biogeography in an Age of Extinction.* Scribner's, New York. An absorbing discussion of many aspects of island biogeography, including its history, modern theory, and implications for conservation.

Shubin, N. 2008. *Your Inner Fish.* Pantheon, New York. A highly readable description of how our ancestry has affected the human body. Written by one of the discoverers of the transitional "fishapod" *Tiktaalik roseae.*

Zimmer, C. 1999. *At the Water's Edge: Fish with Fingers, Whales with Legs, and How Life Came Ashore but Then Went Back to Sea.* Free Press, New York. One of our premier science journalists describes two major transitions in vertebrate evolution: the evolution of terrestrial animals from fish, and the evolution of whales from hoofed mammals.

———. 2001. *Evolution: The Triumph of an Idea.* Harper Perennial, New York. A general treatment of evolutionary biology written to accompany the Public Broadcasting System's televised series on evolution. It is introductory but comprehensive, covering not just the theory and evidence for evolution, but also its philosophical and theological implications.

———. 2005. *Smithsonian Intimate Guide to Human Origins.* HarperCollins, New York. A well-illustrated account of human evolution, including both the fossil record and recent discoveries from molecular genetics.

Evolution, Creationism, and Social Issues

With the exception of some articles in Pennock (2001), I omit references to the writings of creationists and advocates of intelligent design (ID), for their arguments are based on religion rather than science. Eugenie Scott's *Evolution vs. Creationism: An Introduction* describes the various incarnations of creationism, including ID. Those wishing to hear the antievolution side should consult the books of Michael Behe, William Dembski, Phillip Johnson, and Jonathan Wells.

BOOKS AND ARTICLES

Coyne, J. A. 2005. The faith that dares not speak its name: The case against intelligent design. *New Republic*, August 22, 2005, pp. 21–33. A short summary of ID and a review of its public school textbook, *Of Pandas and People*.

Forrest, B., and P. R. Gross. 2007. *Creationism's Trojan Horse: The Wedge of Intelligent Design.* Oxford University Press, New York. A comprehensive analysis and critique of intelligent design.

Futuyma, D. J. 1995. *Science on Trial: The Case for Evolution.* Sinauer Associates, Sunderland, MA. A brief summary of the evidence for evolution, as well as a summary of evolutionary theory and answers to some common creationist arguments.

Humes, E. 2007. *Monkey Girl: Evolution, Education, Religion, and the Battle for America's Soul.* Ecco (HarperCollins), New York. An account of the attempt of intelligent design advocates to insert their ideas into a public school curriculum in Dover, Pennsylvania, and of the subsequent trial that branded intelligent design "not science."

Isaak, M. 2007. *The Counter-Creationism Handbook.* University of California Press, Berkeley. In this useful guide, Isaak briefly presents and refutes hundreds of creationist and intelligent design arguments.

Kitcher, P. J. 2006. *Living with Darwin: Evolution, Design, and the Future of Faith.* Oxford University Press, New York. A spirited defense of Darwinism and suggestions about how it might be reconciled with people's spiritual needs.

Larson, E. J. 1998. *Summer for the Gods.* Harvard University Press, Cambridge, MA. This highly readable account of the Scopes Trial, the first incursion of Darwinism into American courts, corrects many popular misconceptions about the "Monkey Trial." The book won the 1998 Pulitzer Prize in history.

Miller, K. R. 2000. *Finding Darwin's God: A Scientist's Search for Common Ground Between God and Evolution.* Harper Perennial, New York. An eminent biologist, textbook author, and observant Catholic, Miller decisively refutes arguments for intelligent design and then discusses how he reconciles the fact of evolution with his religious belief.

———. 2008. *Only a Theory: Evolution and the Battle for America's Soul.* Viking, New York. An updated critique of intelligent design that not only addresses the "irreducible complexity" argument, but also shows why ID poses a serious threat to science education in America.

National Academy of Sciences. 2008. *Science, Evolution, and Creationism.* National Academies Press, Washington, DC. A position paper by America's most prestigious group of scientists, criticizing creationism and laying out the evidence for evolution. It can be downloaded for free at http://www.nap.edu/catalog.php?record_id=11876.

Pennock, R. T. 1999. *Tower of Babel: The Evidence Against the New Creationism.* MIT Press, Cambridge, MA. Perhaps the most thorough analysis and debunking of creationism, particularly its new incarnation as intelligent design.

——— (ed.). 2001. *Intelligent Design Creationism and Its Critics: Philosophical, Theological, and Scientific Perspectives.* MIT Press, Cambridge, MA. Essays by proponents as well as opponents of evolution, with some provocative back-and-forth arguments.

Petto, A. J., and L. R. Godfrey (eds.). 2007. *Scientists Confront Intelligent Design and Creationism.* W. W. Norton, New York. A series of essays by scientists on paleontology, geology, and other aspects of evolutionary theory that bear on the evolution-creation controversy, as well as discussions of the sociology of the controversy.

Scott, E. C. 2005. *Evolution vs. Creationism: An Introduction.* University of California Press, Berkeley. A dispassionate description of what evolution and creationism really are.

Scott, E. C., and G. Branch. 2006. *Not in Our Classrooms: Why Intelligent Design Is Wrong for Our Schools.* Beacon Press, Boston. A series of essays on the scientific, educational, and political implications of teaching intelligent design and other forms of creationism in American public schools.

ONLINE RESOURCES

http://www.archaeologyinfo.com/evolution.htm. A good (albeit slightly outdated) depiction and description of the various stages of human evolution.

http://www.darwin-online.org.uk/. The complete work of Charles Darwin online.

Includes not only all of his books (including all six editions of *The Origin*), but also his scientific papers. You can find many of Darwin's personal letters at the Darwin Correspondence Project: http://www.darwinproject.ac.uk/.

http://www.gate.net/~rwms/EvoEvidence.html. A large Web site collecting various lines of evidence for evolution.

http://www.gate.net/~rwms/crebuttals.html. A Web site that examines and thoroughly debunks many creationist claims.

http://www.natcenscied.org/. An online set of resources assembled by the National Center for Science Education, an organization devoted to defending the teaching of evolution in America's public schools. It gives updates on ongoing battles with creationism, and includes links to many other sites.

http://www.pbs.org/wgbh/evolution/. A large Web site inspired by the PBS series *Evolution*, this contains many resources for both students and teachers, including discussions of the history of evolutionary thought, the evidence for evolution, and theological and philosophical issues. The sections on human evolution are particularly good.

http://www.pandasthumb.org/. The Panda's Thumb Web site (named after a famous essay by Stephen Jay Gould) deals with recent discoveries in evolutionary biology as well as ongoing opposition to evolution in America.

http://www.talkorigins.org/. A comprehensive online guide to all aspects of evolution. Included within it is the best online guide to the evidence for evolution, at http://www.talkorigins.org/faqs/comdesc/.

Among many good blogs on evolutionary biology, two stand out. One is "The Loom" (http://blogs.discovermagazine.com/loom), the blog of science writer Carl Zimmer. The other is "This Week in Evolution," the blog of Cornell professor R. Ford Denison, at http://blog.lib.umn.edu/denis036/thisweekinevolution/. It presents new discoveries in evolutionary biology and is accessible to anyone who has had a college-level course in biology.

References

Preface

Davis, P., and D. H. Kenyon. 1993. *Of Pandas and People: The Central Question of Biological Origins* (2nd ed.). Foundation for Thought and Ethics, Richardson, TX.

Introduction

BBC Poll on Evolution. Ipsos MORI. 2006. http://www.ipsos-mori.com/content/bbc-survey-on-the-origins-of-life.ashx.

Berkman, M. B., J. S. Pacheco, and E. Plutzer. 2008. Evolution and creationism in America's schools: A national portrait. *Public Library of Science Biology* 6:e124.

Harris Poll #52. July 6, 2005. http://www.harrisinteractive.com/harris_poll/index.asp?PID=581.

Miller, J. D., E. C. Scott, and S. Okamoto. 2006. Public acceptance of evolution. *Science* 313:765–766.

Shermer, M. 2006. *Why Darwin Matters: The Case Against Intelligent Design.* Times Books, New York.

Chapter 1: What Is Evolution?

Darwin, C. 1993. *The Autobiography of Charles Darwin* (N. Barlow, ed.). W. W. Norton, New York.

Hazen, R. M. 2005. *Gen*e*sis: The Scientific Quest for Life's Origin.* Joseph Henry Press, Washington, DC.

Paley, W. 1802. *Natural Theology; or, Evidences of the Existence and Attributes of the Deity, Collected from the Appearances of Nature.* Parker, Philadelphia.

Chapter 2: Written in the Rocks

Apesteguía, S., and H. Zaher. 2006. A Cretaceous terrestrial snake with robust hindlimbs and a sacrum. *Nature* 440:1037–1040.

Chaline, J., B. Laurin, P. Brunet-Lecomte, and L. Viriot. 1993. Morphological trends and rates of evolution in arvicolids (Arvicolidae, Rodentia): Towards a punctuated equilibria/disequilibria model. *Quaternary International* 19:27–39.

Chen, J. Y., D. Y. Huang, and C. W. Li. 1999. An early Cambrian craniate-like chordate. *Nature* 402:518–522.

Daeschler, E. B., N. H. Shubin, and F. A. Jenkins. 2006. A Devonian tetrapod-like fish and the evolution of the tetrapod body plan. *Nature* 440:757–763.

Dial, K. P. 2003. Wing-assisted incline running and the evolution of flight. *Science* 299:402–404.

Graur, D., and D. G. Higgins. 1994. Molecular evidence for the inclusion of cetaceans within the order Artiodactyla. *Molecular Biology and Evolution* 11:357–364.

Hedman, M. 2007. *The Age of Everything: How Science Explores the Past.* University of Chicago Press, Chicago.

Hopson, J. A. 1987. The mammal like reptiles: A study of transitional fossils. *American Biology Teacher* 49:16–26.

Ji, Q., M. A. Norell, K. Q. Gao, S. A. Ji, and D. Ren. 2001. The distribution of integumentary structures in a feathered dinosaur. *Nature* 410:1084–1088.

Kellogg, D. E., and J. D. Hays. 1975. Microevolutionary patterns in Late Cenozoic Radiolaria. *Paleobiology* 1:150–160.

Lazarus, D. 1983. Speciation in pelagic protista and its study in the planktonic microfossil record: A review. *Paleobiology* 9:327–340.

Li, Y., L.-Z. Chen et al. 1999. Lower Cambrian vertebrates from South China. *Nature* 402:42–46.

Malmgren, B. A., and J. P. Kennett. 1981. Phyletic gradualism in a late Cenozoic planktonic foraminiferal lineage; Dsdp site 284, southwest Pacific. *Paleobiology* 7:230–240.

Norell, M. A., J. M. Clark, L. M. Chiappe, and D. Dashzeveg. 1995. A nesting dinosaur. *Nature* 378:774–776.

Organ, C. L., M. H. Schewitzer, W. Zheng, Lm. M. Freimark, L. C. Cantley, and J. M. Asara. 2008. Molecular phylogenetics of Mastodon and *Tyrannosaurus rex*. *Science* 320:499.

Peyer, K. 2006. A reconsideration of *Compsognathus* from the upper Tithonian of

Canjers, Southern France. *Journal of Vertebrate Paleontology* 26:879-896.

Prum, R. O., and A. H. Brush. 2002. The evolutionary origin and diversification of feathers. *Quarterly Review of Biology* 77:261–295.

Sheldon, P. 1987. Parallel gradualistic evolution of Ordovician trilobites. *Nature* 330:561–563.

Shipman, P. 1998. *Taking Wing: Archaeopteryx and the Evolution of Bird Flight.* Weidenfeld & Nicolson, London.

Shu, D. G., H. L. Luo, S. C. Morris, X. L. Zhang, S. X. Hu, L. Chen, J. Han, M. Zhu, Y. Li, and L. Z. Chen. 1999. Lower Cambrian vertebrates from South China. *Nature* 402:42–46.

Shu, D. G., S. C. Morris, J. Han, Z. F. Zhang, K. Yasui, P. Janvier, L. Chen, X. L. Zhang, J. N. Liu, Y. Li, and H. Q. Liu. 2003. Head and backbone of the Early Cambrian vertebrate *Haikouichthys*. *Nature* 421:526–529.

Shubin, N. H., E. B. Daeschler, and F. A. Jenkins. 2006. The pectoral fin *of Tiktaalik roseae* and the origin of the tetrapod limb. *Nature* 440:764–771.

Sutera, R. 2001. The origin of whales and the power of independent evidence. *Reports of the National Center for Science Education* 20:33–41.

Thewissen, J. G. M., L. N. Cooper, M. T. Clementz, S. Bajpail, and B. N. Tiwari. 2007. Whales originated from aquatic artiodactyls in the Eocene epoch of India. *Nature* 450:1190–1194.

Wells, J. W. 1963. Coral growth and geochronometry. *Nature* 187:948–950.

Wilson, E. O., F. M. Carpenter, and W. L. Brown. 1967. First Mesozoic ants. *Science* 157:1038–1040.

Xu, X., and M. A. Norell. 2004. A new troodontid dinosaur from China with avian-like sleeping posture. *Nature* 431:838–841.

Xu, X., X.-L. Wang, and X.-C. Wu. 1999. A dromaeosaurid dinosaur with a filamentous integument from the Yixian Formation of China. *Nature* 401:262–266.

Xu, X., Z. H. Zhou, X.-L. Wang, X. W. Kuang, F. C. Zhang, and X. K. Du. 2003. Four-winged dinosaurs from China. *Nature* 421:335–340.

Chapter 3: Remnants: Vestiges, Embryos, and Bad Design

Andrews, R. C. 1921. A remarkable case of external hind limbs in a humpback whale. *American Museum Novitates* 9:1–6.

Bannert, N., and R. Kurth. 2004. Retroelements and the human genome: New perspectives on an old relation. *Proceedings of the National Academy of Sciences of the United States of America* 101:14572–14579.

Bar-Maor, J. A., K. M. Kesner, and J. K. Kaftori. 1980. Human tails. *Journal of Bone and Joint Surgery* 62:508–10.

Behe, M. 1996. *Darwin's Black Box.* Free Press, New York.

Bejder, L., and B. K. Hall. 2002. Limbs in whales and limblessness in other verte-brates: Mechanisms of evolutionary and developmental transformation and loss. *Evolution and Development* 4:445–458.

Brawand D., W. Wahli, and H. Kaessmann. 2008. Loss of egg yolk genes in mam-mals and the origin of lactation and placentation. *Public Library of Science Biology* 6(3):e63.

Chen, Y. P., Y. D. Zhang, T. X. Jiang, A. J. Barlow, T. R. St Amand, Y. P. Hu, S. Heaney, P. Francis-West, C. M. Chuong, and R. Maas. 2000. Conservation of early odontogenic signaling pathways in Aves. *Proceedings of the National Academy of Sciences of the United States of America* 97:10044–10049.

Dao, A. H., and M. G. Netsky. 1984. Human tails and pseudotails. *Human Pathol-ogy* 15:449-453.

Dobzhansky, T. 1973. Nothing in biology makes sense except in the light of evolu-tion. *American Biology Teacher* 35:125–129.

Friedman, M. 2008. The evolutionary origin of flatfish asymmetry. *Nature* 454: 209–212.

Gilad, Y., V. Wiebe, M. Przeworski, D. Lancet, and S. Pääbo. 2004. Loss of olfactory receptor genes coincides with the acquisition of full trichromatic vision in pri-mates. *Public Library of Science Biology* 2:120–125.

Gould, S. J. 1994. *Hen's Teeth and Horses' Toes: Further Reflections in Natural His-tory.* W. W. Norton, New York.

Hall, B. K. 1984. Developmental mechanisms underlying the formation of atavisms. *Biological Reviews* 59:89–124.

Harris, M. P., S. M. Hasso, M. W. J. Ferguson, and J. F. Fallon. 2006. The develop-ment of archosaurian first-generation teeth in a chicken mutant. *Current Biology* 16:371–377.

Johnson, W. E., and J. M. Coffin. 1999. Constructing primate phylogenies from ancient retrovirus sequences. *Proceedings of the National Academy of Sciences of the United States of America* 96:10254–10260.

Kishida, T., S. Kubota, Y. Shirayama, and H. Fukami. 2007. The olfactory re-ceptor gene repertoires in secondary-adapted marine vertebrates: Evidence for reduction of the functional proportions in cetaceans. *Biology Letters* 3:428–430.

Kollar, E. J., and C. Fisher. 1980. Tooth induction in chick epithelium: Expression of quiescent genes for enamel synthesis. *Science* 207:993–995.

Krause, W. J., and C. R. Leeson. 1974. The gastric mucosa of 2 monotremes: The duck-billed platypus and echidna. *Journal of Morphology* 142:285–299.

Medstrand, P., and D. L. Mager. 1998. Human-specific integrations of the HERV-K endogenous retrovirus family. *Journal of Virology* 72:9782–9787.

Larsen, W. J. 2001. *Human Embryology* (3rd ed.). Churchill Livingston, Philadelphia.

Niimura, Y., and M. Nei. 2007. Extensive gains and losses of olfactory receptor genes in mammalian evolution. *Public Library of Science ONE* 2:e708.

Nishikimi, M., R. Fukuyama, S. Minoshima, N. Shimizu, and K. Yagi. 1994. Cloning and chromosomal mapping of the human nonfunctional gene for L-gulono-γ-lactone oxidase, the enzyme for L-ascorbic-acid biosynthesis missing in man. *Journal of Biological Chemistry* 269:13685–13688.

Niskikimi, M., and K. Yagi. 1991. Molecular basis for the deficiency in humans of gulonolactone oxidase, a key enzyme for ascorbic acid biosynthesis. *American Journal of Clinical Nutrition* 54:1203S–1208S.

Ohta, Y., and M. Nishikimi. 1999. Random nucleotide substitutions in primate nonfunctional gene for L-gulono-γ-lactone oxidase, the missing enzyme in γ-ascorbic acid biosynthesis. *Biochimica et Biophysica Acta* 1472:408–411.

Ordoñez, G. R., L. W. Hiller, W. C. Warren, F. Grutzner, C. Lopez-Otin, and X. S. Puente. 2008. Loss of genes implicated in gastric function during platypus evolution. *Genome Biology* 9:R81.

Richards, R. J. 2008. *The Tragic Sense of Life: Ernst Haeckel and the Struggle over Evolution.* University of Chicago Press, Chicago.

Romer, A. S., and T. S Parsons. 1986. *The Vertebrate Body.* Sanders College Publishing, Philadelphia.

Sadler, T. W. 2003. *Langman's Medical Embryology* (9th ed.). Lippincott Williams & Wilkins, Philadelphia.

Sanyal, S., H. G. Jansen, W. J. de Grip, E. Nevo, and W. W. de Jong. 1990. The eye of the blind mole rat, *Spalax ehrenbergi.* Rudiment with hidden function? *Investigative Ophthalmology and Visual Science* 31:1398–1404.

Shubin, N. 2008. *Your Inner Fish.* Pantheon, New York.

Rouquier, S., A. Blancher, and D. Giorgi. 2000. The olfactory receptor gene repertoire in primates and mouse: Evidence for reduction of the functional fraction in primates. *Proceedings of the National Academy of Sciences of the United States of America* 97:2870–2874.

Von Baer, K. E. 1828. *Entwickelungsgeschichte der Thiere: Beobachtung und Reflexion* (vol. 1). Königsberg, Bornträger.

Zhang, Z. L., and M. Gerstein. 2004. Large-scale analysis of pseudogenes in the human genome. *Current Opinion in Genetics & Development* 14:328–335.

Chapter 4: The Geography of Life

Barber, H. N., H. E. Dadswell, and H. D. Ingle. 1959. Transport of driftwood from South America to Tasmania and Macquarie Island. *Nature* 184:203–204.

Brown, J. H., and M. V. Lomolino. 1998. *Biogeography.* 2nd ed. Sinauer Associates, Sunderland, MA.

Browne, J. 1983. *The Secular Ark: Studies in the History of Biogeography.* Yale University Press, New Haven and London.

Carlquist, S. 1974. *Island Biology.* Columbia University Press, New York.

———. 1981. Chance dispersal. *American Scientist* 69:509–516.

Censky, E. J., K. Hodge, and J. Dudley. 1998. Over-water dispersal of lizards due to hurricanes. *Nature* 395:556.

Goin, F. J., J. A. Case, M. O. Woodburne, S. F. Vizcaino, and M. A. Reguero. 2004. New discoveries of "opposum-like" marsupials from Antarctica (Seymour Island, Medial Eocene). *Journal of Mammalian Evolution* 6:335–365.

Guilmette, J. E., E. P. Holzapfel, and D. M. Tsuda. 1970. Trapping of air-borne insects on ships in the Pacific (Part 8). *Pacific Insects* 12:303–325.

Holzapfel, E. P., and J. C. Harrell. 1968. Transoceanic dispersal studies of insects. *Pacific Insects* 10:115–153.

———. 1970. Trapping of air-borne insects in the Antarctic area (Part 3). *Pacific Insects* 12:133–156.

McLoughlin, S. 2001. The breakup history of Gondwana and its impact on pre-Cenozoic floristic provincialism. *Australian Journal of Botany* 49:271–300.

Reinhold, R. March 21, 1982. Antarctica yields first land mammal fossil. *New York Times.*

Woodburne, M. O., and J. A. Case. 1996. Dispersal, vicariance, and the Late Cretaceous to early tertiary land mammal biogeography from South America to Australia. *Journal of Mammalian Evolution* 3:121–161.

Yoder, A. D., and M. D. Nowak. 2006. Has vicariance or dispersal been the predominant biogeographic force in Madagascar? Only time will tell. *Annual Review of Ecolology, Evolution, and Systematics* 37:405–431.

Chapter 5: The Engine of Evolution

Carroll, S. P., and C. Boyd. 1992. Host race radiation in the soapberry bug: Natural history with the history. *Evolution* 46:1052–1069.

Dawkins, R. 1996. *Climbing Mount Improbable.* Penguin, London.

Doebley, J. F., B. S. Gaut, and B. D. Smith. 2006. The molecular genetics of crop domestication. *Cell* 127:1309–1321.

Doolittle, W. F., and O. Zhaxbayeva. 2007. Evolution: Reducible complexity—the case for bacterial flagella. *Current Biology* 17:R510–R512.

Endler, J. A. 1986. *Natural Selection in the Wild.* Princeton University Press, Princeton, NJ.

Franks, S. J., S. Sim, and A. E. Weis. 2007. Rapid evolution of flowering time by an annual plant in response to a climate fluctuation. *Proceedings of the National Academy of Sciences of the United States of America* 104:1278–1282.

Gingerich, P. D. 1983. Rates of evolution: Effects of time and temporal scaling. *Science* 222:159–161.

Grant, P. R. 1999. *Ecology and Evolution of Darwin's Finches.* (Rev. ed.) Princeton University Press, Princeton, NJ.

Hall, B. G. 1982. Evolution on a petri dish: The evolved ß-galactosidase system as a model for studying acquisitive evolution in the laboratory. *Evolutionary Biology* 15:85–150.

Hoekstra, H. E., R. J. Hirschmann, R. A. Bundey, P. A. Insel, and J. P. Crossland. 2006. A single amino acid mutation contributes to adaptive beach mouse color pattern. *Science* 313:101–104.

Jiang, Y., and R. F. Doolittle. 2003. The evolution of vertebrate blood coagulation as viewed from a comparison of puffer fish and sea squirt genomes. *Proceedings of the National Academy of Sciences of the United States of America* 100:7527–7532.

Kaufman D. W. 1974. Adaptive coloration in *Peromyscus polionotus*: Experimental selection by owls. *Journal of Mammalogy* 55:271–283.

Lamb, T. D., S. P. Collin, and E. N. Pugh. 2007. Evolution of the vertebrate eye: Opsins, photoreceptors, retina and eye cup. *Nature Reviews Neuroscience* 8:960–975.

Lenski, R. E. 2004. Phenotypic and genomic evolution during a 20,000-generation experiment with the bacterium *Escherichia coli. Plant Breeding Reviews* 24:225–265.

Miller, K. R. 1999. *Finding Darwin's God: A Scientist's Search for Common Ground Between God and Evolution.* Cliff Street Books, New York.

———. 2008. *Only a Theory: Evolution and the Battle for America's Soul.* Viking, New York.

Neu, H. C. 1992. The crisis in antibiotic resistance. *Science* 257:1064–1073.

Nilsson, D.-E., and S. Pelger. 1994. A pessimistic estimate of the time required for an eye to evolve. *Proceedings of the Royal Society of London,* Series B, 256:53–58.

Pallen, M. J., and N. J. Matzke. 2006. From *The Origin of Species* to the origin of bacterial flagella. *Nature Reviews Microbiology* 4:784–790.

Rainey, P. B., and M. Travisano. 1998. Adaptive radiation in a heterogeneous environment. *Nature* 394:69–72.

Reznick, D. N., and C. K. Ghalambor. 2001. The population ecology of contemporary adaptations: What empirical studies reveal about the conditions that promote adaptive evolution. *Genetica* 112:183–198.

Salvini-Plawen, L. V., and E. Mayr. 1977. On the evolution of photoreceptors and eyes. *Evolutionary Biology* 10:207–263.

Steiner, C. C., J. N. Weber, and H. E. Hoekstra. 2007. Adaptive variation in beach mice produced by two interacting pigmentation genes. *Public Library of Science Biology* 5:e219.

Vila, C., P. Savolainen, J. E. Maldonado, I. R. Amorim, J. E. Rice, R. L. Honeycutt, K. A. Crandall, J. Lundeberg, and R. K. Wayne. 1997. Multiple and ancient origins of the domestic dog. *Science* 276:1687–1689.

Weiner, J. 1995. *The Beak of the Finch: A Story of Evolution in Our Time.* Vintage, New York.

Xu, X., and R. F. Doolittle. 1990. Presence of a vertebrate fibrinogen-like sequence in an echinoderm. *Proceedings of the National Academy of Sciences of the United States of America* 87:2097–2101.

Yanoviak, S. P., M. Kaspari, R. Dudley, and J. G. Poinar. 2008. Parasite-induced fruit mimicry in a tropical canopy ant. *American Naturalist* 171:536–544.

Zimmer, C. 2001. *Parasite Rex: Inside the Bizarre World of Nature's Most Dangerous Creatures.* Free Press, New York.

Chapter 6: How Sex Drives Evolution

Andersson, M. 1994. *Sexual Selection.* Princeton University Press, Princeton, NJ.

Burley, N. T., and R. Symanski. 1998. "A taste for the beautiful": Latent aesthetic mate preferences for white crests in two species of Australian grassfinches. *American Naturalist* 152:792–802.

Butler, M. A., S. A. Sawyer, and J. B. Losos. 2007. Sexual dimorphism and adaptive radiation in Anolis lizards. *Nature* 447:202–205.

Butterfield, N. J. 2000. *Bangiomorpha pubescens* n. gen., n. sp.: Implications for the evolution of sex, multicellularity, and the Mesoproterozoic/Neoproterozoic radiation of eukaryotes. *Paleobiology* 3:386–404.

Darwin, C. 1871. *The Descent of Man, and Selection in Relation to Sex.* Murray, London.

Dunn, P. O., L. A. Whittingham, and T. E. Pitcher. 2001. Mating systems, sperm competition, and the evolution of sexual dimorphism in birds. *Evolution* 55:161–175.

Endler, J. A. 1980. "Natural selection on color patterns in *Poecilia reticulata*." *Evolution* 34:76–91.

Field, S. A., and M. A. Keller. 1993. Alternative mating tactics and female mimicry as postcopulatory mate-guarding behavior in the parasitic wasp *Cotesia rubecula. Animal Behaviour* 46:1183–1189.

Futuyma, D. J. 1995. *Science on Trial: The Case for Evolution.* Sinauer Associates, Sunderland, MA.

Hill, G. E. 1991. Plumage coloration is a sexually selected indicator of male quality. *Nature* 350:337–339.

Husak, J. F., J. M. Macedonia, S. F. Fox, and R. C. Sauceda. 2006. Predation cost of conspicuous male coloration in collared lizards (*Crotaphytus collaris*): An experimental test using clay-covered model lizards. *Ethology* 112:572–580.

Johnson, P. E. 1993. *Darwin on Trial* (2nd ed.). InterVarsity Press, Downers Grove, IL.

McFarlan, D. (ed.) 1989. *Guinness Book of World Records.* Sterling Publishing Co., New York.

Madden, J. R. 2003. Bower decorations are good predictors of mating success in the spotted bowerbird. *Behavioral Ecology and Sociobiology* 53:269–277.

———. 2003. Male spotted bowerbirds preferentially choose, arrange and proffer objects that are good predictors of mating success. *Behavioral Ecology and Sociobiology* 53:263–268.

Petrie, M., and T. Halliday. 1994. Experimental and natural changes in the peacock's (*Pave cristatus*) train can affect mating success. *Behavioral Ecology and Sociobiology* 35:213–217.

Petrie, M. 1994. Improved growth and survival of offspring of peacocks with more elaborate trains. *Nature* 371:598–599.

Petrie, M., T. Halliday, and C. Sanders. 1991. Peahens prefer peacocks with elaborate trains. *Animal Behaviour* 41:323–331.

Price, C. S. C., K. A. Dyer, and J. A. Coyne. 1999. Sperm competition between *Drosophila* males involves both displacement and incapacitation. *Nature* 400:449–452.

Pryke, S. R., and S. Andersson. 2005. Experimental evidence for female choice and energetic costs of male tail elongation in red-collared widowbirds. *Biological Journal of the Linnean Society* 86:35–43.

Vehrencamp, S. L., J. W. Bradbury, and R. M. Gibson. 1989. The energetic cost of display in male sage grouse. *Animal Behaviour* 38:885–896.

Wallace, A. R. 1892. Note on sexual selection. *Natural Science Magazine*, p. 749.

Welch, A. M., R. D. Semlitsch, and H. C. Gerhardt. 1998. Call duration as an indicator of genetic quality in male gray tree frogs. *Science* 280:1928–1930.

Chapter 7: The Origin of Species

Abbott, R. J., and A. J. Lowe. 2004. Origins, establishment and evolution of new polyploid species: *Senecio cambrensis* and *S. eboracensis* in the British Isles. *Biological Journal of the Linnean Society* 82:467–474.

Adam, P. 1990. *Saltmarsh Ecology*. Cambridge University Press, Cambridge, UK.

Ainouche, M. L., A. Baumel, and A. Salmon. 2004. *Spartina anglica* C. E. Hubbard: A natural model system for analysing early evolutionary changes that affect allopolyploid genomes. *Biological Journal of the Linnean Society* 82: 475–484.

Ainouche, M. L., A. Baumel, A. Salmon, and G. Yannic. 2004. Hybridization, polyploidy and speciation in *Spartina* (Poaceae). *New Phytologist* 161:165–172.

Byrne, K., and R. A. Nichols. 1999. *Culex pipiens* in London Underground tunnels: Differentiation between surface and subterranean populations. *Heredity* 82:7–15.

Clayton, N. S. 1990. Mate choice and pair formation in Timor and Australian mainland zebra finches. *Animal Behaviour* 39:474–480.

Coyne, J. A., and H. A. Orr. 1989. Patterns of speciation in *Drosophila*. *Evolution* 43:362–381.

———. 1997. "Patterns of speciation in *Drosophila*" revisited. *Evolution* 51:295–303.

———. 2004. *Speciation*. Sinauer Associates, Sunderland, MA.

Coyne, J. A., and T. D. Price. 2000. Little evidence for sympatric speciation in island birds. *Evolution* 54:2166–2171.

Dodd, D. M. B. 1989. Reproductive isolation as a consequence of adaptive divergence in *Drosophila pseudoobscura*. *Evolution* 43:1308–1311.

Gallardo, M. H., C. A. Gonzalez, and I. Cebrian. 2006. Molecular cytogenetics and allotetraploidy in the red vizcacha rat, *Tympanoctomys barrerae* (Rodentia, Octodontidae). *Genomics* 88:214–221.

Haldane, J. B. S. Natural selection. Pp. 101–149 in P. R. Bell, ed., *Darwin's Biological Work: Some Aspects Reconsidered*. Cambridge University Press, Cambridge, UK.

Johnson, S. D. 1997. Pollination ecotypes of *Satyrium hallackii* (Orchidaceae) in South Africa. *Botanical Journal of the Linnean Society* 123:225–235.

Kent, R. J., L. C. Harrington, and D. E. Norris. 2007. Genetic differences between *Culex pipiens* f. molestus and *Culex pipiens pipiens* (Diptera: Culicidae) in New York. *Journal of Medical Entomology* 44:50–59.

Knowlton, N., L. A. Weigt, L. A. Solórzano, D. K. Mills, and E. Bermingham. 1993. Divergence in proteins, mitochondrial DNA, and reproductive compatibility across the Isthmus of Panama. *Science* 260:1629–1632.

Losos, J. B., and D. Schluter. 2000. Analysis of an evolutionary species-area relationship. *Nature* 408:847–850.

Mayr, E. 1942. *Systematics and the Origin of Species*. Columbia University Press, New York.

———. 1963. *Animal Species and Evolution*. Harvard University Press, Cambridge, MA.

Pinker, S. 1994. *The Language Instinct: The New Science of Language and Mind*. HarperCollins, New York.

Ramsey, J. M., and D. W. Schemske. 1998. The dynamics of polyploid formation and establishment in flowering plants. *Annual Review of Ecology, Evolution, and Systematics* 29:467–501.

Savolainen, V., M.-C. Anstett, C. Lexer, I. Hutton, J. J. Clarkson, M. V. Norup, M. P. Powell, D. Springate, N. Salamin, and W. J. Baker. 2006. Sympatric speciation in palms on an oceanic island. *Nature* 441:210–213.

Schliewen, U. K., D. Tautz, and S. Pääbo. 1994. Sympatric speciation suggested by monophyly of crater lake cichlids. *Nature* 368:629–632.

Weir, J., and R. Ingram. 1980. Ray morphology and cytological investigations of *Senecio cambrensis* Rosser. *New Phytologist* 86:237–241.

Xiang, Q.-Y., D. E. Soltis, and P. S. Soltis. 1998. The eastern Asian and eastern and western North American floristic disjunction: Congruent phylogenetic patterns in seven diverse genera. *Molecular Phylogenetics and Evolution* 10:178–190.

Chapter 8: What About Us?

Barbujani, G., A. Magagni, E. Minch, and L. L. Cavalli-Sforza. 1997. An apportionment of human DNA diversity. *Proceedings of the National Academy of Sciences of the United States of America* 94:4516–4519.

Bradbury, J. 2004. Ancient footsteps in our genes: Evolution and human disease. *Lancet* 363:952–953.

Brown, P., T. Sutikna, M. J., Morwood, R. P. Soejono, E. Jatmiko, E. W. Saptomo, and R. A. Due. 2004. A new small-bodied hominin from the Late Pleistocene of Flores, Indonesia. *Nature* 431:1055–1061.

Brunet, M., et al. 2002. A new hominid from the Upper Miocene of Chad, central Africa. *Nature* 418:145–151.

Bustamante, C. D., et al. 2005. Natural selection on protein-coding genes in the human genome. *Nature* 437:1153–1157.

Dart R. A. 1925. *Astralopithecus africanus*: The Man-Ape of South Africa. *Nature* 115:195–199.

Dart, R. A. (with D. Craig). 1959. *Adventures with the Missing Link*. Harper, New York.

Davis, P., and D. H. Kenyon. 1993. *Of Pandas and People: The Central Question of Biological Origins* (2nd ed.). Foundation for Thought and Ethics, Richardson, TX.

Demuth, J. P., T. D. Bie, J. E. Stajich, N. Cristianini, and M. W. Hahn. 2007. The evolution of mammalian gene families. *Public Library of Science* ONE. 1:e85.

Enard, W., M. Przeworski, S. E. Fisher, C. S. L. Lai, V. Wiebe, T. Kitano, A. P. Monaco, and S. Paabo. 2002. Molecular evolution of *FOXP2*, a gene involved in speech and language. *Nature* 418:869–872.

Enard, W., and S. Paabo. 2004. Comparative primate genomics. *Annual Review of Genomics and Human Genetics* 5:351–378.

Enattah, N. S., T. Sahi, E. Savilahti, J. D. Terwilliger, L. Peltonen, and I. Jarvela. 2002. Identification of a variant associated with adult-type hypolactasia. *Nature Genetics* 30:233–237.

Frayer, D. W., M. H. Wolpoff; A. G. Thorne, F. H. Smith, and G. G. Pope. 1993. Theories of modern human origins: The Paleontological Test 1993. *American Anthropologist* 95:14–50.

Gould, S. J. 1981. *The Mismeasure of Man*. W. W. Norton, New York.

The Gallup Poll: Evolution, Creationism, and Intelligent Design. http://www.galluppoll.com/content/default.aspx?ci=21814.

Johanson, D. C., and M. A. Edey. 1981. *Lucy: The Beginnings of Humankind*. Simon & Schuster, New York.

Jones, S. 1995. *The Language of Genes*. Anchor, London.

King, M. C., and A. C. Wilson. 1975. Evolution at two levels in humans and chimpanzees. *Science* 188:107–116.

Kingdon, J. 2003. *Lowly Origin: Where, When, and Why Our Ancestors First Stood Up*. Princeton University Press, Princeton, NJ.

Lamason, R. L., et al. 2005. SLC24A5, a putative cation exchanger, affects pigmentation in zebrafish and humans. *Science* 310:1782–1786.

Lewontin, R. C. 1972. The apportionment of human diversity. *Evolutionary Biology* 6:381–398.

Miller, C. T., S. Beleza, A. A. Pollen, D. Schluter, R. A. Kittles, M. D. Shriver, and D. M. Kingsley. 2007. *cis*-Regulatory changes in kit ligand expression and parallel evolution of pigmentation in sticklebacks and humans. *Cell* 131:1179–1189.

Morwood, M. J., et al. 2004. Archaeology and age of a new hominin from Flores in eastern Indonesia. *Nature* 431:1087–1091.

Mulder, M. B. 1988. Reproductive success in three Kipsigis cohorts. Pp. 419–435 in T. H. Clutton-Brock, ed., *Reproductive Success: Studies of Individual Variation in Contrasting Breeding Systems.* University of Chicago Press, Chicago.

Obendorf, P. J., C. E. Oxnard, and B. J. Kefford. 2008. Are the small human-like fossils found on Flores human endemic cretins? *Proceedings of the Royal Society of London*, Series B, 275:1287–1296.

Perry, G. H., et al. 2007. Diet and the evolution of human amylase gene copy number variation. *Nature Genetics* 39:1256–1260.

Pinker, S. 1994. *The Language Instinct: The New Science of Language and Mind.* HarperCollins, New York.

———. 2008. Have humans stopped evolving? http://www.edge.org/q2008/q08_8.html#pinker.

Richmond, B. G., and W. L. Jungers. 2008. *Orrorin tugenensis* femoral morphology and the evolution of hominin bipedalism. *Science* 319:1662–1665.

Rosenberg, N. A., J. K. Pritchard, J. L. Weber, H. M. Cann, K. K. Kidd, L. A. Zhivotovsky, and M. W. Feldman. 2002. Genetic structure of human populations. *Science* 298:2381–2385.

Sagan, Carl. 2000. *Carl Sagan's Cosmic Connection: An Extraterrestrial Perspective.* Cambridge University Press, Cambridge, UK.

Suwa, G., R. T. Kono, S. Katoh, B. Asfaw, and Y. Beyene. 2007. A new species of great ape from the late Miocene epoch in Ethiopia. *Nature* 448:921–924.

Tishkoff, S. A., et al. 2007. Convergent adaptation of human lactase persistence in Africa and Europe. *Nature Genetics* 39:31–40.

Tocheri, M. W., C. M. Orr, S. G. Larson, T. Sutikna, Jatmiko, E. W. Saptomo, R. A. Due, T. Djubiantono, M. J. Morwood, and W. L. Jungers. 2007. The primitive wrist of *Homo floresiensis* and its implications for hominin evolution. *Science* 317:1743–1745.

Wood, B. 2002. Hominid revelations from Chad. *Nature* 418:133–135.

Chapter 9: Evolution Redux

Brown, D. E. *Human Universals*. 1991. Temple University Press, Philadelphia.

Coulter, A. 2006. *Godless: The Church of Liberalism*. Crown Forum (Random House), New York.

Dawkins, R. 1998. *Unweaving the Rainbow: Science, Delusion, and the Appetite for Wonder*. Houghton Mifflin, New York.

Einstein, A. 1999. *The World as I See It*. Citadel Press, Secaucus, NJ.

Feynman, R. 1983. *The Pleasure of Finding Things Out*. Public Broadcasting System television program *Nova*.

Harvard University Press author forum. Interview with Michael Ruse and J. Scott Turner. "Off the Page." http://harvardpress.typepad.com/off_the_page/j_scott_turner/index.html.

McEwan, I. 2007. End of the world blues. Pp. 351–365 in C. Hitchens, ed., *The Portable Atheist*. Da Capo Press, Cambridge, MA.

Miller, G. 2000. *The Mating Mind: How Sexual Choice Shaped the Evolution of Human Nature*. Doubleday, New York.

Pearcey, N. 2004. Darwin meets the Berenstain bears: Evolution as a total worldview. Pp. 53–74 in W. A. Dembski, ed., *Uncommon Dissent: Intellectuals Who Find Darwinism Unconvincing*. ISI Books, Wilmington, DE.

Pinker, S. 1994. *The Language Instinct: The New Science of Language and Mind*. HarperCollins, New York.

———. 2000. Survival of the clearest. *Nature* 404:441–442.

———. 2003. *The Blank Slate: The Modern Denial of Human Nature*. Penguin, New York.

Price, J., L. Sloman, R. Gardner, P. Gilber, and P. Rohde. 1994. The social competition hypothesis of depression. *British Journal of Psychiatry* 164:309–315.

Thornhill, R., and C. T. Palmer. 2000. *A Natural History of Rape: Biological Bases of Sexual Coercion*. MIT Press, Cambridge, MA.

Wilson, E. O. 1975. *Sociobiology: The New Synthesis*. Belknap Press of Harvard University Press, Cambridge, MA.

Illustration Credits

Figures 1–3: Illustrations by Kalliopi Monoyios.

Figure 4: Illustration by Kalliopi Monoyios after Malmgren and Kennett (1981).

Figure 5: Illustration by Kalliopi Monoyios after Kellogg and Hays (1975).

Figure 6: Illustration by Kalliopi Monoyios after Sheldon (1987).

Figure 7: Illustration by Kalliopi Monoyios after Kellogg and Hays (1975).

Figure 8: Illustration by Kalliopi Monoyios.

Figure 9: Illustration by Kalliopi Monoyios (*Compsognathus* after Peyer 2006).

Figure 10A: Illustration of *Sinornithosaurus* by Mick Ellison, used with permission; fossil, with permission of the American Museum of Natural History.

Figure 10B: Illustration of *Microraptor* by Kalliopi Monoyios; fossil, with permission of the American Museum of Natural History.

Figure 11. Illustration of *Mei long* by Mick Ellison, used with permission; fossil, with permission of the American Museum of Natural History; sparrow photograph courtesy of José Luis Sanz, Universidad Autónoma de Madrid.

Figure 12: Illustration by Kalliopi Monoyios.

Figure 13: Illustration by Kalliopi Monoyios after Wilson et al. (1967).

Figure 14: Illustrations by Kalliopi Monoyios, tail photographs from Bar-Maor et al. (1980), used with permission of the *Journal of Bone and Joint Surgery*.

Figure 15: Zebrafish photograph courtesy of Dr. Victoria Prince, human embryo photograph courtesy of the National Museum of Health and Medicine.

Figure 16: Illustrations by Kalliopi Monoyios.

Figure 17: Illustrations by Alison E. Burke.

Figure 18: Photographs by Dr. Ivan Misek, used with permission.

Figure 19: Illustrations by Alison E. Burke.

Figure 20: Illustrations by Kalliopi Monoyios.

Figure 21: Illustrations by Kalliopi Monoyios, fossil distribution after McLoughlin (2001).

Figures 22, 23: Illustrations by Kalliopi Monoyios.

Figure 24: Illustration by Kalliopi Monoyios after Wood (2002).

Figures 25–27: Illustrations by Kalliopi Monoyios.

Index